Nature's Design

Nature's Design

A Practical Guide to Natural Landscaping

by
Carol A. Smyser
and the Editors of
Rodale Press Books

Rodale Press, Emmaus, Pennsylvania

principal author
Carol A. Smyser

contributors
William H. Hylton
Carol Reifsnyder
Amy Zeffarano Rowland
Donald Vining

editors
William H. Hylton
Marcy Posner

copy editor
Jan Barckley

designer
Jerry O'Brien

design assistant
Michael Radomski

illustrators
David Carroll
Mark Schultz
Brian Swisher
Michael Worobec

photographer
Margaret Smyser

Printed in the United States of America on recycled paper, containing a high percentage of de-inked fiber.

Library of Congress Cataloging in Publication Data

Smyser, Carol A.
  Nature's design.

  Bibliography: p.
  Includes index.
  1. Landscape architecture. 2. Landscape gardening.
3. Wild flower gardening. 4. Landscape architecture—
United States. 5. Landscape gardening—United States.
6. Wild flower gardening—United States. I. Rodale
Press. II. Title.
SB473.S59   712'.6   82-330
ISBN 0-87857-343-7   hardcover   AACR2

  4 6 8 10 9 7 5   hardcover

Contents

Introduction ix
  Keys to Natural Landscaping x
    Nature Dictates x
    Native Plants xi
  Why Natural Landscaping? xii
  How to Do It xii
    Step-by-Step Analysis xii
    Design with Plants xiii
  Using *Nature's Design* xiii
    Ecological Analysis xiii
    Functional and Visual Analyses xiv
    Synthesis xiv
    Selecting Plants xiv
    Plan on Paper xv

Section 1: Site Analysis

Chapter 1: Making a Base Map 2
  The Base Map 3
    Using a Survey 3
      Making Your Own Survey 4
    Using a Photo 5
  Drawing the Base Map 6
    Establishing a Scale 7
    Draftsmanship 8
  Mapping Reality 8

Chapter 2: Geology 11
  Geology and the Landscape 12
    Hazards 13
    Foundations 14
      High Water Tables 15
      Glacial Deposits 15
      Clay 15
    Wells and Septic Tanks 16
    Grading 17
      Angle of Repose 17
    Geologic Assets 19
    Vegetation 19
  Your Property: Geological Analysis 20
    Collecting Information 20
    Recording Your Analysis 21

Chapter 3: Physiography 24
  General Information 28
    Topographic Maps 28
      Contours 28
      Slopes 30
  Physiography and the Landscape 30
  Your Property: Physiographic Analysis 31
    Local Physiography 31
      Professional Surveying 31
      Doing Your Own Survey 31
    Recording Your Analysis 34

Chapter 4: Hydrology 36
General Information 37
Hydrologic Cycle 37
Infiltration 38
Runoff 40
Floodplains 40
Groundwater 41
Water Table 41
Hydrology and the Landscape 42
Homes and Runoff 42
Homes and Seasonal High Water
Tables 42
Homes and Grading 43
Wells 43
Drainage 43
Water for Plants 43
Your Property: Hydrologic Analysis 44
Water Pollution 44
Drainage 45
Infiltration 45
Soil Moisture 46

Chapter 5: Soils 47
General Information 48
Soil Formation 48
Soil Composition 50
pH 50
Soil Texture 50
Soil Structure 51
Soil Porosity 51
Soil Water 51
Soil Nutrients 51
Soil and the Landscape 51
Your Property: Soil Analysis 52
Mapping Your Soils 53
Analyzing Soil Profiles 53
Testing for Soil Nutrients 54

Chapter 6: Climate 58
General Information 59
Regional Climate 59
Climatic Regions 60
Solar Radiation 61
Wind 62
Precipitation 62
Temperature 62
Plants and Climate 63
Low Temperature 64
High Temperature 64
Water 65
Frost 65
Wind 65
Sunlight 65
Climate and the Landscape 65
Microclimate 66
Solar Orientation 66
Wind 68

Your Property: Microclimatic
Analysis 70
Solar Radiation 70
Reflection 70
Wind 71
Precipitation 72
Temperature 73

Chapter 7: Vegetation and Wildlife 75
General Information 76
Plant Distribution 76
Succession 78
Weeds 78
Vegetation and the Landscape 78
Wildlife and the Landscape 80
Your Property: Vegetation Analysis 81
Plant Habitats 81
Natural Environments 82
Existing Plants 85
Your Property: Wildlife Analysis 89

Chapter 8: Functional Analysis 92
Your Property: Functional Analysis 93
Energy Efficiency 94
Functional Lists 96
Be Realistic 98
Revise As You Learn 98

Chapter 9: Visual Analysis 99
Diagrammatic Analysis 100
Spaces, Views and Screens 101
Form 104
Texture 104
Color 106
Drawing 107
Tracing Photographs 107

Chapter 10: Synthesis 110
Synthesis: Urban Property 111
Synthesis: Suburban Property 113
Synthesis: Rural Property 114
The Base for Your Design 115

Section 2: Design with Plants

**Chapter 11: Designing Your
Landscape** 118
The Landscape Plan 119
The Site Plan 119
Sketching Plans 119
Drawing the Measured Site Plan 123
Simulating Your Plan 127
The Planting Plan 128
Domestic Gardens 132
Planting Design Cautions 132

The Phasing Plan. 134
   The Construction Phase. 134
   The Planting Phase 134
   Synthesizing the Plans. 135

Chapter 12: Plant Selection 137
   Using Native Plants. 138
      The Benefits of Native Plants. 139
   Ecological Regions. 139
   Vegetation Classifications. 141
   Making Your Choices. 141
      Design with Nature 141
      Covering the Ground. 143
         Meadows. 144
         Prairies. 145
         Ground Covers 150
         Lawns. 151
   Regional Plant Charts. 152
      Northern Coniferous Forest Region. 154
      Eastern Deciduous Forest Region. 167
      Coastal Plain Region. 173
      Southeastern Mixed Forest Region. 176
      Subtropic Region. 178
      South-Central Swamp Region. 181
      Prairie Region. 184
      Rocky Mountain Evergreen Forest
         Region. 189
      Great Basin Region. 192
      Desert Region. 195
      Pacific Forest Region. 198
      California Region. 202

Chapter 13: Functional Uses of Plants 206
   Climate Control. 207
      Shade Trees. 209
      Windbreak Plants. 209
      Insulating Vines. 210
   Erosion Control. 210
      Erosion-Control Plants. 212
      Bank Plantings. 212
      Quickly Spreading and Reproducing
         Plants. 213
      Quick-Growing Plants. 213
   Natural Fertilizer. 214
   Pollution Control. 214
      Pollution-Tolerant Plants. 216
      Aromatic Plants. 217
   Noise Control. 217
      Noise-Control Plants. 218
   Edible Ornamentals. 220
      Edible Native Plants. 220
      Trees for Nut and Seed Production. 220
      Trees for Fruit Production. 221
      Shrubs for Fruit Production. 221
      Trees for Sugars, Drinks or Seasoning. . . . 221
      Shrubs for Miscellaneous Edible Uses. . . . 221

Chapter 14: Aesthetic Uses of Plants 222
   Screening and Privacy Control. 225
      Plants for Screening. 228
   Circulation. 228
      Plants for Barriers. 228
   Flowering Trees. 229
      Flowering Trees. 230
   Form. 230
      Form Plants. 230

Section 3: Landscape Construction

Chapter 15: Working with the Earth 236
   Grading. 237
      Grading Ordinances. 237
      Cut and Fill. 238
      Do-It-Yourself Grading. 238
         Rough Grading. 238
         Finish Grading. 240
   Drainage. 242
      Surface Drainage. 242
         Creating a Swale. 243
      Subsurface Drainage. 244
   Retaining Walls. 246
      Railroad-Tie Walls. 246
         Building the Wall. 248
      Stone Walls. 249
         Drywall Construction. 249
         Mortared Stone Construction. 252
      Masonry Walls. 253
         Bricks and Blocks. 253
         Mortar. 255
         Tools. 255
         Footings. 256
         Laying Up the Wall. 256
   Protecting Existing Plants. 260
      Cutting around Trees. 260
      Filling over Tree Roots. 261

Chapter 16: Paving 263
   Planning. 263
      Walks. 264
      Steps. 264
      Driveways. 266
      Terraces. 266
      Materials Considerations. 267
      Drainage. 267
      Utilities. 268
   Layout. 268
   Loose Aggregates. 270
      Crushed Stone. 270
      Specialty Rocks. 270
      Wood Chips. 270
   Brick. 271
      The Crowned Bed. 271
      Using Headers. 272
      Laying the Bricks. 273

Stone. 275
Concrete. 275
  Ingredients. 276
  Mixing Concrete. 276
  Tools. 277
  Step-By-Step Procedures. 277
    The Foundation. 277
    The Pour. 280
    Finishing. 280
    Curing. 280
  Paving Blocks. 280
  Soil Cement. 281
  Wood Paving. 282
  Steps. 283

Chapter 17: Privacy Fences. 285

Planning. 286
  Boundaries and Legal Matters. 286
  Economics. 287
  Design and Layout. 287
Construction Principles. 287
  Setting Posts. 287
  Building the Fences. 288
    Vertical Board Fence. 288
    Louvered Fence. 290
    Basket-Weave Fence. 290
Gates. 291
  Setting the Posts. 291
  Hinges and Latches. 293

Section 4: Creating and Maintaining Your Natural Landscape

Chapter 18: Preparing the Soil. 296

Improving Soil Texture. 297
  Green Manure Cover Crops. 297
  Mulch. 300
  Compost. 301
    The Indore Method. 301
    The 14-Day Method. 305
    Sheet Composting. 305
    Anaerobic Methods. 306
Fertilizing the Soil. 306
Balancing Soil pH. 308
Organic Soil Builders. 309

Chapter 19: Finding Native Plants. 311

Native Plants from the Nursery. 312
  Trees and Shrubs. 312
    Balled-and-Burlapped Plants. 312
    Bare-Rooted Plants. 314
    Container-Grown Plants. 317

Ground Covers. 317
Lawns. 318
Foraging for Native Plants. 320
  Ground Covers. 322
  Trees. 322
    Evergreens. 325
    Small Deciduous Trees. 325
  Shrubs. 327

Chapter 20: Propagation. 329

Sexual Propagation. 330
  Buying Seeds. 330
  Harvesting Seeds. 330
  Moving Toward Germination. 331
    Stratification. 332
    Scarification. 333
  Germination, Finally. 333
    The Medium. 333
    Watering. 333
    Light. 334
  Seedling Aftercare. 335
  Direct Seeding. 336
Vegetative Propagation. 336
  Rooting Hormones. 336
  Stem Cuttings. 337
    Softwood Cuttings. 338
    Hardwood Cuttings. 340
    Narrow-Leaved and Needled
      Evergreens. 343
    Semi-Hardwood Cuttings. 343
  Layering. 343
  Root and Leaf Cuttings. 343

Chapter 21: Living with Your Natural Landscape. 347

Prairies. 348
Meadows. 350
Woodland Gardens. 352
Lawn. 356
Deserts. 357
City Gardens. 361
Organic Disease Protection. 365
Organic Pest Protection. 366
Inviting Wildlife into Your Natural
  Landscape. 367
  Tips on Controlling Unwanted Guests. . . 375
Choices. 380

Bibliography. 382

Index. 386

Introduction

You probably have your own idea of what landscaping is. A popular conception is that it's the arrangement of plants around a house or other building. You may have started reading this book because you are interested in doing just that.

To a landscape architect, landscaping is much more. To him or her, it is the arrangement of land for human use, and it involves not only the selection and planting of vegetation, but changes to the contour of the landscape, the placement of buildings, walks and roads and much more.

Nature's Design approaches landscaping from the viewpoint of a landscape architect but presents it so that *anyone* can understand and do it. And it presents a special kind of landscaping called natural landscaping. Natural landscaping is ecological landscaping. It lets the environment shape the way humans interact with the landscape.

Landscaping with nature is concerned with the arrangement of natural elements—trees, shrubs, ground covers, soil, water and rocks—and man-made elements—walks, walls, buildings— into attractive and functional outdoor environments. But here the decisions are not based on artificial, arbitrary factors but on the unique characteristics of the site being landscaped. Your property, like every bit of the earth, is a living, growing, evolving ecosystem. The ecosystem is what determines the arrangement or design of a natural landscape.

To landscape with nature, you must ask Nature where and how to do best what you want to do.

If what you want to do is find the perfect site to build your dream house, the process of natural landscaping will help you. It shows you how to study different environments to deter-mine their pros and cons and thereby choose the best possible site—the one that provides all the opportunities that you need to accomplish your plans.

If you don't intend to build but are looking for a home to buy, *Nature's Design* will help you intelligently evaluate the workings of any home-site. You can make sure that the house is well constructed with a stable foundation and adequate drainage. You can evaluate the safety and ampli-tude of the water supply and the safety and effectiveness of the waste disposal system. You can consider the amount of energy that will be required to maintain the home.

If you have no plans to build or move but simply want to improve the appearance of your property, natural landscaping can still do a lot for you. Even if your plans are no more ambitious than adding a few trees or shrubs, *Nature's Design* will help you choose the right plants for your landscape. You may not want to go through the entire process of analysis, but an understanding of your soils, drainage conditions, climate and vege-tation habitats can ensure that the plants you use will thrive and that they are located where they will provide the most benefit at the least cost. You can get even more value by determining what functions you want your new plants to perform and how they will contribute to the appearance of your property.

It is more than likely that once you begin to understand the ecology of your property and its potential as a natural, undemanding and beau-tiful environment, your plans may gradually expand to include a complete naturalization. This doesn't have to take place in one season or one year but can be accomplished slowly throughout your entire lifetime. Returning your landscape to a healthy, biologically stable environment may be one of the greatest contributions you can make to future generations.

A natural landscape is appropriate at any scale, from areas as small as 100 square feet to those as large as several hundred acres. One can be designed for any setting—rural, suburban or urban. In fact, in small urban areas where the effects of man are everywhere, the impact of a natural landscape can be greatest.

Keys to Natural Landscaping

No matter what its size or where it is located, a natural landscape requires an understanding of the unique environmental conditions of its site and the environmental requirements of the plants that are indigenous to that area. These two elements are keys to natural landscaping. Unless it stems directly from the ecological characteristics of the site, and unless it uses native plants, a landscape just isn't natural.

NATURE DICTATES

The first step in developing a natural landscape for your home is to find out what the characteristics of your land are. To do this requires studying the ecological characteristics of your property, including geology, physiography (study of landforms), hydrology, soils, climate, vegetation and wildlife, as well as the effects you have had or wish to have on your landscape.

The present landscape looks as it does because of a long and complex history of natural phenomena as well as man's intervention. Therefore, you will need to determine which characteristics of your property can be attributed to natural processes and which to your interference with these. If you can understand the natural processes you are interfering with, you'll be able to develop a plan that needs less control, thus less maintenance.

You must also realize that your landscape, as it looks now, does not represent a final static condition but rather a balance that exists for the moment. This balance may be controlled by your own forces or, more easily, by natural forces. For example, by keeping a lawn mowed or a hedge clipped, you are constantly working against the forces of nature, and if you wish to maintain this unnatural condition, you'll never be able to stop.

If, however, you decide to stop mowing and let nature take its course, a series of plant communities will take over your yard, continually changing it in a process known as succession. The first pioneer plant communities, probably annual weeds, will prepare the way for plant communities of later successive stages by altering the soil and protecting seedlings. The annuals will then be followed by perennial weeds and grasses and later, depending on the environment, by shrubs and small trees, followed by a woodland of young trees and finally a forest. Undisturbed, this climax forest will maintain and perpetuate itself and provide a stable, healthy and beautiful landscape.

Succession, however, is a slow process, and unless you're planning to be around 200 years from now, your chances of seeing the climax forest are slim. But if you plant an earlier stage of succession—an intermediate stage that is appropriate to your purposes and to the ecology of your land—you can take advantage of natural maintenance and have a beautiful and finished-looking landscape immediately.

Each place has its own distinct character because of the interaction of the highly variable ecological characteristics. The purpose of your landscaping will determine the scale and extent of the ecological factors that must be known. If you are looking for a homesite in several different areas, you will need an overview that shows the individuality of each region. For example, there will be obvious effects of temperature differences between a hillside and a valley bottom that may influence your choice. Would you rather live in a valley with cold air flowing through it or on a hillside where you may have warmer nights but serious erosion? By analyzing any prospective homesite, you can identify problems and opportunities, any areas containing important or delicate natural processes and, finally, the one area most capable of fulfilling your needs.

If you already have a home and are just beginning or continuing a long-term landscape plan, you will need the same kind of information but in much greater detail. Don't make the mistake of assuming that your land is the same as your neighbor's. Ecological conditions often vary within a few square feet, and the success of your landscape plan will depend on how accurately you can locate and understand these variations.

The same holds true for an older property with a mature but nonnatural landscape. If you wish to naturalize an established landscape, you will need to analyze the existing plantings. It would be foolish to cut down every nonnative plant, so you may want to incorporate some existing exotics into your landscape plan. That means judging each plant by its individual merits (or lack thereof) as well as by its contribution to the whole. You must also determine the effects of the existing vegetation on other ecological factors. For example, a large established tree may have altered the microclimate by providing shade and hence cooler areas below it. It may have extended its roots in search of nutrients and water, so that the soil below its canopy spread is different from that beyond.

Regardless of the extent of your landscaping plans, the more you understand about the nature of your property, the better your results will be. At the very least, you must ensure that your use of the land does not lead to disruption of the natural systems and that you do not destroy natural resources and amenities.

NATIVE PLANTS

Choosing vegetation requires further cooperation with nature. The basis of trouble-free planting is using indigenous vegetation. In any area there is always a type of vegetation that would exist without being planted or protected. This native vegetation consists of specific groups of plants that adapted to specific environmental conditions. The oak-hickory deciduous forest occurs in areas of the eastern United States where the winters are cold and dry, the summers are warm and humid and the soils are relatively acid. It does not exist in areas that are cool year-round.

It is important to know what plants nature would produce without your help before you decide how much you want to change or manipulate the natural condition.

By looking closely at an undisturbed natural environment with ecological conditions similar to your own and by observing the vegetation growing naturally, you can determine at firsthand the species that you like and those that will work in your landscape. In addition, you can observe how they grow in the wild. Notice where they occur— at the edge or in the middle of other dense vegetation. See their ultimate size and when they flower. Try to observe them during all stages of growth and during all seasons before making a final decision.

Remember, though, that there are aesthetic principles to consider as well. Because plants are often regarded as intrinsically beautiful things, many people believe that it is enough simply to plant them. This often results in a hodgepodge of jarring and awkard-looking vegetation. Landscape architect Sir Peter Shepheard says that if you want a truly beautiful landscape, you will need to refer to the order found in nature.

Man makes mistakes; nature doesn't. Plants growing in their natural habitat look fit and therefore beautiful. In any undeveloped area you can find a miraculously appropriate assortment of plants, each one contributing to the overall appearance of a unified natural landscape. The balance is preserved by the ecological conditions of the place, and the introduction of an alien plant could destroy this balance.

The lush and varied look, as well as the health and maintenance of a natural or a newly planted landscape, depends on the diversity of the system, explains landscape architect Anne Spirn. Most natural plant communities have a mixture of plants of different ages and sizes that create favorable conditions for each other. In a natural, self-perpetuating woodland, for example, the tall, sun-loving canopy trees provide the shade needed by their young seedling replacements. When there is a gap in the canopy layer, allowing light to penetrate, a smaller, sun-loving understory tree may establish itself. The herbaceous layer of a forest is generally composed of shade-loving ferns, forbs and flowers.

If you were to use exotics in your landscape, it is unlikely that you could afford to buy more than a few different varieties, all of the same approximate size. The starkness of this meager landscape requires tidiness and does not allow for the self-maintaining cycles of nature.

If you don't want to be tied down to landscape maintenance, your design must be as close as possible to the natural landscape of the area. Then, with nature working on your side, you can reduce your effort to a minimum. That means including the natural processes of death and decay as well as birth in your landscape, or, put in practical terms, allowing volunteer seedlings to mature and keeping leaf litter on the ground as a natural soil amendment.

To come to terms with Nature and to make her a partner in your landscape, you must recognize that the same interrelationships that tie other life forms so inescapably to their environment must influence the organization of your activities in the landscape.

Why Natural Landscaping?

If you choose to have a natural landscape, you'll not be alone. Today, for a whole bookful of reasons, there is a growing individual commitment to nature and to the more organic style of life. Many people, if they can afford to, are leaving the city environment and going to rural ones, to beautiful and remote sites. To live close to nature with a life-style that is adapted to the ecosystems is now considered by many to be a greater luxury than living in a man-made environment where nature has been successfully overridden. And even in highly manipulated urban environments, people are beginning to import nature to soften the impact of the man-made world.

A growing number of homeowners in both urban and rural environments have found that natural landscaping provides an alternative to the energy-consuming, high-cost, traditional landscape. It requires time rather than money, intelligence rather than energy, and working with rather than against nature to develop diverse, low-cost, low-maintenance, healthy and attractive landscapes. These homeowners understand and respect the forces of nature and are thereby reaping the benefits of nature's years of experience, avoiding the costs of working against natural systems.

Moreover, by using the design principles of nature, they are employing the best and least expensive landscape designer. Abstractions like color, texture, form and line are worked out to perfection in nature, and the choice of species comes free, complete with a lifetime supply of fertilizer, water and natural insect resistance.

By allowing nature to work out your design, you can make your property look diverse, rich and beautiful in much less time and with much less expense than traditional landscaping requires. Not only is it cheaper to create a natural landscape, it is easier and less expensive to maintain because you don't have to wage a constant battle against nature. And while you are increasing the value of your home by improving its environment, you can use a natural landscape to reduce your household energy consumption, to attract wildlife or to ensure a private and noise-free backyard.

How to Do It

If you're convinced that natural landscaping is the only way to go with your property, then you're ready to embark on a project that will be arduous and time-consuming at first, but rewarding in its beauty. It will be easy to care for once it is established, but you must keep in mind that any natural landscape takes more work to develop than the traditional lawn and foundation-plant landscape.

Natural landscaping does not mean letting everything go. You may have heard of homeowners who simply stopped mowing or weeding and now call their landscapes "natural." The truth is that these so-called no-work, natural gardens will be long dominated by exotic weed species, most of which are pests and look downright ugly. Eventually, in 50 to 100 years, native plants will establish themselves and begin to create an attractive environment, but even then the landscape may not suit the homeowner's needs, simply because there's no design in it.

And design is a critical part of natural landscaping. By using the principles of nature and knowing how they apply to your own environment, you can plan and *design* a landscape that works for you and that is natural and beautiful as well.

STEP-BY-STEP ANALYSIS

The first step of natural landscaping is to learn about the different environmental attributes of your site. This is a big job, but it is educational and can be fun, especially if you're interested in knowing why your land is the way it is.

Because you are designing a landscape that must work for you and your family, you must also analyze what *you* want it to be. The second step, then, is to define what your own needs and desires are. Nature may not allow your landscape to do everything you want it to, or it may make certain combinations of functions impossible. You've got to be able to decide what is most important to you.

Step three requires matching what you have with what you want. You will be working out the best arrangement for an overall plan and finding the best location for each specific purpose. This method of seeking intrinsically suitable sites can operate at any scale, from an entire farmstead to a small urban lot, and all choices can be made with a sound knowledge of the options and consequences.

DESIGN WITH PLANTS

After you have decided what you want to do and where you want to do it, you can begin thinking specifically about *how* to do it.

You can still impose your taste and create the visual effects you want by using the plant species and the successional stage that best meet your needs. If you like free, open space, then you'll use meadow or early successional species. If you like some open space but want it punctuated by trees and shrubs, then use old field species. If you like closed private areas, use late successional forest species.

The best way to decide on individual plants is to look at natural environments that have ecological conditions similar to your own.

This may sound like a lot of work, and it is.

But the amount of time invested in planning your landscape will result in time and expense saved later. Once you've designed and planted an ecological landscape, you can relax. If it is truly ecological, you can sit back and watch the slow but spectacular process of succession.

Using Nature's Design

To landscape your own property, you could hire a professional ecological landscape architect who has studied ecology, design, and natural and social sciences and who knows how to analyze, synthesize, plan and design natural landscapes. With this book, however, you will be able to do your own landscaping. *Nature's Design* contains everything you need to know to plan and create a beautiful, functional and successful outdoor environment using the same techniques that a professional would. It is not arbitrary or confusing. It explains in clear terms the methods employed by landscape architects. It presents a holistic approach.

Nature's Design should be used like a textbook. Read it straight through. Then go back and concentrate on applying the information in each chapter to your own property.

ECOLOGICAL ANALYSIS

The natural factors that contribute to the balance of any environment, as noted earlier, are geology, physiography, ground and surface water, soils, climate, vegetation and wildlife. Although considered individual environmental sciences, these are actually very closely related and interdependent.

If your property has a lot of native vegetation, you may be able to easily identify the ecological conditions of your environment. Most homeowners, unfortunately, have landscapes with little, if any, native vegetation remaining. If this is your case, you may be able to get some clue from how the exotics are responding to their environment. For example, if your rhododendrons are brown or dying, this may indicate an alkaline soil, while dying blueberries may show the soil is too dry. But you won't be able to easily identify all of the ecological conditions. That's why you have to start at the beginning and look at each of the natural factors to see its individual contributions to the ecology of your property. Then you will be able to put them together to distinguish the unique habitats that they create. Because each natural factor is variable and may differ from one area to the next, putting them together may create an infinite number of combinations. That means that there may be many habitats, even in an area as small as an urban backyard.

Section 1 describes these natural factors and tells you how to analyze them. Most of its chapters begin with a checklist of information needed for different kinds of landscaping projects, including, where applicable, locating a house or other structure, grading and planting. Use these checklists as tools to help you determine what information you need to concentrate on, since some of the information may be irrelevant to your landscaping plans or to your property. The introduction to each chapter explains the science and tells you how and why it may be important to your landscape. This is followed by general information that will help you to understand the factors that make up your landscape and thus enable you to make informed decisions, whether you are planning large projects or minor changes. Next is a discussion of how each science affects the landscape around you, and then how you can analyze your property to make the most of its ecological conditions.

By using the general information and the checklist, you will be able to follow easily the step-by-step instructions for analyzing each factor on your property and recording the information on your base map. You will be able to determine how much time, work and outside help you may actually need. As you proceed with the analysis, keep in mind that the more you know about the ecological conditions while you are planning, the more you can sit back and enjoy your landscape once it is designed.

FUNCTIONAL AND VISUAL ANALYSES

The ecology of your property determines what your land would look like or what form it would take without your interference. Your intentions and needs for your landscape determine what you would like your land to look like or what form you would like it to take.

Because ecological landscaping requires defining both nature's and your own intentions and putting them together in the most harmonious manner, you must analyze your needs and wants and record them in the same way that you record the ecological information.

The extent of your needs, as well as the unique features of your site, will make some environmental conditions more important than others.

Chapters on these analyses contain specific guidelines for the information you will need and tell where and how to get it. You'll define the functional needs and wants of your family and the specific requirements of each function. What are your outdoor activities? How much space do they require? How should they relate to your house and to each other? You must look for the factors most beneficial and necessary for every prospective use of your land.

Then study the appearance of your landscape, as it looks now and as you'd like it to look. This will require developing some new ways of looking at the familiar.

SYNTHESIS

Ultimately, all this information about your property and about your desires must be brought together. The geology and the water conditions and the soil and the vegetation all come together physically on your land, and your gathering of facts must too. This is the synthesis.

The professional synthesizes information using a base map with a series of transparent overlays. Each overlay has a different kind of information recorded on it. When all the layers of information are in place, a new perspective on the property being studied is afforded.

Buying the equipment and learning the skills necessary to record and synthesize ecological, functional and visual information just the way a professional landscape architect does is probably not reasonable. But Section 1 will give you alternative techniques that will help you pull together all your information on a single base map.

SELECTING PLANTS

You will now be ready to choose the plants for your landscape.

At this point, you probably can't wait to get on with the project. But before you race ahead and start putting plants in the ground, take some time to weigh your choices. You know you want to use plants native to your region so you don't have to coax along exotic ones. You probably even have some ideas about what you want in ground cover, shrubs and trees. But the plants you choose can do a lot more than just make your home environment pretty. The plants you choose can serve you *and* your environment. Choosing your plants wisely is what much of Section 2 is about.

First of all, there are functional considerations. Plants can do everything in the landscape from helping to moderate the climate around your property to providing a little food. You've merely got to learn how to select those plants that will do the work you want done.

Second, there are aesthetic considerations.

Plants are attractive; you know that. They can beautify your property in the obvious ways, but they can also beautify your vistas by obscuring those aspects you don't want to look at or those you don't want your neighbors or passersby to see. Here you'll find out about all the attractive things plants can do and learn the names of beautiful and beautifully functional native plants that will thrive in your region.

Throughout the section are lists of attractive and functional native plants grouped according to the 12 environmental regions of the continental United States. A description of each region and some information about selected plants native to each are found here. The plant charts will give you some specific recommendations to start your work with.

In choosing the plants to be included in your landscape, you must figure out where, exactly, to put them. Again, the functional and the aesthetic considerations come into play. The preparation of site and planting plans is a time-consuming, trial-and-error process, but it's a vital one. You are far better off experimenting on paper than you are planting and replanting, trying to come up with an appropriate design for your needs and your property.

Weigh your choices carefully.

PLAN ON PAPER

Regardless of your intent, the amount of time invested in this planning stage will save you time and expense later. Although you may have seen beautiful landscapes that were created slowly over the years with no initial study or master plan, they have usually grown through a time-consuming and expensive process of trial and error—and they usually belong to avid gardeners who spend every free minute working on the landscape. It is far easier and cheaper to concentrate the trial-and-error process on paper. This way you will have a useful and attractive landscape immedi-

ately, although it may take years for the process of succession to fill out your plans. And because each decision will affect another, you will want to think it all through before committing yourself and limiting your options or making costly mistakes.

This planning process of ecological design draws from the experience of all the designers who have created successful landscapes—that is, functional *and* beautiful—over the years. In fact, if you were to hire a professional landscape architect, he or she would approach your design in just this way, spending an intense period of time getting to know your site as well as your tastes. By choosing not to rely on professional help, you can save money, time and energy, since you know better than anyone else what you need. And unless you do the ecological study yourself, you will probably never really understand the miraculous natural processes occurring on your property. By following these instructions, you can make your landscape look both professionally designed and uniquely suited to your environment.

After the paper plan is perfected, you will be able to budget the time and expense of the actual construction and planting over any number of years. Sections 1 and 2 will give you the information required to make the appropriate choice of plants and to arrange them in the most effective manner. Sections 3 and 4 give detailed instructions on how to do basic landscape construction, like paths and retaining walls, and on how to obtain and plant trees, shrubs and ground covers yourself.

Although it may take years to complete your landscape, this method will allow you to create a framework that is immediately beautiful and functional and that can be filled in slowly over the years with nature's help. All the while you will have the satisfaction of seeing your maintenance and energy consumption reduced and of knowing that you have contributed to the health of the environment and yourself.

A Gallery of Natural Landscapes

A natural landscape is a surprising landscape. It just doesn't *look* like what you expect a designed landscape to look like. It looks like...well, like a meadow or a grove of trees. If there's a house in it, the house almost invariably looks custom-made. Certainly classy. And yes, expensive. The landscape looks as if it was always there.

And that's where natural landscaping has you.

Look at the landscape on the facing page. Turn the page and view the other color photographs of natural landscapes. You'll find landscapes from all areas of the country — woodlands, meadows, prairies, beachfronts, deserts. If you study the buildings, you'll see that some indeed are custom-built, though they are not necessarily expensive. But you'll also see that some of them are fairly typical American homes: ranchers, split-levels, just generic American houses.

At first glance, you probably get the impression that each of the homes is particularly remarkable. It's an impression lent by the settings, by the natural landscapes.

Those settings can come quite inexpensively. Nature provides the plantings and the design guidelines; you provide the planning and the labor. A million-dollar landscape can be had for your own sweat and labor. It *looks* expensive, but it's not.

And that's another place where natural landscaping has you.

Study the landscapes in the photographs. The landscapes were not always as you see them. The homes were not simply built in the midst of perfect landscapes. Rather, the existing landscapes were modified and refined, excavated and replanted. They were carefully designed to emulate nature, and if they look *so* natural that you can't believe they aren't exclusives from Nature herself, that only confirms how well designed they are.

The natural setting opposite and on page xviii was designed by landscape architect Lewis Clarke to surround his North Carolina home. It exhibits a sympathetic blending of man-made elements and the natural environment. Native plants hug the house and its wooden decks and walks, softening their angularity. As the landscape continues to mature, vines will spread over the trellises and provide relief from the hot summer sun, and, concomitantly, further soften the angles of the house. A successful woodland environment has been created here.

Across the country, and the page, is a natural landscape that's perhaps less grand, perhaps less striking, but certainly no less successful. Here, native California plants have been sited to create both open and closed spaces. Natural materials, such as a well-weathered landscaping tie, have been worked into the landscape to provide inviting places to sit. There's no intimidation in the privacy such spots provide.

A variety of landscapes can be seen on pages xx and xxi. On the left is a colorful landscape, proving both that a natural landscape isn't monotonously green and that you don't have to resort to the use of exotic plants hybridized to yield

(continued on page xxv *)*

North Carolina   Carl Doney

North Carolina
Carl Doney

California
Carl Doney

California   Carol Smyser

California
Carol Smyser

Wisconsin
The Family Handyman

Wisconsin
Cathie Bruner

Connecticut
Margaret Smyser

California   Sally Ann Shenk

North Carolina
Carl Doney

Pennsylvania
Margaret Smyser

Texas
Carol Smyser

Wisconsin
Lorrie Otto

Connecticut
Margaret Smyser

sophisticated hues to have color. The desert landscape at the top of page xxi has more and denser vegetation than you might have imagined a desert could produce. Similarly, the three prairie and woodland landscapes along the right reflect diversity and density of vegetation. A prairie, coincidentally, is seen to be colorful in both bloom and autumn decline. While diversity isn't a key characteristic of the dune-top landscape, a natural landscape in this situation is particularly important, since the grasses stabilize the dune, protecting the structure.

Natural landscaping can come into play successfully both in new construction and in relandscaping situations. On page xxii, you see a house designed for its landscape, which was modified and refined to complement the house. Mature trees were retained, even where they crowded the foundation. And these were supplemented with native plantings that create layers, enfold the house and soften the brute impact of such a functional element as a mailbox.

Opposite this setting, on page xxiii, is a landscape created around a relatively unremarkable suburban home. Once landscaped with a lawn-and-specimen-tree layout, it is now an early successional woodland, complete with a tiny pool stocked with goldfish (the goldfish are a nice touch, even if they aren't strictly, purely *natural*). Had the landscape been designed around a houseless, naturally vegetated plot, it would have been different, but no less successful. So even if you have an existing unnatural landscape, take heart.

For even here, natural landscaping has you again. Natural landscaping *can* work for you, regardless of your location and circumstances. Big tract or little, city or country, desert or wetland, prairie or woodland, river valley or mountaintop, there is a natural environment you can emulate in creating a natural landscape.

Visit a natural environment near your home. Study your property's environmental characteristics. Choose native plants you like. Then design a natural landscape—like those at left—for your home.

SECTION I
Site Analysis

1

Making a Base Map

To make a landscape plan or to study a prospective homesite, you will need to gather and record, organize and synthesize a lot of information. Some of this information will come from asking questions of yourself and your family, some will come from looking at your existing landscape and making judgments about its present condition, and even more will come from outside

sources—government agencies, planning commissions, environmental groups and their publications.

This wealth of information must be gathered and recorded so that it can be put together, or synthesized, to represent a total picture of the place you are studying. To do this, you will need an accurate drawing or map of your property.

Individual copies or tracings of this map will

be used for locating geologic features, soil types, water conditions, plant species and microclimatic conditions. You will then put all of these maps together to see the ecological relationships that exist on your property and to single out distinct habitats. Understanding the individual and accumulated ecological characteristics of these habitats will allow you to produce a responsive design that works for *your* environment.

The Base Map

A base map is a plan or bird's-eye view of your property as it now exists. It shows the locations and exact dimensions of all the man-made features, such as the house, garage, walks, paved areas, utilities and property lines, and all the natural elements, such as trees, shrubs and ground covers. Because you will be recording all the information obtained from your site study, synthesizing this

information and working out your design on this map, it is important that it be clearly and neatly drawn and as accurate as possible.

USING A SURVEY

Although drawing a base map is not that difficult, it is time-consuming and requires careful and accurate measurements. If you have a survey of your property that was made either when the house was built or when you purchased the land, you're a big step ahead. If you are contemplating buying a property, be sure to ask the agent or seller to provide you with an accurate survey of any sites that you are considering.

There are different kinds of surveys, used for different purposes, and hence showing different elements. What you need at this point is a plane survey, which locates buildings, trees and other objects within your property lines. Later, you

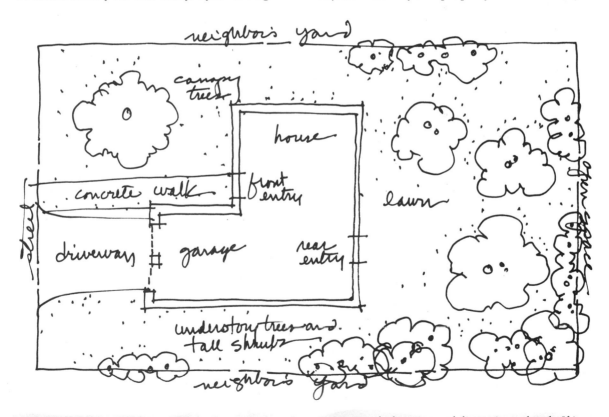

Having a good base map is vitally important to the success of your site analysis. Before you go out and actually measure things, do a rough sketch (above). Include all the features of the existing landscape, estimating the location and dimensions of each. If it helps you to position trees or other landscape elements, quickly pace off distances.

will need a topographical survey, which depicts the third dimension of the ground surface.

Professional surveyors generally use a transit, which gives the compass bearing for any point. Boundary lines are then established in terms of compass bearings and lengths. Elements are located by a method known as triangulation, that is, finding an unknown point by measuring from two known points.

MAKING YOUR OWN SURVEY

You can do your own survey using the same method, but instead of a transit you can use a tape measure, stakes to fix in the ground and a rough sketch of approximate locations.

Begin by setting stakes at the corners of your property. (You can get the record of your property's boundaries from a tax map in your assessor's office.) Then measure from one corner to another around the entire edge of your property and record these dimensions on your sketch. One or more of these lines will now serve as a reference point from which every feature of the landscape can be measured and then located on paper.

Your house is probably the most important fixed element in the landscape, and you will need to locate all of its features that have contact with or extend into the outdoors—windows, doors, porches and decks. To locate your house, if you know its dimensions, you need only measure from two of its corners to two points on the reference line. You will need to measure from all four corners (or more, if it's not rectangular) if you don't know the dimensions.

There are probably other permanent features on your site—garages, walls, drives, walks, trees, shrubs, planting beds or vegetable gardens. It is important to record all of these on your map,

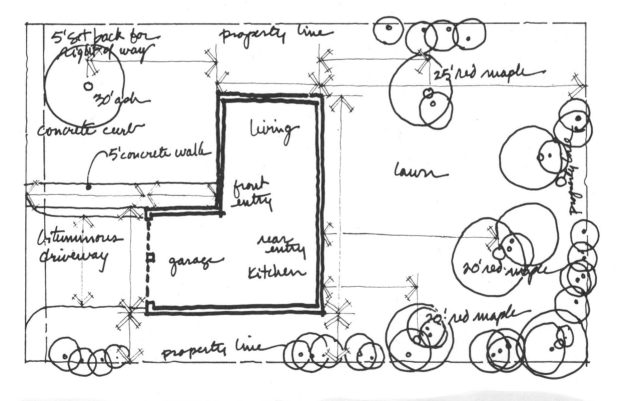

Once the sketch is completed, add arrows showing dimensions and distances that you want to measure accurately (above). The sketch may become messy and cluttered, but it'll be a valuable tool in making and recording the measurements. Get into the habit now of including a legend for each rendition of the map you produce by recording the special symbols and line styles you use in the sketch.

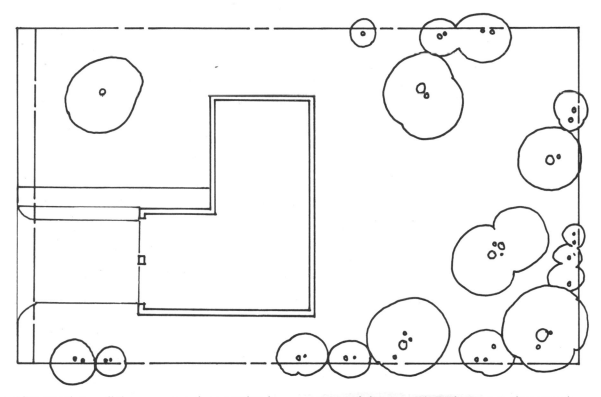

After completing all the measuring, do a new sketch. Draw this one to scale. Include the landscape features shown on the initial sketch, but forget the dimension lines and all the notes (you should know what your *property's features are). Do hang on to the original sketch for the information it contains, but use the new sketch as your base map.*

even if you intend to remove or relocate them. Also try to locate any overhead or underground utilities. Where are the septic tank and water, gas, telephone and electric lines? These may be of critical importance if you are planning any excavation or construction. If there are objects on neighboring properties—trees, pools or buildings —that affect yours, be sure to locate them also.

In making a survey, you are locating a series of points. For a tree, you need to locate only the point of its trunk. You can estimate the spread of its branches and leaves (canopy spread). For a straight drive or walk of known width, locate and then connect two points along one side of it. For a curved one, locate a series of points and then sketch in the curve that connects them. Since you know the width, the other side is easily located. For an irregular form, such as a mass of plants,

locate enough points to be able to sketch in the form. Don't forget to indicate clearly all dimensions on your rough sketch, as these will be scaled and transferred onto your final base map.

USING A PHOTO

If you have a very large property and no survey information, you might be able to find an aerial photograph from which you can trace a base map. Your county or local planning commission may already have photos of your area, and the Soil Conservation Service includes air photographs in their soil surveys. In many areas there are professional aerial photographers who can produce a photograph at whatever scale you need. Or you might enjoy hiring a small plane with a pilot and taking your own photographs. If you use an air

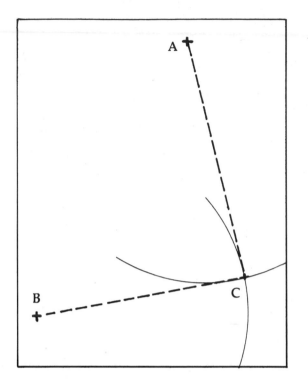

photo instead of a survey, you should keep in mind that there will be some distortion due to the angle at which the camera was held when shooting. You may want to measure the distances between some known points on the ground to determine how severe the distortion is and make adjustments if necessary.

Drawing the Base Map

Assuming that you now have one or more sources of survey information about your property, you are ready to draw a neat and accurate copy of your base map.

Landscape architects have a wide variety of tools and techniques for drawing maps and plans. Generally, they work at a drafting table, which has a flat, clean surface to which a movable straightedge is attached. They have a variety of triangles and templates that allow them to accurately draw any angle or shape on the plan. Most plans are drawn on a good-quality white tracing

If you know the location of your house or property lines, and you want to locate other features, like trees or shrubs, simply measure to them from points on known lines. Thus, to pinpoint the location of C (above), you should measure from known points A and B. No need to worry about measuring perpendicularly; you simply use the distances from C

to A and C to B as the radii of circles with points A and B as their respective centerpoints. Scribe short arcs of these circles on your rough map. Where they intersect is point C. Your job of measuring will be made easier if you have helpers to hold the tape or string and call out measurements while you record the data on your map.

paper or on a sheet of transparent acetate or mylar. Because both of these materials are transparent, they can be reproduced by running them through a blueprint machine, and they allow the draftsman to trace over a rough sketch of his plan. Mylar, although more expensive, has the advantage of greater durability, and because the ink is not absorbed, mistakes can be wiped off.

You too will need a large flat working surface —your dining table will do. You will need some means for drawing straight lines—the most accurate, if your table has a straight edge, is a T square, but a ruler will work; a tool for measuring angles —this could be an expanding triangle or a protractor; paper—it would be helpful to have both thin tracing paper and a better-quality, heavy white tracing or drafting paper; masking tape; sharp pencils; colored pencils; and an eraser. A compass may be helpful in drawing trees or in locating objects using the arcs of circles. All of these supplies can be obtained at a drafting or art supply store.

ESTABLISHING A SCALE

Before you begin the drawing, you will need to establish a scale of measurement, such as 1 inch on the paper equaling 10 feet on the ground. This will, of course, depend on the size of your property and will determine the size of your map. It should be large enough to take notes on and to show individual plants, but not so large as to be unwieldy—you will be taking it outside with you. If you have a lot that is 50 × 100 feet and you used a scale of ½ inch = 1 foot, your plan would be 25 × 50 inches, or about 2 × 4 feet, a good size to work with. But if your property is an acre or more, this scale would be much too large.

Using the appropriate scale, you will need to transfer the actual ground measurements to their equivalent size on paper. Redraw the plan carefully

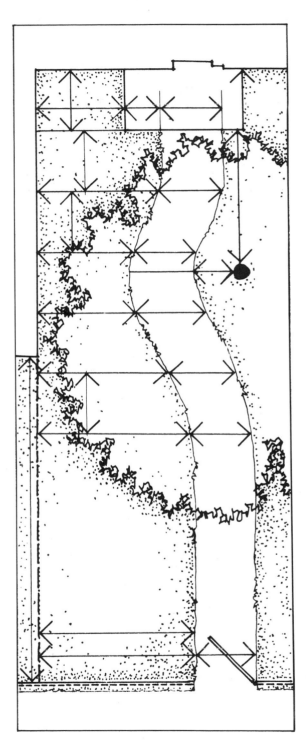

To properly position a curved walk or driveway on your rough map, you must make a whole series of measurements, locating points along its edges. You may have to make two measurements for each point, which is tedious but necessary work. Mark the points on your map, then join the dots.

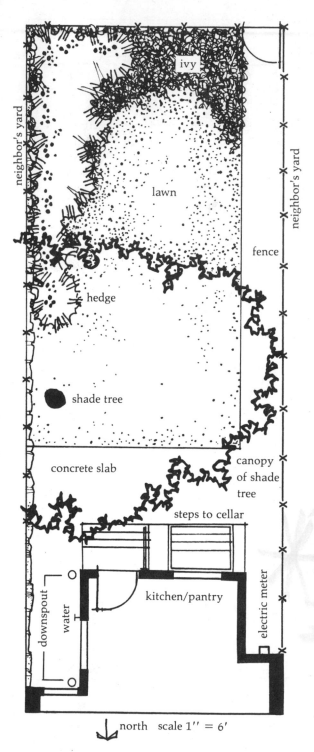

ivy

neighbor's yard

neighbor's yard

lawn

fence

hedge

shade tree

concrete slab

canopy
of shade
tree

steps to cellar

downspout

water

kitchen/pantry

electric meter

north   scale 1″ = 6′

Base Map of the Urban Property: This map shows a typical urban property with a long and narrow back-yard, approximately 20 × 40 feet, closely surrounded by neighboring properties. It has a functional but unimaginative landscape of mostly grass with one large shade tree bordered by a concrete walk and sitting area. The base map is neatly drawn at a scale of 1″ = 6′ and shows the location of all the existing elements, including the location of windows, doors, steps, downspouts and the electric meter.

on tracing paper, being careful to use the correct scale. After you have everything located and sized, you are ready to transfer your map to good-quality, heavy drafting or tracing paper.

DRAFTSMANSHIP

To help make the final draft clear and readable, vary the width of your pencil lines according to the importance of the object you are drawing. The lines used for the walls of your house, for example, should be much heavier than those representing the spread of a tree canopy. Try to represent things simply and clearly, and don't clutter the drawing with irrelevant information. Don't forget to indicate the scale of the drawing and to show which direction is north.

Because you will use this plan over and over, it is important to keep it in good condition. You might tape it to a stiff cardboard backing or keep it taped to your work table. Then buy a roll of tracing paper or acetate, so that you can copy the base and record the information for each phase of the analysis on a separate overlay. You might want to use a different color pen or pencil for each subject, so that when you put all the information together, you can easily see where each bit came from.

Mapping Reality

Although it will soon become obvious to you that the time and effort invested in this initial step of your paper analysis will pay big dividends, a word of caution is necessary. Designing a landscape involves much more than drawing plans that look pretty on paper. Remember that the symbols you have drawn on paper represent objects that actually fill space. Symbols that appear similar on paper may represent things that are different in the landscape. Three circles on paper, for instance, may be related perfectly on the plan. But what is their relationship in the actual landscape when one is a pool (a hole in the ground), another is a raised planter and the third an 80-foot elm?

Landscapes exist in space. They are not flat, and they are not pictures. In addition to having length and width, landscapes have a third dimension—depth, in which the observer can move. Any three-dimensional objects, including trees, shrubs,

walls, fences, benches, paths and terraces, change the space in which they exist. You can view these spaces from many sides as you move about. Keep in mind, then, that the symbols you put on your paper plan are real objects having three dimensions and that the dimension you see on the plan may be the least important.

When your base map is completed, you are ready to begin analyzing your property. The more information you can record on overlays of this map, the more effective your results will be. Remember that the more mistakes you make—and correct—on paper, the fewer you are likely to have in the landscape.

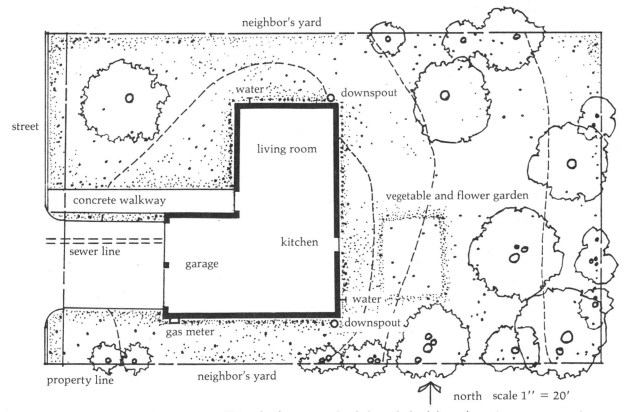

Base Map of the Suburban Property: This suburban property is a newly constructed house, located in a development, with the usual plantings of turf, shrubs and a few small specimen trees. Although it is bordered by neighbors on two sides, a natural wood- *land along the back boundary gives a more spacious feeling and provides a nice backdrop to the property. The map is drawn at a scale of 1″ = 20′. All of the existing landscape features are depicted on the map.*

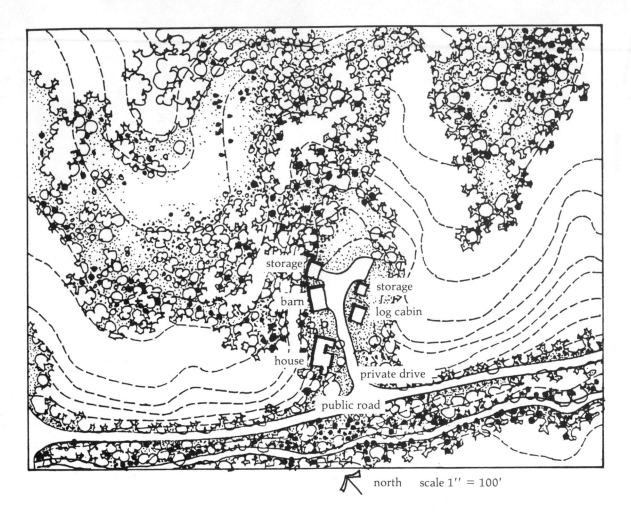

north   scale 1'' = 100'

Base Map of the Rural Property: This is a 52-acre property. The base map is drawn at a scale of 1'' =100' and shows the location of the house and outbuildings, the driveway (which adjoins a gravel township road), vegetation and contour lines. The contour lines were obtained from a professional survey done by the previous owners and were drawn to scale using the grid system.

2

Geology

Geology is the science of the earth. It is the study of all the materials that make up the earth and of the processes that form and transform those materials. Philosopher-historian Will Durant said that civilization exists by geological consent and is subject to change without notice. If you live near a fault zone, you'll have no trouble believing that your life and property are dependent on geologic factors. We've all heard of earthquakes and mud slides that have caused tremendous loss of life and property. These are large-scale geologic events. But even on a less dramatic scale, geology is important to your life and landscape.

Your property is the way it is because of the structure and composition of the underlying materials, their geologic history and the nature and activity of their ongoing geologic processes. The extent to which you can alter your landscape is,

Geological Analysis Checklist

The geological analysis of your property will help you to determine which areas of your land are suitable for different landscaping functions. Because in many cases the geology is not visible, this analysis may point out limitations or opportunities you had no idea existed.

1. *Analyze your area for geologic hazards. Look for:*

   earthquake zones—location of faults
   nature of surface
   deposits and
   bedrock
   steepness of slope
   ground subsidence—natural collapse of
   subsurface rock
   formations
   man-made
   formations
   collapse due to events
   such as pumping
   coastal or stream-bank erosion
   mass movements—landslides, mudflows,
   rockfalls

2. *If you are planning anything from a house to a utility shed, analyze your site for the area best suited for construction. Look for:*
   bedrock and surface
   material—ease of excavation
   foundation strength
   depth to bedrock
   depth to water table
   glacial features

3. *If you need to locate a well or a septic tank, find the area that has a potential ground-water supply for wells, or soils suitable for a septic tank by analyzing your site for:*
   wells—depth to water table
   rock porosity and permeability
   pollution potential
   septic tanks—depth to bedrock
   depth to water table
   drainage characteristics of
   soils

4. *If you need to regrade the ground surface for any reason, analyze your site to find out how extensive the job will be and what the possible consequences are by determining:*
   depth to bedrock
   slope-holding capability of surface material
   possibility of erosion or landslide

5. *Any unique or scenic geological features, such as rock outcrop, should be incorporated into your landscape plan, and any local rock should be used for walls, walks or other features. Determine effects of geology on plant growth. Look for:*
   depth to bedrock
   depth to water table
   temperature variations
   mineral components of soil

in many cases, determined by its geology. Even the choice of a plant species may be influenced by the existing geologic conditions.

If you are engaged in finding a homesite or building a house, you should have detailed and accurate geologic information. At the very least, you will want to know whether your proposed location is free from geologic hazards such as earthquakes, slippage, shrink-swell, frost heave or severe erosion.

If any grading (earth moving) is included in your landscape plans, you must find out if the geology of your property makes it feasible, then what the consequences are. Changing contours may create unstable conditions or erosion problems. If the bedrock is near the surface, it may be impossible or prohibitively expensive to excavate.

On the other hand, you may be able to expose a dramatically beautiful rock edge or wall.

If you are not planning any construction and simply want to make or remake a beautiful garden, you will still need to know the characteristics of your geology, its ability to support structures, its susceptibility to shrinkage, where and to what degree you can change the natural slope and what sort of water absorption the underlying rock provides. All these factors influence the physiography, soils, climate and, ultimately, the vegetation that would occur naturally on your land.

Geology and the Landscape

Although many of the processes that form and transform the earth occur over a period so long that we can barely comprehend them, let alone relate them to our own backyards, there are processes that occur at a rate fast enough to warrant our attention. Earthquakes are the most dramatic and significant of these, but there are others that may be equally important if you live near a pumping station or on a seacoast. Beachfront property is constantly changing, and areas where oil or water is being pumped from the ground are subject to subsidence.

HAZARDS

Everyone knows of the hazards of seismic events associated with the San Andreas fault, but the adjacent Humboldt fault in California is less well known, as is the one in Anchorage, Alaska. There are many more, with varying degrees of probable activity, and many homeowners may be surprised to find that they live in a zone where there is risk of earthquake damage. While faults should be looked for in any region, they become of crucial importance on the West Coast, from southern California to Alaska. Faults are accurately described on geology maps, and it takes little effort to locate them.

The effect of a seismic event, however, is not confined to the fault itself, and cautious home buyers should be familiar with other factors. The effect of an earthquake depends on the distance from the fault, the nature of the geology (the bedrock type) and the types of landforms. People commonly assume that the farther away from the epicenter of an earthquake, the less severe the damage. However, given particular geologic conditions, the distant tremors can actually exceed those near the epicenter. Steep slopes are less likely to be stable than shallow ones and will very likely give way if the tremors are severe. Bluffs along the southern coast of California are notorious for landsliding and should never be considered as a suitable homesite. Very low land that is subject to submersion, such as the land adjoining the

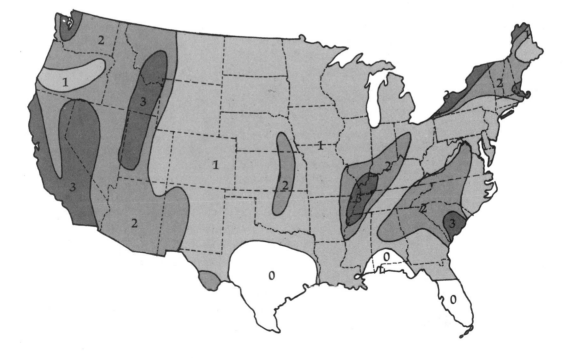

The relative degree of risk of earthquake damage is shown on this seismic risk map. Zone 0 areas are those with a reasonable expectancy of no earthquake damage. Zone 3 areas are those where major destructive earthquakes can occur (and have occurred). In between are Zones 1 and 2, where minor and moderate damage, respectively, are the prospects.

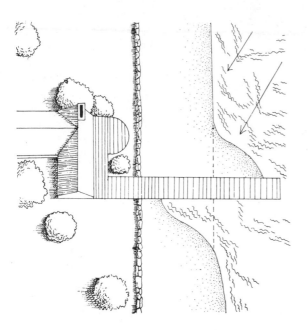

A beach is a dynamic form, and in its natural state, it tends to maintain a balance between input and output. Sand is constantly moving, sometimes down the beach, sometimes landward to form sand dunes. The movement of sediment along the beach is caused by the backwash of waves and is called littoral drift. Any disturbance of the natural balance inherent to the process, such as building on a dune or, as here, constructing a pier, will change the width of the beach by changing its supply of sand. In the case shown, the pier disrupts the ocean's natural current along the coastline (a current known as longshore drift). Typically, sand will accumulate on the upcurrent side of the pier and erode away from the downcurrent side. By understanding littoral drift, you can landscape your beach home in a way that complements what nature does, rather than disrupts or destroys it.

San Francisco Bay, is also a high-risk area for residential construction.

If you live near a coast, you know that some beaches are rising, others are falling. Tides, winds and littoral drifts effect dramatic changes to shore-lines and may cause dramatic changes to your foundation and property.

FOUNDATIONS

If you are planning to build a house, your first task is to ensure that the proposed location is free from geologic hazards. The next step is to determine whether the site is suitable for construction and, if necessary, whether it can provide water and sewage facilities.

The most important determinant of a site's suitability for construction is its ability to support a foundation. Houses require foundations to anchor them to the ground, and if the underlying material is unstable or cannot support the weight of the structure, then obviously the anchor will be unstable as well. In general, igneous rocks, such as granite, and metamorphic rocks, such as marble, provide excellent foundation conditions because they are relatively hard and stable. Some sedimen-

tary rocks, such as sandstones, shales and the harder limestones, will also provide perfectly adequate conditions. But there are some shales that are subject to block faulting, and limestone can present a major hazard in certain areas. Because limestone is water-soluble, caverns are formed below ground, weakening the surface and eventually causing its collapse. The resulting holes, which are common in Kentucky and other limestone areas throughout the United States, are called sinkholes. If your property is underlain by sedimentary rock, be sure to ascertain that it is not block-faulting shale or cavernous limestone.

Good solid rock makes for good solid foundations. But if the bedrock is so far below the surface that reaching it with foundations is impossible, then the nature of the surface material must be studied. This will be particularly true if you live in certain areas of the Coastal Plain—most of Florida, much of Texas, the Carolinas, Georgia, Virginia, Maryland and New Jersey—where rock may be as much as 2,000 feet below the surface. This 2,000-foot depth consists of unconsolidated sediments—sands and gravels—most of which were deposited when this area was below sea level. The land is flat and there is little apparent impediment to building. But because the sediments are permeable and filled with water, you must consider the depth to the water table.

HIGH WATER TABLES

Most of the lowland in the Coastal Plain has a water table on or near the surface many times every year. If you want to have a dry basement, be sure that the seasonal high water table is not less than 10 feet below the surface. In areas where there is year-round saturation of the ground, there may be deep deposits of peat and muck that are unsuitable for foundations. This high water table of the Coastal Plain will affect the construction of wells and septic tanks as well.

GLACIAL DEPOSITS

If you live in the northern states, there is another unique geological factor that may affect your building plans. Here the land was dramatically changed during the glacial period called the Pleistocene, which began 1 million years ago and

ended only 20,000 years ago. It was in this period that great waves of glaciers advanced and receded across North America. They stripped rocks and soils, gouged out holes, deposited tons of rocks, made drainage basins and left a host of characteristic signatures—terminal moraines (masses of material deposited at the lower end of a glacier), kettle lakes (water-filled holes formed when blocks of ice, left buried in sediment by the receding glacier, melted), kames (hillocks formed when blocks of ice containing sediments melted) and eskers (ridges formed by the gravels of streams flowing on or under the glacier). The material left behind by the glaciers, called glacial drift and till, covers the bedrock and determines the suitability of these areas for building.

CLAY

If the composition of the glacial till is rich in clay, there is a great possibility of shrink-swell, frost heave or slippage—any of which can displace

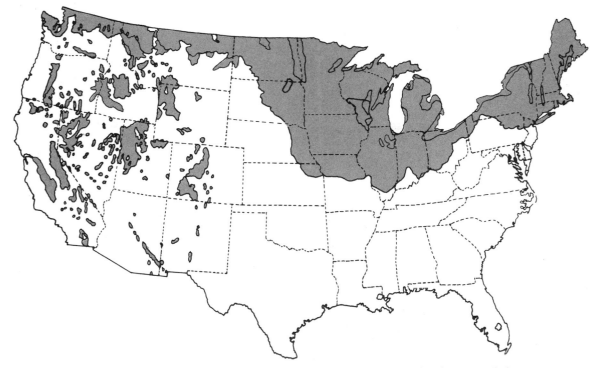

Glaciated areas occasionally present difficult conditions for builders. Getting complete and accurate geologic and soil information is thus important if you live in an area indicated on the map as having been covered at one time by glaciers, and if you are planning to build or add on as a part of your landscaping endeavor. Get the advice of a competent engineer, too.

an entire house. Because clays have the capacity to contain a large percentage of water, they may swell during wet periods and shrink during dry spells. This expansion and contraction of the surface material will rapidly displace foundations, in as short a period as a year. Since clays can have a high moisture content, they are subject to freezing, and because water expands as it freezes, the clays may push up or heave. Frost heave, as this occurrence is called, has sufficient strength to lift foundations out of the ground.

Finally, when sands and gravels overlay clay and clay overlays rock, the entire surface may slip. The sands may move over the clay, and both the sand and clay move over the rock, creating a disaster for anything on the surface. Although this situation is a severe hazard for home builders in the glaciated areas of the United States, it may occur anywhere there is an abundance of clay. If you find this dangerous condition on your property, consult an engineer before building.

If you are building a house, this information should serve to convince you of the importance of knowing what geologic materials lie under the ground on which you want to build. It is possible that there may be two or more formations on your property, one that is suitable for foundations and one that isn't. This will be your first guide in deciding where to locate a new building. When you look at the other ecological conditions of your property—the physiography, soils and water—you will be able to focus on the geologically safe area as the best building site.

WELLS AND SEPTIC TANKS

If your property must provide on-site water and sewage disposal, you will need to determine the water-bearing capacity of the bedrock and the depth and drainage characteristics of the overlying material. Wells require available water, and septic tanks need soil conditions that allow the waste water to percolate gradually. Many beautiful sites, rich in forests and rock outcrops with splendid views, may very well be uninhabitable simply because they cannot provide sufficient water or adequate sewage disposal. Although it is likely that you will depend on an engineer to design and locate these systems, you should know how your geology will affect them.

Igneous and metamorphic rocks are hard and slow to erode and are usually found at high elevations. Because erosion occurs at a faster rate at high elevations, there is often only a thin, sloping layer of soil that is not deep enough for a septic tank. Moreover, hard igneous rocks like granite, gneiss and quartzite have little pore space and do not contain much water except in cracks and fractures. If you have already selected a site that is located on an igneous ridge, you should look for an area where the rock has abundant fractures or where there are two or more rock formations. If the hard layer is covered by a more permeable one, there may be springs and well water in the top layer. But you will also need to find soils that are deep enough to hold a septic tank.

Sedimentary rocks are softer than igneous rocks, erode more easily and are usually found in valleys. They also have larger pore spaces and contain more water than the harder rocks. Therefore, you are likely to find abundant water in sedimentary valleys, particularly those with limestone or sandstone. Because erosion removes material from high ground and deposits it in lower locations, and because the finer material moves faster and farther, the valleys are more likely to have thicker soils suitable for septic tanks. But beware! That perfect valley site with a river bordered by a forest may present great danger for the prospective homeowner. If you notice that the forest has an abundance of water-loving species, it is very likely in the floodplain. Not only are floodplain soils poorly drained and therefore unsuitable for a septic tank, but in time of flood, this area will be occupied by the river.

Cavernous limestone, which is often found in valleys, is a very good source of water, but it too can present problems for water sources as well as for construction. Because water passes freely through the many caverns and fissures, wells are likely to be successful, but pollution can pass through just as easily. That is why there is a frequent occurrence of groundwater pollution in limestone areas. Before you dig a well in a cavernous limestone area, you will need to locate potential sources of pollution and ascertain the direction of the flow of water to make sure that your water is not being contaminated.

The sands and gravels of the Coastal Plain are also rich in groundwater, and as long as you can locate your septic tank above the seasonal high water table, it will drain adequately. Glaciated areas with an abundance of clay are poorly drained and are not suitable for septic tanks. Areas with sands and gravels are so well drained that the septic tank may drain into the well water if they are not located properly in relation to one another.

GRADING

Grading, or earth moving, is required when you need a flat surface on which to build or pave, or when you want to change the shape of the ground for drainage, paths or drives, or to make your yard more private by adding a hill (berm) for screening. Grading involves cutting, which is taking soil away from one location, and filling, which is putting it down at another location. For small areas, it can be done by hand with a pick and shovel. For larger areas, it will probably require mechanical equipment.

Any grading, no matter how slight, alters the natural condition of the surface material and will alter the natural drainage patterns, soils and vegetation. You should always try to keep grading to a minimum. That means locating buildings and paved areas where they require the least change to the existing ground surface. On most sites, however, some grading will be necessary, and to ensure that your grading projects will be successful, you must look at the constraints that may be imposed by the geology of your property.

ANGLE OF REPOSE

All slopes have a maximum angle at which various soil and rock materials can be inclined before failure occurs. This is called the angle of repose, and it is determined by the nature of the surface material, the drainage conditions and the vegetative cover. Remember that grading requires removal of the existing vegetation, and the newly exposed area will be more subject to erosion and landslide. Any new slope should be revegetated as quickly as possible.

In general, clay slopes are most subject to erosion and should be no more than slight to moderate in steepness. Sandy soils will hold a somewhat steeper slope, but no soil can hold the steepness of consolidated bedrock, which in some cases can remain close to vertical.

For the same reason that slopes of consolidated bedrock are stable, they are impossible to grade or cut without blasting. The only way to get a flat surface on exposed bedrock is to fill over and around the top of the rock. Since this fill will have to be brought from somewhere else, this could make an expensive grading job. In any case,

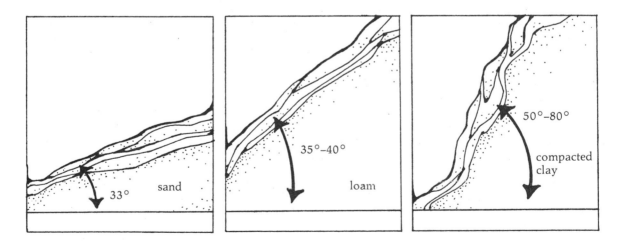

The angle of repose is the maximum angle at which different soil and rock materials can be inclined before they slide or collapse. Dry sand, left, has about a 33-degree angle of repose. Loam, center, a soil composed of sand, silt and clay, has one of 35 to 40 degrees, while well-drained, compacted clay can rise to 50 to 80 degrees.

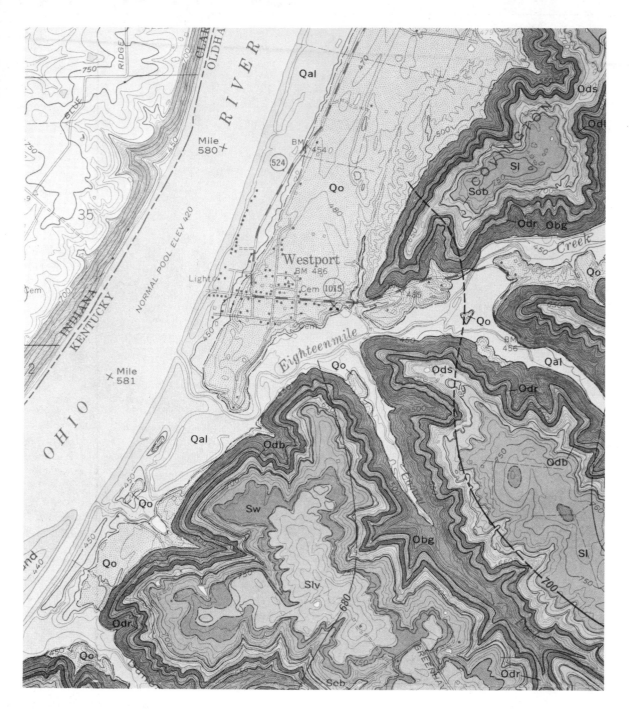

Bedrock geology maps published by the United States Geological Survey are marvels of cartography as well as geology. All sorts of information is compacted and cemented together. There's a base of natural and man-made landmarks—streams, roads, buildings. There are contour lines. And there's color (regrettably missing here). Each rock formation is represented by a different color, delineating the location and the extent of the formation's emergence in the area's geology. The maps are remarkably inexpensive. You should definitely have a quadrangle map covering your area to help you analyze your property's geology.

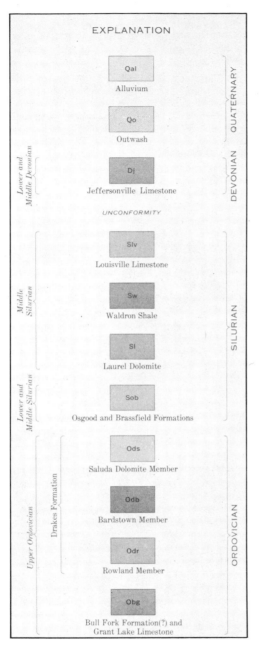

EXPLANATION

QUATERNARY

Qal
Alluvium

Qo
Outwash

DEVONIAN

Dj
Jeffersonville Limestone

Lower and Middle Devonian

UNCONFORMITY

Slv
Louisville Limestone

Middle Silurian

Sw
Waldron Shale

Sl
Laurel Dolomite

SILURIAN

Sob
Osgood and Brassfield Formations

Lower and Middle Silurian

Ods
Saluda Dolomite Member

Odb
Bardstown Member

Odr
Rowland Member

Drakes Formation

Upper Ordovician

ORDOVICIAN

Obg
Bull Fork Formation(?) and Grant Lake Limestone

Every USGS quadrangle map has a legend, although not all legends are the same. Typically, the legend will explain the geologic symbols used on the map. The better legends, as here, summarize the geological information about each formation shown on the map. They list the composition and relative age of each, starting at the top with the youngest and progressing toward the bottom to the oldest. Each formation is named and coded with a color and with letters. The codes are used on the map itself, and the legend is the key that helps you sort them out.

if you plan to do any cutting, be sure that there is sufficient depth to bedrock to allow you to create the desired grade.

GEOLOGIC ASSETS

While exposed bedrock can create problems with grading, it can also be a beautiful and dramatic asset. If it occurs naturally, it should be made one of the most important elements in your landscape plan. Once you understand why and how rocks occur in nature, it is easy to use them with skill. You may even want to create a natural-looking rock outcrop with mosses and lichens and pockets of soil in which you can plant ferns and rock plants. Remember to place the rocks at the same angle that they naturally occur. Also, if there is loose or weathered rock lying on the surface, by all means, use it in the landscape. It will be the cheapest and most appropriate-looking material for walls, walks, patios and houses. (Old fieldstone houses look much more fitting in the landscape than their aluminum-sided replacements.)

VEGETATION

The importance of geology to the plant life of an area is not as obvious as is its importance to building or grading. Except in areas like the serpentine barrens in Maryland, where the unique minerals cause a specialized kind of vegetation, the effects of geology are not as dramatic either. They are, nevertheless, important to understand when analyzing the ecology of your property.

Geology controls the distribution or range of native plants both directly, through its effect on surficial soils and underlying bedrock, and indirectly, through its effect on physiography and climatic variation (see Chapters 3 and 6). Soils, which are the growing medium for plants, provide the nutrients and water necessary for plant life. The kind of nutrients available and the degree of availability depend on the mineral fraction of the soil. This mineral fraction is derived from the parent material or bedrock, and its characteristics determine what plants will survive.

The relationship of geology to the distribution of plants illustrates a reason for using native plants. Unless you are prepared to study the natural environment of every exotic plant you wish to import, you can never be assured of their success.

You may be putting a plant that thrives in a wet, acid environment into your dry, sandy backyard. But plants that occur naturally in your area have adapted to all the natural conditions, including geology. To use native plants that are adapted to your geology, then, you need only understand and identify any geologic variations that may affect plant growth.

Your Property: Geological Analysis
COLLECTING INFORMATION

Your first step in analyzing your property's geology is to obtain information that is pertinent to the geology of your area. There are papers, maps, reports and records available from federal, state and local geological authorities. In addition, your county or local university library may have records of well-drilling data, groundwater availability and information on rock outcrops. Some state highway departments have geological profiles for roadcuts along existing or proposed highways. If you live in an earthquake-prone area, you will want to study the United States Department of Commerce's annual bulletin called *United States Earthquakes.* There is a list of published maps and readily available sources at the end of the book. As you will see, there are several different kinds of maps, and they sometimes require great skill in interpreting.

The kinds of geologic maps that you need will depend on your landscaping plans. At the very least, you will need to obtain a bedrock geology map that depicts the rock formations in your area. A surficial geology map will be neces-

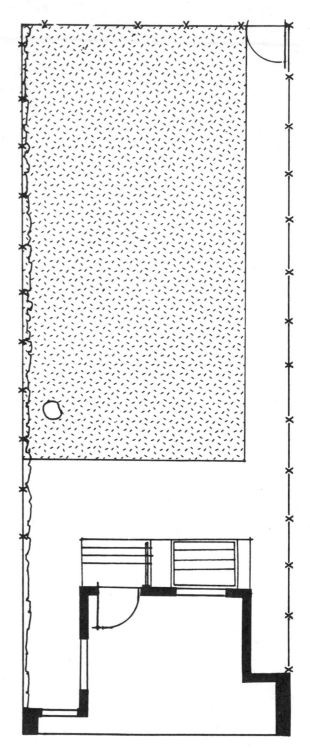

Geologic Analysis of the Urban Property: The geology of this small property is uniform. There are sedimentary and volcanic rocks overlain by old, weakly consolidated terrace materials. This information was obtained from a surficial geology map of the area. Because the homeowners have no construction plans, the only additional information needed will come from the soil survey.

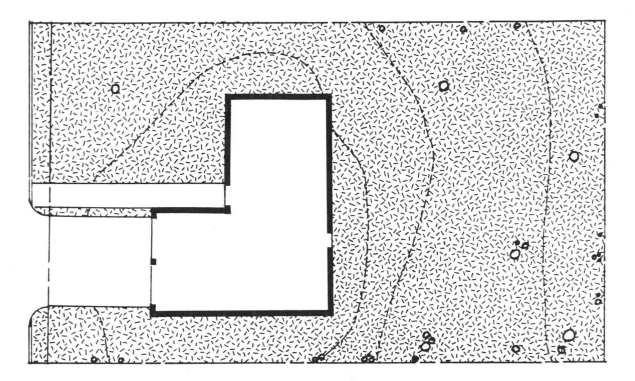

Geologic Analysis of the Suburban Property: This site is underlain by shale and sandstone that is as much as 16,000 feet thick. But between the soil and subsoil and the rock is a thick layer of mixed alluvial materials. In this case, therefore, the engineering characteristics of the soil will be of more importance than those of the very deep bedrock. The soil analysis thus will be important if construction is in the plans.

sary if you live in the Coastal Plain or a glaciated area. If you are planning any construction, you should also get an engineering geology map and a soil survey of your area. The next chapter will explain the need for a topographical map.

RECORDING YOUR ANALYSIS

After obtaining as much published information as possible, you must relate it to your property. Find the exact location of your property on the published map and record the name or names of the formations on a copy of your base map. Note the types of rocks in each formation and their general characteristics. If there are any geologic contacts (places at which two different formations meet) or faults (fractures in the bedrock charac-

terized by displacement on both sides) that exist on your property, you will need to locate them on the copy of your map. Because this map will probably be at a different scale than the geologic map, you will have to estimate the location of the contact or fault as carefully as possible. The next step is to look for clues on your property that confirm the accuracy of the published information or that indicate local variations.

Take your map (with a record of what's supposed to be there) outside, and look for an outcrop or loose rock lying about. If there are no outcrops or rocks visible on your property, look farther afield; you can often see the underlying geology along the side of roads that have been cut into the bedrock. If you find some rock, note its characteristics. Is it hard or soft, stratified or

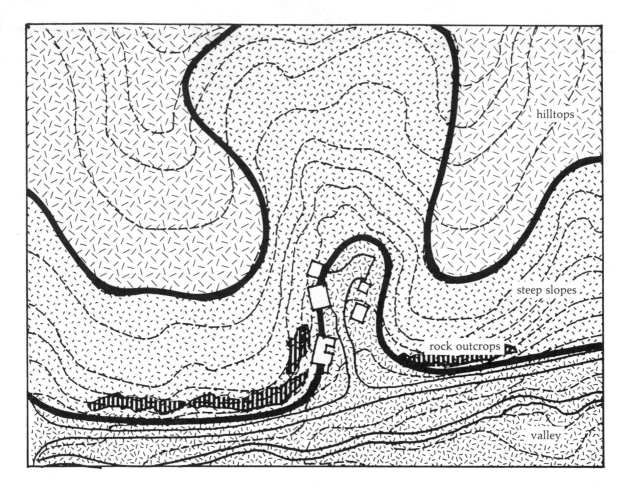

hilltops

steep slopes

rock outcrops

valley

Geologic Analysis of the Rural Property: As is evident from the outcrops, the bedrock on this property is schist and gneiss. There are three geologic areas distinguished mainly by the depth to bedrock. On the steep slopes the bedrock is near to and in many cases *exposed on the surface, whereas in the valley it is 3 to 6 feet below the surface. The hilltops have a depth of 2 to 5 feet to bedrock. This information was obtained from a geologic study prepared by the county planning commission and was confirmed by on-site study.*

nonstratified, coarse or smooth grained, weathered or not? Knowing these characteristics will allow you to refer to a rock identification key and accurately identify the rock.

If there is a geologic contact or fault on your site, look for the physiographic features that might identify where it occurs. If one rock is relatively hard like shale and one is relatively soft like limestone, you will be able to identify the point where they meet by the change in landform from hill to valley. Note the characteristics

of the two formations on either side of the contact. Because these may have a strong influence on your eventual landscape plans, you should try to locate accurately the line of intersection on your map.

If you cannot find any rock and there is no evidence of a contact or fault occurring on your site, you will need to look for other clues that might indicate the bedrock. There may be old stone houses or walls in the neighborhood that have been built from local material. If you live in an area where bedrock is far below the surface, you will need to study the surficial deposits (see Chapter 5).

Once you are satisfied that you have accurately identified the geology of your area, you can turn to one or more of the sources listed at the end of the book to find out the nature of the rock(s). The soil survey, for example, describes engineering characteristics such as foundation strength and depth to bedrock. If you need help or more information, you should contact the geology depart-ment of a local university or your local library. Be sure to record on your map all of the information that you gather.

The geology of your property may itself have implications for your landscape plan, especially if you live near a fault zone or have bedrock on or near the surface. But even if the geology of your property has no direct effect on your plans, it does play an important role in the ecological cycle, and it will help you to understand the other aspects of your environment.

3

Physiography

hysiography is the study of the form of the earth's surface—the mountains, valleys, plateaus and plains. As we've seen, landforms are the product of particular geologic materials and processes—the types of rock, their resistance to erosion and their deformations. Different combinations of rock types result in different landscape forms and structures. Thus, the form of the land is simply the visual expression of the underlying geology. But landforms themselves have important implications for landscaping.

In the United States, different areas of characteristic physiography are called physiographic provinces. Within each province the climate and

Physiographic Analysis Checklist

The physiographic analysis of your property will reveal the features of any small- or large-scale landforms and their possible effects on the climate, drainage and soils of your property.

1. *Analyze your area for physiographic hazards. Make sure to look for:*
   erosion or steep slopes
   floodplains
2. *If you need to regrade the ground surface for any reason, be sure to analyze:*
   degree of slope
   direction of surface drainage
3. *Different physiographic features will create different habitats for plants, so when doing any new planting, be sure to analyze:*
   elevation
   windward or leeward side of slope
   direction of slope
   drainage conditions

geology, and therefore the soils, water and vegetation, are roughly similar. By understanding the nature of your physiographic province, you can begin to see the dynamic interplay of the ecological cycle and how your landscape fits into that cycle.

But there are important differences caused by the location of your property within each physiographic province, and these too may have great impact on your landscaping plans. The climate, soils, hydrology and vegetation of a site located at the bottom of a valley or on a south-facing slope are very different from those features on a hilltop or north-facing slope.

At very high elevations, the effects of physiography produce different climatic conditions. Temperatures are reduced an average of 3°F. for every 1,000-foot increase in elevation, and higher elevations are more likely to have higher wind velocities. Because of the cooling effect of elevation

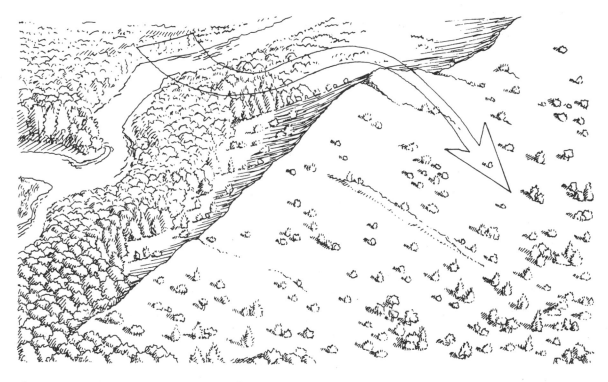

It's important for you to know which side of the hill you are on, if you are on a substantial hill. The windward side—the one facing into the wind—gets more moisture and thus has more vegetation than the leeward side—the one protected from the wind. This may influence your ultimate choice of landscape plants.

Physiographic Regions and Provinces of the Conterminous United States

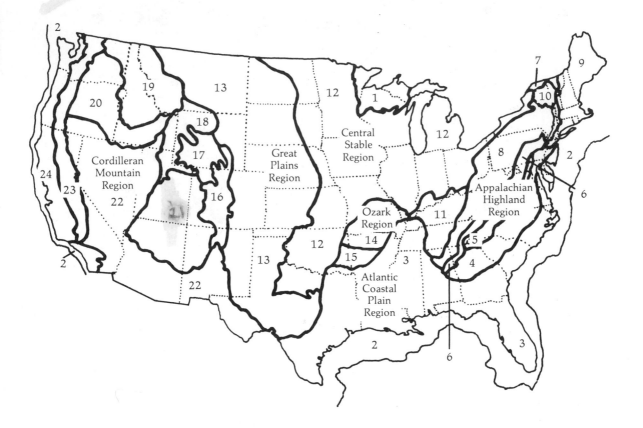

Areas that have similar physiography usually have similar geology, hydrology and climate. Hence, an understanding of your physiography will begin to reveal the interrelationships of the ecological cycle.

Compare, for example, this map of physiographic regions and provinces with the map of ecological regions in Section 2.

Explanation

1. Superior Upland—Hilly area of erosional topography on ancient crystalline rocks.
2. Continental Shelf—Shallow, sloping submarine plain of sedimentation.
3. Coastal Plain—Low, hilly to nearly flat terraced plains on soft sediments.
4. Piedmont Province—Gentle to rough, hilly terrain on belted crystalline rocks becoming more hilly toward mountains.

5. Blue Ridge Province—Mountains of crystalline rock 3,000 to 6,000 feet high, mostly rounded summits.
6. Valley and Ridge Province—Long mountain ridges and valleys eroded on strong and weak folded rock strata.
7. St. Lawrence Valley—Rolling lowland with local rock hills.
8. Appalachian Plateaus—Generally steep-sided plateaus on sandstone bedrock, 3,000 to 5,000 feet high on the east side, declining gradually to the west.

9. New England Province—Rolling hilly erosional topography on crystalline rocks in southeastern part to high mountainous country in central and northern parts.
10. Adirondack Province—Subdued mountains on ancient crystalline rocks rising to over 5,000 feet.
11. Interior low plateaus—Low plateaus on stratified rocks.
12. Central Lowland—Mostly low rolling landscape and nearly level plains. Most of area covered by a veneer of glacial deposits, includ-

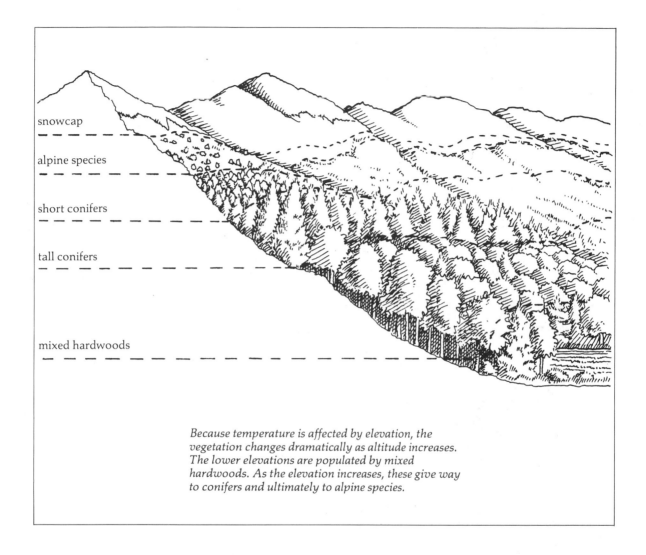

snowcap

alpine species

short conifers

tall conifers

mixed hardwoods

Because temperature is affected by elevation, the vegetation changes dramatically as altitude increases. The lower elevations are populated by mixed hardwoods. As the elevation increases, these give way to conifers and ultimately to alpine species.

ing ancient lake beds and hilly, lake-dotted moraines.

13. Great Plains—Broad river plains and low plateaus on weak stratified sedimentary rocks. Rises toward Rocky Mountains, at some places to altitudes over 6,000 feet.

14. Ozark Plateaus—High, hilly landscape on stratified rocks.

15. Ouchita Province—Ridges and valleys eroded on upturned folded strata.

16. Southern Rocky Mountains—Complex mountains rising to over 14,000 feet.

17. Wyoming Basin—Elevated plains and plateaus on sedimentary strata.

18. Middle Rocky Mountains—Complex mountains with many intermontane basins and plains.

19. Northern Rocky Mountains—Rugged mountains with narrow intermontane basins.

20. Columbia Plateau—High rolling plateaus underlain by extensive lava flows; trenched by canyons.

21. Colorado Plateau—High plateaus on stratified rocks cut by deep canyons.

22. Basin and Range Province—Mostly isolated ranges separated by wide desert plains. Many lakes, ancient lake beds and alluvial fans.

23. Cascade–Sierra Nevada Mountains—Sierras in southern part are high mountains eroded from crystalline rocks. Cascades in northern part are high volcanic mountains.

24. Pacific Border Province—Mostly very young, steep mountains; includes extensive river plains in California portion.

and the fact that moisture-laden air must rise to cross a mountain, precipitation is increased on the windward side of a hill and decreased on the leeward side. This means that moisture-loving plant species will do better on the windward side.

Physiography also affects the availability of surface water and groundwater and the amount and rate of runoff. As we've seen, the configuration of the underlying rocks affects the location of springs and the depth to the water table. Because water flows downhill in the fastest way possible, where it flows from and where it flows to will be determined by the shape of the land. In general, the steeper the slope, the greater the amount of runoff and the more rapid its flow.

This increased water flow on steep slopes causes increased erosion and hence shallow, immature soils. The soils that are carried away by water are generally deposited in the low river valleys and floodplains, producing deep and productive soils. Because the floodplain is unsuitable for a homesite, the soils that exist on upland slopes, where most building occurs, must be protected and stabilized.

The relationship between physiography and the ability of plants to grow well in certain climates is dramatically illustrated by the vertical zonation of plant associations that you can see as you ascend a mountain slope. By climbing a few thousand feet up a mountain, you observe the same changes in species that you would see on a trip to the Arctic. Because mountain ranges run from north to south in the United States, it is possible in the East to travel from a typically southern to a typically northern climate by going not north, but west.

General Information
TOPOGRAPHIC MAPS

Topographic maps show the configuration of the land surface. The United States Geological Survey (USGS) publishes topographic maps for almost all of the United States. The most common of these are the 7½-minute quadrangle maps at 1:24,000 scale. At this scale, 1 inch on the map represents 24,000 inches or 2,000 feet on the ground. These maps cover a four-sided, almost rectangular area

bounded by 7½ minutes of longitude and 7½ minutes of latitude. Because of the converging longitude lines, the actual area covered in each map ranges from approximately 70 square miles for maps of southern states to 50 square miles for maps of areas along the Canadian border.

These topographic maps present a detailed record of a land area and show geographic positions and elevations for both natural and man-made features. They show the shape of the land—the mountains, valleys, plains and plateaus—by means of contour lines joining points of equal elevations above sea level.

CONTOURS

Each contour is a continuous line that never splits or stops. If you want to determine the elevation of a point on a map, you can estimate it by looking at the elevations of the contours around it. Although contours do not cross or overlap, they may appear to coincide on a very steep slope.

Contours that meet on a map indicate a hill or valley. You can tell it's a hill if the numbers increase as the circles get smaller, or a valley if they decrease. Sometimes a map will indicate a specific elevation within these circles.

Evenly spaced contours represent uniform slopes; closely spaced contours represent steep slopes, while those more widely spaced are shallower. Closely spaced contours at the top of a slope indicate a concave surface. If they're closely spaced at the bottom of a slope, they indicate a convex surface.

Contour maps show you in which direction a stream is flowing—water always flows downhill and is always perpendicular to the contour lines. Thus, the contours turn upstream, cross the stream at right angles and then return downstream. In crossing a ridge, however, contours cross at right angles but point downhill rather than up.

The principal value of the topographic map is that it charts the form of the land. It does this by means of contour lines, which connect points of uniform elevation. But the topographic map also shows geographic positions of natural and man-made features.

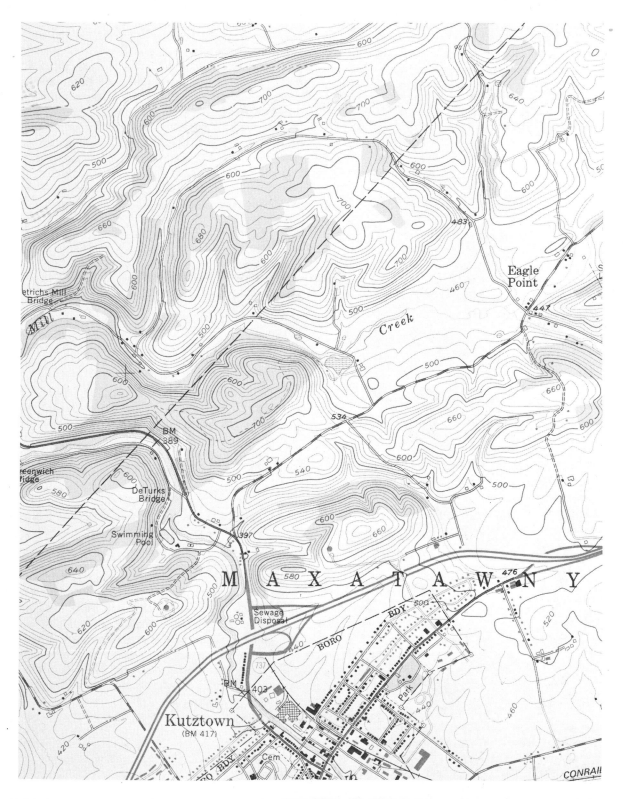

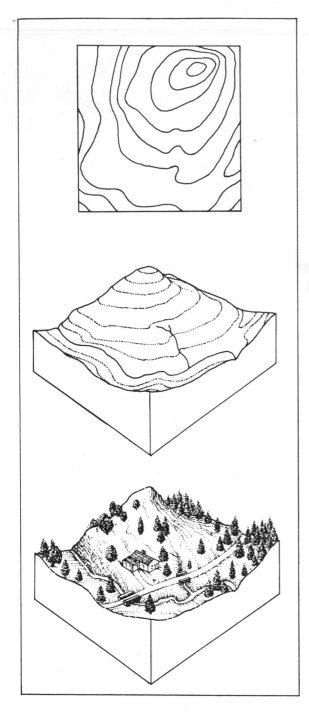

A contour map is a two-dimensional repesentation of a three-dimensional landform. Here the same landform is shown in contours only, top, in a block diagram, bottom, and in a combination of the two, center.

SLOPES

The terms grade and slope are used synonymously and mean the angle of the incline. Slopes can vary from flat, or 0 degrees, to perpendicular, or 90 degrees. The rate of rise or fall of the ground is usually expressed in a percentage and can be determined by measuring the horizontal distance on the ground and the vertical distance, which is the difference in elevation between the contours. You will need to be able to measure slopes to determine drainage conditions and the degree of earth moving required for construction projects.

Physiography and the Landscape

You will need to determine the general physiography of the area in which you live, as well as the local effects of any nearby landforms. Are you within miles of a river valley or surrounded by rolling farmland? Is your property on a plateau? If it seems relatively flat, is it on the edge of a mountain chain or in a large valley? You will have to look as well at the microrelief or minor features, such as small depressions or mounds, and the degree and direction of slopes that occur on your property. Although these may appear to barely slope, they can be the key to keeping water out of your basement. If you are planning to change the grade or the surface of the land for any reason, from building a house or patio to leveling an area for planting, you will have to make sure that the ground surface continues to slope away from your house. It is this slope that insures that water drains away from rather than toward your foundation.

The degree of slope will also play a major part in determining the location and/or cost of your plans. The amount of earth moving required for even minor construction on steep slopes may make these areas costly sites for buildings, roads or even walks. Houses typically require level surfaces with ground sloping away in all directions, and driveways and walks have a maximum angle of inclination beyond which it is difficult to drive or walk.

Your Property: Physiographic Analysis

The first step in analyzing the physiography of your property is to get general information about your area. Most county planning commissions or agencies have maps and information about the surrounding physiographic provinces. Besides writing to your state office of the United States Geological Survey for this physiographic information, check your local college or public library for books about physiography. Look for Charles B. Hunt's *Physiography of the United States* (San Francisco: W. F. Freeman & Company, 1974), which describes in full the geology, soils, hydrology, vegetation and wildlife of each province. Finally, buy a USGS quadrangle map for your area and locate your property on the map.

LOCAL PHYSIOGRAPHY

After analyzing the physiographic features of your locality, you are ready to look at the specific features of your property. If your landscaping plans include no more than adding or relocating plants, you can probably get the degree of accuracy required by estimating slopes. Take out a copy of your base map and locate the low and high points and the extent and degree of sloping areas. Note where there are changes in slope, where it gets steeper or becomes flat.

If you have more extensive landscaping plans, there are three different ways of determining the physiographic characteristics of your property. You can hire a professional surveyor, you can use a USGS topographic map of your area, or you can do your own survey. Whichever method you use, remember to transfer your findings onto the copy of your base map.

PROFESSIONAL SURVEYING

Although estimating the physiography is sufficient for planting and sometimes even for small construction projects like paths, you must make a more precise analysis for anything that requires extensive grading. If you anticipate real difficulties with grading, such as building a house on a steep slope, it may be worthwhile to hire a professional surveyor to prepare a topographic map of your property. Hiring a professional surveyor may be expensive, but it can save a lot of time and may pay for itself in the long run. An accurate description of the existing physiography can help to cut construction costs and allow you to plan for long-term savings by lowering energy consumption or utilizing natural drainage patterns. If you hire a surveyor, be sure to check on his/her qualifications and insist on a contract that spells out what services will be performed for what cost.

DOING YOUR OWN SURVEY

Unless your property is very large, you won't be able to use the USGS map because there won't be enough contours running through your property to allow interpretation. In this case, you will need to do your own surveying on the ground before you can draw the map.

To do your own surveying, you will need a hand level and a folding carpenter's rule or a yardstick lashed to a board. The hand level is a small telescope with a level built in so that you can be sure you are holding it level as you sight

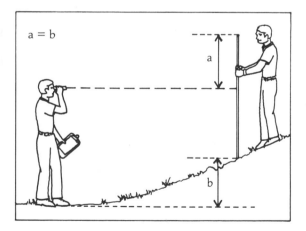

In doing your own survey with a hand level and ruler, always have the person with the stick uphill of the person with the level. The ruler should be adjusted so that its length is the same as the surveyor's height-to-eye level, and it should be held in what may seem to be the upside down position. The dimension read on the ruler when sighting through the level is how much higher the ruler is than the surveyor, and thus the difference in elevation between the two points.

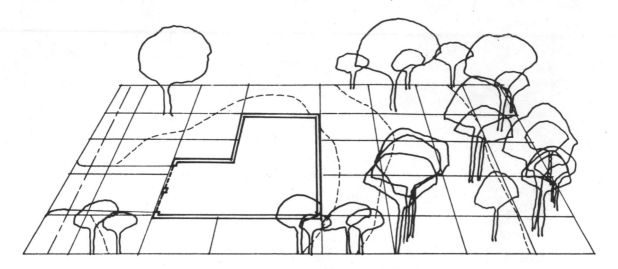

In doing your own survey, readings must be taken in a
systematic fashion. Lay out a grid on the property and,
correspondingly, on the base map. Wherever grid lines
intersect is a measurement point. Take a reading from
each such point to all other points that are uphill of
it. The scale of the grid will affect the accuracy of
the survey: the smaller the grid, the greater the number
of readings and, consequently, the more accurate
the survey.

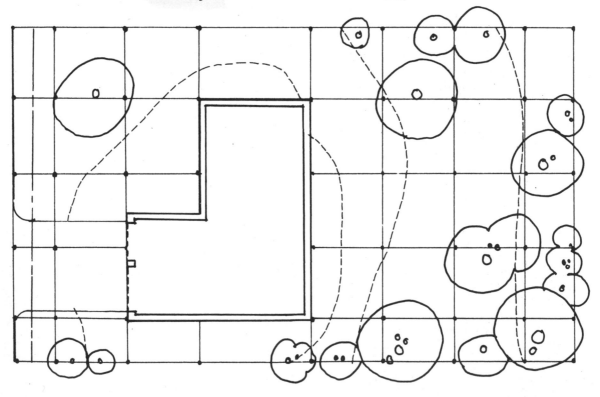

through it. Don't confuse it with a carpenter's or mason's level; it is a surveying instrument. You should be able to get a relatively inexpensive one for your work.

Doing a survey with a hand level is analogous to sketching. You'll get a good sense of your property's grades, but the results won't be as precise as they would be if you'd use a surveyor's transit. The idea is to sight through the hand level to the ruler. The ruler must be adjusted to the eye-level height of the surveyor—that's you—and held upside down, that is, with the 0-inch mark up and the eye-level mark resting on the ground. It must be spotted uphill from the surveyor. You sight through the level and read the measurement. If it is 6 inches, then the spot where your helper is holding the ruler is 6 inches higher than the spot where you stand.

Before you take any readings, you will need to locate stakes in a grid pattern. The distance between stakes will depend on the size of the area to be mapped, the topography—whether fairly uniform or quite varied—and the need for accuracy. (The greater the accuracy required, the smaller the squares must be.)

Although it seems logical that the slope from one stake to the next is uniform, this may not always be the case. If there is an obvious high or

Physiographic Analysis of the Urban Property: Although there is little variation in the physiography of this property, the direction and degree of slope is important. There is a barely perceptible slope to the west and a slightly steeper slope to the rear of the property. These will determine the direction of surface-water runoff.

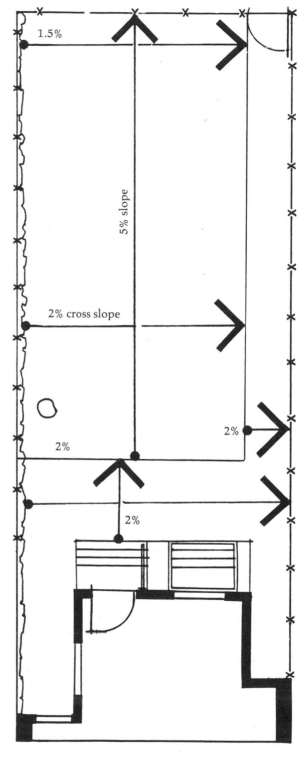

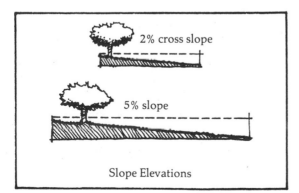

Slope Elevations

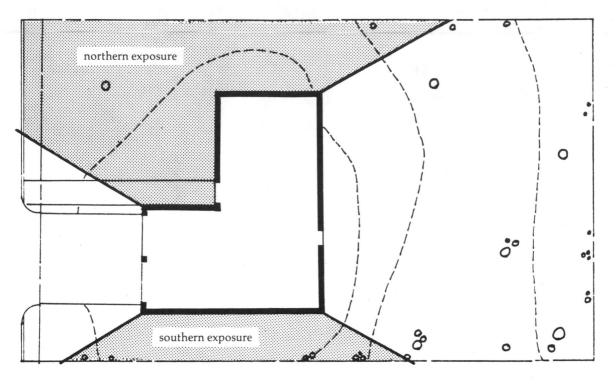

northern exposure

southern exposure

Physiographic Analysis of the Suburban Property: Although there is little variation in the topography, the contour lines determined from a survey of the property indicate that the house is sitting on top of a *small mound with 2 to 5 percent slopes away from it in all directions. There should be no drainage problem around the house, and any landscape plans should ensure that the slopes are not disturbed.*

low spot between stakes, you will need to take an additional reading.

After you've determined the elevation of each stake, you should draw the grid onto your base map and record the elevations. The next step is to draw the contour lines. Remember that these are continuous lines connecting points of equal elevation. Thus, if your grid has 10-foot squares and one stake has a reading of 3 feet 6 inches and another reads 4 feet 6 inches, then the point of the 4-foot contour line will be halfway in between.

To establish the real elevation (the distance above sea level), locate your property on a USGS map and find the closest contour line. If, for instance, it is 440 feet and your property is located on the uphill side of the 440-foot contour, then the 4-foot line on your property is actually 444 feet above sea level.

With the contours mapped, you can go on to calculate the degree of slope and determine where to locate elements so that they require the least grading.

RECORDING YOUR ANALYSIS

Now that you have a contour map, whether you drew it yourself or had it done professionally, you will be able to make landscaping decisions based on accurate measurements of relationships that are often unclear or misleading to the eye. It may surprise you to see that the peak of your roof actually lies on the same contour line as that looming hill across the field. More important, you will be able to use this map to determine the direction of water flow, the probable locations of different soil types, and the physiographic causes

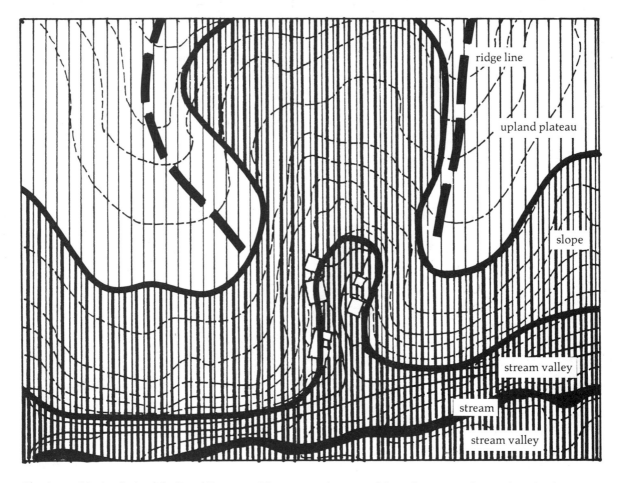

Physiographic Analysis of the Rural Property: The physiography of this property accurately reflects the geologic conditions. There are three general physiographic conditions—the stream valley, the slopes and the plateau. Within these areas there are variations like the direction and degree of slope, which are both *determined from the contour lines. The ridge lines are determined by looking at the contour lines and marking the high points between them. These will determine the drainage divides and hence the direction of runoff. The buildings are all located within the valley bottom and protected by a south-facing slope.*

of small-scale climatic variations. In fact, much of the remainder of your site analysis will build upon this physiographic information. You should, therefore, draw the contours neatly and get several copies made, or be prepared to do many tracings of the contour map.

4

Hydrology

Hydrology is the study of water in relation to the earth—in the soil and underlying rock, on the ground surface and in the atmosphere. The major hydrologic processes are described by the hydrologic cycle, which shows the exchange or movement of water between the earth and the atmosphere. As our population grows and demands on our water increase, it is crucial to realize that this hydrologic cycle is a balanced and finite system. The amount

of water that reaches the earth by precipitation is equal to the amount of water returned to the atmosphere by evaporation and transpiration. It is incorrect to think that increased rainfall is adding to our water supply or that periods of drought signify decreased water supplies.

Whether or not you are fortunate enough to live in an area where there is an abundant and predictable supply of water, there are effects of the

36

Hydrologic Analysis Checklist

The hydrologic analysis of your property will allow you to work with the existing water conditions of your site. It will help you to understand the cause of any water-related problems you now have and help you to change or avoid them.

1. *Analyze your area for water-related hazards. Make sure to include:*
   floodplains—define extent
       limit future building
       protect existing structures
   aquifer recharge areas—protect from pollution or destruction
   erosion—eliminate soil erosion
2. *If you plan to build, determine the area best suited for construction by analyzing your site for:*
   foundations—depth to seasonal high water table
       surface and subsurface drainage
   wells—depth to water table
       water-bearing capacity
       specific yield
       pollution
3. *If you need to regrade, be sure to analyze your site for:*
   drainage—subsurface drainage
       surface grades
       grassed waterways
       runoff
   erosion—revegetate graded soils
4. *Different plants need varying amounts of water. To find out the amount of water available for different species, analyze your property for:*
   precipitation amount
   infiltration
   runoff
5. *Pools or ponds can be a useful and beautiful feature in many landscapes. If you have a wet area, evaluate its potential for a pool or pond.*
6. *If you have a stream on your property, you may need to take measures to protect its banks.*

movement of water both on and off your site. Surface drainage may collect in low spots, creating wet boggy areas, or it may build up against the walls of your house and seep into your foundation or basement. Heavy rains falling on steeply sloping ground may cause serious erosion problems. Or the groundwater you drink and bathe in may become polluted by seepage from nearby septic tanks.

Destroying native vegetation, as man almost always does when he develops virgin land, disturbs the water cycle. Not only does destroying native vegetation decrease the amount and rate of infiltration of water into the soil and increase the amount and rate of runoff, but the native vegetation is often replaced with plants whose water requirements need to be artificially met.

If you want to have healthy plants that eliminate the need for extensive sprinkling or drainage systems, you must understand the hydrologic conditions of your property and use only those plants that are adapted to those conditions. For example, plants found naturally along stream banks or in wetlands, like willows or spicebush, will thrive in a poorly drained yard. If your yard is dry, plants suited to well-drained soils or dry areas will flourish with no need for watering. It is important to locate the different areas on your property that have hydrologic conditions varying from well drained or dry to poorly drained or wet. You may find that your property actually has many different variations in moisture in a small area.

Don't overlook the possibility of using water as an element in your landscape design. Water in the landscape, whether in pools, fountains, streams or ponds, can provide unequaled beauty. Even in a tiny backyard, the addition of a small garden pool or fountain can do much to create a feeling of coolness, greatly appreciated on a hot summer day.

General Information
HYDROLOGIC CYCLE

The hydrologic cycle, the movement of water between the earth and the atmosphere, begins with precipitation in any form—rain, snow, hail, frost or dew. Much of this precipitation soaks into

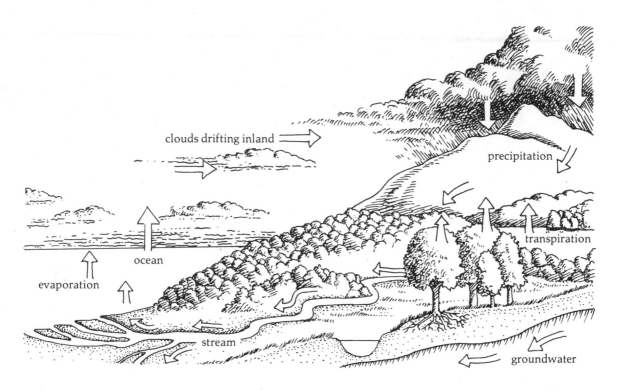

clouds drifting inland ⇒

precipitation

transpiration

ocean

evaporation

stream

groundwater

The hydrologic cycle is the movement of water in the global environment, from the earth to the atmosphere and back again. It is triggered by the heat of the sun and by the pull of gravity. Water moves across and through the earth toward the oceans. During the passage, some of it evaporates. Some of it is taken up by vegetation, which transpires a portion. Even more water evaporates from the ocean. Clouds formed of the evaporated and transpired water move above the land and ultimately return the water to earth as precipitation. Thence the cycle repeats.

the ground by a process called infiltration and becomes groundwater. The water that doesn't soak in runs over the ground surface to lower elevations and collects in streams and rivers that flow to the oceans. From there it evaporates and is restored again to the atmosphere. Evaporation also occurs through the soil surface itself and through plants, which absorb water through their roots and release it through their foliage in a process called transpiration. A large amount of water stays in the ground and moves through the permeable rock layers near the surface, ultimately reaching streams, rivers and the ocean, from where it is again evaporated.

How water moves in a particular area depends on the local variations in climate, geology, physiography, soils and vegetation. We've seen the effects of physiographic features on the amount of precipitation on hillsides and in valleys. All of this precipitation must pass through or over the top layers of the earth, and nearly everywhere this top layer is soil, vegetation or paving.

INFILTRATION

The amount of infiltration depends on the particles of soil and the spaces between the particles. The larger the grains or particles of sand, silt or gravel, the larger are the holes or spaces between them and the more easily can water pass through. When rain falls rapidly on a sandy or gravelly surface, it goes through the sievelike openings into the ground. But when rain falls rapidly on a clay or fine-grained soil, it is absorbed more slowly through the smaller soil spaces, and the water will either stand in puddles or flow over the ground.

The ability of a soil to take in water is also influenced by the type and amount of vegetation

A ridge of the land surface that separates an area of land that drains into one stream from an area of land that drains into another is called a divide. The most famous is the Continental Divide in the Rockies, which separates the land that drains into the Pacific Ocean from the land that drains into the Atlantic Ocean. Divides bound watershed areas. A watershed is the land area that drains into a particular stream. Here you see two divides and sections of three watersheds.

growing on the soil surface. Vegetation helps to prevent erosion because it tends to break the force of falling raindrops and holds the soil particles together, thus preventing the soil from washing away.

The top layer of soil carried away by water erosion contains most of the nutrients necessary for plant and animal life. Loss of this fertile topsoil is serious because it takes hundreds of years to replace. Soils protected by growing vegetation maintain their fertility and are resistant to the erosive forces of rain and running water. This is why the common practice of stripping all vegetation from a newly developed site is so harmful to the soil and why revegetating barren ground as quickly as possible is crucial.

RUNOFF

Water that does not infiltrate runs off and flows to low places as quickly as possible. It drains from the land through channels that begin as small hillside rills and develop into majestic rivers that eventually discharge water into the oceans. Each rill, brook, stream or river receives its water from an area of land that slopes downward toward this drainage channel. These channels, then, occupy the lowest part of the surface area.

FLOODPLAINS

Floodplains are dangerous sites for any construction. Heavy storms increase runoff from the land surface, and thus the flow of streams and rivers is increased. Most of the year water channels have only a moderate amount of water flowing into them. But occasionally there is sufficient rain or melted snow to raise the water to a peak that just fills the channel but does not overrun its banks. A river channel is shaped principally by these full flows, and it is large enough to accommodate them. Sometimes, however, due to suddenly melting

Flooding is a natural characteristic of a stream or river, and the floodplain—delineated here by shading—is the natural means of accommodating the overflow. But building a house on a floodplain is risky. Sooner or later, a flood will damage, if not destroy, the house.

snow or large rainstorms, the channel is not sufficient for the enormous flow of water, and the river floods over its banks. The area occupied by the overflowed water is called the floodplain and is easily identified.

Houses or other structures that are built on the floodplain are sure to be damaged by water at some time or other. Hence, the number one rule in landscaping is: Don't build on a floodplain.

GROUNDWATER

If there is sufficient infiltration of water into the ground, a continuous underground zone of saturation is formed, which is called groundwater. This water accumulates and moves under the surface through pores, holes and cracks in the bedrock. Because many of these openings are caused by weathering, as the bedrock gets deeper there are so few openings that the movement of water becomes almost impossible. Some rocks, however, also have a natural pore space that is not dependent on weathering and that allows the seepage of water to great depths. Sandstone, for example, has large pore spaces and thus allows the water to move easily underground.

Rocks and soils that contain and transmit water are called aquifers. Beneath these aquifers is rock that has become watertight from the pressures of overlying materials. Thus, water seeping down from the rain-soaked surface collects above the impervious layer, filling all the pores and cracks of the aquifer.

WATER TABLE

The top of this saturation area is called the water table. The water table is usually below the surface and can't be seen except in the lowest areas, where it is visible in streams or rivers. The water we see flowing during dry weather usually comes from water in the saturated area.

Because water moves from high to low places, the water table has a surface that is as varied as the surface of the land. Underground water flows downhill, the same way it does above ground. Thus, the lowest point of the water table is exposed at the stream or river that carries away all the water that flows to it (except the water that evaporates). During dry periods, groundwater continues to flow toward the stream, but gradually the water table flattens out.

Many miles may separate the place where rain seeps into the earth's surface to become groundwater from the places where that same water might reappear. This is called the recharge area of groundwater replenishment. Obviously these recharge areas must be protected from decreased infiltration or from pollution.

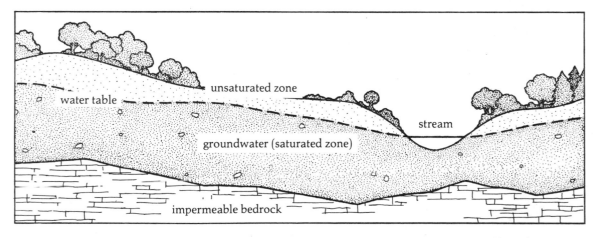

Groundwater is contained in a layer of porous soil or rock called an aquifer. The portion carrying water at any one time is called the saturated zone, and the top of that zone is called the water table. A stream is a part of the water table; were the water table to drop through drought or excessive drainage, the stream would dry up.

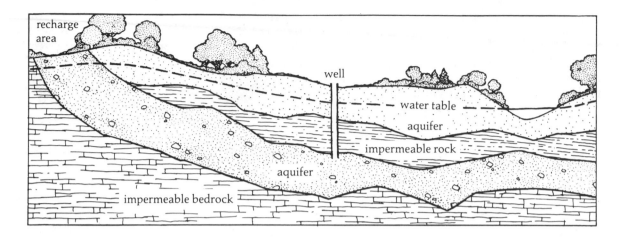

Aquifers are replenished by rain that falls on porous ground and seeps into the saturation zone. The area where this happens is called the recharge area. In some instances, as with the aquifer close to the surface, the recharge area is extensive. But where the aquifer is between impermeable layers, the recharge area may be quite small and located on the periphery of the aquifer.

Hydrology and the Landscape

If you are looking for a homesite, building a home or planning any construction projects, you will want to avoid water problems by taking into account all the hydrologic conditions. The primary point to consider is the extent of any nearby floodplains. In most areas, these have been accurately mapped, and it is often illegal, and always unwise, to build on a floodplain. Check with the local planning commission, the soil and water conservation district office or the Environmental Protection Agency for maps and information regarding the locations of floodplains in your area. If you already have an older building that is located on a floodplain, you should solicit the aid of a United States Department of Agriculture extension service in floodproofing your structure.

In upland areas that are far above any floodplains, flooding can still occur if your house is built in the path of a natural drainageway or in a depression or site that is lower than the rest of the surrounding area. A drainageway or low area may look safe in dry seasons but carry enough runoff water in wet seasons to seriously endanger your house. In housing developments where the landscape has been greatly modified by extensive grading, natural drainageways are often unknowingly blocked or altered. If man-made drainageways or storm sewers are not built to carry the seasonal flow of water, nearby homes may be flooded. Runoff from areas as small as 1 acre can cause flooding.

HOMES AND RUNOFF

Home builders who want to keep the cost of construction within reason should choose a location that has good natural drainage and avoid areas that may be subject to the accumulation or ponding of water or that carry large amounts of storm runoff. Ideally, there should be surface drainage from all sides of a house without your having to do excessive cutting or filling. That means building on an area that is slightly higher than the surrounding ground. If that's not possible, you will have to grade the site to provide adequate surface drainage, and you may have to install subsurface drainage pipes or tiles (see Section 3).

HOMES AND SEASONAL HIGH WATER TABLES

In many areas of the United States, especially where annual rainfall is 20 inches or more, you will need to determine the highest point to which the water table rises during the year; it could flood your basement during certain seasons. On some sites the seasonal high water table may be at or near the ground surface for long periods, and these areas will present difficulties for building. If the water table is 6 feet deep or more, you will probably be relatively safe. You can find the depth to the water table from a soil survey, your local planning commission or by on-site investigation.

HOMES AND GRADING

Remember, too, that areas stripped of vegetation and exposed during construction can cause severe erosion and loss of valuable topsoil. Try to keep grading and the removal of existing vegetation to a minimum. Any areas that must be stripped for construction should be revegetated as quickly as possible. Insist that all topsoil be saved and redistributed after grading, and protect existing trees and shrubs from damage by construction equipment.

WELLS

If you need an on-site water supply, you will want to make sure that there is a high-quality, dependable source of underground water. Although you will want to get expert advice on where and how to locate a well, you can make an initial investigation of the water potential of your property.

DRAINAGE

The easiest and cheapest way to avoid drainage problems is by locating your house and other structures where there is already good natural drainage and making sure that you don't interfere with it. This requires studying the existing drainage conditions before planning your homesite.

Even if your house is several years old and your landscape is well established, still you may have drainage problems inherited from a previous owner or problems that have recently developed because of nearby construction or grading. While you may be able to solve some of the problems yourself, it may be necessary to call in a professional, especially if a system of underground drains is needed to tie in with a public storm sewer.

The easiest way to solve drainage problems is by grading. Remember that water flows to low places in the fastest possible way. If the ground slopes toward the house, water will build up against the walls and seep into the foundation. You should grade your yard so that surface water drains away from the house. A minimum grade of 1 foot in 100 feet is generally adequate. When filling in low areas during grading, use the most permeable soil available. Save the topsoil and spread it over the newly filled and graded areas to help establish vegetation.

Installing suitable downspouts to control roof water may be adequate to prevent water from collecting or ponding in low areas of your yard.

If surface water ponds on your lawn or driveway, you can install small diversions or vegetated waterways to channel off the water. These should be broad and shallow and covered with a tough, dense spreading plant cover.

On lawns, where only a small part is affected by a high water table, a small excavated pond may be a suitable remedy. You can transform the nuisance wet area into an attractive landscaping feature.

If you are planning to add a patio, walk or any paving, be sure that the surface is graded so that water will drain away from the house or any outbuildings. Remember, too, that nonporous paving will prevent infiltration and will increase the amount of runoff. Wood chips, gravel or pebbles, on the other hand, can make an attractive and durable surface while allowing infiltration of rainwater. Also consider laying bricks, flagstones or other pavers over a gravel bed and with sand in the joints. This method also permits infiltration and allows you to grow things in the joints, which will decrease runoff even more.

WATER FOR PLANTS

Once you have ensured that there are no drainage problems that could endanger your house and that any grading you plan does not interfere with the natural drainage of your property, you must determine the amount of water available for plants. Obviously, this depends in large part on the amount of precipitation, which you will determine in your climatic analysis. The average annual precipitation of your area will give you a general idea of the plants to use. But just as in a natural environment, you will find local variations of available water that are caused by small differences in the physiography and soils and that provide micro-habitats suitable for different kinds of plants. To define these habitats, you must observe and test the infiltration and runoff rates of areas with different soils or physiography and rate them according to their relative degree of wetness. Unless your landscape is uniform in every other respect, it is unlikely that there will be uniform water conditions.

You will also need to locate problem areas that might be improved by planting a specific type of vegetation. If, for example, you have a steep slope that is subject to runoff and erosion, you may be able to plant species that will hold back the flow of water. Certain plants develop a heavy, fibrous mat of roots that helps to stabilize the soil and slow down the runoff (see Section 2).

Your Property: Hydrologic Analysis

If you are planning construction or have water-related problems, you will need to obtain information from the sources listed at the end of the book. Depending on the extent of your plans or the severity of your problems, you may need to seek expert advice.

WATER POLLUTION

Armed with as much information as you can get from outside sources, you will need to look at off-site features as well to determine where your water is coming from and possible sources of pollution

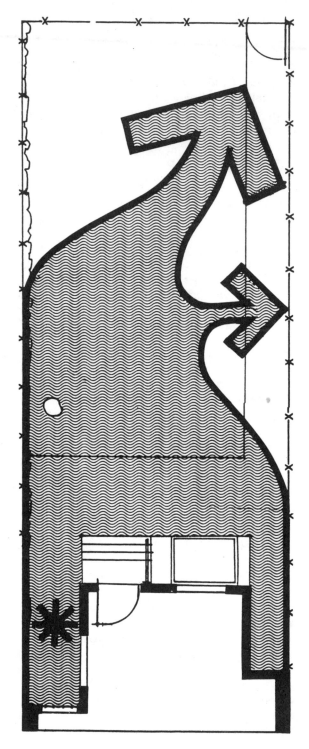

Hydrologic Analysis of the Urban Property: The runoff of surface water follows the direction of the slope, away from the house, toward the southwest edge of the yard, as indicated by the large arrows.

Soil permeability is poor because the clay subsoil slows down the rate of infiltration. This causes puddles of water to stay on the surface after a heavy rainfall—a minor nuisance, since it's only after a major storm.

A more important problem—pinpointed by the large asterisk—concerns water that penetrates the basement walls. The deterioration and settling of the concrete patio that adjoins the house is the cause. The settling has changed the grade and now permits water to run over the concrete toward the house walls, where it seeps through and creates a wet basement.

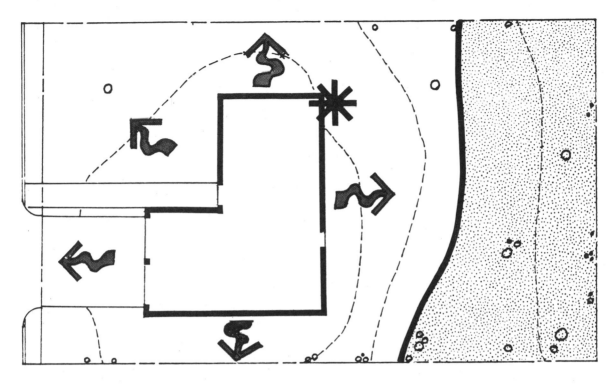

Hydrologic Analysis of the Suburban Property: Surface runoff follows the direction of the slope as indicated by the arrows—away from the house to common grass swales or street gutters. There is a problem—designated by the large asterisk—on the northeast corner of the house where no provisions have been made to carry off the water collected by the downspout. The stippled area at the back of the property is poorly drained and the soil is frequently wet.

along the way. By looking at the physiography of your site in relation to the surrounding area and by determining your watershed area and the location of drainage divides, you can locate where your surface water is coming from and what it is passing over before it gets to you. You can find the source of your groundwater by understanding the geologic characteristics of the area and locating any likely aquifers.

DRAINAGE

Drainage problems that aren't already obvious can be located by observing the movement of water after a heavy rainfall. Look at what happens to water falling from roofs. Does it collect around foundations or walls? And what happens to the water that falls on paved areas like driveways or patios? Note the extent and duration of any puddling.

Record the movement of water on a copy of your base map. Use arrows to indicate the direction of flow. Look for large quantities of runoff that may be coming onto your property and identify the source. Do the same for any water that may be carrying soil off your property. Also record the location of any underground drainage systems.

INFILTRATION

To determine the rate of infiltration, you will need to make several tests in different locations. Find a natural depression, or dig a hole (wide and shallow). Slowly fill it with water. Keep adding water until the soil is thoroughly saturated and there is water standing on the surface. If the water remains for longer than an hour or two, the soil has a poor infiltration rate, and you may have a problem with runoff. Repeat this test at as many locations as possible, especially in areas with different soils

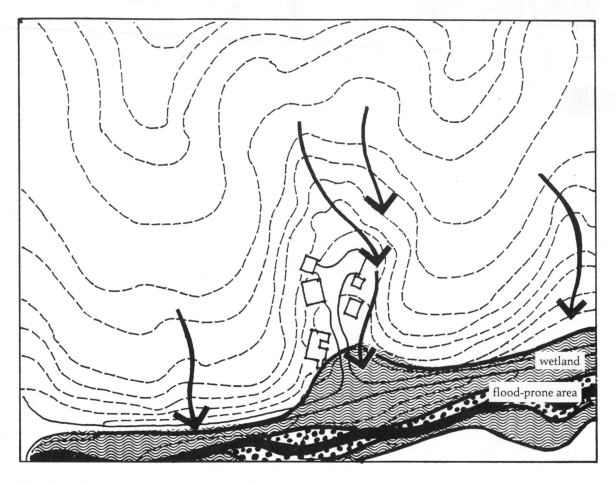

Hydrologic Analysis of the Rural Property: The runoff of surface water flows from high to low point in the fastest way possible following the contours of the ground surface. Arrows indicate the locations of principal drain swales. In those places where it might wash out a road or flow into the house, storm sewers and underground drainage pipe have been provided. There are no major hydrologic problems on this property except during a severe storm, when the stream may flood to as high as the road.

and physiography, and record the results on your base map.

SOIL MOISTURE

If you live in an area of the United States where a lack of water is the problem, you will want to indicate the relative degrees of dryness at different areas of your property. You can test for soil moisture by finding the depth at which various soils remain moist. Again, the more locations you can test, the more accurate your results will be.

By understanding the existing water conditions, you can work with them to prevent any water-related hazards and to plan a landscape that uses water wisely and conservatively. If you have no fear of flooding, have adequate and clean drinking water, and have no drainage problems and no need to water your plants, then you know that your landscape has a balanced water cycle, which you should strive to maintain. If you have one or more water-related problems, this analysis will point out their cause and allow you to design a landscape that eliminates the problems.

5

Soils

Of all the interacting ecological factors of your environment, soil deserves the keenest appreciation and management. It is the natural medium in which plants grow, animals feed, houses are built, roads are laid and through which all kinds of wastes are absorbed. What we do, where we live, what we eat—in fact, everything about our lives—depends on the soil. The quality of our lives is determined in large part by the quality of our soils.

The effect of soil on landscaping is immense, no matter what the scope of the project. For home builders, the determining qualities of a successful site are its bearing capacity, drainage and the stability of its soil surface. Nearly all soils settle under the weight of surface structures, but in most

47

Soil Analysis Checklist

The soil analysis of your property will allow you to distinguish the kinds of soils on your site and the impact of their characteristics on your landscape plans.

> *1. If you are planning to build, find the area best suited for construction by analyzing your site for:*
> *foundations — soil depth*
> *soil texture as it affects*
> *bearing capacity*
> *erosion*
> *drainage*
> *slope stability*
> *septic tanks — soil texture as it affects*
> *drainage*

> *2. If you need to regrade, be sure to analyze your site for:*
> *topsoil protection*
> *soil depth*
> *soil texture as it affects*
> *erosion*
> *drainage*
> *slope stability*
> *3. One of the most important determinants of the success of your plants is the soil. Be sure to evaluate each soil type for:*
> *pH*
> *porosity*
> *texture*
> *structure*
> *water*
> *available nutrients*

cases the amount of subsidence has little effect on the structures themselves. Soils with a low bearing capacity, however, like clayey and water-saturated soils, can become compressed under the pressure of a building's weight, causing severe structural damage.

Grading, which requires removal of vegetation, can obliterate valuable topsoil, cause erosion and alter the water table. Again, clayey soils may present problems that must be taken into account in any grading plans. Because there is much greater runoff on clayey soils, you may need to construct elaborate drainage systems to prevent basement and surface flooding.

Soils and vegetation are mutually dependent on one another. Vegetation plays an important part in the soil-forming process by contributing organic matter to the soil. It also helps to maintain topsoil by stabilizing the ground surface. Soil, in turn, provides the nutrients and water necessary for plant growth. The availability of these, along with the unique needs of individual species, determines what plants can survive and flourish in particular soils.

To find these plants or to discover what you must do to create the soils necessary for the plants you wish to grow, you will have to analyze the structural characteristics and the nutrient content of your soils. The following information gives you the specifics necessary to understand and analyze your soils. The techniques used to change or improve soils are discussed in Section 4.

General Information
SOIL FORMATION

Soil is a complex, carefully balanced natural system with physical, chemical, biological and mineralogical properties. It is formed and modified by factors of climate, parent material, physiography and organisms over vast periods of time. Each of these factors affects the soil-forming process, which in turn influences the properties of the soil itself.

We've already seen how weathering steadily changes the underlying bedrock into unconsolidated fragments. This parent material of the soil has many of the same properties as the consolidated bedrock from which it came.

As weathering of the parent material breaks up the rocks into finer and finer pieces, plants and other organisms move into the weathered rock surface. These grow and die, adding dead organic matter, called humus, which decomposes and becomes part of the soil. New chemicals are formed from humus, making minerals that are physically and chemically different from the original rock.

These processes can be accelerated or delayed by climatic conditions. Temperatures affect the life cycles of plants and animals. Warm temperatures increase their activity and, therefore, their contribution to the soil; cold temperatures reduce or stop it. The amount of rainfall or available water plays a large part in the mineral composition of soil. Water reacts with the original minerals of the parent material and forms new chemical combinations. Some of these dissolved minerals become plant nutrients and are temporarily lost from the soil. However, the more water and nutrients available to plants, the more they will flourish. They will eventually die and decompose, returning the minerals and humus to the soil.

As we've seen, the physiography of the land affects surface erosion. Rain washes off layers of soil, and on steep slopes, where the water flow is faster, it can carry away more soil, and large quantities can be lost.

The final factor in soil formation is time. Few soils can form in less than 1,000 years, and many require up to 10 million years to develop. The age of soil will influence some of its characteristics. Old soils can be infertile due to drainage of minerals for thousands of years. Young soils, which occur in humid regions and on steep slopes, may be shallow and easily eroded.

These factors of soil formation account for the wide variety of soils. There are many climates,

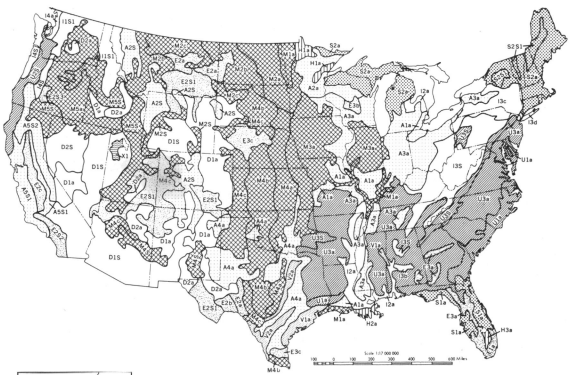

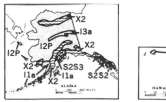

The general soil groups differ because of local features, like physiography, geology, climate and vegetation. Compare this general soil map with maps of other ecological characteristics. The regions each defines, you'll see, are remarkably similar. For the information you need about your soils, check a soil survey for your county.

many combinations of living organisms, many types of rocks, many kinds of land contours and many different soil ages, causing soils to vary widely in their composition and structure.

SOIL COMPOSITION

A basic soil consists of a mixture of sand, silt, organic matter and clay. These different parts of the soil's makeup are generally referred to as fractions: the sand fraction, the silt fraction, the organic matter fraction and the clay fraction. The original composition is formed of the native materials and rock by a process of decomposition.

The sand and silt fractions serve as the chief sources of minerals needed by plants. They occur in different proportions in various soils and feed the plant phosphorus, potassium, calcium, magnesium, manganese, copper, iron, cobalt, zinc, sulfur, sodium, iodine, boron and other nutrients. These minerals are held together in the sand or silt fractions in much the same way as they are in native rocks, but because of silt's extremely fine particles, more surface area is exposed for decomposition and chemical reaction, and, therefore, more minerals are available for assimilation by plants. For this reason, soils with a high percentage of silt are more productive than sandy soils.

The organic matter fraction is made up of residue from vegetable and animal matter deposited in the soil and is chiefly responsible for the soil's nitrogen-producing capacity. This fraction is the most important quality of good soils because it provides a natural home for the millions of bacteriological creatures necessary to plant life. In addition, it serves as a spongy mass to retain water, carbon dioxide and other chemical substances produced in the bacterial world.

The organic material in soil provides a moist coating around each soil particle that creates one of the most active agents for the exchange of mineral elements from soil to plant. Its preservation in the soil is extremely important because without it minerals will be made available to the plant at a much lower rate.

pH

The acidity or alkalinity of a soil is described by the abbreviation pH, which comes from a German term describing the concentration of hydrogen ions. The pH of a soil is expressed in a number somewhere between 3.5 and 8.5, usually around or just below 7.0. A pH of 7.0 means that the soil is neutral. A number below 7.0 means that the soil is acid, while a number greater than 7.0 indicates an alkaline soil. Soil pH can vary greatly, and while most plants can grow in a slightly acid soil, there are some that require alkaline conditions.

Soils near the foundations of buildings are often alkaline because of water washing out the mortar and adding lime to the soil. In a pine woods, the soil will be more acid because of the decaying needles, which leave an acid reaction. Soils at either extreme may not release the available nutrients and should be corrected.

SOIL TEXTURE

The texture of the soil depends upon the relative amounts of different-size particles that combine to make up the soil. These combined particles can be as large as stone and gravel or as small as clay, which cannot be seen even under the strongest microscope.

A typical clay soil is composed of approximately 60 percent actual clay, 20 percent silt and 20 percent sand. The particles in a clay soil are so fine that it tends to be compact, which makes cultivation difficult and interferes with the oxygen supply for plant roots. Water has trouble entering this impervious soil, and runoff is very common during rainfalls.

A typical light sandy soil is composed of approximately 70 percent sand, 20 percent silt and 10 percent clay. The particles in a sandy soil are comparatively large, permitting water to enter the soil and to pass through it so quickly that it often carries nutrients with it and dries out very rapidly. The texture of sandy soils is generally very difficult to modify because huge amounts of organic matter must be added. *Garden*

A typical loam soil is composed of approximately 40 percent sand, 40 percent silt and 20 percent clay, making it an ideal garden soil. It is easily worked and retains water and nutrients, which are slowly absorbed by plant roots. Every gardener should strive for a loamlike soil, and there are soil management techniques that allow you to do so.

A typical adobe soil is a clay soil prevalent in hot, dry areas of the country and is often very hard and cracked. Adobe is the most difficult of all soils for the gardener to cope with. It has all the disadvantages of a heavy clay soil and, being much drier, is more difficult to correct.

SOIL STRUCTURE

A soil's structure refers to the grouping of individual particles into larger chunks or granules. Healthy vegetation requires heavier soils that have good granulation or crumb structure. Sandy soils show little granulation because of the coarseness of their component particles.

Alternate freezing and thawing or wetting and drying, as well as penetration of the soil mass by plant roots, are natural forces that favor the formation of soil granules or aggregates. Such aggregation is most highly developed in soils that are nearly neutral in their reaction: both strongly acid and strongly alkaline soils tend to run together and lose their structural character. Tillage also tends to break down the structure of many soils but can be beneficial if the soil is too compacted.

SOIL POROSITY

Associated with both texture and structure is the soil's pore space, or porosity. This space is large in coarse, sandy soils or in soils with well-developed granulation. In heavy soils containing mostly finer clay particles, the pore space is too small for plant roots or soil water to penetrate readily. Forty to 60 percent of the bulk of a good soil is pore space filled with either water or air.

A satisfactory balance of air, water and soil is necessary for productivity. Too much water slows the release of soil nitrogen, depletes mineral nutrients and hinders proper plant growth. Too much air speeds up nitrogen release beyond the capacity of plants to utilize it, and much of it is lost. Water in overly aerated soil evaporates into the atmosphere and is lost to plants.

SOIL WATER

Soil water occurs in three forms: hygroscopic, gravitational and capillary. Hygroscopic soil water is bound in the soil and is unavailable to plants. Gravitational water normally drains from the pore spaces of soil to become groundwater. If there is excessive drainage and large amounts of water are removed, the plants may suffer from a lack of water. If, on the other hand, drainage is poor, gravitational water may accumulate, causing the soil to become soggy and unproductive. A well-drained soil is generally brown to yellowish brown as far down as 2 or 3 feet, while a poorly drained soil is gray or pale brown down to that depth. Plants depend largely on capillary water, which is the water held in the pores of the soil, for their supply of moisture.

Medium- to fine-textured loams and silt loams provide the best conditions for plant growth. Because they have smaller pore spaces, moisture moves at a faster rate from the lower layers up the root zone. These soils can draw up moisture from greater depths than can either sands or clays. They provide the best conditions of available, but not excessive, soil moisture for plant growth.

SOIL NUTRIENTS

The elements needed by growing plants are supplied by the silt fraction of soils, that portion that results from the slow decomposition of parent material. There may be as many as 100 separate mineral compounds in good soils, but the major plant foods consist of the compounds of nitrogen, phosphorus, potassium, calcium, magnesium, sulfur, carbon, hydrogen and oxygen.

To have a healthy, natural landscape, it is necessary to ensure that your soil, whether you have a small plot or many acres of land, be properly enriched. Dying leaves can be caused as much by a lack of potassium as by a lack of water. A soil test can tell you what nutrients your soils are missing. Their presence or absence in the soil helps us understand the complexity of the relationship between soils and plants.

Soil and the Landscape

A soil's capacity to support a structure, as well as its stability, drainage and erodibility, affects the construction and maintenance of your home. You can determine these properties from the descriptions given in the Soil Conservation Service's soil survey and by on-site investigation. A soil survey will tell you the engineering characteristics of soils, including a rating of each soil's suitability for building as well as its suitability for the disposal of waste from septic tanks.

Although the soil survey's suitability ratings for landscaping can be helpful, you must bear in mind that it takes into account only the traditional landscape of a large lawn surrounded by flower beds and trees. A rocky soil with a high water table, while rated unsuitable for landscaping in the soil survey, can probably be beautifully landscaped with bog plants like arrowhead or pickerel weed and moss-covered rocks.

Your Property: Soil Analysis

The soil survey is an important source of information and should be included in your research, but you

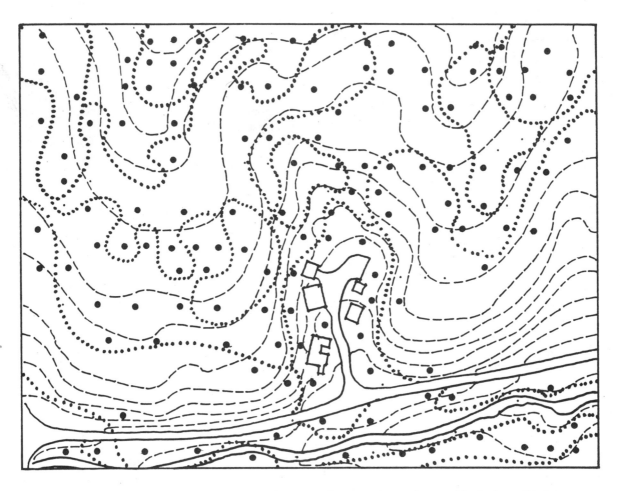

Plotting Soil Testing of the Rural Property: It may be necessary to do more than routine soil testing to get a complete and accurate picture of the soils of a property. Such is the case here, and a copy of the base map is used to plot spots from which to take soil samples for testing. Obviously, each sample must be carefully coded so the test results can be sorted out, recorded and synthesized.

To determine which areas might have different soils that should be separately tested, look at other ecological conditions. On the rural property, the

physiography, geology and hydrology all help distinguish different soil areas. Too, differences in natural and cultivated vegetation may reflect differences in the soils. The dotted lines outline the various soil areas thus evidenced. The scattered dots mark spots from which a sample is to be taken.

Despite the seemingly great number of sampling plots noted here, the property is large enough—52 acres—that even more detailed plotting could be necessary, depending upon landscaping plans.

will also need to do an extensive on-site study to determine your own soil conditions. There are three steps in analyzing your soils: first, define the areas that seem to have different soils; second, study the profiles of the different soils; and third, determine the nutrient content for each soil type.

MAPPING YOUR SOILS

Unless your property was recently covered with a layer of homogeneous topsoil, there will probably be different kinds of soil in different areas. Your first job is to make a rough approximation of those areas with probable differences. The most obvious clue to different soil types is what is growing there. For instance, if an area behind your house has lush growth of burdock, pigweed, purslane and lamb's-quarters, and there is an adjacent area with mosses, skunk cabbage and cattail, you know these areas have different kinds of soil. The first area is probably well drained and fertile with good organic matter content, while the second one is surely wet and possibly acid. The soils from these two areas will have to be tested separately. After you have distinguished areas that appear to have different soils, record their locations on a copy of your base map.

ANALYZING SOIL PROFILES

The next step is to test each of the soils for depth, texture and structure. This means looking at a cross section of the soils to a depth of at least 5 feet. To do this, you must dig a pit or use a soil auger or tube probe to obtain samples from the surface layer to 5 feet below. The core samples will show you the texture of the clay, silt and sand mixture, as well as the structure and the depth of the different layers.

To determine the texture, take a handful of soil from each layer in succession. How does it feel? Sand is gritty, silt is powdery and clay is hard when dry and smooth and sticky when wet. To determine the proportion of each, you should try to mold the soil when wet. If it can be shaped into a thin ribbon or to a fine point, there is a high percentage of clay. If it won't retain any shape, then there is a lot of sand. With a little practice, you will be able to estimate the texture of your soils.

To determine the structure, you can simply look at the particles of soil. Are they loose and granular with a crumblike structure, indicating porous, well-aerated soil? Or are the individual

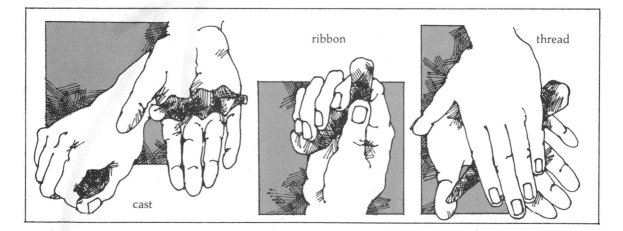

Molding soil in your hand can give you a good indication of the relative amounts of sand and clay it contains. Squeeze a bit of your soil—wet—in your hand. It should form a lump, called a cast. Even wet beach sand will do this. Roll the cast between your hands, and see if it will form a thread. Finally, work the soil between thumb and finger, trying to pinch out a ribbon. Because clay is cohesive and plastic when wet, it can be molded into a long, thin, flexible ribbon that will not break easily. Sand has little, if any, cohesiveness, and though a soil sample with a large percentage of sand will form a cast, it won't form any unbreakable shape. Loam, which has about equal parts of sand and clay, will fail in cohesiveness somewhere between the cast and the ribbon.

particles packed hard and tight, indicating puddled, poorly drained soil?

Record your findings for each soil type on a copy of your map. Also measure the depth of the topsoil and observe the nature of the subsoil in each area. Generally, subsoils will be either mostly clay or mostly sand or gravel, and they may give you a further clue as to the drainage characteristics of the soil.

TESTING FOR SOIL NUTRIENTS

Finally, you should do a chemical analysis of the nutrient content of each of your soil types. There are two ways to find out what nutrients your soil is lacking. You can send a sample to a laboratory or your state's agricultural or land grant college, or you can buy a testing kit and make many of the necessary tests yourself. It doesn't hurt to use both methods so you can double-check the results. A testing kit (available at garden centers or farm stores) will enable you to make frequent tests that may show a variation in nutrient supply from one season to the next.

Testing kits are simple to use and require no knowledge of chemistry or laboratory procedure. You can test for nitrogen, phosphorus, potash and pH.

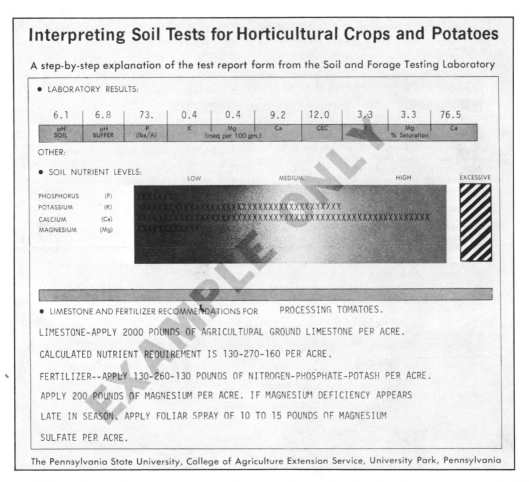

Send a carefully packaged soil sample to your state's land grant college for testing, and you're likely to get a form like this in return. On it are listed the numerical results of the laboratory test. Additional pages explain in layman's terms what the numbers mean. And if what the numbers mean is that your soil needs help, fertilization recommendations—unfortunately in chemical fertilizer terms—are provided.

The most important step in making this test is collecting the soil sample. If you have determined that your whole property has the same kind of soil, then you will need to make only one test, but if there are several soil types, you will need to make a separate test for each. To get a sample that is representative of each soil, dig about 6 inches deep in three to six locations within each area, and mix the samples together. Be sure to keep the samples from different areas separated, and make sure that your collecting shovel or trowel is not contaminated by soils from another location.

The actual test is made by putting a small portion of the sample in a test tube and then introducing one or two reagents. A reagent is a chemical that reacts with the nutrient being tested and shows the quantity of the available nutrient by its color. Color charts are supplied with the test kits, and the final analysis is made by checking the color of the solution in the tube with the test chart.

For a more detailed analysis, along with specific recommendations for improvement, contact your local county extension agent, who will tell you how, when and where to send your samples. If you send samples of several different soils, be sure to indicate on the sample container, as well as on your map, where they were obtained.

The results of the tests will be mailed to you, along with the laboratory's recommendations for soil improvement. Some of these recommendations are made in terms of chemical fertilizers, but you can transpose these recommendations to natural or organic fertilizers by referring to Section 4. A

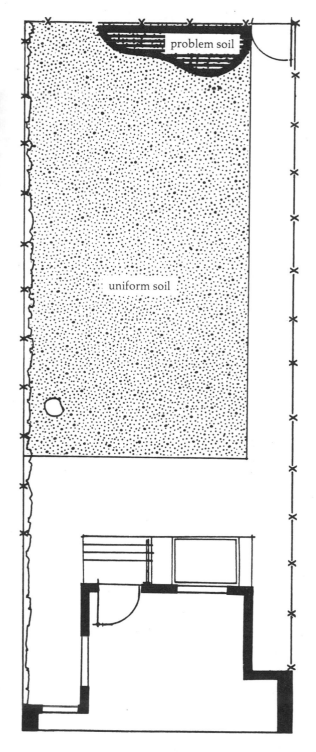

problem soil

uniform soil

Soil Analysis of the Urban Property: The soil is uniform throughout the site—as indicated by the uniform stippling—with the exception of the back side of the property. Here, black stripes delineate an area frequented by neighborhood dogs being walked along the back of the property. The soil in this spot will require improvement and protection to ensure fertility. The general soil type is a moderately well-drained loam that is underlain by a poorly drained clay subsoil. This provides adequate soil moisture in the top layer, but it can also create puddling conditions (see Chapter 4).

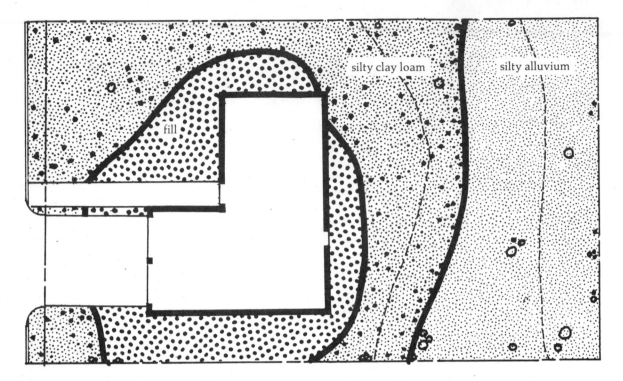

Soil Analysis of the Suburban Property: There are two natural soil types on this property. The first is a fine, silty loam, which has medium acidity and a fine, granular structure in the upper 6 inches. Beneath that it is fine to medium, with a blocky structure. This soil is indicated by the irregular stippling.

The soil at the back of the property is a fine, silty alluvium, which is poorly drained. (Alluvium is any material deposited by running water.) The upper 12 inches is a friable, silty clay loam. Beneath that is a dark, grayish brown, olive brown and brown, firm and friable silty clay loam. This soil is indicated by the even stippling.

There is a third soil type, an unnatural one. It was brought in as fill and contains objects left from construction, including evidence of lime, which accounts for its high alkalinity. This is the dotted area immediately surrounding the house.

general application of compost will correct an overall deficiency of nutrients, while to prevent individual deficiencies, you should apply natural rock fertilizers or other natural supplements.

Once you know the characteristics and locations of the different soils on your property, you can follow one of two courses. You can work with your soils—building where they are naturally best suited for it and planting species that are adapted to soils with similar characteristics—or you can change your soils to make them less wet, more alkaline or better textured.

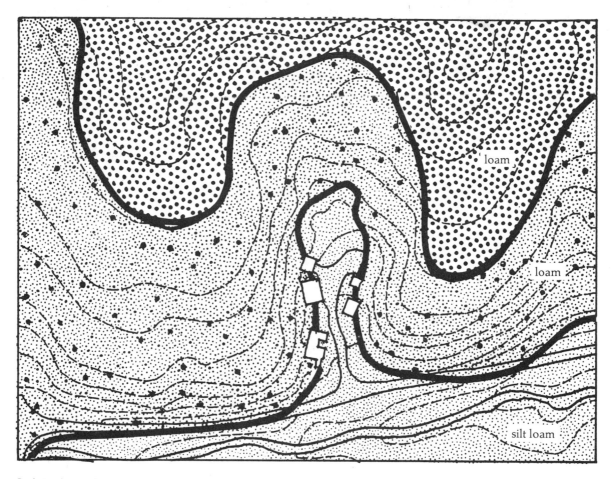

Soil Analysis of the Rural Property: Soil test results, along with the soil survey of the county, indicate that there are general soil types on this property. However, because of the large scale of the mapping area, there may be small areas within the layer grouping that have different soil types. These should be tested later if the soil conditions are important to the landscape plans.

The heaviest stippling delineates an area with a moderate to highly permeable loam. In conjunction with the 3 to 8 percent slopes, the soil is moderately erodible. This particular loam is easy to work, and there is evidence that it had been tilled at one time. The area was most recently used as a pasture, but it is now abandoned.

The soil covering the largest portion of the rural property — delineated by the irregular stippling — is also a loam. This area, however, is more steeply sloped, from 8 to 25 percent, and thus the soil is highly erodible. It has a shallow profile, with much mixing of the surface layers with the upper part of the subsoil. Gullies are common.

The third general soil type is in the stream valley — lightest stippling. It is a silt loam, which in conjunction with 3 to 8 percent slopes is moderately erodible. While the soil is easy to work and is free of stones in most places, it is nevertheless in a floodplain and thus susceptible to flooding.

6

Climate

The daily weather has a powerful influence on our comfort, both physical and psychological. Most of us feel best when it's sunny and clear, and we consider this to be normal weather. Any deviation—an extended rainfall, drought, severe heat or cold—is considered strange and worthy of much discussion. The fact is, however, that these variations in the weather are the norm. Although

there's not much we can do to change the climate, there's a great deal we can do to modify its effects.

Gardeners, from earliest times, have been sensitive to weather changes. When you plant your property, you will have to attune your senses to subtle variations in climate. At the very least, you will want to be certain that the vegetation you plant will survive, since replacing dying

Climatic Analysis Checklist

The microclimatic analysis of your property will enable you to choose plants that will thrive, and will reveal the effects of climate on your energy consumption.

1. Analyze the factors that affect the microclimatic conditions of your site. They are:
solar radiation
wind
precipitation
temperature

2. Analyze the microclimate of your site. Make sure to include the effects of these elements:
landform
vegetation
water
paving
structures

plants can be an expensive proposition. By understanding the effects of climate, you can increase the value of your landscaping efforts even more. With proper manipulation of landscape elements, you can make significant changes in the temperature of your home, reducing your energy consumption considerably.

Unless you live in a very old home, your house is probably not adapted to the local climate. Today we rely on sophisticated heating, ventilating and air-conditioning equipment that uses too much energy that costs us too much money.

But you, as a homeowner with a large interest in the long-term energy needs of your household, can reduce energy costs considerably by a carefully planned landscape. If you are planning to build a home, you have the advantage of being able to design and locate it in the ideal site for climatic and ecological reasons as well as aesthetic ones. If you are not building, there is still a lot you can do to improve the existing conditions.

Your position in relation to the sun is crucial. You will want to be protected from the hot summer sun and exposed to the sun's rays during the cold winter months. Taking advantage of shade and summer breezes can reduce or eliminate the need for air conditioning. In winter, increased solar radiation and maximum protection against northerly winds can substantially reduce heat loss and heating costs.

Although you accomplish these modifications by manipulating your immediate climate (microclimate), to do so requires a thorough analysis of both regional and local climatic conditions. Climate is made up of many measurable factors that vary in different areas of the United States, and in each

of the major climatic regions, people have different landscaping needs or requirements that will make the basic climate more comfortable.

These different climatic regions have great importance to the living part of your landscape. Species like cypress or live oak grow happily in the South but are never seen up North. Traveling, you cannot fail to notice that the plant life looks very different in some areas from that in others. In the Eastern and Pacific states, the landscape may consist chiefly of trees, while in the Prairie states, mainly of grass. All plants are restricted to a more or less limited area where their climatic and other environmental conditions are met.

To ensure a flourishing, maintenance-free landscape, you will need to study both regional and local climatic conditions and analyze how they affect your property.

General Information
REGIONAL CLIMATE

Climatic regions and zones are geographical areas that share common climatic conditions. Many systems have been proposed for classifying climatic regions within the United States, but W. Koppen, a German scientist, developed a simplified classification of climates based on vegetation, which has been the basis of numerous studies of housing, design and climate since it was published in 1931. His classification defines four broad climatic zones—cool, temperate, hot-arid and hot-humid. Each different climatic region merges gradually and almost invisibly into the next. The climatic characteristics of each region are not uniform, and they may vary both between and within regions. In fact, it is not unusual for one region to exhibit at one time or another the characteristics associated with every other climatic region. Yet each region has an inherent character of weather patterns that distinguishes it from the others, and each has different implications for landscaping.

CLIMATIC REGIONS

Landscape Planning for Energy Conservation by Gary O. Robinette (Reston, Va.: Environmental Design Press, 1977) gives the following descriptions of the four climatic regions:

Cool

A wide range of temperature is characteristic of cool regions. Temperatures of −30°F. to +100°F. have been recorded. Hot summers and cold winters, with persistent winds year-round, generally out of the Northwest and Southeast, are the primary identifiable traits of cool regions. Also, northern locations most often associated with cool climates receive less solar radiation than southern locations.

Temperate

An equal distribution of overheated and underheated periods. Seasonal winds from the Northwest and South along with periods of high humidity and large amounts of precipitation. Intermittent periods of clear, sunny days followed by extended periods of cloudy, overcast days.

Hot-Arid

Clear sky, dry atmosphere, extended periods of overheating, and large daily temperature range. Wind direction is generally along an east–west axis with variations between day and evening.

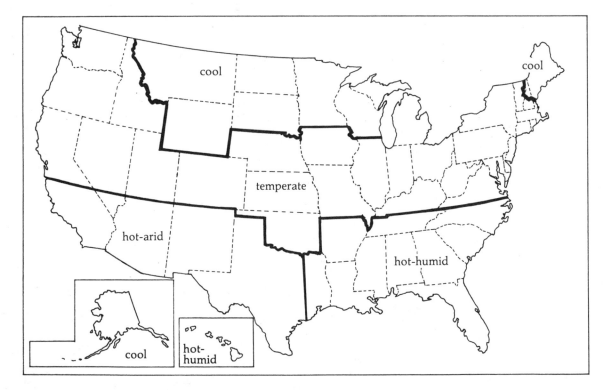

The U.S. can be divided into the four major climatic regions—cool, temperate, hot-arid and hot-humid—as shown. Knowing which region you live in is only the first step in determining the specific microclimatic conditions surrounding your property.

Hot-Humid

High temperatures and consistent vapor pressure. Wind velocities and direction vary throughout the year and throughout the day. Wind velocities of up to 120 miles per hour may accompany hurricanes, which can be expected from east-southeast directions.

Within these regions there are four elements of climate that affect our comfort—solar radiation, wind, precipitation and temperature. Although it is the cumulative effect of these elements that determines the local climate, each must be looked at individually to understand how climate can be controlled.

SOLAR RADIATION

Only about one-fifth of the radiation coming from the sun penetrates the atmosphere to the earth's surface and is received as direct radiation.

The sun's rays strike different areas on the earth's surface with different degrees of intensity, depending on the geographical location, the angle of inclination and the elevation of landforms. The intensity of this radiation is further modified by local features, such as landforms, vegetation, water and architectural elements. This is why the intensity and effect of the sun on your property may be different from that on your neighbor's property across the street or down the block.

Only a part of the sun's radiation—about 20 percent of it—strikes the earth's surface as direct radiation. The rest of the sunlight and heat is absorbed or diffused in the atmosphere and is received on the earth as reflected radiation from atmospheric particles or from materials on or near the earth's surface. Some of this is reflected back into space, some is dissipated within the atmosphere and some is diffused throughout the atmosphere.

The sun's effect is also felt by reflection of light and heat from the ground surface. The intensity of heat varies according to the reflective or absorptive qualities of the materials that the sunlight strikes. Ground materials with high reflective qualities, such as concrete or flagstone, will radiate heat and light, making the surrounding area warmer, and those with low reflective qualities, such as grass or ground covers, will radiate less heat and light and generally be cooler. Since both can be modified by any taller shade-providing elements, such as trees or houses, the absorptive-reflective quality of the surface material is most important in nonshaded areas.

WIND

The actual temperature is often different from what we perceive the temperature to be. It is greatly affected by the wind, which can make a cold day feel unbearably bitter. The windchill factor, included in many wintertime weather reports, is a measure of the wind's effect on temperature.

Wind movement is directed by upright elements in the landscape, like the continental mountain ranges of the Rockies and Appalachians, which divert air masses and control the flow of moisture-laden air.

On this large scale, meteorologists can predict the directions and cycles of wind movement across the country. You can apply these same principles to small-scale wind patterns, in other words, those affecting your property. Wind is obstructed or guided by minor vertical elements in the landscape. By studying the wind patterns on your landscape and the elements affecting them, you can use landforms and architectural materials to alter the airflow over the ground and around or through your house in a desirable manner.

PRECIPITATION

The distribution of rainfall in the United States, like solar radiation and wind patterns, is greatly influenced by large-scale landforms. These landmasses affect the flow of moisture-laden air and aid in trapping and condensing moisture. Warm, moisture-laden air cools as it rises against coastal mountains. This cooling air cannot support the moisture and is forced to release it as precipitation. Most of this falls on the windward side of the mountain, thus creating drier conditions on the leeward side.

Smaller landforms such as high hills, however, cause exactly the opposite precipitation distribution. There is greater rainfall on the leeward side of a slope than on the windward side because the wind carries precipitation over a hill, where it strikes the slope and falls.

On an even smaller scale, plant materials control and alter the impact of rain, sleet and hail, the position and amount of snow, the intensity and location of dew and frost, and the evaporation of moisture from the ground surface. These microclimatic factors, which affect your comfort and your landscaping plans, can be designed to create a desirable microclimate.

TEMPERATURE

The temperature of an area is the result of the combination of the previously discussed climatic forces—solar radiation, wind and precipitation. If you change one climatic force while leaving another in effect, the net result will be a change in temperature. For example, if you provide shade and don't block the wind, you can make an area cooler, or if you control the wind but don't block the sun, the same area will be warmer.

Because plants affect solar radiation, wind, precipitation and humidity, they can be used to control temperature in your landscape. Plants and natural areas generally reduce temperatures by shading sunlight, by absorbing solar radiation and by evapotranspiration. Plants absorb radiation and release it slowly, which can reduce daytime temperatures and prevent heat loss at night. Areas covered with vegetation keep a relatively even temperature throughout the 24-hour period.

On a sunny summer day, solar radiation strikes the surface of a tree canopy, making it the warmest part of the forest. Due to the absorption and reflection of heat by the canopy, the understory is cooler. Successively lower layers receive less heat and consequently are progressively cooler.

By controlling wind, plants also control temperature. Air movement affects human body cooling, not by actually decreasing temperature, but by causing a cooling sensation due to heat loss by convection and increased evaporation from the body. The areas protected by a windbreak will be warmer, especially if they receive direct sunlight.

Patterns of precipitation can be influenced by landforms and vegetation. More rain will fall on the windward side of a towering mountain. As the wind surges up the mountain slope and over the peak, it will dramatically cool and consequently yield up its moisture as rain or snow. But more rain will fall on the leeward side of a small mountain, since the moisture will only be beginning to precipitate as the air mass reaches the mountain's peak and will actually fall after the air mass clears the peak and begins descending the leeward side. While vegetation can't produce such shifts in precipitation, it can alter and mitigate its effects by shielding the ground from direct or even wind-blown impact.

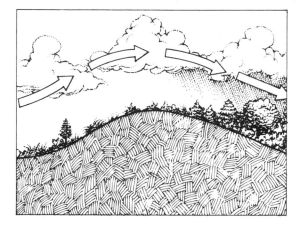

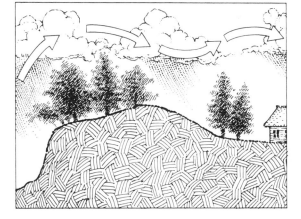

Temperatures change with altitude to a predictable degree—less 1°F. for each 330-foot rise in altitude in summer, and plus 1°F. for each 440-foot rise in winter. The summertime decline in temperature as you ascend a mountain seems reasonable, but the wintertime rise in temperature may not. There is a sound explanation. Cool air is heavier than warm air and behaves somewhat like water flowing toward the lowest points. In hilly and other rough lands, a well-marked local temperature effect is often noted in valleys or depressions into which the cold air sinks during the summer nights.

Cities are generally warmer than the surrounding countryside because of the concentration of city buildings, which store up heat, block winds and slow down cooling. Vegetation can play a large role in modifying the environment of a city by making it more comfortable in both summer and winter. Deciduous trees are preferable because of their ability to intercept solar radiation during the hottest part of the year and not interfere with it during the winter.

PLANTS AND CLIMATE

While plants can help to modify climate, they also act as very sensitive living instruments that continuously integrate all weather factors. They respond to temperature, rainfall and humidity, wind and the amount of sunlight they receive. Slight variations in elevation, landforms, slope, orientation, vegetation cover or man-made structures can create local modification of the general climate, and these small-scale modifications create a microclimate of vital importance to the survival of plants.

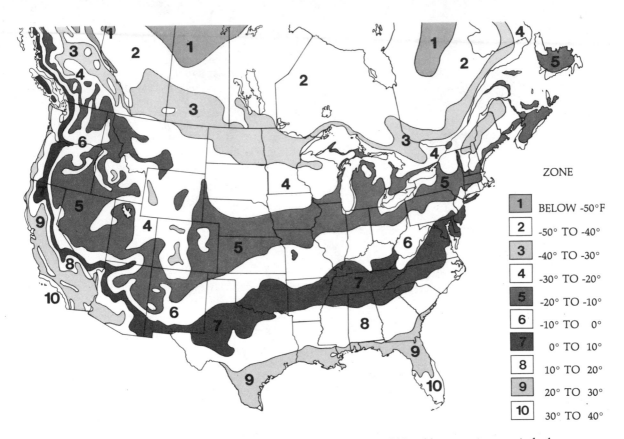

ZONE

1	BELOW -50°F
2	-50° TO -40°
3	-40° TO -30°
4	-30° TO -20°
5	-20° TO -10°
6	-10° TO 0°
7	0° TO 10°
8	10° TO 20°
9	20° TO 30°
10	30° TO 40°

Hardiness zones, as delineated on this map, are used by horticulturists and nurseries in weighing the ability of individual species to weather different regions' climates. Hardiness here is based on the average coldest-day-of-the-year, and thus a plant hardy to

Zone 4 would be able to survive a period when temperatures were −20° to −30°F. (−28.9 to −34.4°C.) But you have to determine if your little pocket of the zone conforms to the overall characteristics of the zone.

The United States Department of Agriculture has developed hardiness zones that are based on average minimum temperatures. These zones or some variation of them are used in countless nursery catalogs and garden books. Plants are classified according to their hardiness or ability to survive cold. However, temperature can vary markedly with the elevation of a few feet or within the distance of a mile. Moreover, the minimum temperature is not the only climatic factor that influences the survival of plants.

LOW TEMPERATURE
Cold temperatures are important in determining the hardiness of plants, but more significant than

cold itself is the fluctuation of temperature. Sudden frosts can be a real danger. A young and moderately hardy woody plant can survive low temperatures if they occur by gradual stages in the fall and are maintained at a fairly even level through the winter. A ten-day to two-week cooling-off period is a great help to plants in the fall. If temperatures drop abruptly, the young plant is caught in its soft and juicy stage, and its tender tissues are broken on the inside by expanding ice crystals.

HIGH TEMPERATURE
Winter damage is not always the result of frozen plant tissues. It can come from evaporation caused by a warm spell, especially in evergreens.

Occasionally in January and February, when the soil is frozen to its greatest depth, there may be a warm and sunny day. If the sun shines on evergreen leaves, which are already low in moisture content in their winterized condition, the little moisture that is left will evaporate, and since the soil is frozen, the roots cannot replace this lost moisture. Rhododendrons have a protective mechanism and avoid this loss by curling their leaves and presenting the smallest possible surface to the sun. But even this is not enough to save them when the temperature change is extreme, and for most plants, the effect of a sudden winter warm-up can be fatal.

The problem faced by southern homeowners is just the opposite of that encountered in the North. Southerners are unable to grow many plants common in northern landscapes, such as birches, because of too much heat or too little cold. Azaleas, which thrive and bloom prolifically in the humid South and throughout the Middle Atlantic states, shrivel and die when they are planted in hot-arid climates, where they are exposed to too high a summer heat and too little winter dormancy.

WATER
Each plant has its own moisture requirements and grows naturally in areas where these requirements are met. Heaths, for instance, need very wet conditions because their roots lack the tiny root hairs found in most plants. Although these roots are finely divided, their absorptive surface is small compared to that of most plants, so the water supply must be greater. Desert plants, on the other hand, store large quantities of water in their fleshy tops during the rainy season and draw on it during the long dry season. They cannot survive too much rain—their roots will rot.

FROST
Frost heave, which results from the expansion of soil water when it freezes, can be a problem in some areas. The greatest danger of heaving is in a clayey soil that is poorly drained to a depth below the frost line. Ice crystals can grow large enough to push up plants. If this process is repeated over and over in the course of a winter as a result of alternate freezes and thaws, the plant may be heaved to the point that its roots die of drying out from wind or exposure to the sun.

Moisture in the air often has a beneficial effect on plants by modifying and preventing temperature extremes. A humid, foggy seacoast provides its own protection against unseasonable frosts. The higher temperature of the seawater warms up the atmosphere and prevents the temperature of the plants from dropping below freezing. However, if the moisture that accumulates on the surface of plants freezes, the weight of the ice can break even huge tree limbs.

WIND
The most spectacular effects of wind damage are seen after a heavy storm, when broken branches and uprooted plants lie all over the landscape. Yet, a heavy storm, even in some of the hurricane districts, can cause less total damage than the steady persistence of a prevailing wind.

Peculiar, gnarled-looking, one-sided trees seen on the tops of tall mountains are produced by winds blowing against them steadily year after year, drying their leaves and their bark and finally killing the whole windward side of the tree. Damage from the wind is greatest in the winter, when the plants become dehydrated as a protection from the cold. Wind increases the evaporation from the surfaces of the leaves, and when the water supply is already depleted, this additional loss can be fatal.

SUNLIGHT
The sun's effect on vegetation is twofold—we've already seen its heating effect, but sunlight alone has an important influence on plant growth. The process of photosynthesis depends on the conversion of sunlight into chemical energy and compounds, including carbohydrates and oxygen. Although only a small amount of the light striking a leaf is used in the process, without any light the process could not be carried out, and life would be impossible.

Climate and the Landscape
In addition to adapting to climate, plants modify it and create new conditions. These changes can create distinctly different pocket environments within a single general environment. These small-

scale or microclimatic differences make it possible for plants with varying climatic requirements to live together. The significance of this for the home landscaper is easy to see. The addition of a shade tree will modify its immediate environment and could spell disaster for any ground cover or sun-loving plants under the shade tree's canopy. What's more, there will be another competitor for the available water and nutrients.

MICROCLIMATE

The microclimates that exist on your property may be far more significant to your landscaping plans than the average minimum temperature. Therefore, if you want to spend more time enjoying your landscape and less time fighting nature, you should study your particular climatic conditions and use plants that grow in areas with similar conditions.

Trees, shrubs, ground covers and turf are among the best exterior solar radiation control devices. Plants may control direct solar radiation by shading the sun or by intercepting reflected radiation from some surfaces.

Each plant variety casts its own distinctive shadow, both in shape and in density. Oaks, maples and beeches cast dark, dense shadows, and trees like honey locusts and willow oaks cast fine, light, lacy shadows. Deciduous trees block out direct sunlight in summer but allow it to pass through in winter, making them useful for both seasons. In temperate zones, tall evergreens on the south and southwestern sides of houses are not good landscaping choices because they will block the winter sun. In arid regions or for summer comfort, use vegetation, landforms or structures like trellises or canopies to shade the west walls and roof from the hot afternoon sun.

Climbing and clinging vines grown on masonry walls act as insulating blankets for hot summer sun and cold winter winds. Differences of 8°F. have been measured on the outer surfaces of shaded and unshaded buildings. Inside differences may be as great as 20°F.

The reflective qualities of the various ground materials on your property will affect the temperature. It is important to remember: solidly paved areas and masonry absorb and reflect heat and cause glare, and light-colored paved areas reflect more than dark ones. Dark colors absorb radiation, and large paved areas can store and radiate heat for many hours after sundown.

Hard mulches, such as marble chips, rocks or bricks, carry more heat to the soil than loose mulches, such as grass clippings, leaves or straw, which act as insulation and reduce the solar radiation that reaches the soil or grass. If you intersperse paved areas with planted ones, there will be less reflection. Permeable paved areas like brick or gravel are less reflective than nonpermeable paving like asphalt or concrete.

SOLAR ORIENTATION

Satisfactory orientation usually is a compromise between conflicting factors, and there are no absolute rules to follow in making the compromise.

So don't despair if the orientation of your house meets none of the preferred criteria. You can use your landscaping efforts to make some significant improvements to a poor orientation. In the temperate zone, expose the south-facing areas and protect them from northern and western weather, especially in winter. You may want to use structural canopies,

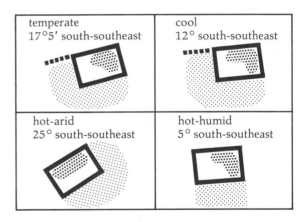

The best orientation for a house, as well as the best layout of the rooms and surrounding landscape, depends upon the climatic region the house is located in. Illustrated are the optimum arrangements for each of the major regions. The dotted areas are the primary indoor and outdoor living areas.

Perspective

By manipulating the elements in your landscape, you can easily reduce the energy needed to maintain a temperate climate in the home. Here is a property—seen in perspective and plan views—that has plantings that help shield the house. For example, the evergreens planted on the earth mound buffer winter winds and help keep snows from drifting against the house. The high-canopy deciduous tree provides shade in summer and filters—but does not block—the winter sun. Deciduous vines trellised over south-facing doorways and windows do the same. A shelterbelt of low deciduous trees guides and filters cooling summer breezes. Similar landscape plantings around your property will create a more favorable microclimate for you in all seasons.

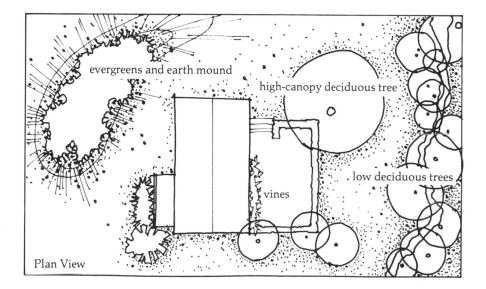

evergreens and earth mound

high-canopy deciduous tree

low deciduous trees

vines

Plan View

which can impede heat loss at night. Maximize activities requiring sun (both indoors and out) on the southern and western sides of the structure and on hard, paved surfaces. In hot areas, use roof overhangs on the southern side of the house. And use the shade of the house, garage or neighboring houses to shade outdoor living areas and circulation paths. Try to use earth forms to shade or screen exposed eastern and western walls. Because light surfaces reflect more than dark ones, a wall painted in a high-key color can send light into a dark, cool area.

WIND

Wind is controlled to a distance of from 2 to 5 times the height of a barrier in front of a wind obstruction and from 10 to 15 times the height leeward of such a barrier. Therefore, the higher the screen, the farther the protection will extend. For example, a 30-foot-high windscreen or shelterbelt may reduce wind velocities for 100 yards in front of the trees and 300 yards downwind.

Screens that allow the wind to go through have lower actual wind reduction near the screen, but the overall effects extend a greater distance

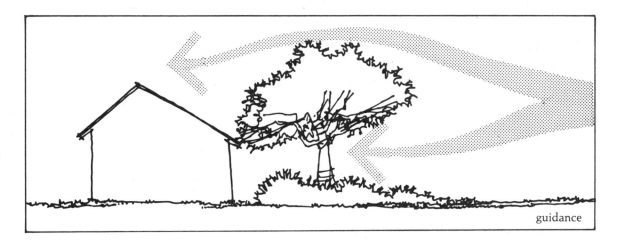

guidance

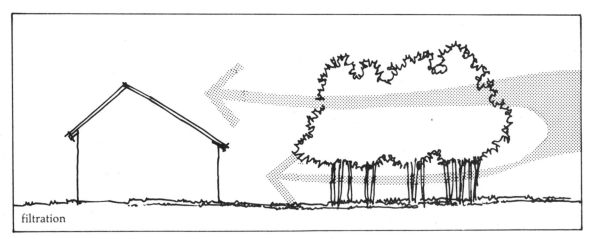

filtration

The location and configuration of a windbreak determine its effect on the wind. By varying the height and density of such a planting, you can achieve a number of different results. A planting that's dense but open at ground level will guide and filter the wind. One that's densest at ground level will obstruct, or at least deflect, the wind.

beyond. Moreover, the turbulence leeward of the windbreak increases with the density of the belt. Therefore, the optimum density is 50 to 60 percent. In other words, the leaves, branches, twigs and trunks should cover 50 to 60 percent of the front of the screen. With this density, narrow screens will afford as much shelter as wider ones of the same penetrability.

Remember that prevailing winds may change direction with the season. A dense coniferous windbreak on the northeast side of a structure may protect it from harsh winter winds and yet direct summer breezes around it. Wind can be guided to the desired location by the angle of planting, and in general, shelterbelts are most effective when placed perpendicular to the prevailing winds.

Coniferous evergreens that branch to the ground are most effective for year-round wind control. However, because cool winds flow downhill at night, dense evergreens placed on a slope can trap and hold cold wind flow, creating cool spaces upwind. Penetrable windbreaks allow cold air to drain away and are important at the foot of sloping gardens and orchards.

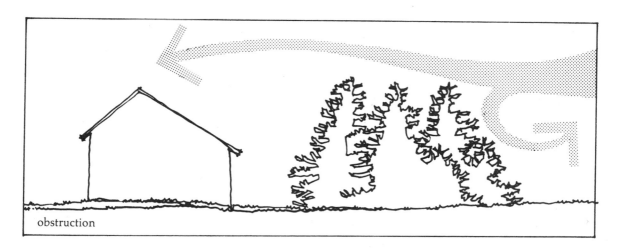

obstruction

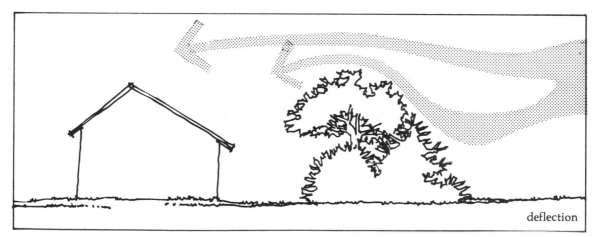

deflection

Your Property: Microclimatic Analysis

SOLAR RADIATION

The first step of your microclimatic analysis is to look at the seasonal patterns of solar radiation on your site. Which areas are exposed, and which are shaded at different times of the day and at different times of the year? Take a copy of your base map with you, and observe the sun and shade during the summer and winter, morning and afternoon. Note how much of the house is shaded, and don't overlook outdoor living areas. If they are hot and sunny or cool and shaded during the hours that you usually use them, remember to record this information.

Begin by showing all the areas that are shaded at one time of the day. Use darker colors to indicate denser shade, and be sure to include the shaded part of the house. Do the same for another

time of day—10 A.M. and 3 P.M. would be reasonable. If there are seasonal differences in your climate, you will need to record these observations during each season. If you can't wait until next winter to complete your landscape plans, you can find out the direction and altitude of the sun for different hours and seasons from the nearest meteorological station or the National Weather Service. With this information, as well as the location and height of all of the elements on your site, you can calculate the shade angle and pattern. After you have recorded this information, you will need to analyze it. If the tall evergreen on the south side of your house provides shade in the winter as well as the summer, it may be wise to remove it.

REFLECTION

Your next step is to analyze the reflective qualities of the surface materials in the nonshaded or exposed areas. You may want to use colors to indicate high, low or medium reflection on another copy of your base map.

Although paving provides a practical surface for outdoor living, its reflective qualities can make it uncomfortably hot on a warm summer day. By using plants and screens, as here, you can screen the direct radiation and thereby lower the temperature.

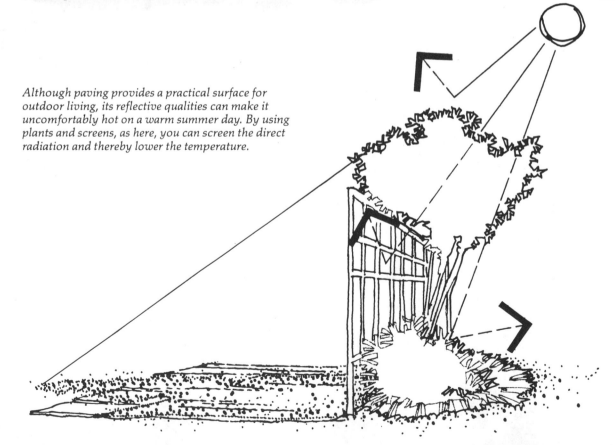

On your map, mark the surfaces that receive shade or protection and those that are exposed to the sun. Look at all of the surface materials of your property as they are affected by summer and winter weather. Indicate elements in the landscape that work to improve the climatic impact as well as those that make it worse.

WIND

Because the winds blowing across your property may be totally different from those prevailing, you will need to do a firsthand study of your wind conditions. Look at how the wind moves on your site—where it flows freely and where and how it is impeded. On a copy of your base map, indicate the direction of seasonal winds. Show where its flow may be diverted or intercepted by existing landscape elements. After indicating these on the map, you can analyze the effects of the existing situation and determine where and how to modify these conditions.

Be sure to consider your total site layout as it relates to summer and winter wind directions and speeds, including the orientation of structures. Also look at the existing protection provided to structures by each other and by vegetation. Note the potential adverse effects resulting from increased

Climatic Analysis of the Urban Property: The regional climate for this area is generally mild. The average annual air temperature is 59°F. (15°C.), and the frost-free season is 260 to 290 days. Winters are cool and moist, and summers are cool and pleasant. The average annual rainfall is 15 to 18 inches. There are frequent sea breezes and early morning fog.

The microclimate is affected by the large tree canopy—indicated by the heavy stippling—that provides partial shade for the south-facing wall and cuts the glare when it overhangs the concrete patio. There is, however, an exposed area of concrete—indicated by the light stippling—that creates an unpleasant glare and reflects unwanted heat to the house in summer. Between the two, at the rear of the yard, is a sun pocket, a vegetated area that gets direct radiation from the sun.

The rear of the property as a whole is sunny and warm and is protected from the northwest winds—indicated by the shaded arrow—by the thick privet hedge. This windbreak also serves to channel the cool northeast breezes—indicated by the unshaded arrow—toward the house.

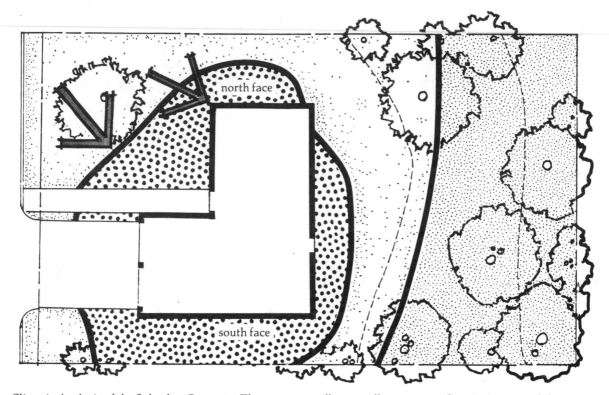

Climatic Analysis of the Suburban Property: The house and landscape as they exist are not very energy efficient. There are cold winter winds from the northwest—the arrows—that are not adequately blocked, and the front of the house is exposed to the late-afternoon summer sun, making it unpleasantly hot. The developer-planted species on the south side of the house are evergreen, and although small now, they will eventually screen out the winter sun, and the summer sun as well. The area affected by these ill-considered plants is indicated by the heavy stippling. The wet soils at the back of the property—indicated by the light stippling—are shaded from the sun's radiation, and air circulation is prevented by the clumped vegetation, thus creating even wetter conditions.

wind speeds around structures and from wind channeling down corridors of buildings, vegetation or roads.

To find the direction of the prevailing winds, tie strips of cloth to several sticks 5 to 6 feet tall. Place them on the north, west and south sides of your house or in any area that seems windy. Keep a chart of observed wind direction for several weeks during each season. Note any odd patterns of erratic wind that may be caused by existing elements in your landscape. Also note the frequency and duration of very high speed winds.

PRECIPITATION

You've already studied some of the effects of precipitation on your property. You can also get information about averages and extremes of rain and snowfall from your local weather bureau to help you plan what to plant. But to improve the microclimate around your house, you will need to look at the effect of moisture on your comfort.

Locate areas on your base map that seem damp and humid or that seem especially dry. Humid areas are often characterized by a lot of overhead plantings, which slow evaporation and increase transpiration, and by a minimum of hard, paved areas. Low windbreaks (6 feet or less) often preserve moisture transpired by turf. Pools and fountains, especially if located on a shady side of the house, can increase the humidity as well.

Areas that receive a lot of sun and that are well ventilated are generally drier. Those that are

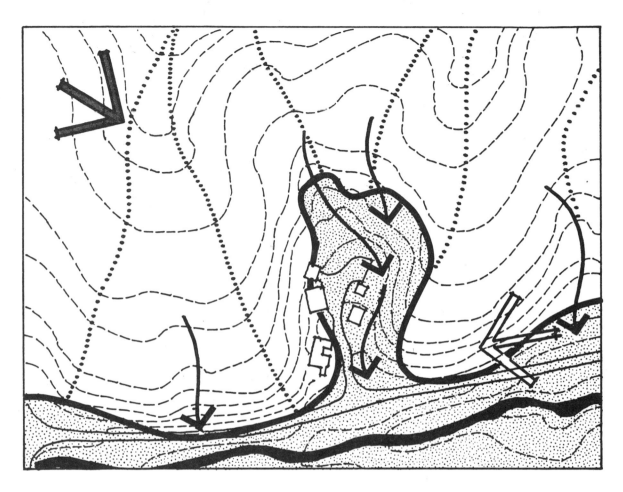

Climatic Analysis of the Rural Property: The general climate of this area is temperate. The winters are moderate, and the average rainfall is 40 + inches. Because the house is located near the bottom of a narrow valley, it is subject to cold air drainage from the higher elevations—shown by the black, serpentine arrows—and because there is a slope on the other side of the stream, there is no way for this cold air to escape, hence a cold-air pocket. This causes fog and dampness and early frost in the lowland. Snow lingers here longer than elsewhere on the property. While causing lower temperatures in winter, it also ensures cool and pleasant summer temperatures. The winter temperatures are somewhat modified by the stairway slope, which protects the house from the northwest winds—the shaded arrow. Moreover, the mature canopy trees in front of the house are deciduous and shade the summer sun while allowing winter exposure. The open arrow shows the direction of summer's cooling breezes.

The hilltop pastures are partly protected from northwest winter winds by the surrounding vegetation, but they tend to be hot and dry in the summer, especially on the south-facing slopes. These slopes are also warmer in the winter.

located high on a hill with well-drained soils or underdrainage systems are also dry. Look for these kinds of clues that might indicate where you have a problem area.

If you live in an area of heavy snowfall, show where the drifts occur and where snow is slow to melt. Also locate frost pockets, if any, and look for factors that may be causing them.

TEMPERATURE

Now that you've looked at the three previous climatic forces as they affect your property, you probably already have a good idea of the areas that are relatively hot or cold. Indicate these areas on a copy of your base map, and note the reasons, which will probably be a combination of radiation, wind and precipitation. For example, warm areas are caused by factors such as plantings or obstructions that act as dams, creating cold air pockets uphill and making the area below warmer. Houses are made warmer by exposing walls and roofs and constructing them of hard masonry or other heat-retaining structural materials. Paved areas on the south side and canopies, which keep night warmth in, also raise the temperature. Areas will be cooler if they have extensive shade provided by coarse-textured, dense trees and if they have ground covers instead of paving. Valley bottoms and locations on the leeward side of water will have lower temperatures.

The final step in analyzing your microclimate is to transfer all of the information from your four or more maps onto one map that will show the whole range of climatic conditions for your property.

Draw a line around each area that has a different combination of conditions.

This map will be a great help in determining the different plant habitats that exist and the vegetation opportunities for your property. It will also show you what areas need to be redesigned to minimize your energy consumption and, at the same time, ensure that you don't destroy any beneficial climatic elements that already exist.

If you are locating activities or structures, or building a house, look at the areas with the most favorable climatic conditions. Don't forget to consider how the addition of your proposed facility will affect the existing conditions.

If you are trying to improve existing conditions, you can see where modifications are necessary (see Section 2). Again, consider the effects of the modifying element on the other climatic conditions. Remember that you will have to compare this climatic data with the other inventory information to see if there may be conflicts or constraints imposed by any of the other factors.

7

Vegetation and Wildlife

The vegetation surrounding your home is the most striking and most important aesthetic factor in your landscaping plans. For many people, adding, removing or rearranging plants is done totally for visual impact. However, vegetation is also a dynamic living part of the environment and plays an important ecological role. In fact, because vegetation will grow and be healthy only in locations where its ecological requirements are fulfilled, you can't separate a balanced environment from its beauty. The appearance of the vegetation on your property is an excellent measure of the effectiveness of your attempts to manage the landscape. It is also a critical indicator of the conditions of the other components of your environment—soils, water, climate, slope and orientation.

75

Vegetation and Wildlife Analysis Checklist

The vegetation and wildlife analysis of your property will allow you to make a planting plan that includes the existing vegetation that should remain and the kinds of plants you will want to add. It will enable you to develop a plan encouraging a diverse population of wildlife.

1. Analyze the existing vegetation for:
   successional stage
   native or exotic
   location, size, health
   appearance
   maintenance required
   energy impact

2. Define plant habitats based on:
   geology
   physiography
   hydrology
   soils
   climate

3. Analyze the existing and proposed vegetation for its potential for wildlife:
   food
   water
   cover

If you are looking for a site to build a house, you can tell a lot about the environment by looking at the vegetation. Plant ecologists who study native vegetation know that certain species (indicator species) need a particular combination of environmental conditions to survive. For instance, red maple, alder, tupelo and willow thrive in poorly drained soils, while oak and hickory grow on warm, dry land, and spruce and fir in cold, moist places.

You can save a large landscaping expense if the existing vegetation is healthy and attractive and if your building plans are designed to maintain that vegetation. While all construction requires some grading, and thus removal of vegetation, you can plan earth moving so that it minimizes destruction, and you can stockpile vegetation for replanting.

If you are planning to relandscape an older house or simply to improve your existing landscape, you will need to analyze the established vegetation in terms of its appearance as well as its functional value. You may find that a perfectly beautiful evergreen is increasing your fuel bills because it's shading out winter sun. You may decide to move it (there are tree-moving machines that can handle trees with trunks up to 6 inches in diameter) or to sacrifice the energy savings for its appearance. Your landscape plan will require many such compromises, and because the compromises must be based on sound information, the analysis of your vegetation is crucial.

Unless you have a barren lot, your vegetation analysis must be twofold. You must analyze the plants and the plant habitats that exist on your property, as well as study the role of vegetation in the natural system—how it is naturally distributed and composed. With this knowledge you will be able to plant species that can maintain and perpetuate themselves, and you will be freed from the need to water, weed, fertilize or otherwise maintain your landscape.

General Information
PLANT DISTRIBUTION

The plant life of one area looks different from that of another because most plants are restricted to distinct environments. This distribution of plants is controlled by the following factors: competition among plants for necessary nutrients, water, space and light; toxic substances secreted by some plants that are lethal to others; synergistic or destructive relationships between certain plants; random distribution of seeds; and sporadic, catastrophic events like fire and storm, which change the character and patterns of different communities in a more or less random manner.

The pattern of vegetation is also affected by degree of slope and the direction it faces (northern slopes are usually cooler and wetter than southern ones), soil type, soil moisture, elevation and other environmental factors.

| crinkled pondweed | yellow water lily | pickerel weed | sedge | cattail | Joe-Pye weed | sedge | buttonbush | sycamore | elm |

The best place to observe the gradation of plant species is at the edge of a pond or lake. Plants respond to the amount of water available, and there the amount of water available changes enormously within a relatively short distance. Consequently, the vegetation mix changes dramatically as you move away from the water's edge to high ground, where the water table is lower.

Plant species have evolved separate niches, each with a distinct pattern of environmental conditions. Every plant grows best in a slightly different habitat. However, there are plants that have a wide range of environmental tolerances and that can therefore exist in many habitats. Red maple, for example, develops well in wetlands yet is also found on dry hilltops.

Although the plants themselves don't move (except to put out runners), they migrate by the movement of wind, water, animals, propulsion, gravity or humans. By chance, seeds may fall near the parent plant and a cluster of the same species will develop, or they may be transported great distances. A good example of migration occurring on your own property is the dandelion seed that floats through the air or the elm tree that is surrounded by many seedlings. Even your dog may be transporting seeds during his daily walk. But the greatest dispersal of plants has been accomplished by man. Some plants, such as barberry, honeysuckle, ailanthus and wild oats, that are native to Europe, were transported by man, found favorable conditions and now grow in the wild here. However, not all transports are successful. If the conditions required for growth are not available or can't be provided, the plant simply won't grow.

SUCCESSION

Vegetation is dynamic, rather than static. Communities of plants (and animals) replace one another over time in a process called a succession. This is a relatively orderly and predictable process that begins with sparse stands of annuals and ends with complex, thick and diverse groups of plants. Each successional stage involves a change in microclimate and site conditions that increases the chances of survival for entering vegetation and decreases the ability of existing species to compete.

Competition is the principal mechanism of succession. Plants are constantly competing with one another for sunlight, for nutrients and for water. When one plant gets an edge, it changes the entire community. In a dry prairie, the ability of one plant to reach deeper into the earth for water and nutrients and higher into the sky for sunlight gives it the edge. And the shallow-rooted, low-growing annual weeds are crowded out. When trees establish themselves in a meadow, the shade they produce will eventually close out the sun-loving species and give harbor to the shade-lovers. The meadow evolves into woodland.

The diversity of successional communities usually enables them to survive even catastrophic events, such as fire. Each species has a different tolerance, and though one or two or three may succumb, others will survive.

This diversity of species is the single most influential characteristic in a plant community. Nature is driven to fill in every biological niche, and rarely, if ever, do you see a bare space in a natural environment. The very existence of a wide variety of species, in itself, assures greater resistance to disease and to the intrusion of alien plants. Thus, a large number of species in an area automatically makes that area both visually pleasing and biologically stable.

In a stable community, the plant population is characterized by long-lived species and species with low reproductive powers. In an unstable population, the opposite is true. Thus, the pioneer plants on vacant lots, which are in an unstable, early successional stage, are weedy annuals, biennials and perennials. These plants are characterized by their strong reproductive powers—the capacity to produce millions of seeds, to self-pollinate or to hybridize with the native population and still remain fertile—and by their efficient dispersal mechanisms, which enable their seeds to travel long distances. Seeds that are dispersed over long distances need to be tolerant of many different conditions, and the more tolerant they are, the more successfully they will grow in disturbed conditions. An unstable environment is indicated in part by an abundance of alien plants, particularly noxious weeds and characteristic disturbance plants, such as poison ivy, honeysuckle and bittersweet.

WEEDS

While the term weed may be difficult to define—one dictionary calls a weed "a plant of no value"—two characteristics of weeds are revealed by succession. One, they grow in areas of severe disturbance, such as where man has cleared the land, and two, they are aliens to the region—exotics.

Therefore, the more disturbed or the more simplified a site, the more susceptible it becomes to the colonization of weed seeds. Or, the more stable and diverse a landscape is, i.e., the later the successional stage, the less invasion by unwanted weedy species.

Vegetation and the Landscape

As we've seen, the species of plants that make up a community in any one location depend on the environmental constraints, the successional stage and the sporadic occurrence of catastrophes. In your home landscape, the occurrence of catastrophic events can usually be controlled (although grading and house building could be considered catastrophic to the plants), and the environmental constraints of your landscape will become obvious as you complete your ecological analysis. Finally, by determining the successional stage of your existing landscape, you can rework it into a later stage that is more stable and self-maintaining.

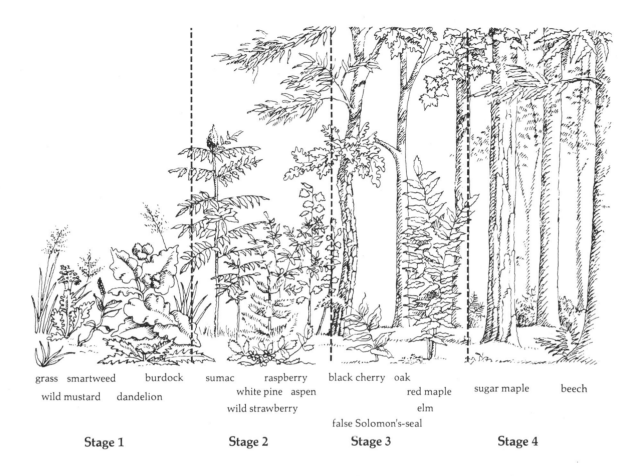

grass smartweed   burdock   sumac   raspberry   black cherry oak

wild mustard   dandelion   white pine aspen   red maple   sugar maple   beech

wild strawberry   elm

false Solomon's-seal

Stage 1   **Stage 2**   **Stage 3**   **Stage 4**

Succession is the change that occurs in an ecosystem as the competing plants respond to and alter the environment. If farmland is abandoned, it will develop slowly—over a period of more than a century—into a climax forest. It will first be a weed patch, Stage 1 in succession.

Gradually, pioneering trees and shrubs will invade. Some Stage 2 species spread by sending out runners, others by wind-blown seeds. As the woody plants grow, their shade strangles the grasses and weeds, though the process may take 20 years or more.

Stage 3 is the subclimax phase and occurs as the seeds of shade-tolerant species are introduced. As these species grow, over a period of 25 to 50 years, they rise above the Stage 2 species and ultimately shade them out.

Stage 4 takes even longer to occur, as much as 50 to 150 years. But if given the time, the climax species, with their high canopies and dense shade, will eventually squeeze out the subclimax species.

Unless there is only topsoil with no plants, you probably have already experienced the first stage of plant succession. The typical lawn, unless it is frequently doused with herbicides, is a grassy, weedy site. Dandelions, crabgrass and various seedlings compete with bluegrass in most home landscapes. (And the weeds would win were it not for the frequent appearance of the lawn mower.) Stage 1, being the most unstable phase of succession, requires a lot of work to maintain. Keeping a landscape in this state is a constant battle with nature's impulse to move on to the next successional stage.

If, however, you've decided to decrease your mowing by planting an edge of shrubs around your yard and have added some specimen trees, your landscape could be classified as being in Stage 2 of succession. And if these trees and shrubs are large enough to produce dense shade, under which ground covers and shade-tolerant species thrive, the effect will be that of a forest or final successional stage.

There are, however, many areas in the United States where the final stage is not forest, but prairie, desert, mountain or shrub land. In these, as in all areas, the early stages are unstable and characterized by weedy species, while the later stages, although still grasses or shrubs, are more stable and self-maintaining. If you want to reduce maintenance and let nature do the work in your landscape, you will need to encourage and plant late successional species.

Wildlife and the Landscape

The traditional landscape practice of removing natural vegetation and replacing it with sterile, nonfruiting exotics is eliminating wildlife habitats. And yet there's no reason why man's habitat can't be a habitat for wildlife, too. Wild creatures need the same elements for survival as humans—food, water, cover for protection, and areas to reproduce and bear young in safety. Wild animals—birds, squirrels, raccoons and deer—are just as much a part of the natural cycle as humans. In fact, wildlife has supplied us with many of our needs for a very long time. As long as you're changing your landscape anyway, why not provide for them?

If you live on or near a naturally vegetated area that provides these essentials, you must be aware of the life and drama that wildlife can add to a landscape. Sharing your living space with other inhabitants of the natural system is easy and can give you a great deal of pleasure.

You can attract many species of wildlife with only a very small garden by providing the essential elements—food, water and cover. The amount, the variety and the quality of these ingredients as supplied by your yard will control the numbers and the kinds of wildlife that will be attracted. Since birds (and other wildlife) vary so widely in their choice of habitat, you cannot hope to attract all species. However, there are general principles of cover and general types of plants that seem to fulfill the requirements of many different species.

You can ensure that food is available by planting species that have berries, fruits or nuts. Choose native plants that provide the same food that birds and other small animals would choose in the wild. Native plantings will provide cover as well as feed, while improving the appearance of your landscape.

But not all native species provide food for wildlife, and when you choose them, you should look for plants with palatable berries that have an abundance of small fruits, pea size or smaller. You should be aware of the time of year that the fruits are produced and try to plant ones that ripen at different times to provide a year-long food supply. It is important to include those that ripen early, those that are ripened by freezing and thawing, and those that can provide food during the cold season when it's most needed. Crab apple, Oregon grape and partridgeberry are good choices. Don't duplicate what's growing in your neighbor's yard. Try to supplement the existing food supply by increasing the diversity of species. For animals other than birds, the most attractive food you can provide is a nut. A wide variety of nut trees will support a wide variety of food-storing animals.

There must always be some form of water available. The best, of course, is a natural stream or pond with cover and food provided nearby. Even in a very small space, a natural pond can easily be constructed.

Animals must have places for protection from predators and from severe weather, and for roosting and nesting. Remember, that doesn't mean a green carpet of clipped grass with a few specimen shrubs. If you are landscaping with nature and following its design principles, you will be providing the preferred habitat of wildlife. Keep in mind the following guidelines: plant clusters of shrubs, not individuals, and make sure they include some thickly branching ones that are at least 3½ feet high, preferably 4 to 5 feet. The more continuous cover you can provide, the more attractive your property will be. If you can design a continuous corridor that links with your neighbor's plantings, you'll be doing even more good.

For the greatest diversity of species, you should capitalize on what ecologists call the edge effect. The number of species and individual animals is greatest at the edges between different environments. Animals that live near the edge can take advantage of both environments. To increase wildlife, create more edges—between mowed area and surrounding woodland, between field and forest. By making the boundaries irregular, you will be creating even more edge space.

Your Property: Vegetation Analysis

To decide on what vegetation to plant for wildlife, shade, food production or any other function

you've decided upon, you will need to analyze what now exists. It may be that your landscape has some areas that are far along in the successional process, while others are being kept in a young successional stage by artificial means, such as mowing and clipping. Your task, then, is to locate these different areas on a copy of your base map.

PLANT HABITATS

For the first part of your vegetation analysis, you must define the plant habitats that exist on your property. Even on a very small property, there will be various combinations of ecological or man-made factors and, thus, different plant habitats. Using the information from your analysis of the geology, physiography, hydrology, soils and climate, as well as close observation of the existing plants, you can distinguish these habitats and locate them on your map. Each habitat will present different opportunities and constraints that will limit your choice of plants. For example, there may be one area that is densely shaded, with wet, acid soils, and another that is sunny, hot, windy and dry. Each condition that contributes to making a habitat unique should be indicated on your map. Remember that the existing vegetation, whether exotic or native, is part of each habitat, and any plans to remove or rearrange vegetation will modify these

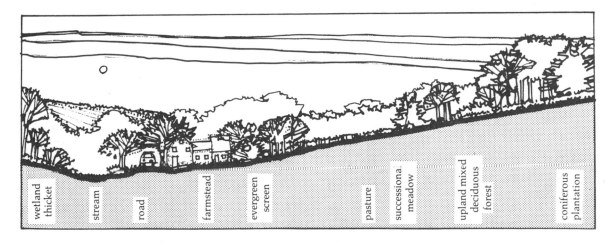

Your property will undoubtedly be surrounded by a variety of plant habitats in different successional stages, as here. It's up to you to analyze your surroundings and record what exists, so that your landscape will be a natural part of its environment.

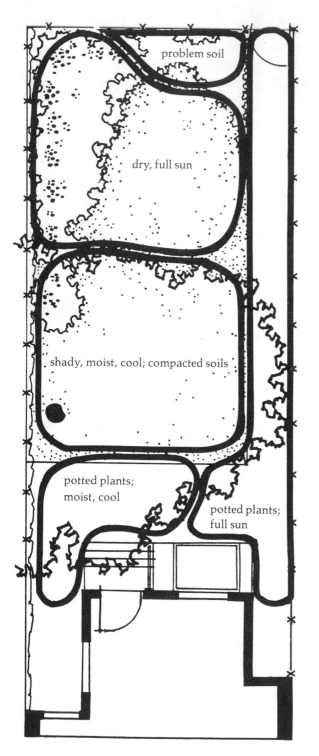

problem soil

dry, full sun

shady, moist, cool; compacted soils

potted plants;
moist, cool

potted plants;
full sun

habitats, as will any new buildings, walls, walks or other additions to your landscape.

Moreover, although you will need to draw lines on your map to separate the areas, in actuality the boundaries are not very precise and often blend into each other. On paper, try to locate the boundaries as accurately as possible, but in planning and planting, you should allow for a transition zone between habitats.

In urban environments, where the original ecosystems have often been destroyed, there are new habitats, which still have ecological characteristics, even though modified by the effects of human interference. City soils, for example, are often highly alkaline as a result of runoff from building debris. The concentration of excrement from domestic animals often results in an increased nitrogen and phosphate content. The concentration of buildings and paved areas accounts for the higher temperatures, increased wind flow and accelerated runoff in cities. Paving also hinders the upward movement of ground and soil water, thus inhibiting evaporation. Air pollutants are responsible for reducing light levels. These factors are just as important in determining plant habitats as natural ones, and when you locate different habitats in urban areas, you will need to be very specific about their effects.

NATURAL ENVIRONMENTS

Once you have identified the different habitats on your property and the factors (natural and man-made) that distinguish each, you are ready to look at vegetation in natural environments with similar conditions.

Plant Habitats of the Urban Property: Because of the small scale and relative uniformity of this property, there are only three distinct plant habitats. The first is the shaded area under the canopy of the maple, which is cooler and wetter than the surrounding area. Any planting in this habitat must be hardy enough to compete with the roots for moisture and nutrients, and, obviously, must be tolerant of shade. The second habitat is the sunlit area behind the tree. Here it is warmer and drier and suitable only for sun-loving plants. The final habitat is the small area to the rear of the property that has problem soils. Nothing will grow here until the soil condition is corrected.

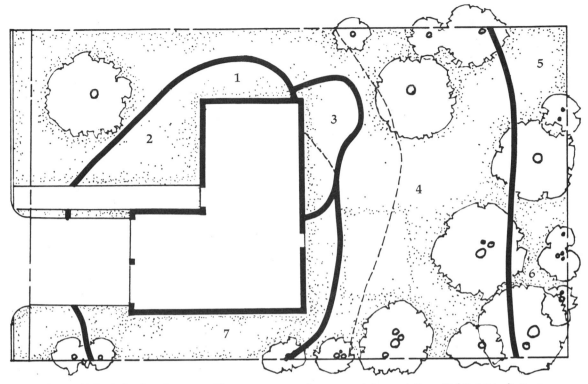

Plant Habitats of the Suburban Property: There are seven distinct habitats for plants on this property. Each has a different combination of ecological conditions, making them each suitable for a different association of plant species.

Habitat 1 is a northwest-facing slope and is shaded from all but the late-afternoon western sun. The appropriate plants for this area would be those found on a northwest-facing slope. Habitat 2 is a west-facing slope and is therefore cooler, although it does receive morning sun. Both of these habitats have two different soil types—the naturally occurring loam and the fill soil, which is somewhat alkaline and better drained than the naturally occurring soil. This creates two subhabitats within each area and further defines

the appropriate vegetation. Habitat 3 is distinct because of the disturbed soil conditions caused by rainwater collection. The soils have become compacted; during storms there is puddling of water, while the rest of the time the soil is dried out and cracked. Provisions for disposing of the water dumped by the downspout would alter this habitat and make it part of Habitat 4, which is the sunniest and driest part of the property. Habitat 5 has poorly drained soil and is somewhat marshy, although it does receive almost full sunlight. Habitat 6 is very wet, and because it is shaded, the air is cool and often damp. Habitat 7 is suitable for those plants that would occupy a south-facing slope and also is subdivided by the two different soil types occurring within it—the two occurring in Habitats 1 and 2.

Suppose, for example, you have a planting area on the north side of a wall in an urban backyard. It's cool and shady, and the soil is fairly acid and wet. You will want to look at the vegetation on an undisturbed north-facing slope. You may find hemlocks, which are obviously too big for your wall landscape, but the smaller shrubs and the ground species may be just the right size. By observing where the plants grow, in the middle of

a forest or at the sunlit edge, you can see which plants would do well in your habitats.

Although you may not be able to use the hemlocks, which provide shade and protection for the other plants, remember that your wall is also shading and protecting the planting area and can, therefore, substitute for a canopy layer.

Using the field guides listed in the Bibliography, identify the plants in each habitat and look up

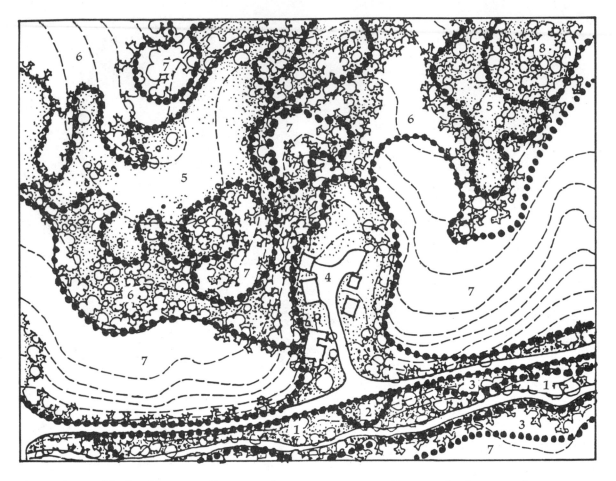

Plant Habitats of the Rural Property: There are eight major plant habitats, each with a different combination of ecological characteristics. These are determined by overlaying all of the previous maps and distinguishing each area that has a different combination of conditions. For example, Habitat 1 differs from 4 because it has a different geology, somewhat different physiography and different soil type. By defining each habitat, it is possible to quickly see the individual characteristics of any place on the property.

Briefly described, the eight habitats are:

1. Dense understory canopy with a limited diversity of woody, wetland species; potential for rich herbaceous layer and water vegetation

2. Mown field; if managed properly, potential for rich color and texture of wetland meadow

3. Nonregenerative deciduous woods; rapacious honeysuckle vines have smothered understory woods; subject to windthrow hazard; needs management

4. Open aspect with poor species diversity, currently demands lots of management; subject to adverse climatic and air pollution conditions

5. Mixed grasses and clumped early successional, pioneer woody species

6. High species diversity with dense lower canopy layers; needs selective cutting and felling

7. Good species diversity; all canopy layers present; occasional windthrown tree; with proper timber management, source of timber and firewood

8. Monospecific coniferous woods; dense canopy, no understory

their growth characteristics. Be sure to note their ultimate size and the color and date of flowering. This information will help you to choose native plants that are both ecologically and aesthetically fit for your landscape.

EXISTING PLANTS

The second part of your vegetation analysis is concerned with the individual characteristics of the vegetation, exotic or native, that exists on your property. You should identify it, locate it and determine its size, health and stability. To determine what should remain and what is to be removed from your property, you will need to analyze further each plant's function in terms of your landscaping purposes.

Probably there are a large number of healthy, attractive and nonnative species around your home. Don't immediately chop them down in favor of native plants. Trees (especially exotics) are costly. They take years to grow. What you already have may serve your purposes well. Furthermore, exotic and native species can coexist quite happily and often visually complement each other.

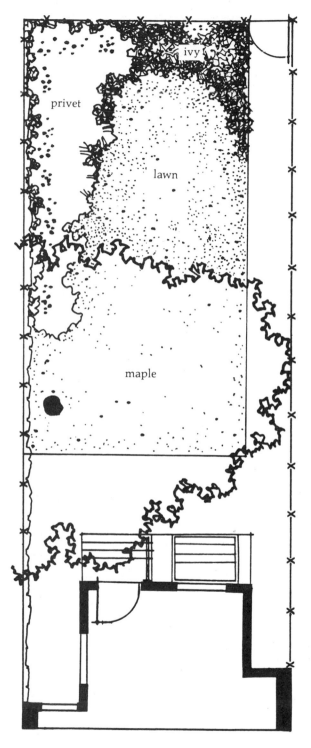

Vegetation Analysis of the Urban Property: The existing vegetation includes a large Norway maple, ivy, privet hedge and an area of grass. The Norway maple is a healthy deciduous tree, about 45 feet high with a broad crown and dense foliage. It is a very adaptable tree that tolerates a wide variety of climatic and soil conditions. However, its characteristically dense and well-developed root system may compete with other plants that are not equally as hardy.

The grass area under the maple is thin and sparsely covered. The shade from the canopy prevents a lush growth, but even though it is unattractive, the grass requires mowing and periodic weeding, which is a nuisance on such a small site.

The privet is a tall deciduous hedge that has outgrown its location. It requires severe pruning to keep in bounds. Because of its age, it appears leggy and woody, rather than green and full. It does, however, provide visual screening and wind blockage, and these functions must be balanced against its unattractive appearance.

The ivy ground cover is an evergreen vine that is tolerant of sun or shade and that is healthy and growing prolifically. Like the privet, however, it requires frequent pruning to prevent its encroachment upon the rest of the yard.

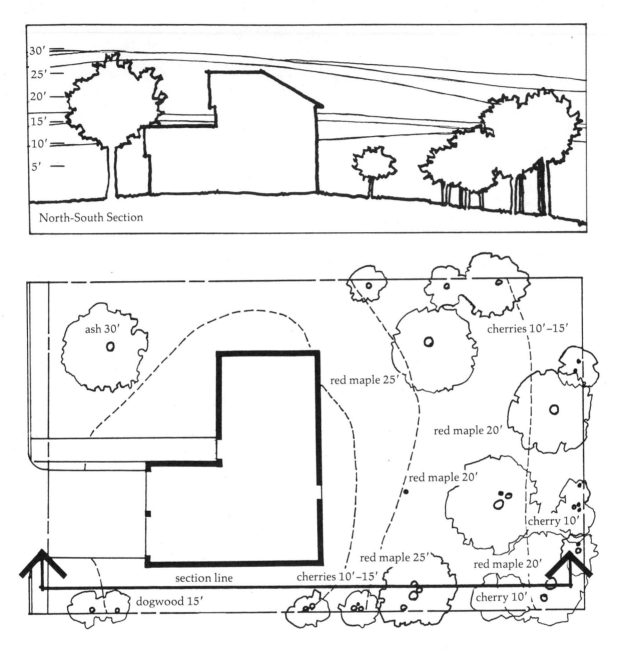

30'
25'
20'
15'
10'
5'

North-South Section

ash 30'

cherries 10'–15'

red maple 25'

red maple 20'

red maple 20'

cherry 10'

red maple 25'

cherries 10'–15'

red maple 20'

cherry 10'

section line

dogwood 15'

Vegetation Analysis of the Suburban Property: The suburban house was only recently constructed. The lawn is newly seeded and isn't well established yet. It consists of ryegrass, clover and various lawn weeds. The trees are those that were saved from the original lowland deciduous forest. They include dogwoods, cherries and an ash, as well as red maples toward the back of the property, where the ground is wet.

Because this family is interested in a landscape plan that will reduce their energy consumption, they have carefully evaluated the height of each tree. A cross section has been drawn, showing the height of the trees in relation to the house. Areas that have shade, or that need shade, can thus be determined.

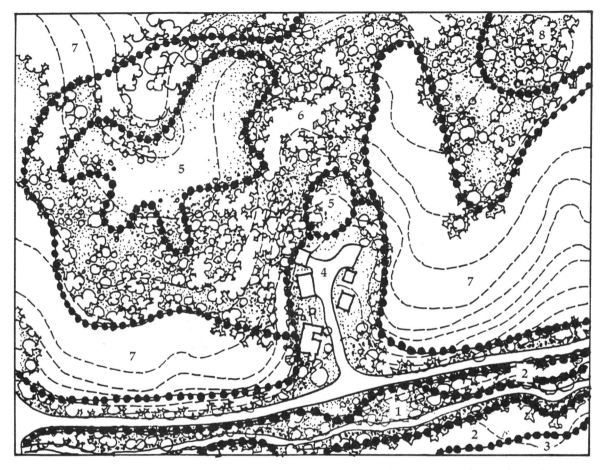

Vegetation Analysis of the Rural Property: There are eight general types of vegetation on this property. The entire site was cleared for farming as recently as 50 years ago, and there are, therefore, no mature woodlands or late successional species. The vegetation types conform to the ecological conditions except where they have been altered by man, as in the pasture, the spruce plantation and the farmstead area.

The area surrounding the house and farm buildings has been landscaped and includes turf grass, exotic rhododendrons, dogwoods, birch and ash, with ground covers and bulbs.

The pastures are seeded and mown to provide forage for farm animals. The spruce plantation was planted 20 to 30 years ago to define the edge of the property. These nonnative species have self-seeded and spread rapidly into the early successional meadow. The early successional woodlands are characterized by an abundance of disturbance species, like poison ivy, honeysuckle and bittersweet. These will remain a problem until the forest canopy becomes more dense and provides enough shade to kill off the vines. The composition of the species in the meadows, thickets and woodlands varies according to the successional stage—how long ago it was abandoned—as well as the soil type, physiography, microclimate and amount of water available.

The general types of vegetation are:

1. Wetland shrub meadow with cherry, witch hazel, willow alder and other species

2. Wetland thicket with ash, red maple, honeysuckle, witch hazel, greenbrier, cherry, willow alder and pin oaks

3. Successional forest with black locust, tulip poplar and cherry, being encroached upon by honeysuckle; in radical state of transition

4. Farmstead with lawn grasses and exotic ornamentals

5. Pasture

6. Upland early successional meadow

7. Upland mixed deciduous forest with sourwood, tulip poplar, oak, red and sugar maples, hickory and dogwood

8. Spruce plantation

It's unlikely that you can afford or even would want to make a total transformation of your landscape immediately. One of the purposes of making a comprehensive plan is to allow you to phase your landscaping over a period of years—to devise a realistic planning and management scheme.

On the other hand, don't be afraid to remove trees or overgrown shrubs that don't work. Each plant must be evaluated on its individual merits (or lack of merit) and on its contribution to your total landscape.

Locate all of the vegetation on your map and take a long, hard look at the contribution of each plant. Once again, the motive behind your landscaping, as determined by the functional analysis (which you'll do next—see Chapter 8), as well as the condition of your site, will determine what you need to know about each species. If you have a large property with a lot of existing vegetation, you may want to use several copies of your base map, one for each category, and use a rating system for each plant. Rate the visual contribution of each plant from beautiful to ugly on one map and the health from hardy to ailing on another. Whether you use one or several maps, the final goal is to get a total record for each plant, which will allow you to decide what to remove and what to retain.

If your motive for landscaping is to create a more beautiful environment, then you should analyze existing vegetation in terms of its visual contribution. Its size, color, texture, structure and location should all contribute to and not distract from the overall scene. Don't forget to account for seasonal variations. If you are interested in a low-maintenance landscape, then you must determine the present and future effort involved in maintaining a species and balance that against

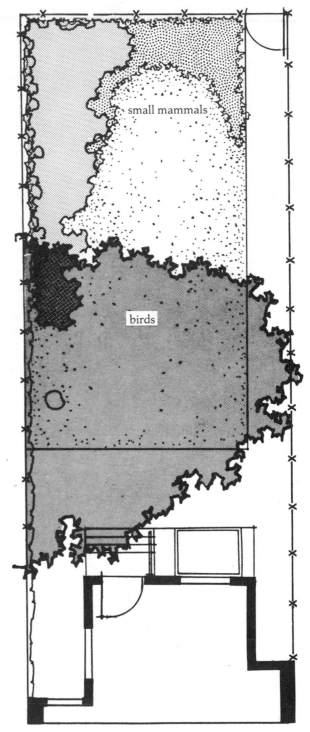

small mammals

birds

Wildlife Analysis of the Urban Property: Because of its urban location, the potential for wildlife attraction is limited. Nevertheless, birds and squirrels have been observed in the tree canopy and even nesting in the privet hedge. Cover is provided by the vegetation—at ground level (stippled area) by the ivy, at shrub level (lightly shaded area) by the privet and at canopy level (darkly shaded area) by the maple. Food is provided by the homeowners, who keep a bird feeder filled. The major lacking element is water; by providing a source of water, the bird population could easily be increased.

any other attributes it might have. If you're interested in reducing your household energy consumption by providing windbreaks or solar controls, you should determine the possible contribution of existing species. If you wish to attract wildlife, look for evidence of species that provide food, water and cover.

You will probably want to analyze existing vegetation for several different reasons.

Your Property: Wildlife Analysis

As you study the existing vegetation, note its real or potential food, cover and shelter. What animals are in evidence now—birds, squirrels, rabbits, chipmunks, snakes, toads, butterflies, foxes, gophers or deer—and where do you most frequently see them?

Indicate on a copy of your base map any areas that may be particularly attractive or very detrimental to wildlife. What can you do to increase the wildlife population?

No matter how small your backyard is—a few square yards or even a window box—it can become a wildlife refuge in miniature. Keep in mind that the more diverse, complete and stable your landscape, the more attractive it will be to wildlife.

If you wish to make a major contribution, convince your neighbors to cooperate and provide

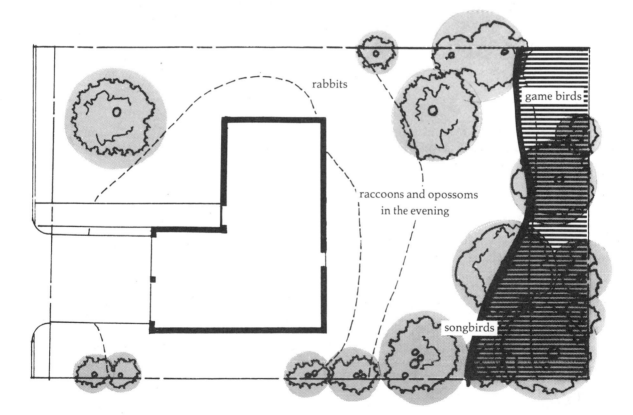

rabbits

game birds

raccoons and opossums in the evening

songbirds

Wildlife Analysis of the Surburban Property: Because of the woodland behind this property and the wet area adjacent to it, there is an abundance of wildlife. Small mammals are often sighted, and there are many bird species nesting in the canopy trees, which are shaded.

Any destruction of the wetland habitat, indicated by the stripes, would destroy one of the necessary elements for wildlife attraction, and care should be taken to enhance and preserve this favorable habitat.

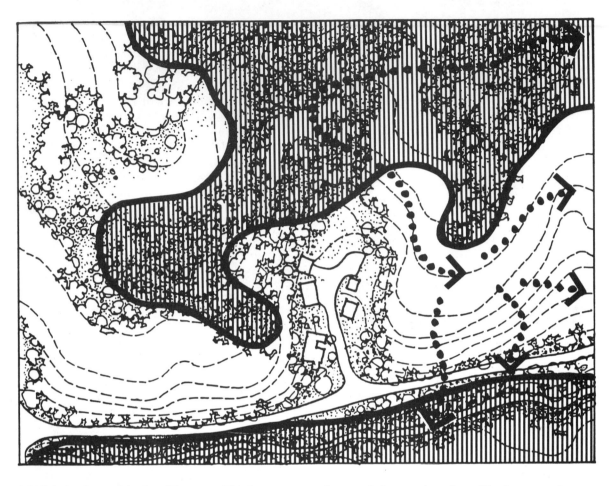

Wildlife Analysis of the Rural Property: This is an excellent environment for wildlife, with all the essentials — food, water and cover, primarily — readily available. Wildlife spottings correlate closely with the existing vegetation. Spotted have been small mammals — groundhogs, skunks, raccoons, rabbits, foxes, squirrels; game birds — pheasant, grouse; songbirds — too many to list; deer; snakes; amphibians; and, in the stream, fish.

 The greatest number of species of both birds and mammals has been observed by the stream, where they obtain water. There is also evidence of wildlife in the upland forest and meadows, where food and cover are available. Both of these areas are shaded on the map. There is movement and evidence of deer sunning on

the west-facing meadow slope. The deer move from here down to the water and back up into the woods for cover. The arrows mark the major discernible trails. There is little wildlife activity around the farmstead area, except for rats attracted by the feed grains and predators such as raccoons and foxes attracted by the chickens.

 While it is difficult to identify particular wildlife habitats by delineating the specific space occupied by a particular species, it is possible to identify existing conditions that are known to be preferred by those species. The preservation or strict conservation of these areas to ensure the continued well-being of these species would certainly be desirable.

larger areas of suitable hatitats. It could be a challenging cooperative project to ensure uninterrupted wildlife corridors, diverse sources of varied food and an unfailing water supply. If you'd like recognition for your efforts, the National Wildlife Federation, through a program called the Backyard Habitat Program, will certify your yard if it meets their requirements as a suitable habitat for wildlife.

This analysis of vegetation and wildlife is probably the most important part of your ecological study. It will allow you to make appropriate decisions about which plants to remove and what to add. The more you can find out about plants that are native to your area—their growth characteristics as well as their ecological requirements—the more beautiful and carefree your landscape will be. And planning your landscape to provide for the needs of wildlife is not only beneficial to the environment but will also enhance your own life.

8 *Functional Analysis*

An ideal landscape is one that is practical as well as beautiful. Very few sites are perfect, and too often we sacrifice practicality for assumed beauty. But what initially seems beautiful may quickly become an eyesore if it conflicts with your family's life-style. Taking care of that large expanse of lush green grass that you once wanted so badly may take up so much of your family's free time that no one wants to look at it anymore.

Preserving and designing beautiful natural habitats does not preclude comfort or human-oriented functions. In fact, practical considerations are even more important in natural landscaping than they are in traditional landscaping because you will be a part of the environment. The goal of landscaping with nature is to find low-cost, natural ways of incorporating all of your needs and wants into the landscape design. This requires defining

Functional Analysis Checklist

This functional analysis of your property will show you whether your existing landscaping does what you want it to do, as well as spell out what you want your landscape to accomplish.

However large or small the changes you want to make, you should complete both steps of the functional analysis.

1. *Analyze what functions your landscape presently accomplishes. You will locate these on your base map and indicate whether they work well or need improvement. Make sure to include, along with work, play and maintenance, functions such as:*
    circulation
    trash collection
    service/delivery
    privacy
    utilities
    security
2. *Make a list of what you want and need in your landscape. Include in your list the reasons for wanting each element, and the physical and ecological requirements needed to support each function. To organize these lists, the functions should be divided into:*
    work
    play/entertainment
    maintenance/living

This will be an ongoing list, and you will add to it or revise it after considering the functional uses of plants described in Section 2.

exactly what your family's present and future needs and desires are, as well as objectively assessing the good and bad functional elements of your site. Obviously, you will need to establish priorities—unless you have a very large property and a landscaping budget to match—and you will certainly have to make compromises. But these can be made fairly easily if you have a clear sense of the options available. If, for example, you'd like a vegetable garden and an area for outdoor entertaining but don't have enough room for both, you may be able to incorporate these two functions into the same area. By designing attractive raised beds for vegetables, with walls that serve as seats and paved areas between (large enough for a table), you could have your vegetables and dinner parties, too. *The important thing is to consider all of the options.*

While you may not be able to predict all of your future needs, it is a sure bet that continued inflation and high energy costs will make increased self-sufficiency and energy conservation both important landscape functions. Therefore, in addition to everything else, you should assess the potential of your site for energy reduction and food production.

The functional analysis of your site will consist of two parts: the first is an analysis of the current functions of your property, including their locations, suitability and performance (i.e., whether they function well or not). The second part is a list of all the functions your family wants to incorporate into your plan—your needs and desires.

Your Property: Functional Analysis

Using another acetate or tracing paper overlay, record all of the existing functional features of your landscape, where they are located and how they work. It might help to use two colors to indicate clearly which features work well and which are problems. The movement of cars, service vehicles and people should be located and the problems or conflicts noted. For example, a shortcut worn into a path indicates that the walk is in the wrong place.

Can you conveniently carry groceries from the car to the house? Does noise from the road affect nearby activities, or do car lights shine in your windows? Is there a problem with privacy or safety? A shaded, heavily screened approach may be good for privacy, but it can be inviting to intruders.

Include the locations of overhead and underground utilities—the well, the septic tank, electric and water lines. Don't forget delivery and service vehicles—does the oil truck have access to your tank?

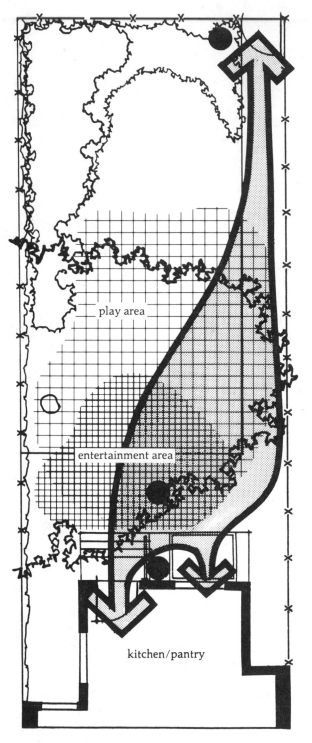

play area

entertainment area

kitchen/pantry

ENERGY EFFICIENCY

Until a few years ago, little thought was ever given to the energy efficiency of a landscape. As a result of our recent energy shortages, we not only need to stop our landscapes from consuming energy, we also need to make them work to reduce energy consumption. This can be done with great success by understanding and applying the principles described later in Section 2. But the first step is to evaluate how efficient or inefficient your landscape is presently.

The energy efficiency checklist will help you determine the environmental impact and energy efficiency of your property. Each of the descriptions is rated with a positive or negative score, and the sum is determined. A perfect score is 56. Although your landscape may be far from perfect now, this evaluation will help you determine what should be changed to increase your energy efficiency and decrease your environmental impact.

By pinpointing the major problem areas in your landscape—an unshaded patio that intensifies

Functional Analysis of the Urban Property: The functional uses of this property were organized according to the former owners' needs. There is an outdoor entertainment and eating area on the patio at the rear of the house and a children's play area, which is no longer needed by the current childless occupants, under the canopy of the yard's large shade tree. It's evident that these two areas overlap. The remainder of the property is given over to high-maintenance plantings—the privet hedge and ivy need constant pruning to control, and the sparse grass requires mowing.

The circulation allows a direct route from the yard's rear service entry to the kitchen and basement doors, as indicated by the arrows. Access is also provided to the electric meter, which must be periodically read by a serviceman. Trash is collected at the front of the house, so there are no provisions for it in the rear.

The analysis reveals that there are provisions for a limited number of functions and that they work in a simple but unimaginative way. The plantings require a lot of maintenance and a lawn mower. The play area is no longer needed for that purpose.

Needed is lighting at both ends of the property, denoted by the black dots. At the yard's rear entry, the lighting is primarily for security. At the house, the lighting would illuminate house and cellar steps for safer passage and the patio for more pleasant and practical use of it after dark.

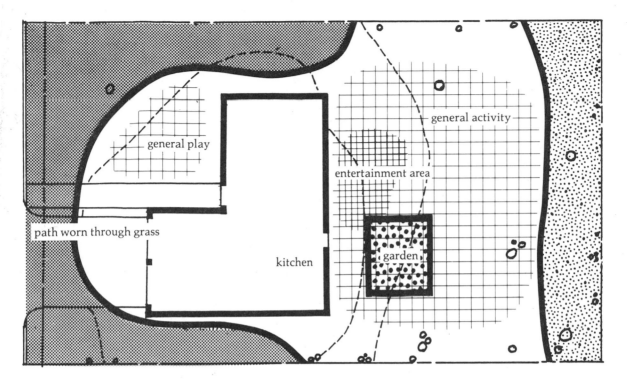

Functional Analysis of the Suburban Property:
Because this is a newly occupied landscape, there is not
yet an orderly arrangement of existing functions.
Activities take place wherever they can.

The driveway, which also serves as a parking
area, cannot accommodate more than two cars.
Because there is no street parking and the family owns
two cars, this is inadequate to accommodate visitors.
The front entry functions poorly. The walk to the
street is never used; instead there is a path worn into
the grass from the parking area. There is also a large
area in front of the house that is essentially wasted.

Although the children sometimes play here, it is not
encouraged because of its proximity to the street.

The back of the house is used for outdoor eating
and entertainment. Unfortunately, there are no formal
provisions for it, though some sort of paved surface
would be desirable. In the interest of cutting down
food costs, the homeowners have started a small
vegetable garden behind the kitchen. They now
realize, however, that this would be an ideal play area
for the children because it can be easily seen from the
kitchen. The back edge of the property is too wet to be
used for any activities.

summer heat in your house or a large evergreen
that blocks the winter sun—you will be able to
decide better how to improve them. But more
important, you will be training your eye to be able
to pick up on the positive aspects of your landscape
that you may have taken for granted. Does an
overhanging wisteria cut down dramatically on
the sun's glare? Or does a clump of shrubbery
provide a screen from traffic noises? As you refine
your checklist, more ideas will occur to you.

FUNCTIONAL LISTS

Have each family member make a list of the
activities and functions he or she would like to
have a place for in the landscape. For example,
your son may want to play basketball, your husband
or wife may desire low maintenance and privacy,
and you may want a special place to grow flowers.
Your family needs can be broken down into three
categories—work, play (including entertainment)
and maintenance. The importance given to each

How to Evaluate Your Landscape in Terms of Energy Efficiency and Environmental Impact

X Before

	+4	+3	+2	+1	0	−1	−2	−3	−4	
	Completely	Mostly	Partly	Slightly	Neither/Nor	Slightly	Partly	Mostly	Completely	
Uses available water								X		Requires watering
Creates richer soil									X	Requires fertilizing
Maintains itself								X		Needs maintenance
Produces its own food			X							Produces no food
Provides wildlife habitats				X						Destroys wildlife habitats
Provides human habitats			X							Destroys human habitats
Provides views and screens		X								Destroys views and screens
Provides beauty				X						Destroys beauty
Controls pollution					X					Creates pollution
Creates silence			X							Destroys silence
Moderates climate and weather				X						Intensifies climate and weather
Uses solar energy			X							Wastes solar energy
Provides natural cooling								X		Requires air conditioning
Controls glare and reflection			X							Creates glare and reflection

+16   +3   −13

A perfect score is 56. Although your landscape may be far from perfect now, this evaluation will help you determine what should be changed to increase your energy efficiency and decrease your environmental impact.

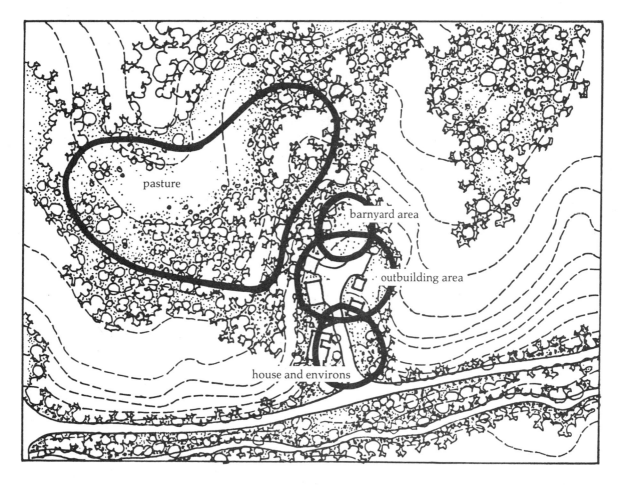

Functional Analysis of the Rural Property: Although this is a large property, it must accommodate many activities. The owners want to expand their farm activities to take advantage of their unused land and to improve the present, inefficient operation.

The barn, which is badly deteriorated, is not large enough to house all the desired animals and is too close to the house. The flies and odors associated with the present animals are nuisances in the house, and additional animals would increase the problem.

The pastures, which are mostly on the hilltops, are too far from the barn and must be supplied with water and animal shelters.

The owners would also like to increase their self-sufficiency by expanding their food production with the construction of a greenhouse and the planting of an orchard.

Other functional concerns relate to the homestead and the human activities that are taking place. The public access road is too close to the house and, though not heavily traveled, does cause some noise, dust and safety problems. Either a visual or physical separation of the road from the house is needed. The owners would like to dam the stream to create a pond for swimming and fishing. This would also provide attractive views from the house.

category should reflect your family's life-style. The play/entertainment category will be important if you have young children or enjoy frequent parties. If you wish to produce your own food and maintain a high level of self-sufficiency, you will focus on the work and maintenance categories.

Along with each function, you should describe the physical and ecological elements necessary for its existence and support. For example, an outdoor dining area should have a stable surface and be large enough to accommodate a certain number of people. You may want it to be private and to be shaded in summer, while a vegetable garden needs a sunny area with well-drained soils.

BE REALISTIC
Your lists should be as extensive as possible, but also realistic. A swimming pool may be your heart's desire, but if there's no room in the budget or in the yard, it would be pointless to include it. These lists, along with information from your other analyses, will allow you to determine what is economically and financially feasible in your landscape plan. It is possible that the existing ecology may not be able to support one or more of your proposed functions. Or it may make building one of your projects prohibitively expensive. If the bedrock is on or near the surface, a garden pool may require costly blasting. On the other hand, your analysis may reveal possibilities that you hadn't considered, such as rock garden using that exposed bedrock.

Before finalizing your lists, be sure to read about the functional and aesthetic uses of plants in Section 2. You may get even more ideas to include in your plan.

REVISE AS YOU LEARN
As you learn more about what can be done in the landscape, your lists of needs will grow. And you will discover that some things you thought you needed, you don't need at all. They may actually prevent your getting the greatest enjoyment from the property. Do you need color? Flowers require a lot of time and labor to keep up, which is okay if you are an enthusiastic gardener. If not, you can get color through fences, terraces, garden furniture, or trees, shrubs and other plantings that require little maintenance. Getting the most use from your outdoor spaces and reducing maintenance may prove more important to you than having all the different kinds of plants you thought you wanted. Your child may even become more interested in attracting wildlife by providing food and cover than in playing basketball on a paved surface.

Because these lists will serve as a program around which your final plan will be designed and your budget developed, you should continue to revise them as you complete your ecological analysis. Even if your original needs remain the same, you may find new ways to accomplish them.

After you have synthesized the ecological information, you will look at each item on this list in light of what exists. This will allow you to arrange the elements of your design in the most effective manner and to satisfy your needs in the easiest and cheapest way. Once you have put together what you want with what you have, you will be able to design a foolproof landscape plan. This plan will be both practical and beautiful— truly functional.

9

Visual Analysis

The appearance of your landscape can be attributed, in large part, to the ecological factors that you have already studied. If the ecology has been modified by man, then the appearance may be attributed to functional needs or desires.

Having analyzed the ecology and functions of your landscape, you should have a pretty good idea of why your property looks the way it does. Your job now is to define the visual aspects and

problems—what you like or don't like in your existing landscape—so that you can determine what needs to be changed.

Our concept of what is beautiful is highly individual and is affected by many factors—our past and what we've been exposed to, our present activities, our attitudes toward life and toward nature. Some of us see a natural meadow as a rich and beautiful landscape, while others find it a

Visual Analysis Checklist

The visual analysis of your property will isolate the elements that make your landscape look the way it does. By understanding the individual elements that make up the total picture, you will be able to see what needs to be changed.

The same techniques you use to visually analyze your property should also be used to study natural environments to gain an understanding of how vegetation looks as it occurs in nature and to adapt this to your landscape.

1. Analyze the existing:
*   spaces—enclosed or open*
*   small or large*
*   views—good or bad*
*   screens—required or unnecessary*
*   forms—of spaces*
*   of ground surface*
*   of vertical elements*
*   texture—smooth to coarse*
*   color—combinations*
*   seasonal changes*

weedy offense. Unless you want a truly wild garden, untouched by human hands, you will be imposing these aesthetic prejudices on the appearance of your property, and by doing so, you are not only imposing a design, you are modifying a living system.

How you change the appearance, then, should be determined by the ecology of your environment. Whether you want a formal, highly structured design or one that is casual and unstructured, you must observe the rules of nature. What this means is that no matter how much you love a water-needing species, it won't survive if you have only a hot, arid environment. Or if you want a dark, shaded glen, you can't expect hay-scented ferns or brightly flowering shrubs to exist without sun. Designing with nature requires using only those plants that are suited to the environment you have.

To design a beautiful landscape, you must understand how nature uses form, color and texture in its compositions. While these design principles and their relationships may seem esoteric, arty or just plain incomprehensible, it is helpful to look at the individual elements that make up the scene. Abstracting these will help you to understand what makes your landscape look the way it does and how to change it.

You don't need a degree in design to observe a natural environment. The best basis for understanding composition is looking at nature itself. Each ecosystem is not only a community of plants, but also a consistent vocabulary of forms, colors and textures that ultimately create an unmistakable atmosphere. Yet each one has variations that can provide design examples for you to emulate in your landscape. By observing and using nature's designs, we can all master the rules of landscape design.

Your job is made easier by having the advantage of knowing your tastes and knowing your property. There are disadvantages to this, however. Your landscape problems may have been around so long that you can't help but overlook them. Or you may *think* that you know the solutions as well as the problems.

Now is the time to drop any preconceived ideas and analyze your site as though you were looking at an unknown property. You will be amazed at the changes in attitude this fresh look produces.

There are three different techniques that are used by professional landscape architects that will be helpful to you in analyzing your own property or any other natural environment that has features you want to incorporate into your plan. They are, first, the diagrammatic analysis of spaces, views, screens, form, texture and color; second, drawing; and third, tracing photographs. These methods of recording what you see will help you to understand what contributes to the composition of your landscape and to the harmony of all natural landscapes.

Diagrammatic Analysis

You will need to make several overlays for your base map to define spaces, views, screens, form,

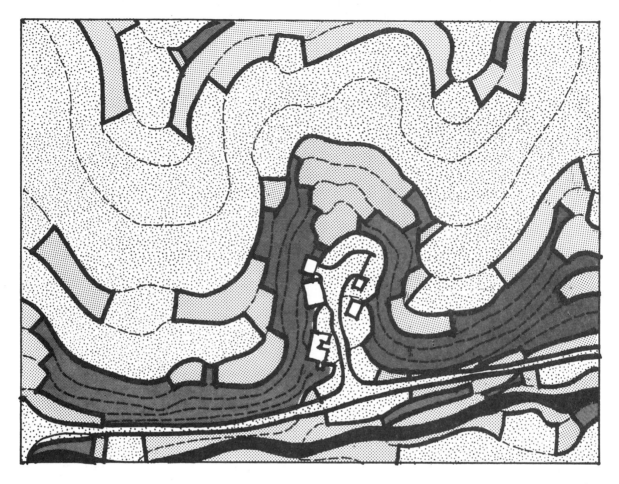

Landform Analysis of the Rural Property: This property has a strong form derived from the topography — an obvious valley bottom enclosed by two bluffs. A stream runs through the valley bottom, adjoined by a township road. Domestic buildings are on both sides of an access road intersecting this township road. Although other kinds of form could be

analyzed, the landform analysis is most relevant to this size property.

Key information depicted on the map is the degree of slope. The areas with the dark shading are those areas with 15 to 25 percent slopes. The light shading denotes 5 to 15 percent slopes, while the stippling denotes 0 to 5 percent slopes.

texture and color as they now exist in your landscape. As you are defining and locating these elements on your map, you will also be deciding whether you like or dislike them. Eventually, after you have synthesized all this information, you will see how to change them. For example, if your property is one large space with long open views to the horizon, but you prefer smaller, confined spaces, you will need to design screens of plants or architectural elements that define and enclose spaces. Medium-tall evergreens or a brick wall could be used to make that enclosure.

SPACES, VIEWS AND SCREENS

You have already recorded the major existing elements on your base map. Using just this plan and a tracing paper overlay, you can analyze the spaces created and their relationships. Look at how your landscape is organized and the spaces that are formed. It is likely that along with the obvious spaces enclosed by walls or vegetation there will be implied spaces that are defined by a change in ground texture or a partial enclosure. Whether real or implied, the elements that are responsible

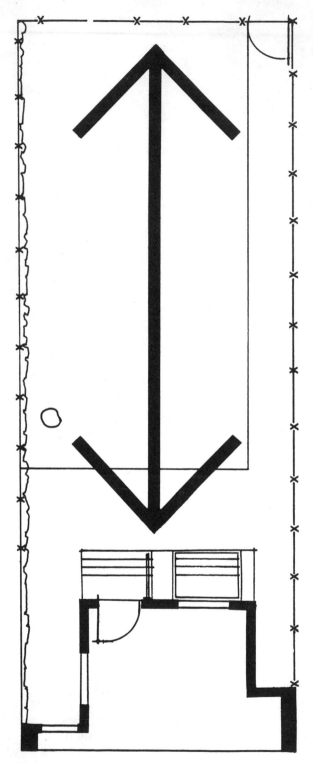

Form Analysis of the Urban Property: The shape of the property is long and narrow, and this dominant form is emphasized by the fences running along the sides of the property and by the parallel concrete walk. The arrow drives this point home. The only elements providing variety to this rectilinear form are the large canopy tree and the privet hedge.

Seen in perspective (facing page), it is clear that the shade provided by the canopy serves to break up the monotony of this long, narrow space. The privet hedge, while not attractive in itself, softens the strong lines of the property boundary. There is very little variety of color, no flowering plants and no spring/ summer interest. The property needs greater diversity of form, color and texture, which should de-emphasize the rectangular property lines and provide screening where needed.

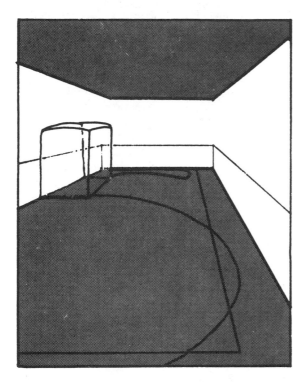

for creating the space will also determine its feeling. A brick terrace surrounded by a 6-foot stone wall makes a very confined and private space, while the same terrace in the middle of an open field would be very different.

Whichever space you prefer, large and open or small and enclosed, its sense of proportion can make you feel comfortable or not. What are the sizes and shapes of the spaces on your property? We all can recognize pleasant or awkward proportions. If sizes and shapes are either too equal or extremely unequal, the sight of them is disconcerting or just plain monotonous.

Draw the spaces that occur on your property and indicate whether they're enclosed or not. Jot down what the feeling is, what creates it and whether or not you like it. Be as specific as possible. This analysis will be very important in determining your final design.

The same elements that define spaces can also define views. Heavily enclosed spaces will screen your views both into and out of the enclosed area. This may be desirable if you don't want to look at the neighbors' swimming pool, but it could be undesirable if you want to keep an eye on the kids' play area.

On the same map locate what you see from the windows of your house and from the most heavily used outdoor areas. Locate neighboring views that should be screened or attractive views that should be opened up. How much of a screen or opening is needed to change the view will be determined by the angle of sight and the distance of the screen from the observer. In general, the closer you locate the screen to the observer, the smaller it needs to be. Again, the more specific you can get, the more helpful it will be to your final design.

As you look at spaces and views, you will begin to notice patterns that are created by different shapes, textures and colors in the landscape. Is there a dominant pattern to your landscape that is expressed by form, texture or color? What are the exceptions to this pattern? Although these design elements are so closely allied that they can be frequently difficult to distinguish, it is helpful to look at each separately.

FORM

There are many types of form in any landscape, and each has a bearing on the overall appearance of a place.

First, there is form in the lines laid out on your plan and the spaces that are created by paving, architectural elements or vegetation. The shape of these may be rectangular or curving, or a combination of the two.

If the form is created by a series of geometric shapes arranged symmetrically, with the house as the focus, the landscape will appear highly formal. If, on the other hand, the forms are made up of winding, languid curves serpentined over the garden in various directions, the landscape will be informal. Because there are very few geometric forms in nature, naturalistic landscaping usually results in an informal design.

A second type of form in the landscape is contour. The shape of the ground creates forms that can play a large part in your design. The surface of your land is determined on a large scale by the physiographic region in which you live. Whether it is perfectly flat as in the Plains states or ruggedly varied as in mountainous areas, its character must be recognized and will influence your plan.

On a smaller scale, ground forms can be altered by paving, grading and walls. A raised terrace with a broad, low flight of steps from one level to the next contributes horizontal lines that can continue the lines of the building and vertical lines that can add interest and variety. Mounds or berms of earth can greatly alter the natural physiography.

The third kind of form in the landscape is the shape of every plant in the garden. This form can be dominated by the shapes of individual species or by masses of plants growing together. These vertical forms cannot be seen on your plan, which shows only horizontal elements. To analyze these requires observation and the use of sketches or photographs. Rhythm may be achieved by a repetition of one form, either in planting a series of the same plant or a series of plants with similar form. You can create accent or emphasis by an interruption in the rhythm using a contrasting form.

Good composition relies on simplicity, sequence, balance and scale similarity. Although it generally takes years of experience to develop skill in using form, you can learn quickly by observing nature. Examples of rhythm created by repeating forms are evident everywhere. A coniferous forest, a prairie grassland, a bank of ferns—all repeat the dominant species over and over, creating a subtle rhythm that is punctuated here and there by a contrasting form. These accent plants occur where a change in the ecological conditions provides an environment for a different kind of species. A flowering dogwood may appear in the midst of a forest where a tree has fallen and allows light to penetrate. Nature's designs are always based on sound ecological determinants. They look beautiful, not because of an arbitrary decision to add bright flowers, but because the environment is appropriate and fitting for a contrasting kind of species. By using natural forms to create nature's kind of rhythm and accent in your landscape, your design will stand up to the best.

TEXTURE

Texture means the degree of smoothness or roughness of elements in a landscape. The appearance of a rough or smooth texture is produced by the variations of size, structure and shape among the parts of the plants. Some trees, shrubs and ground covers have a smooth appearance caused by small, dense foliage, while others look rough because of large, open foliage and visible trunks and branches.

Texture can change with the seasonal variations of the plants. Take, for instance, the dogwoods. In the spring before the leaves appear, their red, yellow and gray bark makes a beautiful and dramatic background texture, and as the summer continues, there is still a hint of these shades of bark showing through the green leaves but giving another type of texture. Moreover, plants constantly change their characteristics with age and location. When young, the bark will have a soft texture, but it will become coarser as the tree matures. The texture of plants is also influenced by their location, soil and moisture content. A plant growing in a wet environment may have a very different texture from the same species growing in a dry environment.

As you look at your existing landscape, you

Texture Analysis of the Rural Property: The only place where texture is a concern on a property of this size is where it is part of an aesthetic composition, such as the entrance to the house. The analysis reveals there is a good harmony, with the large rhododendron of medium texture balanced by the smaller shrub of coarse texture. It gives just the right combination for interest and variety, but not so much as to be confusing.

This information can be reduced to a perspective schematic, as seen at right, by tracing the outlines of buildings and plants, then using different symbols for different textures. Here the gradations from fine textures to coarse ones are obvious.

will need to decide whether there's too great a variety of textures, creating a discordant effect, or whether too little variety makes your garden look uninteresting and bland.

COLOR

The subtle color combinations found in nature are nearly always superior to those man tries to create. Although a lot of work has been directed toward producing bigger, brighter and more exotically colored flowers, some of which are spectacularly beautiful in themselves, using them successfully requires great skill.

Moreover, many color schemes are designed for a brief flowering season only, and flowers are the most transient part of the landscape picture. No matter how rich the flower beds in any garden, green is the predominant color in summer. In fall, it may be brilliant yellow, gold, red and brown. In winter, it becomes gray and brown, with bright colors supplied mostly by berries, birds and evergreens. You will be surprised how beautiful a minimal amount of flowers can be against the background of a continually changing natural color scheme.

Looking at the spaces, views, screens, form, texture and color on your base map, you will be able to understand your present landscape and how to work with it. You should analyze each element on a separate copy of your map.

Visual Analysis of the Urban Property: The visual analysis shows that screening—indicated by the striped band—is needed to create privacy for the patio and to block undesirable views of the alley behind the property. The existing privet hedge provides a screen where it is needed, but because of its age, it is not attractive. If it's removed, it must be replaced with something that will serve as a screen. There is a nice short view—indicated by the arrows—from the kitchen windows to the rear of the property that should be preserved. The area shaded by the canopy tree appears dark and cool in contrast to the fully exposed, sunlit spaces and adds variety and interest to the landscape. From the sunny area of the yard, there is an interesting long view—again, arrows indicate this—of the city skyline. The break in the proposed screening preserves this special view.

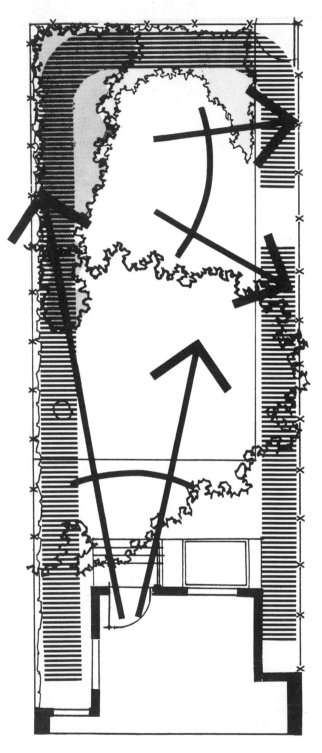

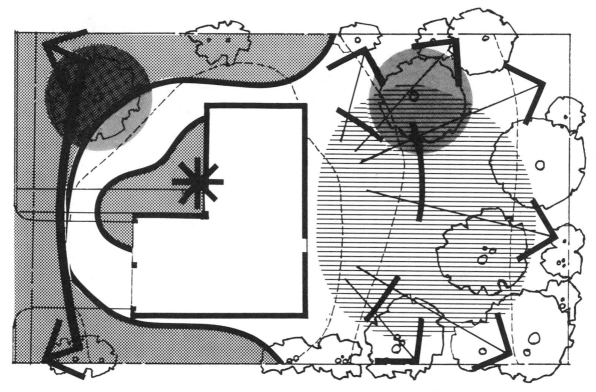

Visual Analysis of the Suburban Property: The biggest problem with this property, visually, is the front yard. It is just one large, open space. There's no sense of entry, no distinction between the entranceway and the rest of the front yard. There's no separation of the parking area from the rest of the front yard. The entire space seems to bleed into the development. This property is not separated from any of the other properties: those next to it and those across the road from it. Screening from the road and the neighbors is needed. On the map, this need is indicated by the heavy, arced bar with arrows on either end.

Two worthwhile elements in the front yard are noted on the map. The tall ash tree, noted on the

vegetation analysis, is marked with a double canopy to denote it as special. The large asterisk denotes visually appealing architectural detailing around the front door.

Moving along the sides of the house into the rear yard, you find shaded bars denoting the need for screening to provide privacy.

The views to the back of the property are good and should be maintained, as indicated by the arrows. The area shaded by the horizontal lines has a pleasantly enclosed nature to it, and the small crosshatched area is the spot most easily observed from the rear windows of the house, making it the best area for supervised play. A particularly handsome red maple is noted, as was the ash in front.

Drawing

The second technique of visual analysis is drawing. Take a pad and pencil outdoors and find a comfortable seat that gives you a good view of your property. You may need to try several locations. Look carefully at what is there and draw it. You will see the vertical lines, patterns and relationships that were not obvious on your base map. As you try to represent accurately what you see, you can't help but notice textures, dark areas (shadows and shade), light areas, masses and empty spaces. That's

why, even if your finished drawing doesn't look like your property, this experience will be useful. Drawing makes you look closely at the subject and forces you to see much more than the obvious.

TRACING PHOTOGRAPHS

If you feel that freehand drawing is too difficult for you, try tracing photographs. While color slides can be used, it is better to use black-and-white photographs so that you're not distracted

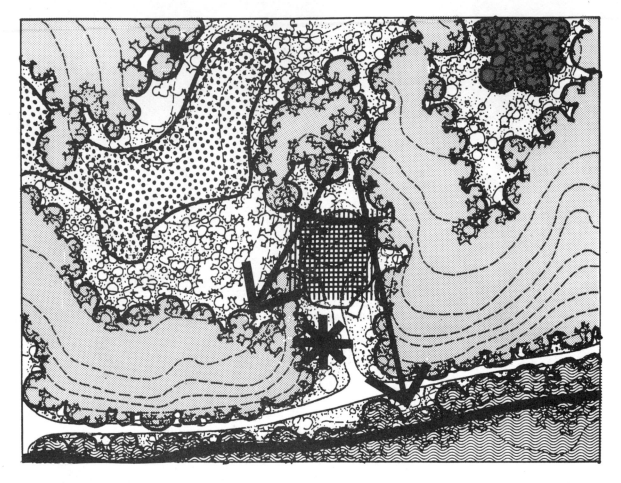

Visual Analysis of the Rural Property: There are three different kinds of spaces and accompanying views here. From the broad, open-spaced hilltop meadows (stippled area), there are expansive views over other hilltops. Here the scale is large, and the feeling one of freedom and openness. The exact opposite is the confined space within the woodlands (darkly shaded area). Here the view is only to the next tree. The space is very enclosed, and the feeling is one of confinement.

Between these extremes is the domestic space bounded by the slopes. Within this space, there is some

degree of openness, but the views are limited and the scale is intimate.

These observations are delineated on the map. So too are other visual elements. The asterisk denotes that the farmhouse on the property is a picturesque historic structure. The cross just into the trees bordering the hilltop meadow marks the highest spot on the property. The crosshatched spot in the farmstead area indicates an undesirable view, that of the deteriorating barn and surrounding barnyard.

by the individual colors of plants. This technique will make flowers appear as a certain shade on the gray scale and allow you to look at the structure of the overall design instead of the beauty of each

plant. Later on, these photographs will be very helpful when you begin to design. By tracing over the photographs of the existing landscape with your proposed changes, you can see what the design will actually look like. For example, if you plan to take away your overgrown foundation plants and replace them with low-growing shrubs and ground covers, you can draw this change over a photo of your house and see how you like it.

Remember that these techniques are tools to help you look closely at your landscape and to understand what it is that makes any landscape appeal to you. The diagrams and drawings allow you to put your observations on paper and come back to them later when you begin to design.

Don't forget that seasonal changes will create significant differences in the appearance of your property—views will change and spaces will be less well defined with the winter loss of foliage. And while you're deciding what is good or bad about the appearance of your own property, you should also be studying natural landscapes and the principles of nature's design.

10

Synthesis

Synthesizing your site analysis is an important step in the landscape process. It is a transition from the information-gathering stage to the planning-and-design stage. It requires putting together one drawing with all the information that you have previously recorded on individual maps or overlays. The synthesis drawing will then show the ecological characteristics of your property and where one area differs from another.

This will be the base on which your landscape design is developed, and its use will ensure that your plan responds to and is guided by the ecology of your site. No matter what the scope of your plans, the synthesis will guide you so your design works with nature.

The next step, after drawing the synthesis map, is to go back to the list of needs and wants that you made in Chapter 8. These lists should be reviewed and revised in light of your new knowledge of the landscape. The ecological factors required for each element on the list will then be matched with the ecological factors described in the synthesis. The combination of the factors needed matched with the factors existing will show you the best location for each element you want. There may, however, be conflicts that will require you to make choices. These will depend partially on your values but also on the degree of constraint or opportunity provided by the different areas represented on your synthesis map.

The synthesis map will be the basis for your planting plan too. Each habitat on the map has different conditions and is therefore suitable for a different vegetation group. Your synthesis map will reveal the boundaries of each habitat and the characteristics that distinguish one area from another. It will allow you to see the opportunities and constraints of your property and to work out a plan that is ecologically fit for your environment. The synthesis thus will indicate a planting scheme by defining the areas that require different planting approaches.

To synthesize all of the information, put a piece of tracing paper over each of your maps, beginning with geology and including each of the ecological subjects as well as the functional and visual analyses. On the tracing paper overlay, record the relevant information from each of the individual maps.

If there are two or more different geologic conditions, draw the line that divides them. Or, if there are any distinct geologic features, show where they are located.

Do the same for physiography, hydrology, soils and so forth. Anything that distinguishes one area from another should be noted and lines drawn to show where conditions differ. When you encounter information that is not variable or which can't be drawn on the plan, it should be noted on a separate piece of paper.

Because you will be adding a lot of different information to this map, it may get cluttered and messy. You may want to devise a color and symbol system that will help to keep it readable. Be sure to record what the colors or symbols stand for. For example, each natural factor can be assigned a color. Arrows, stars or other symbols sketched in color can show where individual elements occur, while color shading can be used to show general areas affected by natural factors.

After you have traced all of the information from each of the analysis maps, you should have many lines, each of which defines a different habitat. Now color each distinct habitat and write down what its features are—what makes it different from the other habitats.

Keep in mind that the actual boundaries of each habitat are generally not as precise as a pencil line drawn on paper. In reality, each habitat gradually merges into the next, and you really should allow for a transition zone.

To get a better idea of how the synthesis is done, look at the synthesis maps for the three example properties on the following pages. Then page back through the chapters in this section and study the information recorded on the analysis maps for each property. Analyze what information was put onto each synthesis map and what was left off.

Put yourself in the position of actually drawing each synthesis map. Here's how you would do it.

Synthesis: Urban Property

The synthesis map of the urban property does not have a great variety of information, even though at first glance it seems to be a welter of arrows and symbols. The ecological factors are fairly uniform and therefore don't present the kinds of restraints that varied slopes, soils and climatic conditions would. When put together on one map, nevertheless, the ecological factors combine to show clear opportunities and constraints that will influence any landscaping plans.

As each map is overlaid individually and then cumulatively, it becomes easy to see what information is relevant and must be recorded on the synthesis.

The geologic analysis revealed uniform conditions that will have little direct effect on any landscaping plans. Therefore, it isn't necessary to make any notations on the synthesis overlay.

Although there are no large-scale physiographic variations, there is a slope that controls the direction of runoff. This is noted on the synthesis map, because any grading must maintain that slope to provide for surface drainage.

Indicating the direction and degree of slope

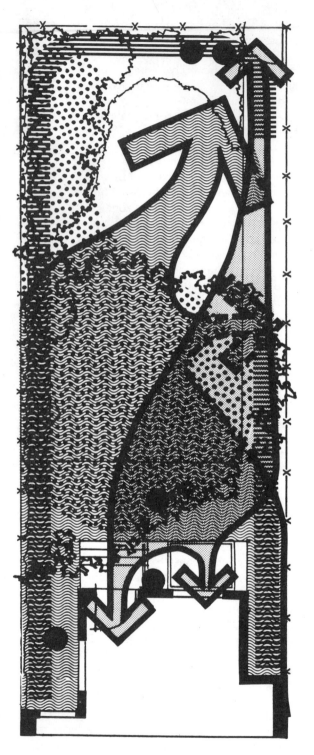

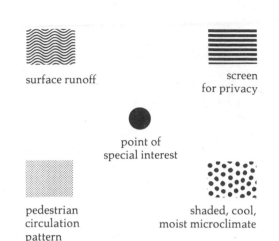

surface runoff

screen
for privacy

point of
special interest

pedestrian
circulation
pattern

shaded, cool,
moist microclimate

also shows the major hydrologic consideration—the direction of surface water flow. The (hydrologic) problem of water seeping into the foundation walls is also noted on the synthesis map.

The soils are uniform and present no major constraints, but it is noted that there is a clayey subsoil that slows down the infiltration of water. One small area with problem soils is indicated.

The microclimatic analysis is included in the synthesis by noting the glare from the concrete patio, the shade of the canopy tree and the direction of summer breezes and winter winds.

Three vegetation habitats are next traced onto the synthesis. Because these were derived by studying the other ecological factors, they are roughly similar to what's already there. The characteristics of the individual species are also noted. Although it's not necessary to record any wildlife information on the map, it is noted that water must be provided to attract more species of birds.

The information from the visual analysis is overlaid, and the areas that need to be screened are marked, as are the areas where views should be maintained. It is also noted that the hedge is unattractive and that there is a need to break up the long narrow space.

Finally, the functional analysis is added. All of the plantings except the canopy tree require a lot of maintenance. The need for night lighting is recorded. And while the existing circulation pattern is already shown on the base map, the points that must be gotten to and from are recorded on the synthesis. Any change in circulation thus can be analyzed when the design is being worked out.

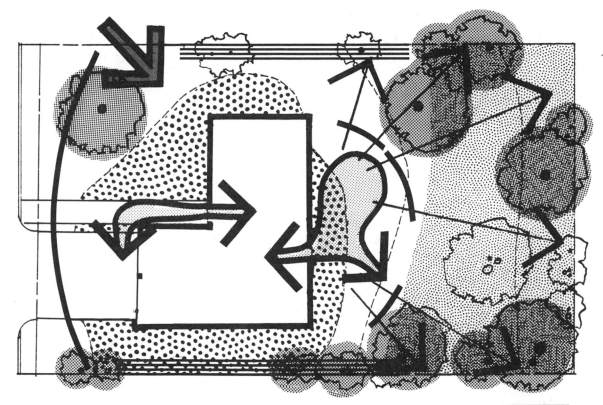

With all of this information compiled, this synthesis drawing is ready to be used as the information base for the design. Together with the list of needs and wants, it will be used to work out a landscape plan. That plan, by the way, can be seen in Chapter 14.

Synthesis: Suburban Property

The suburban property is a little larger, and the greater amount of information that's available here is more of a challenge. It takes some time to do properly. The value of carefully conceived symbols and color codes becomes evident. You'll find it worthwhile to sketch in pencil and to stop periodically to clean up and simplify. As you become certain that areas of the map will not be changed by the addition of new factors, turn to your colored pencils or pens and finalize those areas.

The geology of the suburban property is uniform and therefore not recorded on the synthesis overlay.

The physiography is included by tracing the contour lines onto the synthesis overlay.

fill soil

northwest winds

screen open views
for privacy
and setting

desirable
views

screen
for privacy

pedestrian
circulation
pattern

wet soils

desirable trees

The surface drainage follows the direction of slope and that is already recorded by means of the contour lines. The only additional hydrologic information included is the problem area caused by the undirected downspout water.

The lines that divide areas with different soil types are traced.

The results of the microclimatic analysis are added. The northwest winds, hot summer sun and south-facing side of the house are all indicated.

The condition of the existing vegetation is noted and the plant habitats are drawn. As in the urban synthesis, these habitats will conform with much of the information already located. The wildlife information is not drawn, but it is added to the notes.

At this point, the property has been defined in terms of its ecology, and all that remains to do is to add the functional and visual information. Before this information is added, the drawing may need to be cleaned up. You see only the completed synthesis map for the suburban property, but if you were actually drawing your own synthesis map, you might find it a mess of lines and arrows. Take the time periodically to clean up and simplify.

To do this, look at the spaces divided by each line and analyze what it is that makes one area different from the next. Using colored pencils or pens, color in each area that is distinct and unique. In some cases, you may find that the lines are close enough together to be compromised into one without losing practical accuracy. For example, if the line that indicates a change from a north-facing area to an east-facing area is within a few feet or yards of a line separating two different soil types, these could be combined into one line that would simplify, and thus clarify, the drawing. There is always a transition zone between habitats that allows for a gradual change of conditions and hence a gradual change of plant species.

After the map is made more readable, the suburban functional and visual analyses are added. The front walk is unnecessary, and the path indicates where a walk should be located. The parking area is noted as being too small, and the children's play area and the outdoor entertaining area are noted as being best located behind the house. Screens that are needed and views that are to be maintained are shown. Finally, it is noted that the front entrance needs a sense of enclosure and greeting.

As you can see, the cumulative record of all this information is well on the way to giving form to the landscape plan.

Synthesis: Rural Property

Because of the larger size of the rural property, there is a much greater diversity of ecological factors and thus much more information to be included on the synthesis map.

The areas with different geologic conditions are recorded first, then the physiographic analysis is overlaid. As can be expected because of the interdependence of physiography and geology, the dividing lines of the physiographic areas are the same as the geologic ones. The direction of the slopes are indicated, and those areas with very steep slopes are located.

Information taken from the hydrologic analysis includes the boundaries of the flood-prone area, the direction of runoff and the locations of collection points for surface water.

The different soil types are recorded and the microclimatic factors noted, including the direction of winds and the cold air drainage down the valley.

When the vegetation habitats are traced onto the synthesis, many of the previously drawn lines are repeated. Now you can easily see the dependence of each ecological factor on the others. This is what causes overlapping lines. Habitats emerge.

As with the suburban synthesis, the drawing was cleaned up and refined before adding the functional and visual information. (If you have even more varying information, you may find it necessary to refine or even redraw the synthesis after including the functional and visual analysis. You do need a final readable version.)

On this property, the functional analysis includes problems associated with animal husbandry and homesteading, as well as the degree of maintenance needed and of energy consumed. Much of this information is recorded in the notes rather than on the drawing itself.

The major visual concern is limited to the area surrounding the house and the need for a visual buffer between the house and the road.

Although there are many opportunities and options for landscape development on this large site, there are also important constraints that are recorded on the synthesis.

The Base for Your Design

In every case, no matter what the size of the property, the synthesis should serve as the total picture of the existing site. The information recorded on this map allows a person without any special skills or training to make intelligent decisions about the use of the landscape. The synthesis makes it clear where it's easiest, cheapest and most desirable to do anything, including building a house, planting a vegetable garden or adding a terrace. It further defines all of the conditions available for vegetation, thus allowing you to use plants that have requirements that can be met by those conditions.

With your synthesis completed, you are well on your way to enjoying nature's design in your landscape. The next steps are to choose plants and to fill in the details of your design.

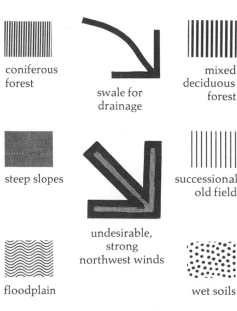

coniferous forest

swale for drainage

mixed deciduous forest

steep slopes

undesirable, strong northwest winds

successional old field

floodplain

wet soils

SECTION II
Design with Plants

11 Designing Your Landscape

Yyou're ready—*finally*—to put everything together on a plan that will serve as the blueprint for your landscape. Having thoroughly analyzed your site and defined its opportunities and constraints, you are ready to start "designing."

The creation of a design is an eclectic, sometimes frustrating, trial-and-error process. You do it on paper. You use one pencil and a half-dozen erasers.

But even though you're doing paperwork, you'll be getting exercise, for you'll be walking around your property again and again, scrutinizing the reality of what you've got analyzed on your various maps. You'll also be taking nature walks, studying plants and plant associations, gathering ideas and information for your landscape.

The design stage is when you get immersed in vegetation. You waded among the plants a little in doing your vegetation analysis, but now you will dive right in. You have to learn your options, and you have to analyze them.

You have to learn about plants native to your ecological region. The following chapter will introduce you to each of the 12 regions that comprise the 48 contiguous states. The vegetation charts in that chapter will give you a starting point in your vegetation studies. You'll also learn, in Chapters 13 and 14, how plants can make functional and aesthetic contributions to the landscape. Although you may think you know a lot about the aesthetic qualities of plants, you may be surprised at what you learn.

At any rate, this section of *Nature's Design* focuses on design. Since plants are intrinsic to natural landscape design, plants are the dominating subject of this section. As you read this chapter, you'll have to consult plant books, like field guides to wild flowers and trees, and you'll have to get out and around, taking notes, sketching, taking photographs.

You'll have to ruminate on what you learn, sifting out what works for you and your site and incorporating it into your final landscape plan.

The Landscape Plan

Ultimately, you'll prepare a landscape plan, a package with two principal elements: a site plan and a planting plan. If you are being thoroughly methodical about it, the plan should also include a phasing plan. The whole works should be documented by your site analyses and notes on the vegetation you select for your landscape.

Both the site plan and the planting plan are detailed drawings, done on copies of your base map.

The site plan has to do with the physical, man-made elements in the landscape. It should show the location, size, shape, arrangement, groupings and composition of all the structures, including retaining walls or fences. Likewise, it should show the location, size and composition of paths, walks or informal trails, the driveway and parking area, if such exist, and any recreational areas, such as patios, decks or pools. Even artificially lighted areas should appear on the site plan.

Although the planting plan will zero in on the plants, you do have to include some pretty specific information about plants on the site plan. What you have to do, using the site plan, is work out the interplay between plant elements and everything else. Natural landscaping won't allow you to be so inflexible as to ink in all the constructed features, like walks and drives and buildings, then fill in around them with plants.

In natural landscaping, the ecology of the site speaks, the constructed features speak and the plants speak. A harmonious chorus results. All elements must have a say, so all elements must interact on your paper plans.

After the site plan is worked out, you turn to the planting plan. This plan shows all the plants, including the trunk and canopy size of trees and shrubs and the extent of ground covers. Species are listed. In doing this plan, you must make your plant selections. It is from this plan that you do your planting.

The Site Plan

Don't expect to complete the site plan in one try. Most designers start with a piece of tracing paper laid over the site analysis. Using a soft pencil, they begin by sketching in approximations of the design. Long before they consider individual species, they locate plant masses and slowly define shapes, sizes and the relationships of all the elements of the design. They continually refine the drawing on overlays, and only after a great many sketches do they make up their minds about individual elements.

This is the process of thinking with a pencil. Every idea is sketched, no matter how quickly or crudely, allowing you to see the overall plan on paper and to work out any conflicts on paper.

SKETCHING PLANS

You will begin your design by arranging all of the elements included on your want list on an overlay of your analysis. This sketch will probably show only blobs with arrows and scribbled notations. Every element must first be assessed in terms of the underlying analysis, then further assessed in terms of the design decisions. Do the elements blend harmoniously? Or do they collide?

Consider all the ramifications of each decision you make. You find the perfect place for a vegetable garden, for example. How does that siting couple with your desire to shade the house? Can you provide summer shade for the house without affecting the garden?

A common problem provides another example. The best location for the patio—the place where it's easiest to construct (nearly level, with well-drained soils) and most convenient to the house—lacks privacy from the neighbors. If this problem is yours, it means you must allow space for a privacy barrier, or you must relocate the patio to a spot where it may be more difficult to construct but where you would have the desired privacy without enclosure.

Once you have an initial concept for your plan, you will begin thinking about spaces and circulation patterns. Go back to your visual analysis and review your conclusions about the spaces formed in your landscape. Are your preferences for wide open vistas or for small, intimate spaces?

Site Plan for the Urban Property: The site plan clearly reflects the needs and desires of the homeowners but also works with the constraints and opportunities of the site. The final plan represents an attractive, private and low-maintenance landscape that solves the problems that were revealed in the site analysis.

The concrete slab bounding the rear of the house is to be covered with brick paving, sloping away from the house. Not only will this solve the drainage problem, it will also look better and diminish glare, which was a problem with the concrete.

Behind the new patio, an informal and delightful entertainment area has been situated in the shade of the existing Norway maple. It includes a small pool that adds to the pleasantness of the area and provides water for birds. The existing lawn is to be replaced with informal stone paving and low-maintenance, shade-loving plants. Privacy is to be achieved by fencing the sides of the yard and planting vines to climb the fence and visually soften its edges.

The productive garden area is located at the rear of the yard, where the soil is better drained and there is plenty of sun. Raised beds, which create topographic interest, are used for flower and vegetable gardening, and the area is surrounded by a gravel path, which separates the garden activity from the rest of the yard. The work area is made efficient and practical by the addition of a screened compost bin.

The plan provides well-defined spaces for and separation of all the desired activities, while creating interest and diversity within a very small area.

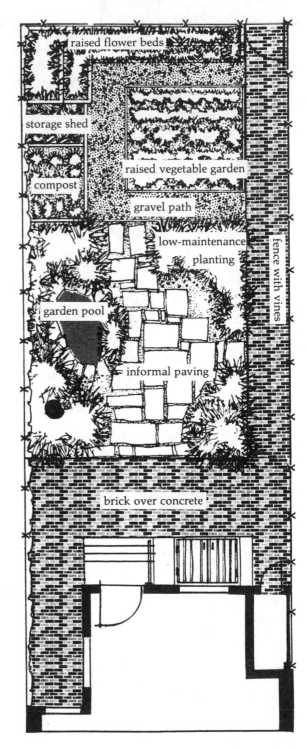

raised flower beds

storage shed

raised vegetable garden

compost

gravel path

low-maintenance planting

fence with vines

garden pool

informal paving

brick over concrete

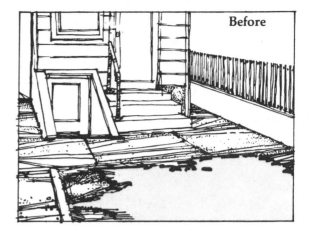

Before

"Before," this urban backyard was rife with problems. The bare earth and concrete were unattractive. They provided no variety of color, texture or form. The concrete's surface had crumbled, and part of the slab had settled, creating drainage problems. Glare from the concrete was unpleasant on sunny days. The open cellarway was not particularly attractive or safe. And there was no privacy from neighboring yards.

All of these problems were brought out in the site analysis and were addressed in the site plan. The "after" sketch shows just how attractive the planned solutions are.

After

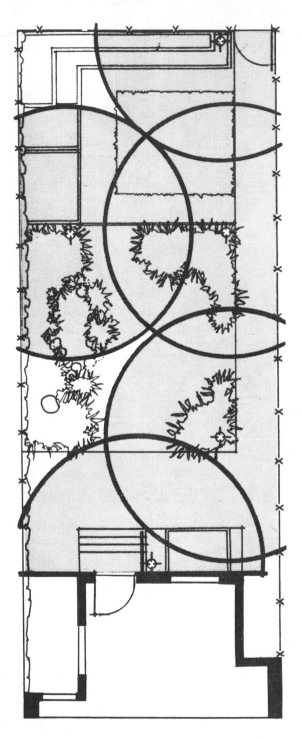

This will determine whether you regulate the spaces in your design subtly, by controlling the direction of movement or by changing elevation, or whether you do it more obviously, by providing enclosures of walls, fences or plantings.

Rough out a circulation pattern for your entire plan. What places or spaces must you move to and from? What are the most convenient routes? Paths, walks or drives should all appear to be plausible and convenient routes to destinations. A curved walk usually looks silly unless it's curving around something.

Outdoor light is an oft-overlooked but essential element in every landscape plan. There are many varieties of easily installed outdoor lights, which can be used to achieve many different effects. With the urban property, the desire was to create intimacy and separation of spaces, but at the same time to improve safety by lighting as many areas as possible. Ground lights are used, and the ranges of their illuminations were carefully plotted. Placement was thus designed to cover as much area as possible, while bathing critical areas with as much light as possible by overlapping light spreads at those spots.

After completing this rough approximation of your plan, go back through it and review your decisions in terms of functional needs. Can you solve the drainage problem that previously existed? Can that privacy screen also serve as a windbreak?

DRAWING THE MEASURED SITE PLAN

If you are certain you have solved all of the existing problems and haven't created any new ones, you can begin to get more specific. Get out a ruler and measure spaces. If your patio is 10 × 20, that will allow 10 feet for a planting buffer. But if you enlarge the patio, you must reduce the width of the planting, and you might have to consider a fence instead.

By following this method of graphic trial-and-error, you can avoid the expense of making your

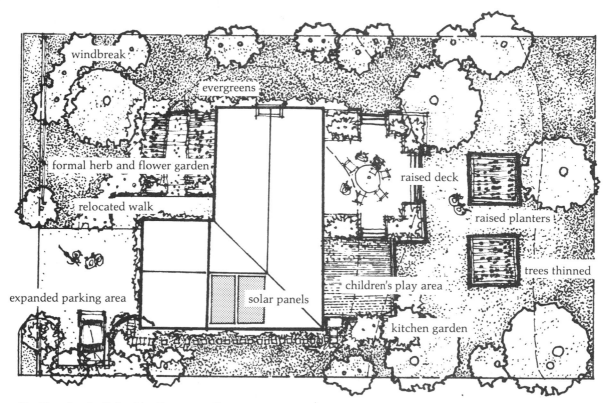

Site Plan for the Suburban Property: The owners of this property have come up with an economical plan that will both save on energy and provide a sense of place, a setting, for their home.

The front entrance will be formalized, enclosed and even made productive by adding an herb and flower garden as part of the entrance. The old walk from the street to the front door will be replaced by a shorter one from the expanded parking area.

Evergreen plantings on the north and northwest are designed to break the wind and protect the house.

Outdoor living and playing areas—for adults and children—are added to the back of the house, where they can be screened from neighboring yards yet still have pleasant views of the forest beyond. The children's play area is located just beyond the kitchen,

where it can be easily seen and supervised from inside the house. This play area is enclosed by planters that will nurture a modest kitchen garden, with a few vegetables and some herbs. Steps lead to the raised wooden deck. It is shaded by the house and the existing vegetation. Raising it allows air circulation almost completely around it. The deck provides a pleasant warm-weather living area and circumvents the need to deal with the problem soils adjacent to the house at this spot.

The poorly drained soils at the back of the property are exposed by pruning and selective removal of existing vegetation. Raised planters are used to provide a controlled, well-drained area for vegetable growing.

These before and after sketches of the suburban property depict how the awkward-looking house can be integrated with the landscape. The addition of trees and shrubs softens the architecture and makes the house appear to be a part of the environment rather than an intruder in it.

Moreover, the additional trees and shrubs reduce the energy needs of the household. The conifers screen the house from cold winter winds, while the deciduous trees screen the house from the hot summer sun.

Before

Before and after sketches of the rear of the suburban house show how a pedestrian, uninviting space can be transformed into a useful and attractive place for work and play. By extending bits of the architecture into the landscape, as was done with the deck and planters, it is usually possible to achieve more unity and better integration of building and landscape.

After

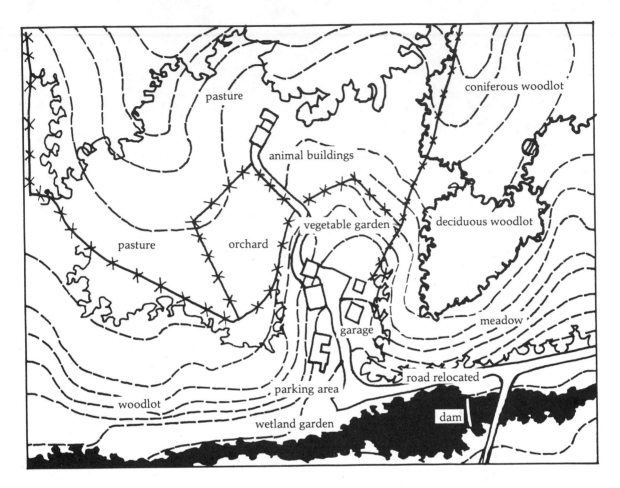

pasture

coniferous woodlot

animal buildings

vegetable garden

deciduous woodlot

pasture   orchard

meadow

garage

road relocated

parking area

woodlot

dam

wetland garden

Site Plan for the Rural Property: A major concern of the property owners is providing pasture and sound shelter for farm animals. The pastures, in the plan, are located where the ground is not too steep, where the soils are well suited for pasture crops and where they will be accessible but not too close to the house. The pasture area will be fenced in sections so the animals can be rotated periodically. The buildings will be designed to hunker into the slope, shielding themselves from the northwest winds, while facing into the southern sun. The buildings will be easily accessible to the pastures, of course.

An orchard is planned for the south-facing slope behind the house. The woodlots will be maintained for fuelwood.

Many of the visual and functional problems will be solved by relocating the public road to the south

side of the stream. The portion of that road from the house west will be abandoned to nature, while the portion from the house east will be converted into a private access drive and parking area.

Damming the stream will create a pond, which will be surrounded by a wetland garden. This will be a lovely and productive recreation area. A large vegetable garden will be located near the barnyard, an area with naturally fertile and well-drained soils. Since the barnyard will continue to house pigs, a terrific supply of fertilizer will be right by the garden.

The plan itself shows the relationships of all the elements on the site, but the scale of it precludes a lot of detail. Individual areas will have to be isolated, and larger-scale, heavily detailed plans prepared for each of them.

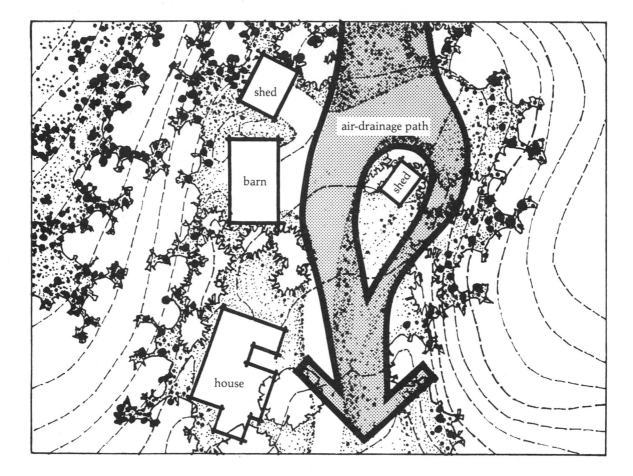

mistakes on the ground. If there are areas that require a lot of detailed planning—for example, a patio surrounded by a wall and rock garden, or a deck, which requires construction details—you should try to isolate it and work at a larger scale. Before deciding on materials and methods of construction, skim through the construction section to get ideas and see what's involved in using the various materials. Some are easier and/or cheaper to use than others. Your ultimate goal is to show the exact location and size of every element and to draw the details needed to carry out their construction.

SIMULATING YOUR PLAN

A three-dimensional simulation of your design will allow you to see the vertical, as well as

Energy Reduction Plan for the Rural Property: When this stone home was built 250 years ago, it was positioned in front of a steep, south-facing bank. This sheltered location provides protection from cold winter winds. With mature deciduous trees providing shade, it remains pleasantly cool in the summer. Because the protected location is also in a valley, there are problems with cold air drainage, fog and early frost. These are alleviated somewhat by the plantings surrounding the house.

With the exception of summer shade directly in front of the house, the area is kept open and unshaded. This creates a solar pocket, where the transpiration process during the day generates some evaporative cooling and reradiation of absorbed heat tends to stabilize otherwise cool evening temperatures. Coniferous plantings upwind of the domestic buildings will guide cold-air drainage, control snow drifting and, in summer, will decrease the amount of rainfall reaching the ground, thereby deterring excessive runoff during heavy storms.

horizontal, relationships between elements and make corrections where necessary. This simulation of your plan can be carried out by a full-size mock-up on your property. Use stakes and strings to measure and mark off areas. Use boards, brown paper or anything else you have around to represent paving, walls or fences. Lay out as much as you can, then walk through it. Sit on the proposed patio, use the proposed walks, look at the proposed pond from your window and evaluate all of them. You'll almost certainly see things that weren't obvious on your proposed plan.

This technique of using your actual property as the plan on which you design is the best method for visualizing your plan. Although it requires time and effort, it is an extremely valuable tool that almost guarantees success.

The Planting Plan

The planting plan identifies each species and tells whether it exists in your garden now or whether it's something you intend to plant. This plan requires putting together all of the information

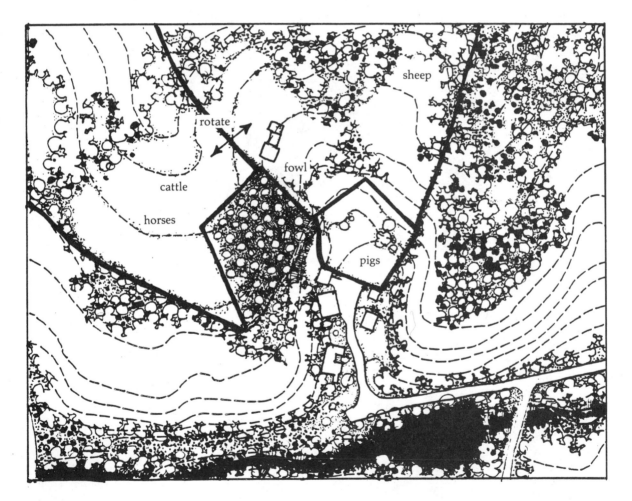

Animal Husbandry Plan for the Rural Property: As noted, the scale of the site plan for the rural property was such that additional detail plans would be necessary. This detail depicts the specific accommodations for the farm animals. While the plan obviously *doesn't have building construction details, it does show exactly where the fences and buildings will be positioned. It can be seen that the plan is workable, in that it separates the stock from, yet keeps it reasonably accessible to, the living area.*

Planting Plan for the Urban Property: The yard has two distinct planting areas. The raised planters at the back are for cultivated flowers and vegetables, while the area closest to the house is designed as a cool, natural retreat. Because the soils are poorly drained and the area is shaded, a number of water- and shade-loving species are used. Most of these are forbs or small shrubs with the largest—the redbud—reaching a height of 15 feet at maturity. This may need to be cut back at some point in the future. Although there may seem to be too many for such a small area, the number listed will create immediate enclosure and provide the diversity found in nature. The owners plan to collect as many plants as possible and experiment with their placement, but this plan will serve as a starting point and provide guidelines for the general layout of the plan.

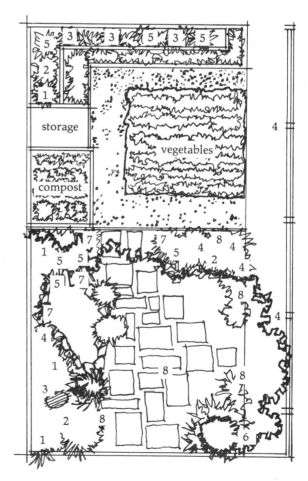

The list of plants, keyed to the plan, is as follows:
1. *Clematis*
2. *Twinberry*
3. *Blueberry*
4. *Potentilla*
5. *Redbud*
6. *Sweet shrub*
7. *Manzanita*
8. *Assorted forbs:*
    yellow star tulip
    satin flower
    California poppy
    adobe lily
    plantain
    iris
    lupine
    primrose
    giant trillium
    fuchsia
    California Indian pink

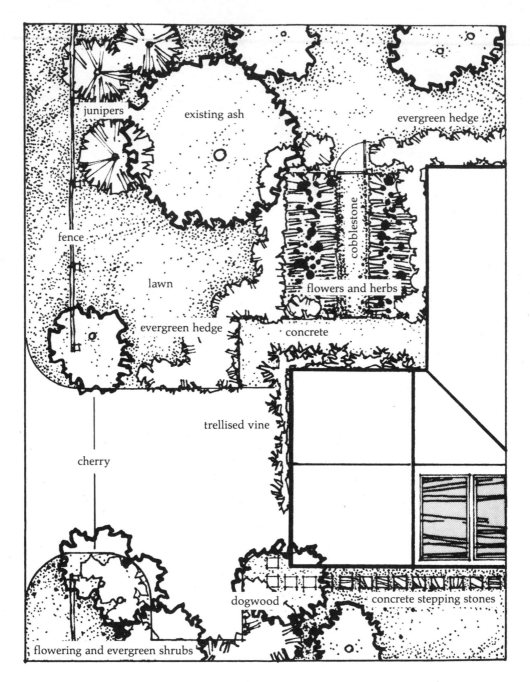

Planting Plan for the Suburban Property (detail): A relatively small number of plants, carefully placed, can maximize energy reduction and, at the same time, create interesting spaces. Here in the suburban property's front yard, plants are positioned where they will screen and buffer. The species used depends on the position. Flowering dogwoods and cherries are appropriately used in sunny locations where deciduous trees are desirable. Junipers and other evergreens provide year-round screening and are used where windbreaks are needed. Flowers and herbs will be beautiful in the summer but are best used in front of or in combination with evergreens to provide year-round interest.

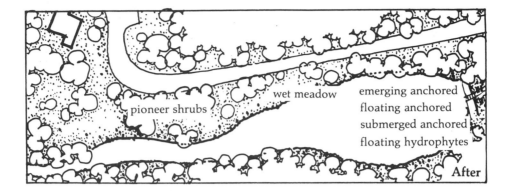

After

wet meadow

pioneer shrubs

emerging anchored
floating anchored
submerged anchored
floating hydrophytes

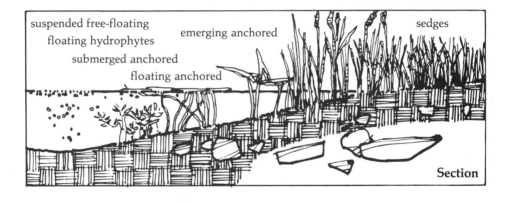

suspended free-floating
floating hydrophytes
submerged anchored
floating anchored

emerging anchored

sedges

Section

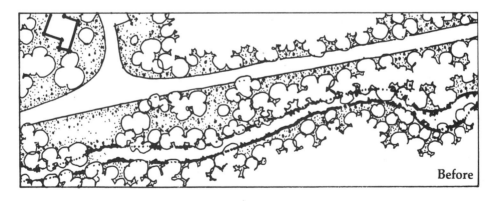

Before

Planting Plan for the Rural Property (detail): The wetland garden is shown in this three-part detail from the overall planting plan. Here you see "before" and "after" plan views, as well as a "section" of the pond's edge. The plan is still being developed, as can be deduced from the lack of a list of particular species that will be incorporated into the garden. Types of plants are listed, however, along with their prospective locations. Doing this is a logical step in the development of the planting plan.

Ultimately included in the species selected will doubtless be: suspended free-floating—algae and some duckweeds; floating hydrophytes—some duckweeds, water hyacinth; submerged anchored—macroscopic algae, stonewort, eel grass; floating anchored—water lilies; emerging anchored—arrowhead, bur reed, cattail, bulrush.

from your analysis, choosing species and locating them so that they will accomplish your goals. Again, don't expect to finish this plan in one try. You must start with a general approximation of what you think will work, then continue to refine it until you feel satisfied that you have the best design possible.

Begin by putting your recently completed plan, which shows the areas that will be planted, on top of your plant habitat map. You will see the existing conditions for each planting area. For example, the front yard may be a sunny, well-drained, south-facing habitat, the area where you will be screening the patio may be cold and shady with acidic soils, while the backyard may be wet and clayey. Just label each area where you expect to be planting. Then jot down the various conditions that exist in each area. The list for each area will "define" the habitat.

After each habitat is defined, you will again consider your functional and aesthetic needs. Do you want to attract wildlife? Are you interested in reducing energy consumption?

If you have decided that energy reduction is one of your major goals, you will start by locating plants where they will best protect your house. The location will determine the size and shape of plants needed, and knowing this allows you to look for species that fit that bill. And because you know your plant habitats, you can narrow your choice to those species that are attractive and will provide you with a carefree, natural landscape.

DOMESTIC GARDENS

If you are including food- or flower-producing or other domesticated plants in your scheme, you will need to distinguish where they will be. First, evaluate the needs of the plants. Then find the habitat on your property that best fulfills those needs.

In the case of vegetables, you'll need an area that is sunny, well-drained and has fertile soils. If you don't have such an area, you'll need to create it. It might mean cutting down shade trees or fertilizing and conditioning the soil.

Unlike your natural garden, the domesticated one includes plants that are not native and whose needs must be provided by you. Continual maintenance will be necessary and must be considered as you locate the domestic garden.

Make sure it is easily accessible and that there is a nearby storage area for tools and supplies. In most cases, it is desirable to visually and physically separate the domestic and natural gardens. Remember that native vegetation will attract wildlife that could be a nuisance in the vegetable garden.

PLANTING DESIGN CAUTIONS

As you complete your planting plan, you should also consider some potential problems that arise from the improper selection or placement of some plant species.

A few plant-related problems can result from the close proximity of natural and nonnatural or man-required facilities. Roots of some trees such as elm, willow, poplar and maple can clog sewer lines. The problem is common where a break in the line allows water to escape into the surrounding soil. Contrary to popular belief, roots do not *seek out* water, so much as they develop quickly where there is a lot of water available in the soil. The roots can grow into the break and make it larger. But if the sewer and drain lines are intact and functioning properly, there will be no trouble with tree roots.

Shallow-rooted plants can cause a different problem. If trees or large shrubs are planted too near a sidewalk or paved area, their growing roots can crack the pavement and lift it out of the ground.

Tree branches should be considered if you have overhead utility lines. Use plants with a height maximum or a branching pattern that won't interfere with the lines. Keep in mind, too, that a tree that hangs over the house will probably fill the rain gutters with leaves each fall.

The fruits on some plants may be a problem if they fall near the house. The fruit of the horse chestnut is toxic if eaten in any quantity. Ginkgo fruits produce an unpleasant odor as they decompose. The volume of fruit may be a nuisance, as with some crab apple varieties.

Even flowers can create problems that must be considered. The male flowers on the ailanthus have a strong, unpleasant odor. The pollen from several other species irritates many people, and petals dropped from flowering trees can make walkways dangerously slick.

While these potential problems are annoying and certainly deserve consideration, they gen-

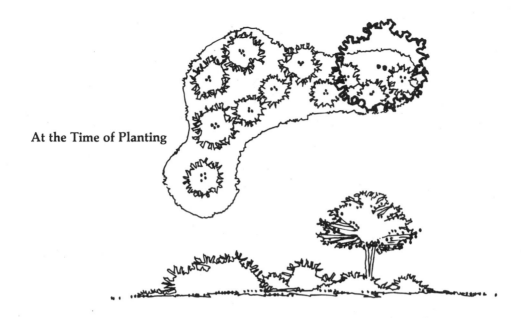

At the Time of Planting

Plants grow. This is both a blessing and a curse. It's swell to have manageably sized trees and shrubs to transplant from forest to homesite, knowing they'll grow and fill out. But planning for low maintenance is challenging when you aren't sure just how big the plants will ultimately be. You don't want to have to prune and prune and prune; you don't want to cut or dig out plantings that you spent money and time establishing. So a part of your planting plan should be perspective sketches of selected plant groupings, one suggesting what the plants will look like when first planted and another suggesting their appearance at maturity. You'll then be better prepared to plant the right number of plants in a thoughtful spacing and pattern.

At Maturity

erally aren't serious and can be prevented by researching, observing and getting to know the species you are planting.

As you complete your planting scheme, consider the vertical relationships that aren't seen on the plans. The height needed for adequate screening or shading is one thing, but how does that relate to the other elements in your plan? Drawing a quick cross section with a vertical scale will show whether you are blocking views or obstructing circulation. Better still, you can return to the sketches and photographs you created as parts of your site analyses and sketch on the proposed additions.

Finally, don't forget that the size of vegetation does not remain constant. Draw the full-grown size as well as the planting size of each species. This will ensure that you avoid the common mistake of siting plants too close to each other or to structural elements.

The Phasing Plan

When your site and planting plans are drawn to your satisfaction, prepare a phasing plan. It need not be elaborate; an overlay on each of the site and planting plans will do. What a phasing plan is, quite simply, is a plan of attack. If you are energetic and have time on your hands, you may well do the whole job at one time. But if you are like most of us, you'll do a little bit at a time, perhaps stretching the work over several years.

And the phasing plan merely indicates when you are going to do what.

Try to estimate honestly how much work you can accomplish during a working-outdoors season. Factor in where you will be getting your planting materials, as horticulturists love to call trees, shrubs and other plants. If you'll be buying most of them, your means may be more of a determinant of how much you do each year than your time or energy. Then break down your planting plan into seasons.

THE CONSTRUCTION PHASE

Certain work you'll do right off. Usually, the construction work should be completed before you do a lot of planting. Why run the risk of injuring your plants? Put in the drainage system,

the walks and drives, the walls and fences, then do the planting.

On the phasing overlay of the site plan, indicate the site modification and construction work that must be done. Then, perhaps using color, show the sequence in which the work will be done. Common sense may recommend that certain jobs be done in a certain order, so listen to what yours tells you. Why do any job twice? Next, perhaps in the key, jot down the sequence and, if you are schedule oriented, some deadlines. If you are going to do a set number of projects the first season, note which ones. Mark the jobs to be done the next season. And the next. Until the whole of the site work is done.

THE PLANTING PHASE

Turn then to the planting plan and its phasing overlay. Don't worry about the existing vegetation, unless you have to tear it out (and that work is more likely to be site work). Address the plants you have to add to the landscape. Just as you did with the site work, sketch in all the work to be done, color it according to the sequence in which it *should* be done, then note when you will do each bit of planting.

As you do the plant phasing, keep in mind that you don't want to leave any ground bare too long. You may want to plant a green manure cover crop, just to protect and hold the soil, never mind the soil-enrichening benefits. As you subsequently move across your landscape with shovel, plants and watering can, you can turn under the green manure planting a little bit at a time.

What may hit you now—perhaps for the first time—is the great disparity between what you've been planning and what you will have when the planting is done. Probably the natural settings you studied in your design and plant selection research had a preponderance of mature plants. There were saplings in the forest, to be sure, but there were substantial *trees*, too. And now you realize that it'll be literally years before your landscape looks exactly as you've envisioned it.

Don't despair. Your landscape will come around. The framework of plants that you provide will encourage self-propagation. Seedlings will volunteer, plants will grow, and in the process they will teach you even more about your natural landscape.

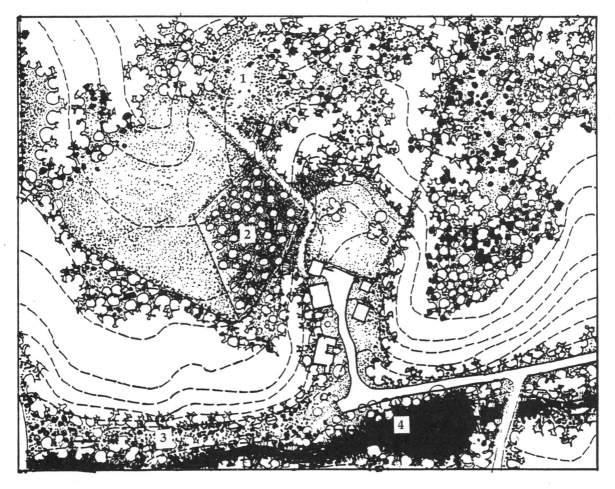

Phasing Plan for the Rural Property: Because there is so much to do, it would be both physically and financially impossible for the owners to carry out their landscaping plan all at one time. Therefore, they'll do it over a period of years. While a timetable hasn't been set, the work has been split into four stages so it can all be done in an orderly fashion.

The first stage will be the clearing and fencing of pastures, the construction of adjacent livestock housing, the selective cutting in the fuelwood forest areas and related work.

Planting the orchard will be the second stage.

Moving the public road, helping nature reclaim the right-of-way west of the house and finishing off the remainder of the road as a private drive and parking area will be the third stage.

The fourth and final stage will be the construction of the dam on the stream and the development of the wetland garden.

SYNTHESIZING THE PLANS

In any case, you should bring the two phasing plans together and synthesize them. While the site work usually *is* done first, as noted already, it doubtless is possible to integrate some of the planting with the construction. Laying one overlay atop the other will let you see where work overlaps, where priorities overlap. You may want to revise the construction schedule so that those important barrier plantings can be dug in and set to growing.

It may be vexing to be scratching with pencil on paper at this point, more so now than at any other time throughout the project, but it is important not to let down now. You are trying to save money, you are trying to save work. Figuring out the right phasing plan is an essential part of those savings.

When your site and planting plans are drawn to your satisfaction, and your phasing plan is purged of problems, you are due some congratulations and—undoubtedly—a long rest. You've completed the long but rewarding process of landscape planning. You are ready now to begin the physical transformation of your landscape.

All of the time you've spent researching, analyzing and planning—even if it's been a year or more—has been time spent well. You'll see this to be true someday, if you don't see it now.

But even the most careful analysis and the most thoughtful design can have shortcomings. If you come upon problems in the physical work that comes next, don't be reluctant to put down your shovel and take up your eraser and pencil once again. Be chary of adjustments, but don't be inflexible.

12

Plant
Selection

Plants are the most important elements in your landscape. They are the heart of natural landscaping. Now, perhaps for the first time, as you study plants and begin to pick those particular ones that you'll have around your home, you begin to feel as if you really *are* involved in a landscaping project.

Now is the time to concentrate on plants. You still have a lot of research and study ahead of you.

First of all, you have to learn what plants are.

You have to learn what they can do. They can perform valuable functions far beyond mere decoration. They can help you reduce energy consumption, control erosion, have a quieter place in which to live; they can even provide food, fuel or income.

Second, you have to find out what plants are specifically suited for your landscape. This is a key point. For your landscape to be natural,

137

you've got to use plants indigenous to your ecological realm, and you've got to choose wisely of those plants.

Such is the business of this chapter.

Using Native Plants

Indigenous plants are referred to as natives, while those that are imported are called exotics. Every plant is native to somewhere—except maybe hybrids that have been developed for bigger and brighter flowers, droopier branches or more variegated leaves. For the most part, exotics are simply transported natives.

Before nurseries and landscaping became big business, the few foreign species that made their way into home landscapes must have actually

black oak   dogwood   pignut hickory   mountain laurel   white oak   black cherry   northern wild raisin (viburnum)   hickory

The Eastern Deciduous Forest is dominated by tall, broadleaf trees that provide a continuous and dense canopy in summer. Lower layers of small trees and shrubs develop only weakly. In spring, a luxuriant layer of herbs develops quickly but is greatly reduced when the trees reach full foliage and shade the ground. Common trees of this forest are oak, beech, birch, walnut, hornbeam, hickory, basswood, maple, elm, ash, tulip tree and sweet chestnut. Other species grow in poorly drained areas, and conifers appear as second-growth vegetation.

seemed exotic. Now the reverse is true: our native plants, some of which are nearly extinct, seem exotic to many (especially to nurserymen who've never even heard of some and will never stock them until the demand makes it profitable).

There certainly are a lot more homeowners familiar with weeping cherry and pachysandra than with serviceberry or partridgeberry. Plants that were at one time exotic and unusual have now become overused and monotonous in most home landscapes throughout the country.

There's nothing wrong with exotics themselves. Without them we'd have very bland diets, fewer fabrics and fewer medicinal drugs. Many are quite beautiful and make a large contribution to lovely landscapes. But their overuse has created problems, which natural landscaping and a commitment to native plants can solve.

THE BENEFITS OF NATIVE PLANTS

One of the benefits of using native plants is the expression of the individuality and unique beauty of any particular place in the world. Vegetation that is native to Iowa is different from vegetation that is native to Florida, and both of those kinds of vegetation are different from Utah's. Sadly, landscaping in any of those places looks pretty much the same. And it is more than the designs that make it so, it's the plants that are used. Think how much more interesting a trip across the country would be if you could see the uniqueness of each environment expressed in its residential areas.

A second benefit of using native plants is the improvement in the biological health of the environment. The same popular exotics used over and over again from East to West are dangerously prone to insects and disease. Just as intensive single-crop agriculture creates an unstable condition by upsetting natural controls, so does simplification of natural landscapes. Planting a diversity of native species will provide natural checks and balances and will add richness to our landscapes. And it will make a further contribution to the health of the environment by providing food and cover for native wildlife. The typical suburban sprawl, with its miles of bluegrass dotted with spindly, nonfruiting specimen trees, is not very attractive to the colorful birds and lovely animals that used to be around.

By far the most important reason for using native plants has to do with Charles Darwin's theory that only the fittest survive. Plants that are native have evolved through billions of years of competition. There has been a long process of trial and error that has resulted in those species that are most fit for each environment. When you plant a native species, you are employing all of evolutionary history. You can't find a better reason for choosing a plant than that gained from 3 billion years of experience.

Ecological Regions

As you've seen, there's more to landscaping with native plants than just going to a nursery and asking for a native plant. A native species is not only indigenous to a particular area, like southeastern Pennsylvania, it is indigenous to a particular environment, like a sunny, dry alkaline, south-facing slope.

Your site analysis has revealed the given conditions of your property. Now you must find the plants that are right for those conditions.

To help you do this, charts listing plants native to each of 12 ecological regions of the continental United States are included at the end of this chapter. You'll find them to be a jumping-off point for you, rather than an exhaustive encyclopedia of native plants.

To use the charts, you must first know what ecological region you live in. The map of the regions should show you instantly which region you're in. The regions, by name, are:

> Northern Coniferous Forest
> Eastern Deciduous Forest
> Coastal Plain
> Southeastern Mixed Forest
> Subtropic
> South-Central Swamp
> Prairie
> Rocky Mountain Evergreen Forest
> Great Basin
> Desert
> Pacific Forest
> California

marsh   cottonwoods   blue-eyed   sycamore   red osier   osage
milkweed   grass   orange
                  prairie
                  fringed
                  orchid

The Prairie Parklands are found along the eastern edge of the Prairie Region. Tall grasses, together with some broad-leaved herbs, naturally dominate the prairies, with trees and shrubs being almost totally absent. But in the Parklands area, stretching from Illinois south to the Gulf Coast, prairies characteristically intermingle with groves and deciduous forest strips. Here trees — mostly elms, sycamores, bur oaks, eastern cottonwoods, hackberries, redbuds and buckeyes — grow near streams and on north-facing slopes.

Just as the boundaries of the habitats of the property are indistinct, and just as those habitats blend into one another, so, too, do these regions blend into one another. There's a description of the characteristics of the region heading each chart. By comparing your analysis with the regional characteristics, you'll be able to figure out which region you're in, should there be any question.

The charts are based on plant lists developed by vegetation expert Carol Reifsnyder. It was she who defined the regions. If you were to conduct a national site analysis following the approach of this book, overlaying geology, climate, soil, vegetation and other information, you'd end up with the regional habitats shown. Since each region has a common set of environmental conditions, each has a common vocabulary of plants. The plants listed under each region are native to it and have needs that are fulfilled by that general environment.

Vegetation Classifications

All plants have a relative growth habit that serves as the basis for their classification into the broad categories of trees, shrubs, vines, herbs or forbs, and grasses.

Trees are woody plants with one main stem (trunk) and are at least 12 to 15 feet tall at maturity. A tree has a well-developed head of foliage (crown), and its trunk is several inches or more in diameter. Its leaves may be evergreen, or they may be deciduous and be shed annually. Most cone-bearing trees like pines are evergreen, with needlelike leaves, but there are also some broad-leaved evergreens, like the hollies and rhododendrons.

Shrubs are also woody plants with deciduous or evergreen leaves, but they are differentiated from trees because they have several stems growing from a clump and because they are generally smaller than trees. Vines may also have woody stems, but they do not have a distinct crown of upright branches.

Herbs are much smaller than trees or shrubs, generally not more than 2 to 3 feet high, and they are not woody, at least not above the ground. Forb is another name for any herbaceous plant other than grasses. A forb can be annual, biennial or perennial. Grasses differ from forbs in that they have narrow leaves, hollow-jointed stems and clusters of flowers borne in smaller spikelets.

Among these general classifications there are tremendous variations. There are thousands of trees, each with a single stem and well-developed crown, but each species has different characteristics that determine how it looks and what functions it can perform. Whether you choose a tree or shrub, and the particular species you select, will depend on your functional and aesthetic needs.

Making Your Choices

To make your selections you will need to observe firsthand how individual plants grow. Take your knowledge of your own habitats into the field or forest along with a plant identification guide and look for natural areas with conditions similar to your own.

If you have a bare, steep, north-facing slope with thin, well-drained soils, then look for the same conditions in a natural area.

If it is a woodland, you may find that hemlocks are the dominant tree and that they exist in all sizes, from seedlings to mature canopy trees. You may also find an understory of mountain laurel, rhododendron and some wild azaleas. Christmas ferns may be abundant, and there may be carpets of partridgeberry. In the openings created by wind-felled trees and at the forest edge where sunlight is available, there may be flowering dogwoods and abundant shadblows.

You must identify all of these plants and note their relative positions and microenvironments. Keep in mind that species that have similar needs occur together. When you see a change in species composition—like a dogwood in the middle of hemlocks—it reflects a change in the environmental conditions. In the case of the dogwood, the change is a sunny habitat instead of a shady one.

Most likely, you will have different habitats on your own property—different solar aspects, different degrees of slope, different soils and varying degrees of moisture. For each of these habitats you will need to find a natural equivalent, populated by native plants. So, for example, you might look for a population of aquatic plants for a pond, including floating plants like water lilies, water-edge plants like cattails, marsh mallow and mertensia, and water-loving trees like the swamp maple. Or you may look for a flat, sunlit meadow with grassland flowering plants like black-eyed Susans and cornflowers, or a dry, warm, south-facing slope dominated by oaks.

Each of these natural environments with their attendant plant communities must be observed and recorded before you can develop the planting plan for your landscape. Only after you have identified environments with their appropriate plants can you pick and choose the species you want in your landscape.

DESIGN WITH NATURE

This knowledge of plants and their habitats allows you to change your environment to suit your preferences. If you would like many dogwoods, then you must provide the sunny conditions they require. If you wish a field of skunk cabbage, then you must create a wet meadow, and if you want flag iris, you will need to provide even wetter conditions.

As you grow in skill, associating factors of

Understanding succession will help you in selecting plants for your landscape. If left untouched, land in many areas of the country will evolve from bare ground to climax forest. This drawing illustrates how succession works, as weeds first cover the earth, only to be crowded out by grasses, then by grasses and *forbs. Shrubs will elbow their way in, and eventually trees of increasing size will grow and shade out any but the shade-loving species. If you want open spaces, choose grasses and forbs. If you want a climax forest, choose trees and hope you live a long, long time.*

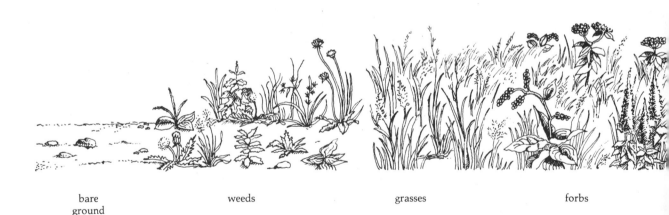

bare
ground

weeds

grasses

forbs

slope, aspect, soil, water and microclimate with plants and their successional stages, you will be able to perceive the essential attributes of plant communities.

You can impose your taste and create the visual effects you want by using the successional stage that best meets your needs. If you like free, open space, then you'll use meadow or early successional species. If you like some open space but want it punctuated by trees and shrubs, then use old field species. If you like closed, private places, use late successional forest species.

shrubs   woodland

COVERING THE GROUND

A special part of selecting plants for your landscape is selecting something to cover the ground. That's an obvious part of landscaping. Yet we're so used to having lawn surround the homeplace that trying to figure out what you're going to fill up all that empty space with—and not have it be fescue or its ilk—is like watching television with the set switched off.

But yes, there really are options. Depending upon where you live, you can create a meadow or a prairie in your own yard. Regardless of where you live, city or country, east or west, north or south, you can choose a native ground cover that isn't lawn.

MEADOWS

If you live in the East, your lawn can be a meadow. A "meadow" in ecological circles denotes a grassland in an area of high rainfall. And that's what you have in the East: an area of such high rainfall that it supports a temperate-zone rain forest. The "climax" vegetation is a mix of hardwood and coniferous trees—"climax" being what eventually would form a permanent cover over the land if humans didn't interfere. In the eastern United States, the natural cover is forest occasionally broken up by patches of meadow. In the drier Midwest, the natural cover is a prairie.

In order to replace your unnatural cover of traditional lawn grass, you first have to readjust your own sense of "lawnscaping": wind-whipped grasses, Queen-Anne's-lace and sky blue chicory in place of close-cropped grass; bird songs in lieu of lawn mower stutter. Meadows, unlike traditional lawns, are areas in a constant stage of transition; their elements are of varying height, color and character—reacting to the seasons and climate with a unity that is at once random and uniform. They are, in our suburban world of developments and manicured lawns, anomalies. They do not "belong," and for that reason, to be appreciated they must be accepted for what they are rather than for what they are not.

It must be understood, too, that no two meadows are the same. But they have in common a wide diversity of plant material, each species finding its own place, shading out or being shaded by its neighbors until a balance is achieved. In a man-made meadow, this diversity can be promoted or controlled, depending upon the pretreatment of land and the degree and form of maintenance that is applied thereafter. So your locale, preferences and the extent to which you want to become involved in the life cycle and development of the meadow are aspects to consider when deciding what kind and how much of a meadow you will be comfortable with.

The following lists species that can be used in a meadow garden. Some of them could be used as a ground cover to replace a grass lawn. The list is meant to supplement those species described in

the vegetation charts. If you are not sure which are native to your area or appropriate for your environment, look them up in a regional or general guide for identifying native plants.

Acer circinatum—Vine maple
Amsonia Tabernaemontana—Bluestar
Arctostaphylos columbiana—Hairy manzanita
A. densiflora 'Howard McMinn'—Sonoma manzanita
A. Hookeri—Monterey manzanita
A. Uva-ursi—Common bearberry
Aronia melanocarpa—Chokeberry
Artemisia ludoviciana var. *albula*—Silver king
Asclepias tuberosa—Butterfly weed
Aster spp.
Baccharis pilularis—Dwarf baccharis
Baptisia australis—Wild blue indigo
Ceanothus gloriosus—Point Reyes ceanothus
C. griseus var. *horizontalis*—Carmel creeper
Celastrus scandens—American bittersweet
Chelone obliqua—Shellflower
Clematis virginiana—Virgin's bower
Coreopsis auriculata—Coreopsis, tickseed
C. grandiflora—Coreopsis, tickseed
C. verticillata—Coreopsis, tickseed
Corylus cornuta—Beaked hazel, beaked filbert
Dennstaedtia punctilobula—Hay-scented fern
Echinacea purpurea—Purple coneflower
Elymus glaucus—Blue wild rye
Filipendula rubra—Queen-of-the-prairie
Gaultheria Shallon—Salal
Gaylussacia baccata—Black huckleberry
Gramineae spp.—Grasses
Helenium autumnale—Sneezeweed
Hibiscus Moscheutos—Common rose mallow
Hydrangea arborescens—Wild hydrangea
Ilex verticillata—winterberry
Juniperus communis—Common juniper
Kalmia angustifolia—Sheep laurel
K. latifolia—Mountain laurel
Liatris scariosa—Blazing-star

L. spicata—Blazing-star
Linum perenne subsp. *Lewisii*—Prairie flax
Lupinus polyphyllus—Lupine
Lysimachia ciliata—Loosestrife
Mahonia Aquifolium—Oregon grape
M. nervosa—Long-leaf mahonia
Monarda didyma cvs.—Bee balm, Oswego tea
Oenothera fruticosa 'Youngii'—Sundrops
O. missourensis—Sundrops
Paeonia californica—Peony
Panicum virgatum—Switch-grass
Papaver californicum—Western poppy
P. nudicaule—Iceland poppy
Parthenocissus quinquefolia—Virginia creeper
Penstemon spp.—Beard-tongues
Phlox subulata—Moss pink
Physostegia virginiana cvs.—Obedience
Prunus americana—Wild plum
Rhus integrifolia—Lemonade berry
Ribes viburnifolium—Current
Robinia hispida—Bristly locust
Rubus spp.—Brambles, including blackberries, raspberries and dewberries
Rudbeckia laciniata cvs.—Coneflowers
Spartina pectinata—Prairie cordgrass
Spiraea latifolia—Meadowsweet
Thelypteris noveboracensis—New York fern
Thermopsis caroliniana—Carolina lupine
Tradescantia virginiana cvs.—Common spiderwort
Vaccinium angustifolium—Lowbush blueberry
Wisteria frutescens—Wisteria
Yucca filamentosa—Adam's-needle, needle palm
Y. glauca—Soapweed

PRAIRIES

If you live in the Midwest, you can have a prairie. The prairies originally stretched from Indiana west to the Rockies and from Canada into the top of Texas. They were not all the same kind of prairie, and they did not contain the same plants, but they covered a big chunk of the country. Today, prairie restoration is possible within that chunk of the United States. East of Indiana, however, increased rainfall and increased evaporation make prairie establishment too difficult to attempt.

Unlike the traditional lawn, which enjoys an eternally evergreen spring, a prairie follows the seasons, each plant in the rich community emerging and disappearing in turn, in flux around the stalwart grasses. Unless you have seen some remnant or restored prairie, you may not realize how rich in plants is a piece of prairie. Natural remnants may contain as many as 200 species of grasses and forbs. (Anything that is not a grass is a forb, generally an herb or broad-leaved plant. The forbs have flowers, many of them quite showy.) After the spring burn, which is the only authentic way to maintain a prairie, the young grasses are short but lush green. Small plants and flowers appear among the low grasses in early spring. By summer the grass is much taller, shading out the low-growing early forbs. These are soon replaced, however, by blooming plants as tall as the grasses, a second wave of color among the green spikes. As fall approaches and the grasses begin to sere, a third rank of forbs matures—*Silphiums* and *Asters*—to tower above the drying grasses. The prairie at this time can be 6 to 10 feet tall.

There not only is change in a prairie planting but also movement, wildlife and surprises. One plant seems to invite another. Birds and animals leave "gift" seeds behind them that germinate and find a place in the prairie community. The result is a freshness, the regeneration of a living thing that recombines its member parts in new ways to produce a changing picture. There is movement, too, and sound: the wind in the grasses. And there is life: birds, butterflies and bees find a home. The suburban prairie patch may even have its resident groundhog.

Obviously, a key part of establishing your own prairie is the choice of plants. You have lots and lots of species to choose from.

The following list contains species that are native to the prairie. They are divided into groups based on the amount of moisture in the soil, from Wet Prairie to Dry Prairie. Although some of these species are described in the vegetation charts, others have been included to increase your choices if you are designing a prairie landscape.

Wet Prairie

Allium canadense—Wild garlic
Andropogon Gerardii—Big bluestem grass
Anemone canadensis—Canada anemone
Apocynum cannabinum—Indian hemp
Asclepias syriaca—Common milkweed
Aster novae-angliae—New England aster
A. simplex—Panicled aster
Calamagrostis canadensis—Bluejoint grass
Camassia scilloides—Wild hyacinth
Comandra Richardsiana—False toadflax
Desmodium canadense—Canada tick trefoil
Dodecatheon Meadia—Midland shooting-star
Dryopteris Thelypteris—Marginal fern
Equisetum arvense—Common horsetail
Erigeron strigosus—Daisy fleabane
Eupatorium perfoliatum—Boneset
Fragaria virginiana—Wild strawberry
Galium boreale—Northern bedstraw
G. obtusum—Meadow bedstraw
G. tinctorium—Dye bedstraw
Gentiana Andrewsii—Bottle gentian
Habenaria leucophaea—White fringed orchid
Helianthus grosseserratus—Saw-tooth sunflower
Heuchera Richardsonii—Midland alumroot
Houstonia caerulea—Bluets
Hypoxis hirsuta—Yellow-eyed grass
Iris Shrevei—Wild blue flag
Lathyrus palustris—Marsh vetchling
Liatris pycnostachya—Prairie blazing-star
L. spicata—Spike blazing-star
Lilium michiganense—Western Turk's-cap lily
Lobelia spicata—Pale lobelia
Lysimachia quadriflora—Narrowleaf loosestrife
Monarda fistulosa—Wild bergamot
Oenothera perennis—Small sundrops
O. pilosella—Prairie sundrops
Oxypolis rigidior—Cowbane
Pedicularis canadensis—Wood betony
Phlox pilosa—Downy phlox
Pycnanthemum virginianum—Common mountain mint

Ratibida pinnata—Grayheaded coneflower
Rudbeckia hirta—Black-eyed Susan
Salix humilis—Prairie willow
Saxifraga pensylvanica—Swamp saxifrage
Solidago gigantea—Late goldenrod
S. Riddellii—Riddell's goldenrod
Spartina pectinata—Prairie cordgrass
Spiraea alba—Meadowsweet
Thalictrum dasycarpum—Purple meadow rue
Tradescantia ohiensis—Common spiderwort
Veronicastrum virginicum—Culver's root
Viola cucullata—Blue marsh violet
Zizia aurea—Golden Alexanders

Wet to Moderately Wet Prairie

Allium canadense—Wild garlic
A. cernuum—Nodding wild onion
Amorpha canescens—Lead plant
Andropogon Gerardii—Big bluestem grass
A. scoparius—Little bluestem grass
Anemone canadensis—Canada anemone
Asclepias syriaca—Common milkweed
Aster azureus—Azure aster
A. ericoides—Heath aster
A. laevis—Smooth aster
A. novae-angliae—New England aster
Baptisia leucantha—Cream false indigo
Blephilia ciliata—Downy wood mint
Cacalia tuberosa—Tuberous Indiana plantain
Calamagrostis canadensis—Bluejoint grass
Camassia scilloides—Wild hyacinth
Cicuta maculata—Spotted cowbane
Cirsium discolor—Pasture thistle
Comandra Richardsiana—False toadflax
Desmodium canadense—Canada tick trefoil
Dodecatheon Meadia—Midland shooting-star
Elymus canadensis—Canada wild rye
Equisetum arvense—Common horsetail
E. laevigatum—Kansas scouringrush
Euphorbia corollata—Flowering spurge
Fragaria virginiana—Wild strawberry
Galium boreale—Northern bedstraw

Gentiana Andrewsii—Bottle gentian
G. crinita—Fringed gentian
Geranium maculatum—Wild geranium
Habenaria leucophaea—White fringed orchid
Helianthus grosseserratus—Saw-tooth sunflower
H. laetiflorus—Rigid sunflower
Heuchera Richardsonii—Midland alumroot
Lactuca canadensis—Canada wild lettuce
Lathyrus palustris—Marsh vetchling
L. venosus—Showy vetchling
Lespedeza capitata—Roundheaded bush clover
Liatris pycnostachya—Prairie blazing-star
Lilium michiganense—Western Turk's-cap lily
Lithospermum canescens—Hoary puccoon
Monarda fistulosa—Wild bergamot
Panicum Leibergii—Prairie panic grass
Phlox pilosa—Downy phlox
Polytaenia Nuttallii—Prairie parsley
Prenanthes racemosa—Smooth white rattlesnake root
Pycnanthemum virginianum—Common mountain mint
Ratibida pinnata—Grayheaded coneflower
Rhus glabra—Smooth sumac
Rosa spp.—Prairie roses
Rudbeckia hirta—Black-eyed Susan
R. subtomentosa—Sweet coneflower
Salix humilis—Prairie willow
Silphium integrifolium—Wholeleaf rosinweed
S. terebinthinaceum—Prairie dock
Smilacina stellata—Starry false Solomon's-seal
Solidago gigantea—Late goldenrod
S. graminifolia—Grassleaf goldenrod
S. rigida—Stiff goldenrod
Sorghastrum nutans—Indian grass
Spartina pectinata—Prairie cordgrass
Spiraea alba—Meadowsweet
Spiranthes cernua—Nodding ladies'-tresses
Sporobolus heterolepis—Prairie dropseed
Thalictrum dasycarpum—Purple meadow rue

Tradescantia ohiensis—Common spiderwort
Vernonia fasciculata—Common ironweed
Veronicastrum virginicum—Culver's root
Vicia americana—American vetch
Zizia aurea—Golden Alexanders

Moderately Wet Prairie

Allium cernuum—Nodding wild onion
Amorpha canescens—Lead plant
Andropogon Gerardii—Big bluestem grass
A. scoparius—Little bluestem grass
Anemone cylindrica—Prairie thimbleweed
Antennaria neglecta—Pussy-toes
Apocynum androsaemifolium—Spreading dogbane
A. cannabinum—Indian hemp
Asclepias Sullivantii—Sullivant's milkweed
A. syriaca—Common milkweed
A. tuberosa—Butterfly weed
Aster azureus—Azure aster
A. ericoides—Heath aster
A. laevis—Smooth aster
A. novae-angliae—New England aster
Baptisia leucantha—White false indigo
B. leucophaea—Cream false indigo
Bromus Kalmii—Prairie Bromegrass
Carex Bicknellii—Bicknell's sedge
C. Meadii—Mead's sedge
Castilleja coccinea—Scarlet painted-cup
Ceanothus americanus—New Jersey tea
Cirsium discolor—Pasture thistle
C. Hillii—Hill's thistle
Comandra Richardsiana—False toadflax
Convolvulus sepium—Wild morning-glory
Coreopsis palmata—Prairie coreopsis
C. tripteris—Tall coreopsis
Desmodium canadense—Canada tick trefoil
D. illinoense—Illinois tick trefoil
Dodecatheon Meadii—Midland shooting-star
Echinacea pallida—Pale purple coneflower
Elymus canadensis—Canada wild rye
Eryngium yuccifolium—Rattlesnake-master
Euphorbia corollata—Flowering spurge
Fragaria virginiana—Wild strawberry
Galium boreale—Northern bedstraw
Gentiana puberula—Downy gentian

Helianthus grosseserratus—Saw-tooth sunflower

H. laetiflorus—Rigid sunflower

H. occidentalis—Western sunflower

Heliopsis helianthoides—Oxeye

Heuchera Richardsonii—Midland alumroot

Hypoxis hirsuta—Yellow-eyed grass

Krigia biflora—False dandelion

Lactuca canadensis—Canada wild lettuce

Lathyrus vernosus—Showy vetchling

Lespedeza capitata—Roundheaded bush clover

Liatris aspera—Rough blazing-star

L. ligulstylis—Rocky Mountain blazing-star

L. pycnostachya—Prairie blazing-star

L. spicata—Spike blazing-star

Lilium philadelphicum—Wood lily

Lithospermum canescens—Hoary puccoon

Lobelia spicata—Pale lobelia

Monarda fistulosa—Wild bergamot

Oxalis violacea—Violet wood sorrel

Panicum Leibergii—Prairie panic grass

P. oligosanthes—Scribner panic grass

P. virgatum—Switch-grass

Parthenium integrifolium—Wild quinine

Pedicularis canadensis—Wood betony

Penstemon Digitalis—Smooth penstemon

Petalostemon candidum—White prairie clover

P. purpureum—Purple prairie clover

Phlox pilosa—Downy phlox

Physostegia virginiana—False dragonhead

Polygala Senega—Seneca snakeroot

Polytaenia Nutallii—Prairie parsley

Potentilla arguta—Prairie cinquefoil

Pycnanthemum virginianum—Common mountain mint

Ratibida pinnata—Grayheaded coneflower

Rhus glabra—Smooth sumac

Rosa spp.—Prairie roses

Rudbeckia hirta—Black-eyed Susan

R. subtomentosa—Sweet clover

Salix humilis—Prairie willow

Silphium integrifolium—Wholeleaf rosinweed

S. laciniatum—Compass plant

S. terebinthinaceum—Prairie dock

Sisyrinchium albidum—Common blue-eyed grass

Smilacina stellata—Starry false Solomon's-seal

Solidago missouriensis—Missouri goldenrod

S. rigida—Stiff goldenrod

S. speciosa—Showy goldenrod

Sorghastrum nutans—Indian grass

Sporobolus heterolepis—Prairie dropseed

Stipa spartea—Needlegrass

Tradescantia ohiensis—Common spiderwort

Veronicastrum virginicum—Culver's root

Vicia americana—American vetch

Viola pedatifida—Prairie violet

Zizia aptera—Heartleaf meadow parsnip

Moderately Wet to Dry Prairie

Amorpha canescens—Lead plant

Andropogon Gerardii—Big bluestem grass

A. scoparius—Little bluestem grass

Anemone cylindrica—Prairie thimbleweed

A. patens—Pasque flower

Antennaria neglecta—Pussy-toes

Artemisia caudata—Beach wormwood

A. ludoviciana—Louisiana wormwood

Asclepias syriaca—Common milkweed

A. tuberosa—Butterfly weed

A. verticillata—Whorled milkweed

Aster azureus—Azure aster

A. ericoides—Heath aster

A. laevis—Smooth aster

A. oblongifolius—Aromatic aster

A. ptarmicoides—White upland aster

A. sericeus—Western silvery aster

Bouteloua curtipendula—Sideoats grama grass

Cirsium Hillii—Hill's thistle

Comandra Richardsiana—False toadflax

Coreopsis palmata—Prairie coreopsis

Delphinium virescens—Larkspur

Erigeron strigosus—Daisy fleabane

Euphorbia corollata—Flowering spurge

Gentiana quinquefolia—Stiff gentian

Hedeoma hispida—Mock pennyroyal

Helianthus laetiflorus—Rigid sunflower
H. occidentalis—Western sunflower
Koeleria cristata—Junegrass
Kuhnia eupatorioides—False boneset
Lespedeza capitata—Roundheaded bush clover
Liatris aspera—Rough blazing-star
L. cylindracea—Cylindric blazing-star
Linum sulcatum—Grooved flax
Lithospermum canescens—Hoary puccoon
L. incisum—Narrow-leafed puccoon
Monarda fistulosa—Wild bergamot
Oenothera biennis—Common evening primrose
Panicum Leibergii—Prairie panic grass
P. oligosanthes—Scribner panic grass
P. perlongum—Longstalked panic grass
Petalostemon candidum—White prairie clover
P. purpureum—Purple prairie clover
Physalis virginiana—Ground cherry
Potentilla arguta—Tall or prairie cinquefoil
Ratibida pinnata—Grayheaded coneflower
Rudbeckia hirta—Black-eyed Susan
Sisyrinchium campestre—Blue-eyed grass
Solidago nemoralis—Oldfield goldenrod
S. rigida—Stiff goldenrod
Sorghastrum nutans—Indian grass
Sporobolus heterolepis—Prairie dropseed
Stipa spartea—Needlegrass
Tradescantia ohiensis—Common spiderwort
Viola pedata—Bird-foot violet
V. pedatifida—Prairie violet

Dry Prairie
Amorpha canescens—Lead plant
Andropogon Gerardii—Big bluestem grass
A. scoparius—Little bluestem grass
Anemone cylindrica—Prairie thimbleweed
A. patens—Pasque flower
Antennaria neglecta—Pussy-toes
Arabis lyrata—Lyre-leaved rock cress
Arenaria stricta—Rock sandwort
Artemisia caudata—Beach wormwood
Asclepias verticillata—Whorled milkweed
A. viridiflora—Short green milkweed

Aster azureus—Azure aster
A. ericoides—Heath aster
A. laevis—Smooth aster
A. oblongifolius—Aromatic aster
A. ptarmicoides—White upland aster
A. sericeus—Western silvery aster
Bouteloua curtipendula—Sideoats grama grass
Castilleja sessiliflora—Downy yellow painted-cup
Comandra Richardsiana—False toadflax
Coreopsis palmata—Prairie coreopsis
Desmodium illinoense—Illinois tick trefoil
Erigeron strigosus—Daisy fleabane
Euphorbia corollata—Flowering spurge
Geum triflorum—Prairie smoke
Hedeoma hispida—Mock pennyroyal
Helianthus laetiflorus—Rigid sunflower
H. mollis—Downy sunflower
Koeleria cristata—Junegrass
Kuhnia eupatorioides—False boneset
Liatris cylindracea—Cylindrical blazing-star
Linum sulcatum—Grooved flax
Lithospermum incisum—Narrow-leaved puccoon
Monarda fistulosa—Wild bergamot
Muhlenbergia racemosa—Green muhly grass
Oenothera biennis—Common evening primrose
Panicum perlongum—Longstalked panic grass
Penstemon pallidus—Pale penstemon
Petalostemon purpureum—Purple prairie clover
Physalis subglabrata—Tall ground cherry
P. virginiana—Lance-leaved ground cherry
Potentilla arguta—Prairie cinquefoil
Psoralea esculenta—Prairie turnip
Rosa spp.—Prairie roses
Ruellia humilis—Hairy ruella
Scutellaria parvula—Small skullcap
Sisyrinchium campstre—Blue-eyed grass
Solidago nemoralis—Oldfield goldenrod
S. rigida—Stiff goldenrod
Sporobolus heterolepis—Prairie dropseed
Stipa spartea—Needlegrass

Verbena stricta—Hoary vervain
Viola sagittata—Arrow-leaved violet

GROUND COVERS

Ground-cover plants are abundant. There's one for every situation and every climate, roughly 450 of them if you survey the literature. A true ground cover is a plant that is low and self-spreading, forming a dense colony that resists invasion by weedy plants. The most practical of these are evergreen and root themselves as they spread, holding the soil beneath them in a tangled web. In nature, they function as a protective "blanket" over the soil, preventing its erosion and shielding its moisture from the sun's evaporative rays.

The "classic" ground covers are all evergreen, low, widely adapted, undemanding, boldly spreading and tolerant (to a greater or lesser degree) of drought.

In selecting one of the following plants, all you must do is choose the species native to your region. Then you can maintain an area with a low-growing profile and still eschew lawn.

Andromeda Polifolia—Bog rosemary
Antennaria rosea—Pussy-toes
Arctostaphylos Hookeri var. *franciscana*—Laurel Hill manzanita
A. Uva-ursi—Common bearberry
Arenaria spp.—Sandworts
A. verna—Moss sandwort
Artemisia Stellerana—Beach wormwood
Asarum spp.—Wild gingers
Baccharis pilularis—Dwarf baccharis
Campanula rotundifolia—Harebell
Ceanothus gloriosus—Point Reyes ceanothus
C. griseus var. *horizontalis*—Carmel creeper
Celastrus scandens—American bittersweet
Chimaphila umbellata—Pipsissewa
Clematis virginiana—Virgin's bower
Clintonia borealis—Clintonia
Comptonia peregrina—Sweet fern
Coptis groenlandica—Goldthread
Cornus canadensis—Bunchberry
Dicentra Cucullaria—Dutchman's-breeches
D. eximia—Fringed bleeding-heart

D. formosa—Pacific bleeding-heart
Dichondra micrantha—Dichondra
Epigaea repens—Trailing arbutus
Fragaria chiloensis—Beach strawberry
F. vesca var. *americana*—American strawberry
F. virginiana—Virginia strawberry
Galax urceolata—Galax
Gaultheria hispidula—Creeping snowberry
G. humifusa—Western wintergreen
G. ovatifolia—Oregon wintergreen
G. procumbens—Wintergreen
G. Shallon—Salal
Gaylussacia brachycera—Box huckleberry
Geranium maculatum—Wild geranium
Hypericum spp.—St.-John's-worts
Iris cristata—Crested iris
Juniperus communis var. *depressa*—Common juniper
J. communis var. *saxatilis*—Common juniper
J. horizontalis and varieties—Juniper
Kalmia angustifolia—Sheep laurel
Leiophyllum buxifolium var. *prostratum*—Sand myrtle
Leucothoe axillaris—Leucothoe
Linnaea borealis—Twinflower
Mahonia Aquifolium—Oregon grape
M. nervosa—Longleaf mahonia
M. repens—Creeping barberry
Maianthemum canadense—Canada mayflower
Mertensia virginica—Virginia bluebell
Mitchella repens—Partridgeberry
Myrica pensylvanica—Bayberry
Pachysandra procumbens—Allegheny spurge
Parthenocissus quinquefolia—Virginia creeper
Paxistima Canbyi—Pachistima
Phlox divaricata—Blue phlox
P. nivalis—Trailing phlox
P. ovata—Mountain phlox
P. procumbens—Trailing phlox
P. stolonifera—Creeping phlox
P. subulata—Moss pink
Pieris floribunda—Mountain andromeda

Podophyllum peltatum—Mayapple
Polemonium reptans—Jacob's-ladder
Polygonatum biflorum—Solomon's-seal
Potentilla spp.—Cinquefoils
Ranunculus repens—Creeping buttercup
Rhus aromatica—Fragrant sumac
Salix spp.—Dwarf willows
Sanguinaria canadensis—Bloodroot
Satureja Douglasii—Yerba buena
Shortia galacifolia—Oconee-bells
Smilacina racemosa—False Solomon's-seal
Symphoricarpos orbiculatus—Coralberry
Taxus canadensis var. *stricta*—Ground hemlock
Tiarella cordifolia—Foamflower
Trillium spp.—Trilliums
Uvularia grandiflora—Bellwort
Vaccinium angustifolium—Lowbush blueberry
V. Vitis-idaea—Cowberry
V. Vitis-idaea var. *minus*—Mountain cranberry
Vancouveria hexandra—Barrenwort
Viola spp.—Violets
Waldsteinia fragarioides—Barren strawberry
Zauschneria californica—California fuchsia

LAWNS

You've bought a book on natural landscaping. You've analyzed and tested your soil to see what native species will thrive, and you've planned it all out on paper. You feel pretty enthusiastic about the project, and then you discover something's "wrong." You want some lawn.

You need not feel like a traitor to the environmental movement. There are many good reasons why a patch of lawn deserves to be part of your landscape plan. You may want an area for family picnics or for the kids to play touch football. You may like the idea of garden parties that wander right off the patio into the backyard. Maybe you love to play volleyball or badminton.

Whatever your reasons, relax. A small area where family and friends gather to work or play together, to affirm and renew their ties to one another and nature, has a psychological value that cannot be overestimated. If a lawn serves this purpose for you, spend the money and put in the effort to create and maintain it in good conscience.

Don't kid yourself. It will be a lot of work. You will save yourself unnecessary labor and frustration, however, if you select grass varieties well suited to your climate and soil conditions. Also consider the amount of traffic your lawn will bear, the slope of the lawnbed, the amount of light and shade, and the exposure. Have an idea of the way you'd like your lawn to look and how short or high you intend to mow it.

If you live in the North, you may select bent grass, Kentucky bluegrass, rough bluegrass, or tall or red fescue. These varieties thrive in mild weather (from 60° to 80°F./15.6° to 26.7°C.) but may wilt and go dormant above 80°F. (26.7°C.) if adequate water is not supplied.

The grasses that Southerners use for their lawns are adapted to higher temperatures. If the mercury drops to 50°F. (10°C.) or below, they wilt and turn brown. At 70° to 75°F. (21.1° to 23.9°C.), they present a carpet of living green to the world that invites barefoot walking. And under the soil, a network of horizontal roots (rhizomes) spreads rapidly, starting new plants and thickening the stand. The warm-climate grasses include Bermuda grass, carpet grass, centipede grass, St. Augustine grass and zoysia.

In those areas of the South where winter temperatures fall to 50°F. (10°C.) or below, home-owners often overseed their dormant lawnbed with Italian ryegrass. Planting this quick-growing annual makes it possible for many warm-climate gardeners to have a green lawn year-round.

If you live in an arid region, Bermuda grass and St. Augustine grass will grow for you if you are willing and able to supply them with constant water. This is not only a great expense, but a great extravagance of one of our most precious natural resources. If you choose instead to sow buffalo grass, love grass or grama, you will be rewarded with a lawn that is less carpetlike but able to thrive in desert conditions. It will serve your needs without draining your well or the local reservoir.

Growing a healthy lawn demands the same forethought and preplanning as any other landscape design. Indeed, it may not be natural to force rhizomatous plants to propagate vegetatively by frequent, repeated mowings, but at least you can choose the variety of grass best adapted to endure such treatment in your climate and soil conditions. Working *with* nature—even to this small degree—will raise your chances of successful planting.

Regional Plant Charts

New awareness and appreciation of our native flora is growing. Many of these plants have become dangerously scarce and are taking on a new attractiveness to nature lovers. But this interest can have both a positive and negative effect. It can help replenish a species and increase its range. But it can also further destroy the most sought-after and rarest species. Experienced gardeners can help immensely by collecting and sowing seeds, caring for these plants and vigorously opposing careless habitat destruction. On the other hand, if they are not experienced, they can add to the problem by thoughtlessly digging up specimens best left in the field.

It is impossible to list all or even most of the plants native to the United States. Those that have been included in the accompanying charts are considered most suitable for landscaping, and while this is a good place to learn familiarity with native plants, it is not meant to be all-inclusive. By all means, go out and look at what's growing in a natural environment and decide for yourself what species you like.

The plants are listed alphabetically by scientific name in the categories of trees, shrubs and forbs within each of the 12 major ecological regions. Each region, which is briefly described, has generally consistant environmental conditions and uniform plant life. But there are many different environments within any region, and there may be areas in one region that are similar to those in another.

Ecoregion Map

Northern Coniferous Forest Region

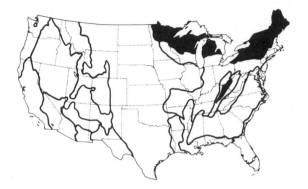

Only small areas of the Northern Coniferous Forest Region occur in the United States. These are found in the New England mountains, around the Great Lakes and along a narrow, broken band reaching into the southern Appalachians. Separate lists for each area are included here.

Precipitation over the region is moderate (to 40 inches) but transpiration, due to the predominance of needle-leaved conifers, is low. Diversity, both in the canopy and in the herbaceous layer, is low, but there is a full shrub layer (although made up of only a few species) and abundant moss. Soils are of glacial origin and are impoverished.

The appearance of this forest does not change dramatically with the change of seasons. There are a few deciduous species mixed in with the conifers, but not enough to give the forest a colorful appearance in autumn, nor to allow sufficient light penetration for showy herbaceous bloom in spring. An exception to this are the boggy areas in the Midwest.

There are several valuable ornamentals from these communities. These should be planted in like environments to produce the best results. Often, by limiting their natural range, diseases can be avoided.

Appalachian Area (high elevation)

The southern extension of the Northern Coniferous Forest reaches to North Carolina and is the highest elevation area of the Appalachian Mountain chain. Although the area is small, it is important as a haven for several unusual species. Climate, geologic history (as a nonglaciated region), and soils work together to produce a rich flora. Ferns and herbaceous material thrive on the upper elevations of the mountains, where conifers such as Fraser fir are endemic.

TREES

Name	Habitat	Growth Characteristics	Notes
Abies Fraseri Fraser fir	Cool; rich, light loamy soil in mountains	Open symmetrical crown; rigid branches; height to 60', diameter to 2½'	Short-lived in cultivation; rather unusual and scarce. Attracts squirrels, deer and chickadees
Acer pensylvanicum Striped maple	Moist slopes; in shade of taller trees	Small, upright branches, often shrubby; interesting longitudinally striped bark; height to 40'	May be hard to find commercially
A. spicatum Mountain maple	Moist, rocky hillsides, western slopes of mountains	Upright branches, often shrubby and rounded; height to 40'	Attractive understory tree
Tsuga caroliniana Carolina hemlock	Rocky stream banks at elevations of 2,500'–4,000'	Narrow pyramidal head; pendulous branches; height to 200'	Attracts a variety of birds and small mammals. Frequently planted ornamental

FORBS

Name	Habitat	Growth Characteristics	Notes
Cypripedium Calceolus Yellow lady's-slipper	Swamps, wet grasslands; moderately acid soil	Deep yellow flower with purple spots, bronzy petals; height to 2'	Very difficult to propagate; needs cool conditions. Showy, fragrant flower worth the trouble. Can be purchased at nurseries

FORBS (continued)

Name	Habitat	Growth Characteristics	Notes
Pedicularis canadensis Early wood betony	Clearings, damp meadows; moderately acid soil	Fernlike leaves; whorl of tubular yellow flowers; height to 14''	May be hard to find, as it is not a typical wild-flower species in demand Unusual and desirable for wild garden
Trillium sessile Toad trillium	Open, rich woods	Mottled leaves; brownish green flowers; height to 8''	More interesting than pretty
T. undulatum Painted trillium	Woods, swamps; cold, acid soil	Red, pink blotch-bronzy leaves; white flowers; height to 20''	The showiest of native trilliums, very beautiful

Great Lakes Area

This forms a narrow strip of dense vegetation extending from New England west to the Rockies. The portion around the Great Lakes consists of fairly tall conifers mixed with deciduous trees. This area has many low, boggy areas, which are a major habitat for sedges, orchids and other moisture-loving plants. The soils are organic peats, clays and silts. The growing season is three to four months.

TREES

Name	Habitat	Growth Characteristics	Notes
Larix laricina American larch, tamarack	Moist bottomlands in South; well-drained uplands in North	Narrow, pyramidal in forest; graceful, contorted with broad, open, picturesque head in open; height to 60'	Propagate by seeds; rapid grower Attracts crossbills, grouse, chipmunks and squirrels, rabbits and deer
Picea glauca White spruce	Stream banks, lake borders, rocky slopes	Open pyramid; graceful, thick, up-sweeping branches; height to 70'	Propagate by seeds; cannot tolerate heat, dryness Attracts crossbills, chickadees, porcupines and deer Disagreeable foliage smell
P. mariana Black spruce	Bogs	Pyramidal; open, irregular crown; often twisted; dark green shining needles; height to 30', rarely 100' diameter to 1'	Propagate by seeds Attracts many songbirds, porcupines and deer
Thuja occidentalis American arborvitae	Swamps, rocky stream banks	Narrow, compact head; short, often buttressed trunk; interesting red-orange bark; scalelike leaves; height to 60'	Propagate by seeds Attracts pine siskins and deer

SHRUBS

Andromeda glaucophylla Bog rosemary	Bogs and shallow pools	Spreading evergreen shrub; slender leaves; pink flowers; height to 2'	Propagate by seeds, cuttings or layering Unsuited to warm areas Attractive shrub that can spread into large patches under favorable conditions
Chamaedaphne calyculata Leatherleaf	Bogs, peaty soils, cool conditions	Much-branched evergreen shrub with horizontal branches; height to 3'	Propagate by seeds only slightly covered, by layering or suckers

FORBS

Aster macrophyllus Big-leaf aster	Edge of bogs, clearings, woods	Purple-white flowers from August to September; height to 5'	Propagate by seeds sown in spring for bloom the following summer Aster best suited to cold, acid conditions
Cypripedium reginae Showy lady's-slipper	Wet woods, bogs	White sepal and petal; rose pouch 1'–3'	Grow in acid, cool, moist garden Leaves and stems may be irritating to skin

FORBS (continued)

Name	Habitat	Growth Characteristics	Notes
Habenaria dilatata Leafy white orchid	Cold swamps, bogs, grasslands	White, slender inflorescence; height to 2½'	
H. Hookeri Hooker's orchid	Bogs	Yellow-green blossom from early summer to early autumn; height to 16''	
H. obusata Blunt-leaf orchid	Cold bogs	Greenish white blossom from early summer to early autumn; height to 8''	
Listera cordata Heart-leaf twayblade	Cold bogs and mossy woods	Heart-shaped leaves; purple-bronzy green flowers (small and few); height to 6''	Fragile, susceptible to pests More unusual than showy
Smilacina trifolia Bog Solomon's-plumes	Cold, wet bogs; acid, peaty soil	Few leaves; small white flowers clustered on stalk, in late spring; red berries; height to 1'	

Pinus Strobus   *Vaccinium angustifolium*   *Arethusa bulbosa*

New England Area

Representatives of these associations are found in the mountainous regions of the Northeast. The climate is cold and moist, the soil infertile and the growing season short. Although the species listed here do appear elsewhere, this environment is optimum for their development.

TREES

Name	Habitat	Growth Characteristics	Notes
Abies balsamea Balsam fir	Edge of streams, edge of bogs in mountains	Slender pyramidal crown; straight trunk; regular whorls of branches; height to 60'	Propagate by seeds Short-lived but rapid grower; adaptable; fire-prone Attracts grouse, hares, deer, moose and porcupines
Acer rubrum Red maple	Swamps, floodplains, upland ravines, shady cliffs, mountain coves	Upright; narrow crown; red twigs and flowers; autumn foliage scarlet; height to 120', diameter to 4'	Propagate by mature or stratified seeds, also green-wood cuttings or layering Attracts songbirds, squirrels, cotton-tail rabbits, snowshoe hares, white-tailed deer and moose

TREES (continued)

Name	Habitat	Growth Characteristics	Notes
Betula papyrifera Paper birch	Near rushing waters, clear, cold lakes and bogs, deep, rocky woods on cool soil; sun tolerant	Erect and slender while young, graceful, pendulous branches at maturity; interesting peeling bark, varies from creamy white to bronze; filmy green leaves; height to 60'	Propagate by seeds sown immediately or stratified, by layering or green-wood cuttings Seeds and buds are eaten by numerous game birds and songbirds
Picea mariana Black spruce	Bogs	Pyramidal; open, irregular crown, often twisted; dark green shining needles; height to 30', rarely 100', diameter to 1'	Propagate by seeds Susceptible to wind, as shallow rooted; wind breakage common Attracts many songbirds, porcupines and deer
P. rubens Red spruce	Along the edges of streams and bogs (associated with Balsam fir), well-drained uplands and mountain slopes	Pyramidal crown; straight trunk; regular whorls of branches; height to 70', diameter to 2'	Propagate by seeds
Pinus Banksiana Jack pine	Infertile soil; open, wind-swept areas	Small, gnarled evergreen; crooked, knotty trunk can appear ragged; height to 70'	Propagate by seeds; short-lived, about 60 years Attracts nearly all game birds, rabbits, hares, squirrels, chipmunks and black bears
P. resinosa Red pine	Rocky acid, sandy loams with high moisture; often in association with white pine	Symmetrical, oval crown; bark interesting, irregular diamond-shaped plates; height to 100', diameter to 3'	Propagate by seeds Usually forms groves, sometimes pure forests
P. Strobus White pine	Acid, rocky soil where there is heavy snow-fall, plentiful moisture; also sandy loams and fertile, well-drained soil	Pyramidal crown; straight bole with whorled branches beginning at 30' or more; height to 100' (has been known to reach 240')	Propagate by seeds; grows with vigor and rapidly Forms pure stands Attracts game birds, many songbirds, rabbits, hares, squirrels and chipmunks
Populus tremuloides Quaking aspen	With conifers, on logged or fireswept areas, in silted-in sloughs and around mountain lakes, barrens, infertile areas	Tall, with narrow, rounded crown; slender branches; restless, musical leaves; autumn foliage beautiful; height to 60', diameter to 2'	Propagate by hardwood cuttings or suckers, rarely seeds; fast growing, short-lived and disease-prone Attracts ruffed grouse, sharp-tailed grouse, deer, moose, bears, snow-shoe hares and rabbits
Salix nigra Black willow	Riparian, slowly moving streams; moist areas	Irregular crown; several trunks; much branching; bends toward water; height to 50'	Propagate by hardwood cuttings or suckers; easily grown; fast growing, will root if twig touches ground Attracts grouse, ptarmigans, deer, moose, beavers, muskrats, snow-shoe hares and porcupines Useful for flood protection
Sorbus americana American mountain ash	Cool mountainous areas, swamps, rocky hillsides	Narrow, rounded crown; slender trunk; conspicuous white flowers, scarlet fruit; brilliant autumn foliage; height to 30'	Propagate by ripe or stratified seeds or layering Attracts grouse, ptarmigans and moose

SHRUBS

Name	Habitat	Growth Characteristics	Notes
Chamaedaphne calyculata Leatherleaf	Peat bogs	Evergreen; low; height to 5'	Propagate by seeds, suckers or layering
Gaylussacia baccata Black huckleberry	Bogs, dry, sandy woods, rocky woods	Deciduous; upright branches; height to 3'	Propagate by seeds, layering or division

SHRUBS (continued)

Name	Habitat	Growth Characteristics	Notes
Ledum groenlandicum Labrador tea	Cold bogs; peaty soils, high moisture, very acid	Evergreen; rounded top; height to 3'	Propagate by seeds sown in spring, by layering or division. Suited to long winters, with little summer heat
Vaccinium angustifolium Lowbush blueberry	Open rocky woods, clearings; strongly acid, dry	Deciduous; widely spreading; height to 2'	Propagate by division or cuttings, sometimes by seeds. Attracts songbirds and mammals. The commercial blueberry
V. Oxycoccos Small cranberry	Cold sphagnum bogs	Evergreen; trailing; height to 1½'	Propagate by division or cuttings, sometimes by seeds. Fruit, which ripens in late summer and autumn, has commercial value

FORBS

Name	Habitat	Growth Characteristics	Notes
Arethusa bulbosa Swamp pink, dragon orchid	Sphagnum bogs, swamps; needs moisture, strongly acid soil	Grasslike leaves; pink, purple and white solitary flower, 1'' to 1½'' long; showy	Beautiful and well worth extra effort
Calypso bulbosa Fairy-slipper orchid	Cold, damp, moderately acid woods; soil high in organic matter	Solitary white (purple-blotched) 1'' flower from May to June; showy plant; height to 6''	Difficult to grow, requires cool, pest-free conditions. Relatively scarce in the wild
Coptis trifolia Goldthread	Damp woods, bog; cool conditions; acid soil	Evergreen; 3-lobed leaves; small, white, 5-petaled flowers (similar to buttercup); height to 6''	Propagate by seeds; moderately easy if cool conditions and acid soil are provided. Excellent ground cover in cool, wild garden
Cornus canadensis Bunchberry	Swamps, deep woods; strongly acid, organic soil	Small, yellow-green flowers surrounded by 4 showy, white bracts in early spring; red fruit; height to 8''	Propagate by cuttings; needs cool conditions and acid soil. Provides food for wildlife
Dentaria laciniata Cut-leaved toothwort	Woods, slopes on moderately acid soil; moist conditions	3-whorled leaves; pale pink flowers, ½'' long, clustered near top of stem; height to 15''	Propagate by seeds
Pyrola elliptica Thin-leaved pyrola, shinleaf	Woods; moderately acid, organic soil	Basal leaves, 5''–10'' long; nodding, white ⅔'' flowers at top of stem	Propagate by cuttings or division; easy in acid woodland gardens

John Hamel

A Gallery of Native Plants in Natural Environments

Carl Doney

John Hamel

Margaret Smyser

Carl Doney

Cathie Bruner

John Hamel

Sally Ann Shenk

162   Carol Smyser

Carl Doney

T. L. Gettings

Carl Doney

John Hamel

Carl Doney

Carl Doney

Carl Doney
John Hamel
Carl Doney

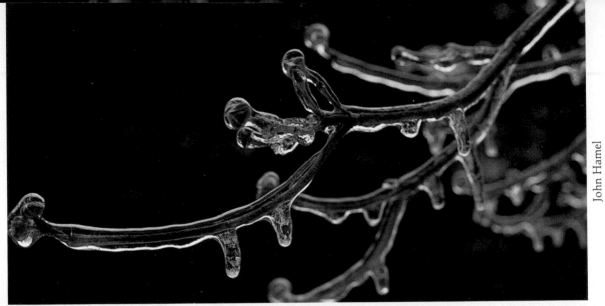

John Hamel

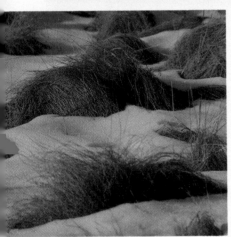

T. L. Gettings

T. L. Gettings

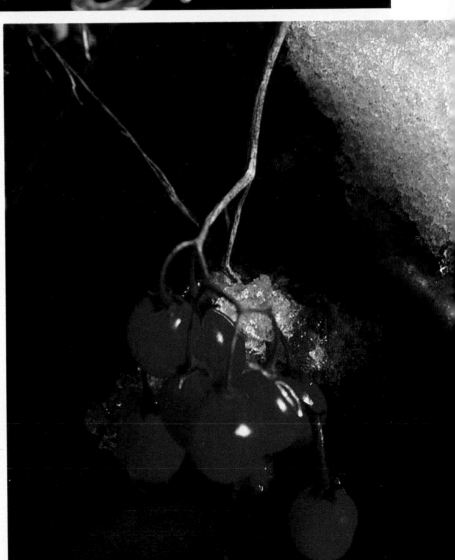

Eastern Deciduous Forest Region

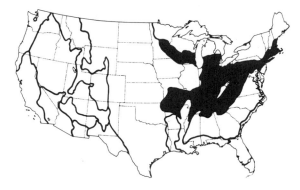

The Eastern Deciduous Forest Region extends from the southern tip of Maine south to northern Alabama and Georgia and west to western Indiana, with a northern arm crossing Wisconsin and Minnesota and a southern arm encompassing the Ozark area of Missouri and Arkansas.

Most of the area is rolling, but some parts are nearly flat, and in the Appalachian Mountains the relief is high (up to 3,000 feet). The northern parts of the region have been glaciated, but not the southern. Elevations range from sea level to 2,500 feet; a few isolated peaks are higher than 4,500 feet.

The Eastern Deciduous Forest receives adequate precipitation in all months, with an annual average of 35 to 60 inches. A strong annual temperature cycle brings cold winters and warm summers. The average annual temperature is 40° to 60°F. (4.4° to 15.6°C.).

Winter deciduous forest, sometimes called temperate deciduous forest, is characteristic of this region. It is dominated by tall, broadleaf trees that provide a continuous and dense canopy in summer but shed their leaves completely in winter. Lower layers of small trees and shrubs develop weakly. In spring a luxuriant low layer of herbs quickly develops, but this is greatly reduced after the trees reach full foliage and shade the ground.

Appalachian Oak Forest Area

This is the most complex and the richest area within the Eastern Deciduous Forest. Its milder climate, geologic history and topographic diversity are responsible for the numerous plant habitats within a relatively small area. There are granite mountains, sedimentary ridges and valleys, and limestone plateaus that have been home to land plants since early Paleozoic times. It includes southern New England, much of Pennsylvania and the Southern Highlands.

TREES

Name	Habitat	Growth Characteristics	Notes
Aesculus octandra Yellow buckeye	Upland woods	Rounded crown; large capsules; brown, fissured bark; showy yellow flowers; large shrub (often), but can rise 60'–90'	Propagate by seeds sown in autumn or stratified
Chionanthus virginicus Old-man's-beard, fringe tree	Rich, moist soil of flood-plains; Appalachian Mountains, 4,000'	Narrow crown; stout branches; fragrant, showy white flowers borne in loose panicles; autumn foliage yellow; height to 30'	Propagate by seeds sown in autumn or by layering in autumn; needs good drainage. Late to put out leaves in spring
Cladrastis lutea Yellowwood	Rich limestone soils on slopes, ridges near streams	Open crown; ascending branches; bark silvery gray or light brown, lighter-colored branches; normally flowers alternate years; autumn foliage yellow; height to 50'	Propagate by seeds sown in spring or by root cuttings
Franklinia Alatamaha Franklin tree	Stream banks; either acid or alkaline soils (possible prefers alkaline)	Upright; white, brilliant orange and red flowers appear in autumn; height to 30'	Propagate by cuttings or seeds
Halesia carolina Silver-bell, silver-bell tree	Stream banks and slopes	Rounded crown; trunk sometimes divided; white flowers (sometimes pink tinge); interesting 4-winged fruit; height to 40'	Propagate by ripe or stratified seeds, layering or root cuttings

TREES (continued)

Name	Habitat	Growth Characteristics	Notes
Magnolia tripetala Umbrella-tree	Stream banks, edges of swamps in moist, rich soil	Slender trunk; stout, contorted branches; 20'' leaves clustered at twig tips; creamy flowers with unpleasant odor	Propagate by seeds sown in autumn or stratified
Pinus pungens Table Mountain pine	Rocky, gravelly mountain slopes	Narrow crown; straight trunk; pendulous branches to ground; height to 60'	Propagate by seeds, sometimes cuttings Attracts game birds, rabbits, hares, squirrels and chipmunks
Robinia Pseudoacacia Black locust	Dry, sandy slopes or rich, moist, deep soils (not particular)	Open, oblong crown; flowers in white, drooping racemes very fragrant; fruit a brown pod; height to 75'	Propagate by seeds sown in spring, by suckers, root cuttings or division Attacked by pests, especially when planted out of its native area
Stewartia ovata Mountain camellia	On stream banks and wooded slopes; rich soil	Small tree; large, showy, camellia-like flowers in July; height to 25'	Hard to propagate, difficult to find in nurseries
Tsuga caroliniana Carolina hemlock	Mountains, steep slopes above 3,000'	Graceful evergreen; height to 70'	Propagate by seeds Very rare, occurs in localized areas of the Smokies

SHRUBS

Name	Habitat	Growth Characteristics	Notes
Gaylussacia brachycera Box huckleberry	Sandy woods, wooded slopes; dry acid soil	Creeping evergreen; white, pink or red flowers from May to June; height to 15''	Propagate by seeds, layering or division Rare, a colony exists in Pennsylvania Fruits attract ruffed grouse
Leucothoe Fontanesiana Dog-hobble, switch ivy	Rocky, wooded mountain slopes; moist, acid soils	Graceful semievergreen; spreading with arching branches; white, bell-shaped, fragrant blossoms from April to May; height to 3'	Propagate by seeds sown in greenhouse, by division or root cuttings
Pieris floribunda Fetterbush	Slopes and balds	Narrow, upright evergreen; nodding white flowers from March to June; height to 6'	Propagate by seeds, layering or ripewood cuttings under glass Often cultivated, readily available
Rhododendron arborescens Smooth azalea, sweet azalea	Moist, rocky woods, along streams, swamps and bogs	Deciduous; upright; can be straggly (pick specimen for shape); foliage glossy green turning red in autumn; white, sometimes pink, flowers from late May to July, very fragrant; height to 15'	Propagate by seeds sown in pans of sandy peat Browsed by deer
R. calendulaceum Flame azalea	Oak, pine woods, mountain balds	Deciduous; showy clusters of yellow, scarlet or orange flowers from April to June; height to 15'	Propagate by seeds sown in pans of sandy peat Often cultivated, so readily available
R. catawbiense Catawba rhododendron, mountain rosebay	Rocky slopes, mountain tops (over 3,000'); acid soils	Thicket-forming shrub; lilac-purple, spotted green flowers in showy clusters from April to June; oblong fruits; height to 10'	Propagate by seeds sown in pans of sandy peat
R. minus Piedmont rhododendron	Slopes and along streams	Evergreen; magenta-pink blossoms in early summer; height to 8'	Propagate by seeds sown in pans of sandy peat
R. Vaseyi Pink-shell azalea	Floodplains, swamp edges and mountain tops	Deciduous, bushy shrub; pink-spotted yellow or orange blossoms from May to June; height to 15'	Propagate by seeds sown in pans of sandy peat Very local native distribution, but acclimates readily in cultivation
Spiraea corymbosa Spiraea	Damp, rocky slopes and stream banks	Deciduous; slender, much branched; wandlike branches; coarsely toothed leaves; corymbs of white flowers from June to July; height to 3'	

FORBS

Name	Habitat	Growth Characteristics	Notes
Aristolochia durior Pipe vine, Dutchman's-pipe	Rocky slopes; medium acidity	Shrubby vine; large leaves; maroon-green blossoms from May to June; height to 30'	Propagate by seeds, layering or cuttings; vigorous grower
Asarum canadense Wild ginger, snakeroot	On slopes, rocky or loamy soils; neutral pH	Low spreading; beautiful, large, lustrous green leaves, paired; single flower below leaves, maroon-green blossoms in April; height to 8''	Propagate by seeds or division
Claytonia caroliniana Carolina spring-beauty	Upland woods	Mat-forming colonies from tuberous roots; white and pink striped blossoms from March to May	Propagate by seeds
Dicentra eximia Turkey corn, wild bleeding-heart	Rocky woods, slopes	Neat, nonspreading, multibranched, semisucculent; beautiful, finely cut leaves; pink-red blossoms from May to August; height to 16''	Propagate by division or seeds Does well in cool, semishaded garden
Galax urceolata Wandflower, wand plant	Wooded slopes	Evergreen; slender, naked stalk; glossy, dark basal leaves; stalked white flowers above them from May to July; height to 2'	Propagate by division
Hepatica acutiloba Sharp-lobed hepatica	Rich, often calcareous woods	Hairy stems; 3-lobed leaves; white, pink or red flowers on naked stalks above leaves from March to April; height to 9''	Propagate by seeds or division Rarer form of *H. americana*
Heuchera americana Rock geranium	Open woods, rocky slopes; well-drained, medium acid soil	Good ground cover; tiny but numerous white-bronze blossoms from May to June; height to 2'	Propagate by seeds or offsets
Hydrastis canadensis Goldenseal, orangeroot, turmeric	Well-drained wooded slopes; rich, moist, neutral soil	Bold basal leaves; solitary greenish white flower from April to May; height to 1'	Propagate by seeds or division
Hydrophyllum virginianum Virginia waterleaf	Rich woods; moist	White–pale purple flowers below maplelike leaves from June to July; stamens extend beyond petals; height to 20''	Propagate by seeds or division
Panax trifolius Dwarf ginseng	Mountains, moist woods; neutral soil	Delicate 3-stalked leaves; white-pink blossom in an umbel from April to June; height to 8''	Propagate by stratified seeds

Oak-Hickory Forest Area

This is the climax forest of the eastern United States and is characterized by tall, broad-leaved vegetation that grows in moderate moisture. Winters are cold and moderately dry, while summers are warm and humid. Precipitation is generally adequate throughout the year, but markedly increased in spring and summer. Soils are acid podzols. Streams and bottomlands are common and are richly vegetated. The area extends west from the western foothills of the Appalachians to the Ozarks of Missouri and Arkansas.

TREES

Name	Habitat	Growth Characteristics	Notes
Acer saccharum Sugar maple	Moist slopes in cooler areas	Wide-spreading, rounded crown (can be 80' across); shallow rooted; excellent autumn color; height to 120'	Propagate by mature or stratified seeds sown in spring Attracts game birds, songbirds, mammals and browsers

TREES (continued)

Name	Habitat	Growth Characteristics	Notes
Betula nigra River birch	Floodplains of slow-draining rivers	Many trunks; graceful, arching limbs; papery, exfoliating bark; height to 90′	Propagate by seeds sown immediately or stratified, sown on sand Holds banks, preventing erosion, controlling flooding
Carpinus caroliniana American hornbeam	Deep rich soils along the borders of streams, swamps	Bushy, slightly pendulous branches; gray-blue sinewy bark; brilliant scarlet-orange in autumn; height to 40′	Propagate by seeds sown in autumn Excellent understory tree Provides food for birds and squirrels
Carya ovata Shagbark hickory	Rich, deep, moist soil	Rounded crown; columnar trunk; pendulous branches; bark distinctive for shaggy appearance; height to 90′	Propagate by stratified seeds sown in spring or by root sprouts; hard to transplant; slow growing Source of nuts Attractive to waterfowl, game birds, songbirds and browsers
Cornus florida Flowering dogwood	Best in rich, moist soils but will invade fields, climb mountains, pioneer on burned or logged areas	Understory tree of many shapes; rounded, bushy crown; reliable and glorious blooms; deep red autumn color; beautiful fruit; height to 40′	Propagate by mature-wood cuttings or layering Excellent winter food supply for songbirds
Fagus grandifolia American beech	Second terrace, moist soils; deep, rich loams; cool, shady locations on limestone	Columnar silhouette, but at least 40′ wide; shallow root system; coarsely serrated leaves; beautiful copper color in fall; height to 100′	Propagate by mature or stratified seeds sown in autumn; needs ample room Provides food for squirrels and chipmunks, also birds and browsers
Fraxinus americana White ash	Deep, sweet loams, lots of moisture but well drained; plenty of sun	Wide crown; open shape, light shade; graceful, far-reaching limbs; gold fall color; height to 175′	Propagate by stratified seeds sown the following year; easy to transplant
Juglans nigra Black walnut	Rich, moist soils of second terraces and hillsides	Broad, domed crown; straight trunk, free of branches near ground; wide limbs; height to 150′	Propagate by seeds; fast growing Attracts woodpeckers and squirrels
Liriodendron Tulipifera Tulip tree, tulip poplar	Moist, rich soils of terraces and slopes, well drained	Narrowly pyramidal; straight trunk free of branches near ground; large leaves; cup-shaped flowers; height to 200′	Propagate by stratified seeds sown in spring; rapid grower, disease-free, but culture difficult Provides food for cardinals, purple finches and squirrels
Prunus pensylvanica Wild red cherry, pin cherry	Early successional tree on lumbered or burned area	Narrow; white flowers appear before the leaves; fiery red autumn color; height to 40′	Propagate by seeds sown in autumn or by stratified seeds sown in spring Intolerant of pollution Provides excellent food for songbirds, game birds, mammals and browsers
P. serotina Black cherry, wild black cherry	Upland forests, old fields	Forest trees are tall, straight; others variable, often gnarled; height to 100′	Propagate by seeds sown in autumn or by stratified seeds sown in spring Provides excellent food for songbirds, game birds, mammals and browsers
Quercus alba White oak	Ridges, plains or uplands; gravelly, sandy, rich, moist soil	Wide-spreading branches, almost rounded outline when mature; height to 150′	Propagate by seeds sown in autumn; taprooted, hard to transplant; plants dug from wild rarely survive; slow growing; can live for 500 to 800 years Provides excellent food for ducks, game birds, songbirds and mammals
Q. coccinea Scarlet oak	Light, dry soil, often sandy; dry, gravelly uplands	Narrow, open crown; delicate, graceful twigs; glossy green leaves; autumn foliage brilliant scarlet; height to 80′	Provides excellent food for songbirds, game birds and mammals

TREES (continued)

Name	Habitat	Growth Characteristics	Notes
Q. palustris Pin oak, Spanish oak	Moist bottomlands; deep acid soil	Pyramidal outline; pendulous lower branches, twiggy; autumn foliage scarlet; height to 75'	Propagate by seeds sown in autumn; easy to transplant
Q. velutina Black oak, yellow-barked oak	Dry, gravelly uplands, ridges, on glacial drift	Narrow crown; uneven outline; beautiful dark green shining leaves; brilliant autumn color; height to 150'	Propagate by seeds sown in autumn; hard to transplant

Quercus alba   Kalmia latifolia   Mertensia virginica

SHRUBS

Kalmia latifolia Mountain laurel	Moist, acid, rocky soils, sometimes swamps	Evergreen; leaves crowded at branch tips; handsome buds and flowers, blooms profusely	Propagate by seeds, cuttings of half-ripened wood or layering; transplant in spring; specimens dug from wild seldom thrive
Rhus copallina Shining sumac	Open woods, thickets, fence rows, old fields; poor, dry soil	Erect; treelike in South; beautiful, shining foliage; red, hairy fruits; autumn color scarlet; height to 20'	Propagate by seeds, root cuttings or layering
R. typhina Staghorn sumac	Uplands, abandoned fields; poor, dry, sandy soils; sun	Deciduous; upright; develops into large clumps; crimson fruits; red autumn color; height to 30'	Propagate by seeds, root cuttings or layering; rapid grower Provides food for many songbirds, game birds, small mammals and browsers Useful in soil-erosion control
Sambucus canadensis American elderberry	Rich, moist woods	Medium-size shrub, coarse but attractive; height to 12'	Propagate by seeds or cuttings; easily grown but invasive
Viburnum acerifolium Maple-leaved viburnum	Variable conditions, moist to dry, rocky woods	Deciduous shrub with handsome maplelike leaves; creamy white flowers from May to June; autumn foliage pink-magenta; height to 6'	Propagate by stratified seeds or hardwood cuttings; needs some sun to flower but can tolerate dappled shade Provides food for deer, rabbits and grouse

FORBS

Acorus Calamus Sweet flag	Stream banks and pond edges, shores	Hardy perennial; leaves rise from horizontal rhizome; irislike or grasslike; yellow-green fleshy flower spike, up to 4'' long; height to 6'	Propagate by division

FORBS (continued)

Name	Habitat	Growth Characteristics	Notes
Arisaema triphyllum Woodland Jack-in the-pulpit, Indian turnip	Woods and swamps of the Piedmont	Green-purple and striped, fleshy flower spike with overhanging flap; height to 3'	Propagate by seeds or offsets
Aster patens Late purple aster	Dry, open woods, clearings	Deep blue-violet flowers from August to October; height to 3'	Propagate by seeds sown in spring for bloom the following year or by division
Geranium maculatum Wild geranium	Open woods; moderately acid, rich soil	Leaves deeply lobed; 1¼'' lavender flowers from late spring to summer; height to 2'	Propagate by seeds or roots
Goodyera pubescens Downy rattle-snake plantain	Pine, oak, wooded slopes; acid, organic soil	Gray-green leaves with conspicuous veins; small white flowers along stalk in summer; height to 15''	Propagate by seeds or division; difficult Should not be removed from woodland, very scarce
Hedyotis caeruea Quaker-ladies, bluets	Grasslands, open woods; moderately acid soil	Bright blue 4-petaled flower with yellow center in spring; height to 1'	
Hepatica americana Round-leaved hepatica, liverleaf	Well-drained wooded slopes; moderately acid	White-pink-blue-lavender flowers in early spring; height to 6''	Propagate by seeds or root division
Lilium philadelphicum Wood lily	Grasslands, shrubs in sandy, gravelly, acid soil	Bright green whorled leaves; upright orange-red flowers in summer; height to 3'	Propagate by offsets in early autumn or by seeds; strongly acid soil and natural conditions must be maintained
Mertensia virginica Bluebells, Virginia bluebells	Open woods and bottomlands	Semisucculent; nodding, bell-like flowers, pink bud turning blue from March to May; height to 2'	Propagate by seeds as soon as ripe; tubers available commercially
Podophyllum peltatum Mayapple, mandrake	Open, damp woods; neutral, acid soil	Large umbrellalike leaves; solitary white flower beneath in late spring; height to 1' or more	Propagate by seeds or division
Polygonatum biflorum Solomon's-seal	Wooded stream banks, limestone ridges in rich soil	Paired, greenish yellow flowers from April to June; height to 3'	Propagate by division
Trillium grandiflorum White wake-robin	Swamps and woodlands in Piedmont uplands; various soils	White flowers turning pink in spring; height to 1½'	Propagate by seeds or division; plants require moisture and partial shade
Viola pedata Bird-foot violet	Open woods, grasslands; sterile soil, very strongly acid	Deeply divided fan-shaped leaves; very low; lilac flowers in spring	Propagate by seeds sown in autumn or by division
V. rotundifolia Round-leaved yellow violet	Open woods; neutral, acid soil	Fan-shaped leaves; bright yellow flowers with brown stripes in spring; height to 1'	Propagate by seeds sown in autumn or by division

Coastal Plain Region

Coastal plains extend all along the eastern seaboard. They are level areas of marine-deposited material that contain features such as beaches, tidal flats, bottomlands and swamps. There is similarity of form and pattern among vegetation associations, but there is variation in species, depending on climate, microclimate and elevation.

Soils are a mixture of sands, silts and clays. Water tables are often barely subsurface or surface much of the year, and hydric species are common. Water-tolerant conifers and hardwoods are widespread, with a dense understory of vines, mosses and acid-loving shrubs.

There are hundreds of colorful forbs in the bogs, meadows and old fields, some of which are suitable for landscaping purposes.

TREES

Name	Habitat	Growth Characteristics	Notes
Carya aquatica Bitter pecan, water hickory	Swamps	Large, symmetrical tree with scythelike leaflets; height to 100'	Propagate by stratified seeds sown in spring or by root sprouts; not readily transplanted Attracts waterfowl and small mammals, especially foxes
C. pallida Sand hickory	Dry, sandy soils of upper coastal plain	Oval crown; height to 100'	Propagate by stratified seeds sown in spring or by root sprouts Attracts foxes, chipmunks and squirrels
Liquidambar Styraciflua Sweet gum	Bottomlands; sandy soils	Oblong crown; slender branches; interesting fruit; brilliant scarlet in autumn; height to 140'	Propagate by seeds, which may not germinate until the second year
Magnolia virginiana Sweet bay	Wet, sandy soil, acid	Slender, attractive form, understory tree; lustrous leaves, persistent in South until spring; flowers fragrant; colorful seeds, pods; height to 60'	Propagate by seeds sown in autumn or stratified, or by green cuttings under glass Provides food for sapsuckers, woodpeckers, vireos, towhees, squirrels and mice
Nyssa sylvatica Pepperridge, sour gum, black gum	Prefers moist, rich soil, but is also found in uplands	Narrow crown; sometimes crooked with brushy branching; glossy leaves turn glorious scarlet in autumn; height to 90'	Propagate by seeds sown at once or stratified, sometimes by layering
Pinus palustris Longleaf pine, southern yellow	Gravel, sands, thin soils, high water table	Small, open crown; long, straight trunk; 6''–10'' cones; height to 100'	Propagate by seeds
P. rigida Pitch pine	Dry, rocky soil	Irregular, wide crown; whorled branches, sometimes drooping; height to 75'	Propagate by seeds; vigorous grower Provides food for game birds, songbirds and mammals
P. virginiana Jersey pine	Rocky, infertile sandy soils; abandoned fields	Flat crown; widely spaced branches in whorls; height to 45'	Propagate by seeds; tolerant of difficult conditions; rapid grower Provides food, shelter for game birds, songbirds and mammals
Populus nigra Black poplar, swamp poplar	Mixed in swamps, lowland forest	Narrow, rounded crown; aromatic twigs and buds; height to 90'	Propagate by hardwood cuttings or suckers, sometimes by seeds; fast growing

Nyssa sylvatica

Clethra alnifolia

Iris prismatica

TREES (continued)

Name	Habitat	Growth Characteristics	Notes
Quercus Falcata Spanish red oak	Moist, loamy ridges, old fields and flats	Long, straight trunks; height to 80'	Propagate by hardwood cuttings or suckers, sometimes by seeds
Q. laurifolia Laurel oak	Sandy soils, scattered in swamps	Semievergreen; symmetrical, rounded crown; height to 60'	Propagate by hardwood cuttings or suckers, sometimes by seeds Attracts squirrels, small mammals and songbirds
Q. phellos Willow oak	Wet, sandy soils along streams and in swamps, can be grown in upland	Pyramidal crown; beautiful pale yellow autumn color; height to 60'	Propagate by stratified seeds or seeds sown in autumn Attracts wood ducks, mallards, quail, squirrels and woodpeckers
Taxodium distichum Bald cypress	Swamps, depressions, stream banks, ponds	Pyramidal (youth); wide-spreading, rounded crown; strongly buttressed trunk; height to 150'	Propagate by seeds Becoming scarce, as habitat is being destroyed

SHRUBS

Name	Habitat	Growth Characteristics	Notes
Alnus maritima Seaside alder	Near coast, along ponds, stream banks	Narrow, round-topped crown; mostly shrubby; interesting, drooping catkins; height to 30'	Propagate by seeds dried in autumn and sown in spring, also by cuttings or suckers Provides food for beavers, deer, rabbits and small birds Useful for controlling erosion
Baccharis halimifolia Groundsel tree, groundselbush	Swamps, sandy areas, beaches, also Piedmont (brackish)	Semievergreen; upright, stiff and leggy; flowers small daisies; fruits have conspicuous silky hairs; height to 20'	Propagate by seeds or cuttings; easy to transplant
Clethra alnifolia Sweet pepper-bush, summersweet	Wet woods, swamps; acid, peaty soils	Deciduous; upright; clump forming nonevergreen heaths; white flowers from July to August; height to 8'	Propagate by seeds sown in spring, by layers or division (green-wood cuttings under glass)
Comptonia peregrina Sweet fern	Sterile, peaty, sandy soils of the Coastal Plain, uplands	Deciduous; many-branching, woody shrub; forms stands; looks like a fern; height to 5'	Propagate by seeds, root cuttings or division; difficult to propagate
Leiophyllum buxifolium Box sand myrtle	Pinelands	Evergreen and multibranched; dense clusters of white flowers; height to 2½'	Propagate by seeds in a cold frame or by layering
Lindera melissifolia Jove's fruit	Pond borders, swamps	Fragrant leaves; tiny yellow flowers; height to 6'	Propagate by ripe seeds, green-wood cuttings under glass or layering Provides food for deer, wild birds and rabbits

SHRUBS (continued)

Name	Habitat	Growth Characteristics	Notes
Myrica cerifera Wax myrtle, candleberry	Wet, sandy pinelands and bogs	Upright; grows in colonies; height to 6'	Propagate by seeds, layering or suckers Attracts small birds, quail and wild turkeys Useful to control erosion
M. Gale Sweet gale	Cool swamps	Erect; height to 4'	Propagate by seeds, layering or suckers; grows best in peaty soil
M. pensylvanica Bayberry	Dry, sandy soils, dunes	Upright; height to 6'	Propagate by seeds, layering or suckers Provides food for many wild birds
Rhododendron canescens Florida pinxter, hoary azalea	Moist, sandy woods, swamps, floodplains	Deciduous; fragrant, pink-white flowers; height to 10'	Propagate by seeds or cuttings
R. prunifolium Plum-leaved azalea	Moist woods, ravines	Deciduous; dark green leaves; bright red flowers in July and August; height to 10'	Propagate by seeds or cuttings
R. viscosum White swamp azalea	Bogs, along streams	Deciduous; large, finely toothed leaves; white–pale pink flowers; height to 10'	Propagate by seeds or cuttings
Zanthoxylum clava-Herculis Hercules'-club	Dry sand hills, woods	Interesting, almost tropical appearance; large leaves	Propagate by seeds, suckers or root cuttings

FORBS

Name	Habitat	Growth Characteristics	Notes
Aletris farinosa Unicorn root, star grass	Bog edges, open woods, sterile grasslands; strongly acid soil	Erect perennial; tends toward colonizing; small, tubular white flowers spaced along 1'–2' stalks; height to 2'	Propagate by seeds or division; strongly acid soil essential
Arisaema triphyllum Jack-in-the-pulpit	Moist areas, swamp, bog margins	3-parted leaf; dark, fleshy flower spike; height to 2'	Propagate by seeds or natural offsets
Aster spectabilis Showy aster	Sandy soils near coast	Violet flowers in fall; height to 2'	Propagate by division or cuttings; seeds may not come true
Drosera rotundifolia Round-leaved sundew	Wet, acid sandy/peaty soil; bogs, swamps, along streams	Small white flowers in summer; height to 2''	Propagate by seeds, division, cuttings or rhizomes
Gentiana autumnalis Pine-barren gentian	Wet pine barrens	Gorgeous blue open flowers, fringed petals, from August to October; height to 1½'	Propagate by seeds or root division; difficult, prone to fungus disease
Helonias bullata Swamp pink	Swamps, bogs, in acid, humusy soil	Lilylike leaves; pink flowers with blue anthers in spring	Propagate by division; fairly easy in moist, acid soils
Iris prismatica Slender blue iris	Moist grasslands, bogs, in strong acid, sandy soil	Beautiful lavender flowers with yellow sepals in early summer; height to 2'	Propagate by division of rhizomes or by seeds
Polygala lutea Yellow milkwort	Bogs, wet, sandy flats	Dense, small yellow-orange flowers in summer; biennial; small rosettes yield next season's blooms; height to 10''	Propagate by seeds
Solidago odoro Sweet goldenrod	Sterile, sandy soil	Fragrant, showy yellow flowers in summer; height to 3'	Propagate by seeds (blooms in second year); can become weedy if soil is too rich

Southeastern Mixed Forest Region

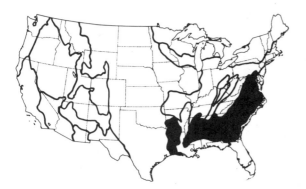

The Southeastern Mixed Forest occurs on the upland Piedmont in the southeastern portions of the United States. The trees are tall, broad-leaved and evergreen species with a rich shrub understory. There are many of the same species as found in the Eastern Deciduous Forest and Coastal Plain regions. Pines are very common, and some unusual species are found mixed in with other hardwoods.

The climate is mild with hot, humid summers and only rare freezes in the winter. Precipitation may reach 60 inches a year in some areas.

TREES

Name	Habitat	Growth Characteristics	Notes
Asimina triloba Pawpaw	Rich woods and alluvium	Upright; large, light green leaves; green-maroon flowers; edible fruits; height to 30'	Propagate by seeds sown in autumn or stratified, by layers or cuttings
Cotinus obovatus American smoke tree	Dry uplands, limestone glades	Shrubby; widespread, pendulous branches; flowers appear like smoke; brilliant autumn color; height to 35'	Propagate by seeds, root cuttings or layers
Ilex cassine Dahoon, cassina	Moist, fertile soils; sometimes on sandy ridges	Rounded crown; slender ascending branches; shrublike; clusters of bright red berries; height to 30'	Propagate by cuttings or stratified seeds
Magnolia grandiflora Southern magnolia	Rich bottomlands, slopes with other hardwoods	Straight trunk; showy, fragrant white flowers; height to 90'	Plant in protected areas, as winds and rain can tear leaves and flowers
Osmanthus americanus Devilwood	Stream banks, swamps; rich, moist soil	Narrow crown; yellowish white, fragrant flowers; height to 70'	Propagate in summer by cuttings
Pinus echinata Shortleaf pine	Dry upland soils	Narrow, pyramidal crown; bark scaly plates; height to 100'	Propagate by seeds Provides food for game birds, rabbits, hares, squirrels and chipmunks
P. Taeda Loblolly pine	Old fields, along streams, mixed with hardwoods	Open crown; long, straight trunk; height to 110'	Fast growing for long periods
Quercus falcata Spanish red oak	Dry, infertile soils of the uplands	Rounded crown; wide-spreading branches; height to 80'	
Ulmus serotina September elm	Limestone soils; bottomlands	Rounded crown; flowers and fruit appear in autumn; height to 40'	Propagate by seeds sown when ripe or by layering; transplants easily Very rare Provides food for songbirds, game birds, squirrels, rabbits, deer and muskrats

SHRUBS

Name	Habitat	Growth Characteristics	Notes
Aristolochia tomentosa Birthwort	Bottomlands	Vigorous climber; yellowish flowers from May to June; height to 30'	Propagate by cuttings, layering or seeds

SHRUBS (continued)

Name	Habitat	Growth Characteristics	Notes
Clematis Viorna Leather flower	Rich, moist soils that are well drained	Climbing; reddish purple flowers from May to August; height to 10'	Propagate by stratified seeds, layering, division or cuttings
Crataegus Marshallii Marshall's hawthorn	Wet areas, along streams	Small tree–shrub; white blossoms in April; fruits like small apples appear in May; height to 20'	Identification of hawthorns is confusing and difficult; they freely hybridize among themselves Provides food for mammals

FORBS

Name	Habitat	Growth Characteristics	Notes
Actaea pachypoda White baneberry	Rich woods	Bright green, compound, toothed leaves; raceme of delicate, ephemeral white flowers in April; white berries, may be poisonous; height to 2'	Propagate by seeds sown in late autumn or by root division in the spring
Asarum virginica Heart-leaf	Moist or dry woods	Spreading; thick, elongated, heart-shaped, evergreen leaves; inconspicuous flower, no petals, from March to May; height to 6''	Propagate by seeds or division
Canna flaccida Golden canna	Freshwater swamps, wet woods, marshes	Erect perennial from rhizomes; large leaves; height to 4'	Propagate by seeds or division of rhizomes Unusual and rare
Centrosema virginianum Climbing butterfly pea	Thin woods, open areas; dry, sandy soils	Climbing perennial; compound leaflet(s); bright pink–white showy flower from March to September	Propagate by seeds
Hisbiscus Moscheutos Swamp rose mallow	Brackish marshes, swamps	Erect perennial; white, sometimes pink, flowers from May to September; height to 2'	Propagate by seeds or division; needs lots of water
Lobelia elongata Purple lobelia	Marshes, swamps, fresh to brackish	Slender perennial with narrow leaves; blossoms from July to November; height to 3½'	Propagate by division or basal offsets; available from wild-flower nurseries
Passiflora incarnata Wild passion-flower	Deciduous woods, roadsides	Vine; unusual multiblossoms, purple, sometimes white, from June to September; edible fruits	Propagate by seeds or cuttings
Ruellia pedunculata Ruellia	Open woods, dry soils of uplands, dry woods	Erect, opposite-leaved perennial, somewhat coarse; light purple blossoms from April to September; height to 3'	Propagate by cuttings, seeds or division
Sarracenia leucophylla Pitcher plant	Low, wet grasslands, bogs	Erect perennial; nodding purplish red-veined white flowers from March to April; quite showy; height to 3'	Propagate by cross-pollinated seeds; available at many nurseries Carnivorous species
Spigelia marilandica Indian pink	Rich woods	Erect perennial; bottle-shaped, brilliant red flowers from April to June	
Thermopsis caroliniana Thermopsis	Open areas, thin, deciduous woods, higher elevations	Upright, unbranched perennial; showy yellow flowers from May to July; height to 5'	Not difficult to cultivate; available from wild-flower growers
Tipularia discolor Cranefly orchid	Not particular, wet to dry, hardwoods to pine	Erect; inconspicuous, pale-colored flowers from June to September; height to 2½'	Common orchid from a corymb Should not be dug from wild

Subtropic Region

The Subtropic Region, despite its very small size—it encompasses only the southern quarter of Florida—has an exceedingly rich and interesting plant life. The flora includes elements of Appalachian and Coastal Plain flora, as well as the rich, tropical West Indian flora. The geology consists of maritime limestones and sands. The soils are sands, clays and mucks, and the climate is Antillean—warm and moist.

While South Florida has one of the most diverse flora, it also has an extensive array of introduced plants, many of which have become serious pests. Its benign climate permits nonnatives to grow rampantly. Lacking natural predators, these should be planted with extreme caution, if at all. Since there is a wealth of native species, there is no need to bring in additional species.

TREES

Name	Habitat	Growth Characteristics	Notes
Annona glabra Pond apple	Along streams and swamps; sometimes pure stands	Widespread crown; contorted branches; trunk consists of a swollen base and narrower bole; yellow-brown 5″ fruit; height to 50′	Propagate by seeds Exotic-looking understory tree; readily grown
Avicennia nitida Black mangrove	Low, muddy shores washed by tides	Widespread, rounded crown; stilt-like roots; height to 30′ (less at northern end of range)	Propagate by seeds Assists land building by accretion Attracts aquatic creatures and birds
Bumelia celastrina Saffron plum	Upland areas, dry woods and thickets; sun/part shade	Rounded crown; graceful, drooping branches with thorns; very fragrant white flowers; height to 20′	Moderately difficult to get established Makes an excellent, impenetrable hedge Provides food for many birds and small mammals
Bursera Simaruba West Indian birch, gumbo-limbo	Sun/shade, hardwood hammocks near tide-water; sandy soils	Rounded crown; horizontal, spreading branches; bark scaly and reddish brown; compound deciduous leaves; upright racemes of greenish flowers appear before leaves; height to 60′	Takes root and grows very quickly
Coccoloba Uvifera Sea grape	Sandy shores and beaches; sun/shade; any soil	Shrubby; height to 25′	Propagate by seeds or cuttings; available at nurseries Susceptible to whitefly and borers Provides fruit for birds
Erythrina herbacea Cardinal-spear	Shell ridges, sandy soils, woods, thickets; sun/partial shade	Shrubby tree with whitish bark; bright red flowers in March before leaves; height to 30′	Propagate by seeds, wood cuttings or transplants Slow growing; makes a good hedge
Ficus aurea Golden fig, strangler fig	Mixed hardwood hammocks	Starts as parasite engulfing host tree; broad, rounded crown; may attain tremendous width; height to 60′	Propagate by layering; can be started from seeds; easy to root (even in water) Roots very invasive Provides fruit for birds and mammals; good nesting tree

TREES (continued)

Name	Habitat	Growth Characteristics	Notes
Lysiloma latisiliqua Sabicu	On hardwood hammocks, sandy soil near salt-water	Wide, flattened crown; horizontal branches; compound leaves; height to 60'	Propagate by seeds or layering
Persea Borbonia Red bay	Rich, moist soils of swamps and flood-plains, mixed with conifers	Beautiful evergreen tree; dense pyramidal crown with ascending branches; aromatic leaves; blue-black fruit; height to 70'	Propagate by seeds or cuttings Fruit attracts birds
Pinus Elliottii Slash pine	Coastal area, hammocks and along streams, swamps	Rounded crown of horizontal (some-times ascending) branches; height to 100'	Propagate by seeds; rapid grower; very vigorous Provides seeds for songbirds and game birds
Sabal Palmetto Cabbage palmetto, cabbage tree	Uplands in sun or shade	Narrow, rounded top; straight bole; height to 50'	Propagate by seeds in mud; easy to transplant even older trees Attracts birds and mammals
Sideroxylon foetidissimum Mastic	Uplands, woods, sun/shade	Rounded crown; ascending branches; leaves flutter (like aspen); height to 70'	Difficult to find; slow growing Provides fruit for birds Becoming scarce; worth growing despite difficulty

Coccoloba Uvifera

Serenoa repens

SHRUBS

Name	Habitat	Growth Characteristics	Notes
Ardisia paniculata Marlberry	Upland woods and thickets, also moist lowlands; sun	Columnar with graceful ascending branches; white, fragrant starlike flowers clustered at branch tip; height to 25'	Propagate by seeds or small seedlings; slow growing
Chiococca alba Snowberry	Sandy soils of upland woods and thickets, usually in light shade	Small shrub to vine; yellow flowers in clusters at leaf axils; white berries in February and March; height to 10'	Propagate by seeds; can be transplanted
Eugenia axillaris White stopper	Upland ridges, woods, thickets, sandy soils near tidewater	Small shrublike tree; scaly bark; inconspicuous white flowers at leaf axils; sweet black berry; height to 30'	Propagate by seeds or cuttings; moderate growing rate Berries attract birds
Serenoa repens Saw palmetto, scrub palmetto	Pine forests, upland sandy soils, roadsides, thickets; sun	Forms large colonies; fanlike, deeply incised leaves with sharp spines; fragrant, creamy-white flowers in upright racemes; height to 25'	Propagate by seeds; can be transplanted Excellent for wild, thickety garden; invasive roots
Sesbania punicea Sesban	Coastal Plain, waste places, hedgerows, roadsides; sun	Compound, dark green leaves; orange-red flowers in drooping clusters; height to 5'	Propagate by seeds

SHRUBS (continued)

Name	Habitat	Growth Characteristics	Notes
Sophora tomentosa Silverbush	Upland woods and thickets	Gracefully arching branches; drooping yellow racemes; height to 8'	Propagate by seeds or small plants; moderately rapid grower May be poisonous to wildlife
Zamia integrifolia Coontie	Well-drained, sandy soils; prefers sun and acid soils	Fernlike foliage radiating out from central point; showy fruit, brown pods/red seeds; height to 3'	Propagate by seeds sown in shallow, protected sand or by suckers when plant is dormant; slow growing

FORBS

Name	Habitat	Growth Characteristics	Notes
Bacopa caroliniana Fragrant bacopa	In muds along the shores of streams, in shallow water	Prostrate; lemon-scented leaves; blue, bell-shaped flowers year-round; height to 5''	
B. Monnieri Water hyssop	Moist depressions, shallow ponds	Succulent plant with creeping stems; forms mats; white/pink, bell-shaped flowers from April to November; height to 5''	Fast growing for difficult places; salt tolerant
Clematis baldwinii Pine hyacinth	Damp pinelands and prairies, fertile	Erect, solitary herb; bluish pink bells blossom in winter and spring; fruit conspicuous as feathery plumes; height to 1½'	Propagate by stratified seeds, layering, division or cuttings
Coreopsis leavenworthii Tickseed	Moist pinelands, disturbed areas, roadsides	Clumps of erect stems; composite flowers at tip, yellow rays with brown disc, bloom year-round; height to 3'	Propagate by seeds, cuttings or division
Crinum americanum Southern swamp crinum	Marshes and ditches; high moisture and sun	Solitary plant with straplike basal leaves; exquisite, fragrant flower, 6 petaled, white and reflexed, others purple, in spring and summer; height to 32''	Propagate by bulb offsets, rarely by seeds; does not transplant well
Cuthbertia rosea Roseling	Open scrublands of palmetto, oak and pine	Erect, grows in clumps; delicate grasslike leaves; pink, crinkled 3-petaled flowers in summer; height to 1'	Not difficult if grown in well-drained, acid soils in sun
Epidendrum conopseum Green-fly orchid	Hardwoods and cypress trees in association with Resurrection fern	Purplish leaves; gray-green, ½''-wide blossom from January to August; height to 8''	Difficult to grow from seed
E. tampense Florida butterfly orchid	In trees of forests and hammocks	Epiphytic; stalks bear 3 to 40 flowers in spring and summer; pseudo-bulbs; height to 30''	*Not to be collected*
Tillandsia fasciculata Wild pineapple	On cypress trees (lives on but is not parasitic)	Stiff, curved leaves; red, green, yellow bracts/violet petals from April to October; height to 2'	Propagate by suckers or sprouts
Zephyranthes grandiflora Zephyr lily	Moist, open pinelands, marsh borders	Stout stalk; basal leaves; white/pink, 3'', 6-petaled flower in spring; blossom lasts only 1 day, usually following a rain; height to 1'	Propagate by bulb offsets

South-Central Swamp Region

Some of the flattest, lowest and youngest land in the United States is along the Mississippi River and its Delta and along the Gulf Coast. It is swamp and bottomland country, with cypress, tupelo, red maple, pumpkin ash, overcup oak and bitter pecan as major tree species. Many of these water-lovers occur in other regions, but nowhere are they so prominent as in Louisiana, east Texas and Arkansas.

Precipitation is high, up to 60 inches a year, and occurs evenly throughout the year. Soils are deep and black, with high fertility. The availability of water, the moderate climate and the vegetation all make this a major wintering area for countless bird populations.

TREES

Name	Habitat	Growth Characteristics	Notes
Acer rubrum var. *Drummondii* Drummond red maple	Deep swamps	Narrow crown; erect, slender branches; bright scarlet flowers and fruit; height to 35'	Propagate by mature or stratified seeds sown in spring Controls erosion by holding banks Many species eat buds; excellent nesting tree
Fraxinus tomentosa Pumpkin ash	Deep river swamps	Narrow, open crown; stout branches; buttressed base of trunk; large leaves for an ash; height to 120'	Attractive landscaping tree if water conditions can be duplicated Winged fruit eaten by many birds and mammals
Gleditsia aquatica Water locust, swamp locust	Deep swamps; often growing together in dense groves	Heavy, contorted branches; stout spines 3''–5'' long on trunk and branches; height to 60'	Propagate by seeds, which should be soaked in hot water prior to planting Needs copious water, but an attractive ornamental that grows fast and has an unusual shape An understory tree to cypress
Nyssa aquatica Cotton gum, tupelo gum	Deep swamps, standing water with cypress	Narrow crown; straight trunk; height to 100'	Propagate by seeds sown in autumn or stratified, or by green-wood cuttings under glass
N. sylvatica Pepperridge, sour gum, black gum	Prefers moist, rich soil, but is also found in uplands	Narrow crown; sometimes crooked with brushy branching; glossy leaves turn glorious scarlet in autumn; height to 90'	Propagate by seeds sown at once or stratified, sometimes by layering
Populus heterophylla Swamp cotton-wood	Rich bottomlands	Clean straight bole, branching at 50'–60'; height to 90'	Propagate by hardwood cuttings or suckers, rarely by seeds Rapid grower; needs high water table Useful for flood and erosion control but limited as an ornamental
Quercus lyrata Overcup oak	Wet, poorly drained clay soils	Irregular open crown; buttressed trunk; drooping branches; large, deeply cut leaves; distinctive acorn; autumn foliage brilliant yellow, orange, scarlet; height to 100'	Propagate by seeds sown in autumn or stratified Very slow growing Vigorous, disease-free and long-lived; excellent ornamental Excellent winter food for many species
Q. prinus Basket oak	Generally moist soils	Compact crown; silvery bark; pinkish foliage in spring, lustrous, dark in summer and deep red in autumn; height to 100'	Propagate by seeds Long-lived, frequently cultivated Sweet, edible acorn attracts mourning doves, wild turkeys and deer

TREES (continued)

Name	Habitat	Growth Characteristics	Notes
Q. virginiana Live oak	Sandy soils (sometimes clay)	Wide crown; massive limbs; narrow, persistent leaves; height to 60′	Propagate by seeds, layering or cuttings Easily transplanted; rapid grower
Taxodium distichum Bald cypress	River swamps, wet banks and depressions	Tall, tapering, buttressed trunk; produces "knees" in wet areas; beautiful soft, light green deciduous foliage; height to 150′	Propagate by seeds

Quercus virginiana   *Forestiera acuminata*   *Nelumbo lutea*

SHRUBS

Name	Habitat	Growth Characteristics	Notes
Cephalanthus occidentalis Buttonbush	Along streams, in swamps, ponds	Upright; attractive deciduous foliage; fragrant, white, ball-shaped flower clusters on long stalks; height to 10′	Propagate by seeds, mature-wood cuttings in autumn or green-wood cuttings in spring Provides food for waterfowl and browsers Tolerant of high water table
Crataegus viridis Green hawthorn	Inundated stream banks, swamps	Rounded, compact head; fluted trunk; forms dense thickets; white flowers in April and May; autumn foliage brilliant scarlet; height to 35′	Propagate by ripe or stratified seeds; takes 2 years to germinate Disease-prone Excellent nesting shrub; provides food for many species of birds
Forestiera acuminata Swamp privet	Along streams, pond edges and swamps	Treelike appearance; forms thickets; small deciduous leaves; inconspicuous yellow-green flowers; purple fruit; height to 25′	Propagate by seeds or layering Provides food for ducks, quail and songbirds Good for the thickety, wild garden, not as a specimen
Hypericum galioides Bedstraw St.-John's-wort	Low, wet pinelands and swamps	Low evergreen shrub; small, bright yellow, 5-petaled flowers in clusters from June to August; height to 4′	Propagate by seeds, green-wood cuttings, division or suckers
Itea virginica Sweetspire	Swamps, stream edges	Deciduous; slender, graceful, with wandlike branches; small white flowers in narrow, upright clusters; foliage brilliant scarlet in autumn; height to 8′	

GRASSES/FORBS

Name	Habitat	Growth Characteristics	Notes
Amsonia Tabernaemontana Bluestar, amsonia	Wet soils of prairie and pinelands	Round cluster of star-shaped flowers from April to May; height to 3′	Propagate by seeds; difficult to move

GRASSES/FORBS (continued)

Name	Habitat	Growth Characteristics	Notes
Boltonia asteroides Boltonia	Wet soils, alluvium	Multibranched, erect perennial; numerous lavender-white flower heads from September to October; height to 6'	Propagate by seeds
Cyperus esculentus Nut grass, nut sedge	Damp, sandy soils	Perennial with narrow, straplike leaves; yellow-brown spikes from August to October; height to 2'	Propagate by division, tubers or seeds sown in spring Can become troublesome as rampant grower
Hymenocallis caroliniana Spider lily	Marshy banks of streams, freshwater swamps, ditches	Erect, fleshy herb; fragrant, showy, glossy leaves; delicate white-purple blossoms from summer to early fall (after leaves have dried up); height to 3'	Propagate by seeds or offsets Does well in garden if water is plentiful
Iris virginica Southern blue flag	Marshes, wet grasslands, shallow water, neutral to moderately acid soil	Shallow rhizomes send up grasslike leaves; flowers in clusters bloom only briefly; height to 3'	Propagate by division Good perennial plant for wet, wild garden
Juncus effusus Soft rush	Peaty swamps and thickets	Slender, wiry perennial; irregular clusters of flowers between 2 thin leaves at top of stem from July to September; height to 2'	Propagate by seeds or division; spreads rapidly
Kosteletzkya virginica Seashore mallow	Fresh to brackish marshes and shores	Erect; gray-green coarse leaves; rose-colored, 5-petaled flower, 4'' across, from July to September; height to 3'	Propagate by seeds or cuttings; easily grown in neutral muddy soil
Lobelia siphilitica Great lobelia	Alluvial soils, swamps, wet grounds	Erect perennial; racemes of pale blue to white flowers from August to September; height to 3'	Propagate by seeds or purchase from nursery; divide plants each spring
Nelumbo lutea American lotus	Ponds, quiet streams, estuaries, freshwater	Fleshy, round leaves; yellow, rounded, 8'' blossoms during the summer; height to 3'	Propagate by division of rhizomes or by seeds sown in shallow pan; easily grown and very desirable Moderately attractive for waterfowl, game birds, songbirds and mammals
Nemastylis acuta Prairie iris	Sandy soils of pinelands	Erect perennial from bulb; strongly parallel, veined leaves; delicate, light-blue flowers from April to May; height to 2'	Propagate by bulb offsets or seeds; short-lived
Nuphar advena Cow lily, spatterdock	Swamps, tidal waters, ponds, fresh muddy water	Fleshy, large round leaves; yellow, 3'', 5- to 6-petaled blossoms from June to August; height to 6'' above water	Propagate by seeds Rapid spreading, only for larger ponds
Nymphaea odorata Fragrant white water lily	Lakes, ponds, stream margins	Fleshy flower held above the water; rounded, deeply notched leaves; white-pink blossoms in summer	Propagate by seeds; easily and extensively cultivated
Pontederia cordata Pickerel weed	Fresh marshes and swamps, shallow water, mud	Erect, stout stems; fleshy heart-shaped leaves; lavender-blue spikes from June to August; height to 3½'	Propagate by division; a must for large bog gardens
Sagittaria graminea var. *platyphylla* Arrowhead, swamp potato	Swamps, marshes, along bayous in shallow water	Erect, fleshy, long-stemmed plants from tubers; 3-petaled, white 1½'' flowers from July to September; height to 3'	Propagate by seeds, division or underground tubers Desirable plant for bog gardens Attractive to waterfowl, marsh birds and shorebirds
Typha latifolia Common cattail	Fresh to intermediate marshes	Upright with narrow leaves; minute flowers on long spikes from May to July; height to 8'	Propagate by division Valuable winter cover; provides food for muskrats and geese Controls erosion

Prairie Region

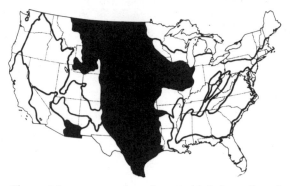

The prairie occurs as a broad vertical belt from Canada to Texas at mid-continent. Grass is the principal vege-

tation, and its height correlates closely with moisture availability. Broad-leaved flowering forbs are generously scattered throughout the grasslands, and most bloom in late summer. Few trees and shrubs occur here, and those that do are largely concentrated in depressions and along swales and streams.

Twenty to 40 inches of rainfall, with balanced evaporation, falls in this region. Soils are deep, friable and fertile, and the topography is gently rolling.

The major divisions of this region are (1) Prairie Parkland, which occurs from Illinois to the Gulf Coast, (2) Prairie Brush, which extends from the western end of the Coastal Plain to the Great Plains, (3) the Great Plains, which includes Oklahoma, west Iowa, the Dakotas, Nebraska, Kansas, Montana, Wyoming and Colorado, where water is not adequate for demands.

TREES—Prairie Brush

Name	Habitat	Growth Characteristics	Notes
Carya illinoinensis Pecan	Rich floodplains	Symmetrical; broad, rounded crown; buttressed trunk; height to 150′	Propagate by stratified seeds sown in spring; rapid grower Prey to tent caterpillars, bark beetles Provides nuts for birds, squirrels, opossums, raccoons and peccaries
Cotinus Coggygria Smoke tree	Rocky woodlands, limestone soils	Widely spreading crown; pendulous branches; scaly bark; hazy appearance of flowers looks like smoke; height to 35′	Propagate by seeds, root cuttings or layering Commonly cultivated; never abundant in wild
Juniperus Ashei Ashe juniper, Ozark white cedar	Limestone hills, forming dense breaks	Rounded crown; bushy tree with several trunks; aromatic shredding bark; height to 40′	Propagate by seeds or cuttings Useful for erosion control and windbreaks
Maclura pomifera Osage orange	Varied; rich bottomlands, old fields	Open, rounded crown; short trunk with ascending branches; attractive orange bark; height to 50′	Propagate by seeds Provides food for bobwhites and squirrels Use male for landscaping to avoid the large green fruits, which can be messy
Ulmus crassifolia Cedar elm	Limestone soils, slopes and bottomlands	Rounded or narrow crown; pendulous, winged, corky branches; small, toothed leaves; height to 90′	Propagate by ripe seeds, layering in autumn Provides food for songbirds and game birds Immune to Dutch elm disease; tolerates dry spells

TREES—Prairie Parkland

Name	Habitat	Growth Characteristics	Notes
Aesculus glabra Ohio buckeye	Rich, moist soil of floodplains, mountain slopes	Tall, straight bole; blunt, pendulous branches; pale yellow-green, upright racemes of flowers; height to 70′	Propagate by seeds or stratified seeds sown in autumn Fruit and flaking bark poisonous
Celtis occidentalis Hackberry	Riverbanks, hillsides	Rounded crown; slender trunk; height to 60′	Propagate by seeds, layering or cuttings in autumn Provides food for birds and mammals Can withstand harsh conditions

TREES—Prairie Parkland (continued)

Name	Habitat	Growth Characteristics	Notes
Cercis canadensis Eastern redbud	Edges of streams, rich bottomland soil; fertile sandy loam	Understory tree; wide, flat crown; straight bole; heart-shaped foliage; scaly, red-brown bark; showy pink-purple (rarely white) flowers on branches before leaves; bright yellow autumn color; height to 50′	Propagate by seeds sown in spring (in heat) or by layering
Platanus occidentalis Sycamore, buttonwood, American plane	Borders of lakes and rivers, rich bottom-lands	Open, irregular crown (sometimes to 100′); massive; huge, spreading limbs; often a divided, clay-colored trunk with flaking bark; height to 170′	Propagate by seeds, layering or cuttings under glass; transplants well Provides food for finches and mammals Frequently disfigured by anthracnose
Quercus macrocarpa Bur oak, mossy-cup oak	Low, rich bottomlands	Broad crown (70′); massive branches; often as broad as tall; tremendous root systems; height to 170′	Propagate by seeds sown in autumn or stratified Provides food for waterfowl, marsh and game birds and songbirds

TREES—Great Plains

Name	Habitat	Growth Characteristics	Notes
Bumelia lanuginosa Chittamwood, false buckthorn	Along streams; limestone soils	Rounded crown; tall, straight trunk; resembles live oak but loses its leaves; height to 80′	Transplants easily when small; slow growing but durable
Populus Sargentii Great Plains cottonwood	Along streams	Broad, open crown; widely spreading branches; massive trunk; height to 90′	Propagate by hardwood cuttings or suckers, rarely seeds; resilient and vigorous though short-lived Provides cover and seeds for woodpeckers, starlings, owls, bluebirds and meadowlarks
Prosopis glandulosa Mesquite	Variable	Loose crown; divided trunk; slender branches; scaly, red-brown bark; pinnately compounded foliage thin and lacy; thick taproot can extend 40′ down; fragrant, greenish white flowers; height to 50′	Propagate by seeds Provides food for livestock, game birds, some other birds and mammals
Quercus macrocarpa var. *depressa* Shrubby bur oak	Dry uplands	Shrubby with corky branches; height to 8′	Propagate by seeds sown in autumn or stratified

SHRUBS

Name	Habitat	Growth Characteristics	Notes
Amorpha canescens Lead plant	Dry hillsides and prairies	Deciduous subshrub; purplish blue blossoms in terminal racemes up to 6″ long from June to August; height to 3′	Propagate by seeds or cuttings. May be difficult to find
A. fruticosa var. *angustifolia* Bastard indigo	Stream banks, open woods, rich thickets in moist calcareous soils	Deciduous; violet purple blossoms in terminal racemes from April to June; height to 9′	Propagate by seeds, suckers or layering Excellent for flood control
Cornus sericea Red-osier dogwood	Wet, swamp areas, shores and thickets	Spreading, ascending, bright red branches; cyme of white showy bracts from May to August; white with lead-colored fruit; height to 9′	Propagate by mature-wood cuttings or layering; vigorous grower
Prunus angustifolia Chickasaw plum	Dry thickets and woods, waste places	Twiggy, thicket forming; white blossoms from March to April; height to 25′	Propagate by seeds sown in autumn or stratified until spring Edible fruit for game birds, songbirds and mammals, especially foxes

SHRUBS (continued)

Name	Habitat	Growth Characteristics	Notes
P. Munsoniana Wild-goose plum	Stream banks; rich alluvial soils	Forms dense thickets; thin, glossy leaves; white petals from April to May	Propagate by seeds sown in autumn or stratified until spring

Carya illinoinensis   *Prunus angustifolia*

FORBS

Name	Habitat	Growth Characteristics	Notes
Allium cernuum Nodding wild onion	Sunny, partially shaded; rocky or gravelly slopes	Solitary; fleshy stem and leaves; white/pink/purple flowers in umbels in summer; height to 1'	Propagate by bulbs planted in autumn, which increase rapidly, by seeds sown in spring or by offsets
Anemone caroliniana Prairie windflower	Sandy or gravelly prairies, openings; calcareous soil	Erect stems; basal leaves; greenish white to purplish blossoms from April to June; height to 10''	Propagate by seeds, division or bulbs
A. cylindrica Long-headed anemone, thimbleweed	Dry, well-drained slopes; sterile soils	Finely cut leaves at about 1½' on erect, stout stalk; greenish white sepals in summer; whole plant woolly with dense gray hairs; height to 3'	Propagate by seeds or division in early spring
Arenaria stricta Rock sandwort	Gravel slopes, prairies; neutral, dry soil	White blossoms in summer; height to 10''	Propagate by division, cuttings or seeds; readily grown
Asclepias incarnata Swamp milkweed	Wet grasslands, floodplains	Red/purple, ⅜'' blossom from July to August; height to 4'	Propagate by seeds; difficult to transplant
Aster sagittifolius Arrow-leaved aster	Moist grasslands, low places, waste areas	Upright; blossoms with light blue/purple or yellow rays in fall; height to 4½'	Propagate by seeds or spring division (for bloom the following year)
Baptisia bracteata Wild indigo	Dry grasslands; neutral soil	Divided leaves; drooping flowers in light yellow racemes from May to June; height to 32''	Propagate by seeds or division; readily grown in dry, sunny areas
B. leucantha White wild indigo	Rocky areas, dry, sandy soil	Erect, bushy plant; compound leaves; white blossoms from June to July; height to 6'	Propagate by seeds or division; easily grown perennial for sunny, dry, well-drained areas
Callirhoe digitata Wine cup, poppy mallow	Dry plains and prairies; rocky limestone soils	Branching, slender herbs; deeply incised leaves; bloom from April to July; height to 20''	Propagate by seeds; easily grown
Castilleja coccinea Indian-paintbrush	Gravelly or sandy prairies; full sun	Perennial; scarlet blossom from May to June; showy bracts; height to 15''	Difficult to cultivate because of its parasitic nature

FORBS (continued)

Name	Habitat	Growth Characteristics	Notes
Delphinium virescens Prairie larkspur	Prairies, open woods; neutral to slightly acid soil	Erect, stout stems, unbranched; narrow leaves; whitish blue, 2'' blossoms in summer; height to 4'	Propagate by seeds for bloom the following year, also division
Desmodium canadense Canada tick trefoil	Wet prairies	Tall, branching plant; 3-parted foliage; pink/purple flowers in terminal racemes from July to August; height to 6'	Propagate by seeds
Echinacea angustifolia Narrow-leaved purple coneflower	Dry prairies, barrens	Erect, slender stem; solitary flowers with drooping, purple/crimson rays and yellow disc from May to October; height to 2'	Propagate by seeds or division; vigorous; can be transplanted
E. purpurea Purple coneflower	Dry prairies, openings, open woods, eroded lands	Coarse, stiff stems; solitary 3'' flowers with purple/pink rays and brown discs from June to October; height to 5'	Propagate by seeds or division; can be transplanted
Eryngium Leavenworthii Leavenworth's eryngo	Dry, open areas	Erect, stout stem; spiny, thistlelike leaves; metallic violet blossom from July to October; height to 4'	Propagate by seeds or division of clumps
Euphorbia corollata Flowering spurge	Prairies, clearings, fields, roadsides, open woods	Upright; branching near end of stem; inflorescence of white petallike flowers from June to October; height to 3'	Propagate by seeds; easily grown
E. marginata Snow-on-the-mountain	Dry grasslands; neutral soils	Erect; annual; green flowers with showy white bracts from summer to autumn; height to 2''	Propagate by seeds; easily grown Milky sap may cause skin burns
Eustoma grandiflorum Prairie gentian	Low, limestone prairies, rich meadows	Erect; purple-blue, 3'' bloom from May to August; height to 3'	Propagate by seeds; cannot be transplanted
Filipendula rubra Queen-of-the-prairie	Moist grasslands, thickets; neutral to mildly acid soil	Bushy; coarse divided leaves; numerous fragrant pink flowers in a terminal inflorescence from May to July; height to 5''	Propagate by seeds or division; easily grown
Gaillardia pulchella Blanket flower	Dry prairies, openings, wide distribution	Multistemmed; numerous red, yellow-purple flowers with purplish brown disc from May to September; height to 15''	Propagate by seeds or cuttings; easily grown
Geum triflorum Three-flowered avens, prairie smoke	Dry to wet prairies; sandy soils	Branched stem; lobed leaves; white ½'' flowers in summer; pink plumed fruit; height to 2'	Propagate by seeds or division; easily grown
Helianthus salicifolius Prairie sunflower	Sandy soils of prairies, roadsides, plains	Erect stems, multibranched; flowers in compact heads from June to September; height to 3'	Propagate by seeds; easily grown Attractive to birds
Isopyrum biternatum Midland isopyrum	Moist soils in grasslands and woods; neutral soil	Few leaves; delicate, short-lived flowers in spring; pear-shaped fruits; height to 16''	Propagate by seeds or division
Liatris punctata Blazing-star, button snakeroot	Dry prairies, hillsides, plains	Perennial; upright; multiflowered spikes with purple bristly flowers from August to October; height to 2½'	Propagate by seeds or division; easily grown
Lupinus texensis Texas bluebonnet	Prairies, dry openings	Erect; palmate leaves; deep blue flowers with dense racemes in May; height to 2'	Propagate by seeds Readily available seeds; somewhat hard to grow

FORBS (continued)

Name	Habitat	Growth Characteristics	Notes
Mentzelia decapetala Prairie lily	Dry upland prairies, rocky plains	Erect, coarse, branching plants; creamy flowers open in the evening from June to August; height to 2'	Propagate by seeds
Penstemon arkansanus Arkansas beard-tongue	Sandy open prairies	Perennial; erect; white, slightly purple, 2'' trumpet-shaped flowers in loose racemes from May to July; height to 3'	Propagate by seeds; easily grown
P. Cobaea Cobaia penstemon, beard-tongue	Plains, prairies, rocky openings, ledges	Erect; sparingly branched; stout stems; white, purple, violet tubular flowers in terminal clusters from May to June; height to 2'	Propagate by seeds
Petalostemon purpureum Purple prairie clover	Prairies, dry, open woods, hillsides	Upright; rose, crimson flower from June to September; height to 3'	Propagate by seeds; easy to grow
Phlox pilosa Hairy phlox	Prairies, dry woods, openings	Slender stems; clusters of blue/pink flowers at stem tip from April to June; height to 1½'	Propagate by seeds
Salvia coccinea Scarlet sage	Limestone hills, grasslands	Erect perennial; square stem; red flowers arranged in raceme in summer; height to 2½'	Propagate by seeds
Sisyrinchium campestre Blue-eyed grass	Dry, upland meadows, prairies; sunlight	Erect; blue/purple/white, 6-petaled flower with yellow eye from May to July; height to 16''	Propagate by seeds
Sphaeralcea coccinea Prairie mallow	Sandy plains	Erect, 5-petaled, reddish orange, yellow-eyed ¾'' flower, densely clustered at stem terminus, from May to August; height to 1'	Propagate by seeds, division or softwood cuttings
Stillingia sylvatica Queen's-delight	Prairies, rocky hillsides on sandy soils	Terminal spikes on stout stems; bright green sessile leaves; yellow blossom from May to July; height to 4'	Propagate by seeds
Verbena bipinnatifida Dakota vervain	Gravelly prairies; limestone soils	Forms mats; bluish/reddish/purple flowers from April to September; height to 1½'	Propagate by seeds
Veronia Baldwinii Western ironweed	Rich, low ground, prairies, pastures	Much branched; clusters of purple, ½'' terminal flowers from July to September; height to 6'	Propagate by seeds, division or cuttings
Yucca glauca Soapweed	Dry plains; sandy soils	Perennial; rigid stem; creamy white, 2½'' flowers from April to June; height to 1½'	Propagate by seeds, offsets, cuttings, stems, rhizomes or roots; easily grown

Rocky Mountain Evergreen Forest Region

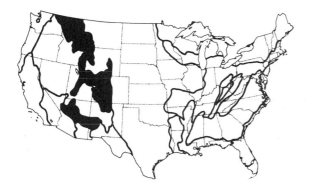

This is a beautiful, rugged area of high peaks, shallow soils and extensive evergreen forest. Vegetation zones correlate closely with altitude. There are mostly stunted trees, grasses and forbs in the alpine zone above 11,500 feet. From 11,500 to 9,000 feet there is the dense forest of Engelmann spruce and firs of the Canadian Zone. The Transition Zone, which consists of lodgepole pine, aspen, yellow pine and Douglas fir extends to 6,500 feet.

The climate of the area depends on altitude. Snowfall at the top may exceed 20 feet, while at lower altitudes, precipitation may be meager. Frost-free areas vary from 40 days to 120 days.

Soils at higher elevations, where precipitation is greater, are acid, but become more alkaline at lower, drier elevations. Mostly soils are shallow and, in places, highly erodible.

TREES

Name	Habitat	Growth Characteristics	Notes
Abies lasiocarpa Alpine fir	High, mountainous areas, cold and humid on variable soils	Pyramidal; height to 100'	Propagate by seeds Tolerates poor soil, wet or dry conditions, cool temperatures
Picea engelmannii Engelmann spruce	Highest forest environment, cold and humid on moderately deep soils	Pyramidal crown; graceful pendant branches; forms great forests; height to 160'	Propagate by seeds; slow growing, long-lived; vigorous Foliage has unpleasant odor Seeds attract Fremont chickaree, western chipmunk and rodents; ideal for nesting, roosting and winter cover
P. pungens Colorado spruce, Colorado blue spruce	Dry mountain ridges, 6,000'–11,000'	Pyramidal; height to 100'	Propagate by seeds; grows quickly Susceptible to many pests; loses lower branches when mature Provides nesting, roosting, winter cover and food for songbirds, game birds, squirrels and other mammals
Pinus contorta Lodgepole pine	Mountainous regions on fairly dry, cool eastern or northern slopes	Pyramidal shape; straight bole; closed cones that open with fire; height to 100'	Propagate by seeds Tolerates poor soils and harsh conditions; does not prune well
P. flexilis Limber pine	Eastern slopes, 5,000'–12,000'	Pyramidal when young, flat topped when mature; height to 75'	Propagate by seeds Attracts songbirds, game birds, mammals and browsers
Populus tremuloides Quaking aspen	Moist sandy and gravelly soils of hillsides in Rockies, prefers deeper soils	Loose and open rounded crown; slender trunk; pendulous branches; beautiful white bark; yellow autumn color; height to 90'	Propagate by hardwood cuttings or suckers; occasionally by seeds Large specimen susceptible to storm breakage and disease Provides food for grouse, browsers, rabbits, beavers and porcupines
Pseudotsuga Menziesii Douglas fir	Mountainous regions of moderate, humid climate on well-drained soils	Pyramidal; dense; unique pendulous cones; height to 300'	Propagate by seeds; grows moderately fast; can be pruned Fairly free of disease Provides food for grouse, songbirds, mammals and browsers (especially white-tailed deer)

Pseudotsuga Menziesii

Arctostaphylos Uva-ursi

SHRUBS

Name	Habitat	Growth Characteristics	Notes
Arctostaphylos Uva-ursi Common bearberry	Dry, open woods; gravelly, sandy soil (typically with Ponderosa pine)	Prostrate, matted evergreen shrub; numerous leathery leaves; pink/rose tubular blossoms from May to June; height to 1'	Propagate by seeds, cuttings of half-ripened wood or layering; withstands dry conditions well; requires poor soils to grow well Valuable ground cover Provides valuable winter food for wildlife
Crataegus rivularis River hawthorn	Streamsides, ponds, hillsides to 8,500'	Deciduous; shrubby; beautiful, fragrant white flowers in clusters in May; small, dark purple, apple-like fruit; height to 25'	Propagate by seeds sown when ripe or stratified; easily transplanted
Fragaria vesca Strawberry	Moist soils up to timberline, woods and meadows, rocky areas	Attractive deciduous ground cover; spreads by runners; blooms all summer; height to 1'	Propagate by division of runners; not difficult to grow in open, stony, well-drained places
Juniperus communis Common juniper	Poor, rocky soil	Irregular, open head; slender branches; reddish bark; aromatic fruits; height rarely to 20'	Propagate by seeds Controls erosion
Kalmia poliifolia Bog kalmia	Wet soil, timberline, cold climate	Slender, erect; pink/rose blossoms from June to August; height to 24'	Propagate by seeds sown in pans, by cuttings of half-ripened wood or layering Won't survive transplanting from the wild
Lonicera ciliosa Honeysuckle	Moist soil; woods, hillsides	Trailing, climbing, attractive ornamental; more or less evergreen; yellow/orange bloom from May to July	Propagate by seeds sown in autumn or stratified, by cuttings or layering
Paxistima myrsinites Oregon box wood	Rich, moist, acid soil; semishade	Densely matting; evergreen leaves; brown/yellowish/red inconspicuous blossoms from May to June	Propagate by seeds, layering or cuttings under glass Requires shade; excellent ground cover in acid, moist soil
Sambucus pubens American red elderberry	Moist streamsides, woods, grassy areas	Deciduous, shrubby; beautiful white flowers in flat clusters from June to July; edible fruit from August to September; height to 10'	Propagate by seeds or cuttings, sometimes by suckers Attracts songbirds and grouse
Shepherdia canadensis Buffalo berry, soapberry	Dry, alkaline soils, open areas	Rangy; silvery foliage; beautiful berries in early summer; height to 7'	Propagate by seeds sown in autumn or stratified Needs both sexes to produce berries Inclines to leggy growth; may be pruned

SHRUBS (continued)

Name	Habitat	Growth Characteristics	Notes
Vaccinium scoparium Grouseberry, little-leaf huckleberry, also *V. ovalifolium* blueberry	Thickets, open woods and peaty slopes	Erect; broomlike branches; small leaves; exfoliating bark; bears fruit from July to September; height to 5½′	Propagate by division, layering or cuttings; needs acid soil

FORBS

Name	Habitat	Growth Characteristics	Notes
Anemone multifida Anemone	High valleys and mountains	Slender stemmed with basal leaves; purple-red blooms from mid-July to mid-August; height to 1′	Propagate by seeds sown in cool, moist, partially shaded areas
Aquilegia caerulea Blue columbine	Moist to wet soil on rockslides and outcrops, shady open woods	Slender stem; rounded, deeply incised leaves; 2″ flowers with white/blue sepals and cream/blue petals from June to August; height to 2′	Propagate by seeds Easy to grow in shady, well-drained, moist soil
Chimaphila umbellata Pipsissewa, prince's pine	Moist, coniferous woods, along streams, to about 8,000′	Evergreen semishrub; leathery, dark green leaves; white/pink, nodding, waxy flowers from June to August; height to 14″	Difficult to transplant; needs acid soil and shade
Clintonia uniflora Bride's-bonnet	Moist soils under conifers, occasionally along streams	Slender stalk; fleshy, rounded, straplike leaves; spreading; blooms from May to July; height to 8″	Propagate by root division or seeds in shaded areas; cool, moist but well-drained areas
Erythronium grandiflorum Avalanche lily	Moist, rich soil, to 12,000′	Leafless stem; oblong basal leaves; yellow, nodding flower from April to August	Propagate by seeds or offsets Will thrive with ample water, cool temperatures and rich soil
Gentianopsis thermalis Western fringed gentian	Wet soils up to 13,000′, meadows, hillsides near water	Annual; bluish purple 1″ flowers from June to August; height to 16″	Propagate by seeds as soon as ripe, by cuttings or root division Prey to pests and fungus in gardens
Ipomopsis aggregata Scarlet gilia	Dry soils up to timberline; variable, does well on ridges, valleys, meadows	Biennial; trumpet-shaped scarlet 1½″ flowers (sometimes pink/orange/white) from May to July; height to 3′	Propagate by seeds; blooms the following year Unpleasant leaf odor
Phlox multiflora Phlox	Open woods, grassy meadows; moist to medium-dry soil	Matting; short, upright branches with many flowers from May to July; height to 1′	Propagate by seeds or division of clumps Does well in moist, partially shaded garden with good air circulation
Xerophyllum tenax Elk grass, bear grass	Open mountain meadows, slopes	Slender stem; grasslike leaves; large raceme of white flowers from June to September (depending on elevation); height to 3′	Difficult to cultivate Does not flower each year Provides seeds for elk, small rodents, goats, bears and other mammals

Great Basin Region

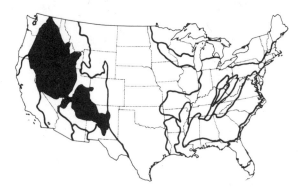

Nevada, Utah, Colorado, Arizona and New Mexico have 200,000 square miles of basins with interior drainage and mountains rising steeply out of the plains. Sagebrush is the dominant shrub, while shadscale, rabbit bush and greasewood also occur on the poorly drained, highly alkaline soil. Small mammals such as squirrels, rabbits, kangaroo mice, wood rats and foxes are common.

There is a fairly wide range of temperatures here, with hot summers and moderately cold winters. Precipitation is low, with a maximum of 20 inches annually and almost no rainfall to counteract summer heat. Water is scarce, with demand exceeding supply throughout the Great Basin.

TREES

Name	Habitat	Growth Characteristics	Notes
Acer Negundo Box elder	Damp soils of canyons, along streams	Rounded crown; short irregular trunk; wide spreading branches, height to 40'	Propagate by seeds sown soon after maturity or stratified and sown in spring Hardiest of maples, withstanding wide temperature extremes and dry soils, but short-lived Provides food for mice, squirrels and birds
A. saccharum subsp. *grandidentatum* Big-tooth maple, Rocky Mountain sugar maple	Damp soils of canyons, along streams	Rounded crown; wide spread branches; beautiful red autumn color; height to 50'	Propagate by seeds sown soon after maturity or stratified and sown in spring Provides food for deer and livestock
Amelanchier utahensis Serviceberry	Dry areas and hillsides of pinyon-juniper, 2,500'-7,000'	Shrublike; edible fruits	Susceptible to a rust
Cercocarpus montanus Mountain mahogany	Canyons, hillsides of pinyon-juniper; 4,300'-6,800'	Stout branches, wide spreading; height to 25'	Interesting seed with tapering plume

Cercocarpus montanus

TREES (continued)

Name	Habitat	Growth Characteristics	Notes
Fraxinus anomala Single-leaf ash	Dry, rocky soils; hillsides and canyons	Shrublike; reddish bark; thin, leathery leaves; height to 20'	Controls erosion
Juniperus monosperma Cherrystone juniper	Semiarid, rocky soils, grows in areas of lower elevations than *Fraxinus anomala*, 3,000'-7,000'	Gnarled trunk; branches near ground; height to 30'	Propagate by seeds or cuttings Common scrub tree
J. scopulorum Colorado red cedar, Rocky Mountain juniper	Mountain slopes, foothills, mesas, 5,000'-9,000'	Conical shaped; drooping, flattened branches; shreddy bark; height to 40'	Aromatic
Pinus monophylla Single-leaf pinyon, pinyon pine	Dry, gravelly slopes and mesas, 7,000'	Rounded crown; pendulous branches; height to 50'	Propagate by seeds
Populus Fremontii Fremont cotton-wood	Moist soils along streams	Flattened crown; wide spread branches; gray-brown trunk; height to 100'	Propagate by hardwood cuttings, suckers or seeds Largest tree in the Great Basin; rapid grower

SHRUBS

Name	Habitat	Growth Characteristics	Notes
Agave utahensis Utah agave	Arid, well-drained lands	Succulent basal leaves with spines; 20' yellow flower spikes appear once, after 8 to 10 years	Propagate by suckers, root division or stem buds Plant dies after flowering
Arctostaphylos pungens Mexican manzanita	Chaparral, dry plains	Twisted shape; bluish green evergreen leaves; nodding pink flowers from March to April; height to 5'	Common shrub
Artemisia tridentata Common sage-brush	High plains; fertile soil	Rounded shrub; grayish silver leaves; purple shaggy bark; greenish yellow flower from summer to fall; height to 12'	Propagate by seeds or division; strongly aromatic
Ceanothus Greggii Redroot desert ceanothus	Lower elevations of pinyon-juniper, 3,000'-5,300'	Rounded, compact; rigid branches; opposite gray-green leaves; white, rarely blue/pink fluffy clusters of fragrant flowers from March to April, sometimes through summer; height to 5'	Propagate by seeds sown in autumn or by cuttings Deer attracted to leaves
Chamaebatiaria millefolium Desertsweet	Rocky, gravelly soils, pinyon-juniper area, 4,000'-7,000'	Compact; rounded and much branched; profusion of tiny daisy-like flowers from July to November	Propagate by seeds or cuttings of half-ripened wood
Echinocereus viridiflorus Green pitaya	Dry slopes of pinyon-juniper belt	Tiny-ridged cactus; green flowers encircle plant from May to June; sharp spines; height to 3''	Propagate by seeds
Fallugia paradoxa Apache-plume	Dry chaparral, mesas and washes, 3,700'-8,000'	Somewhat straggly; evergreen leaves; white flowers from April to October can be very large if rain is plentiful; seeds with fluffy plumes; height to 5'	Propagate by seeds
Ipomoea leptophylla Bush moonflower	Dry slopes up to 7,000'	Low-spreading shrub; forms dense clumps; narrow leaves; magenta flowers in summer; height to 2'	Propagate by seeds; can become rampant Huge root enables plant to store water and withstand long periods of drought
Philadelphus microphyllus Mock orange	Dry, gravelly soils	Much branched; flaking bark; white flowers from June to July; height to 4'	Propagate by seeds, cuttings, layering or suckers

SHRUBS (continued)

Name	Habitat	Growth Characteristics	Notes
Sarcobatus vermiculatus Greasewood	Wet, alkaline soils; 1,000'-6,000'	Spreading branches; succulent leaves; inconspicuous green flowers from June to September; height to 10'	Valuable winter food for many creatures
Symphoricarpos oreophilus Mountain snow-berry	Higher elevations of the foothills, dry, gravelly soils of canyons	Erect, multibranched shrub; paired tubular pink flowers from May to August; waxy white berries; height to 4½'	Propagate by seeds, cuttings, suckers or division

FORBS

Name	Habitat	Growth Characteristics	Notes
Aquilegia triternata Red columbine	Rocky slopes	Solitary erect perennial; red/yellow nodding flowers from June to October; height to 1'	Requires some shade, moisture
Claytonia rosea Spring-beauty	Shady areas with rich, moist soil	Succulent plant from bulb; pink flowers from April to May; height to 4''	Propagate by seeds
Datura meteloides Datura	Lower elevations	Creeping annual; forms clumps; white flowers from May to October open night/morning; height to 4'	Propagate by seeds
Epipactis gigantea Helleborine	Moist rich soil of pinyon-juniper areas	Slender stems; irregular greenish flowers with purple veins from June to July; height to 3'	Difficult to propagate by seeds; cannot be transplanted satisfactorily
Geranium caespitosum Wild cranesbill	Rich soils in the pinyon-juniper belt	Slender stems, branched; incised leaves; beautiful pink flowers from June to September; interesting seed pods; height to 2'	Propagate by seeds Provides forage for sheep
Ipomopsis aggregata Skyrocket gilia	Well-drained slopes, 5,000'-8,000'	Upright solitary plant; pink/red tubular flowers near end of stems from June to August; 3-parted capsules; height to 8''	Propagate by seeds
Monarda pectinata Horsemint	Sandy soils	Perennial; square stems; white flowers clustered with leaves along stem from August to October; height to 4½'	Propagate by spring division; slightly aromatic
Pedicularis racemosa Lousewort, wood betony	Shady, well-drained slopes of pinyon-juniper, 7,000'	Basal, fernlike leaves; purplish, irregular flowers in a spike in June; height to 20''	May be hard to cultivate; partially parasitic on other plant roots
Penstemon Palmeri Wild snapdragon	Arroyos, roadsides, sandy soils, 6,500'	Perennial; attractive white-tinged pink flowers from May to September; height to 4½'	Propagate by seeds or division
Petrophytum caespitosum Rock spiraea	Rocky limestone slopes, appears as if growing without soil, in sun	Low, matting perennial; spikes of fluffy white flowers about 5'' from July to September; height to 3''	Propagate by seeds or division; rare; may be difficult to find
Townsendia exscapa Easter daisy	Dry hillsides, mesas, to 7,000'	Mat forming; covered with purplish flowers from March to July; height to 5''	Propagate by seeds

Desert Region

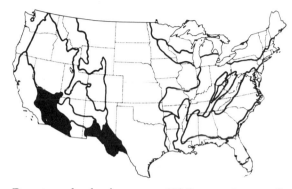

Deserts are lands of extremes. While water is normally very scarce (often less than 7 inches a year), rains can be torrential, causing severe flash flooding. In the summers the sun is very strong and shade almost nonexistent; in the winters there can be bitter cold and piercing winds. Substrates range from cementlike pavements to drifting sands and are frequently highly alkaline.

The plants that live in these environments have made many fundamental adaptations, such as widespread or deeply penetrating root systems, succulent, water-conserving leaves and stems, and seeds that are viable for many years.

There are two major desert areas in the United States. These are (1) the American Desert, which includes the Mojave, the Colorado and the Sonoran deserts of California, Arizona, Nevada and Utah; and (2) the Chihuahuan Desert, which includes southern New Mexico and western Texas.

In the American Desert, precipitation is between 2 and 10 inches annually and does not occur predictably anywhere in the province. In Death Valley, temperatures up to 134°F. (56.7°C.) have been recorded, and occasionally frosts have occurred during the winters.

In the Chihuahuan Desert heavy but brief rains occur during the long and hot summers. In winters, though short, below-freezing temperatures may occur.

TREES

Name	Habitat	Growth Characteristics	Notes
Bursera microphylla Elephant tree	Dry, gravelly or rocky areas; extreme acidity	Reddish brown twigs; enlarged trunk; shredding bark; spicy odor; blue fruits; height to 30'	Stores water in swollen trunk and branches
Carnegiea gigantea Giant saguaro	Warm, arid areas near arroyos	Upright; definite trunk; showy white flowers; height to 50'	Extremely difficult to cultivate; does not survive transplanting Long-lived (up to 250 years); becoming rare
Cercidium floridum Blue palo verde	Along washes of warm deserts, low sandy areas, rocky hillsides	Broad crown; green bark; small compound leaves; yellow flowers from April to May; large brown pods; height to 30'	Leafless during most of the year
Dalea spinosa Smoke tree	Sandy arroyos	Shrublike; few leaves; pale, silvery color of trunk and branches gives it the appearance of smoke; deep blue, pealike flowers; height to 20'	
Olneya Tesota Ironwood	Along gravelly or sandy arroyos below 2,000'; hot southern desert	Wide-spreading crown; blue-green leaves; purple, drooping flowers; height to 27'	One of the largest trees of the desert
Yucca brevifolia Joshua tree	High deserts (3,000'-4,500'), dry slopes, hot, dry areas	Weird, contorted branches; dark brown bark; stiff, bluish green leaves; cream colored/reddish flowers in tight clusters; height to 30'	Provides food for red-shafted flickers, downy woodpeckers, flycatchers, titmice and wood rats
Y. elata Soapweed yucca	Dry, hot deserts, high plains, arid grasslands, gravelly mesas	Trunklike stem; green/white leaves; fragrant white flowers in panicles from May to June; height to 30'	Easy to grow
Y. Torreyi Torrey yucca	Dry, hot deserts	Usually single trunk; smaller than *Yucca elata* with more slender and longer leaves; height to 24'	Easy to grow

Dalea spinosa   *Baileya multiradiata*

SHRUBS

Name	Habitat	Growth Characteristics	Notes
Artemisia tridentata Common sagebrush	Throughout arid Southwest	Erect, much branched; inconspicuous greenish white flower; height to 8'	Vigorous and good for very difficult places; not very ornamental
Dalea Schottii Indigo bush	Hillsides, rocky arroyos	Erect, multibranched; beautiful lavender pealike flowers; height to 8'	Propagate by seeds
Dasylirion Wheeleri Sotol, spoon flower	Rocky areas	Erect, straplike, gray-green leaves; blossoms from May to July; height to 15'	Indicator species of Chihuahuan Desert
Justicia californica Chuparosa	Arroyos, rocky places	Compact, rounded shrub; leaves drop during hot weather; unusual-shaped red flowers bloom after rains; height to 3'	Propagate by seeds or cuttings Attracts hummingbirds
Larrea divaricata Creosote bush	Very adaptable, sands to gravels, varying temperatures	Waxy yellow flowers bloom sparsely throughout the year, profusely in spring; fuzzy fruits; height to 8'	Very vigorous Strong, musty odor after rain
Lophocereus Schottii Senita	Arid, hot areas	Ascending branches form clumps; long, twisted bristles look like hair; pink flowers produced at night; height to 15'	Sometimes produces 100 upright stems; edible fruits
Opuntia arbuscula Bush cholla	Sandy arroyos and also heavy soils, 900'-4,100'	Cylindrical cactus; greenish yellow/red flowers in spring; showy red fruits; height to 10'	Easy to cultivate; fast growing in areas of higher rainfall
O. Bigelovii Teddy-bear cholla	Hot, dry, rocky hillsides	Erect, with a trunk and lateral branches; yellow-green or white/red flowers; height to 5'	Pots readily and is easily cultivated Extremely painful spines make an impenetrable barrier
O. ramosissima Pencil cactus	Alluvial soils	Upright; multibranched; cylindrical stemmed; small yellow-green flowers; attractive fruit with long silvery spines; height to 8'	Vigorous; roots easily
Sphaeralcea ambigua Desert mallow	Not particular but does best in well-drained soil	Erect; apricot-colored blooms during spring and summer; height to 3'	Propagate by seeds, division or cuttings; easily grown
Yucca aloifolia Spanish-bayonet	Hot, dry areas	Clumps of sharply pointing leaves; conspicuous, waxy white bell-shaped clusters of flowers from July to August; height to 25'	Desirable and easily cultivated

FORBS

Name	Habitat	Growth Characteristics	Notes
Abronia fragrans Sand verbena	Sandy plains	Much branched; widely spreading (or trailing); fragrant white/pale lavender flowers opening in late afternoon from April to June; height to 3'	Propagate by seeds sown in spring; easily grown
Allium Drummondii Wild onion	Unshaded, barren areas and deserts	Bulb; basal leaves; odorless, dainty white/rose-pink flowers in umbels from April to May (sometimes repeat in fall); height to 6''	Propagate by seeds sown in spring or by bulb offsets in spring or fall; easy to cultivate
Baileya multiradiata Desert marigold	Gravelly deserts	Sturdy, yellow daisylike flowers bloom throughout the year; height to 1'	Propagate by seeds; vigorous grower
Coreopsis Bigelovii Bigelovii coreopsis	Open, well-drained areas	Perennial; erect; opposite leaves; blooms from April to June; height to 2'	Propagate by seeds sown in sunny, well-drained places; profuse bloomer
Dichelostemma pulchellum Blue-dicks, wild hyacinth	Sandy, gravelly deserts; infertile soil	Upright; branched; tall stemmed; white/mixed colors, 6-petaled tubular flowers in summer; height to 2'	Propagate by seeds or bulb offsets
Echinocactus horizonthalonius Eagle-claws, mule-crippler cactus	Hot, dry areas	Globose to columnar; pink to rose flowers bloom profusely throughout summer; height to 1'	Propagate by seeds; easily grown; reliable
Eremalche rotundifolia Desert five-spot	Dry, sandy, well-drained soils	Upright; opposite branching, rounded leaves; hairy stems and leaves; globe-shaped, pink/lilac, dark violet spotted flowers in summer	Propagate by seeds
Linanthus aureus Golden gilia	Well-drained, sunny areas	Annual; erect; loosely branched; occurs in dense colonies; corymbs of yellow flowers; height to 20''	Propagate by seeds
Mammillaria Heyderi Coral cactus, pancake pincushion	Rocky plains	Tiny; appears flattened, with radial spines; creamy white, many-petaled flowers encircle the plant; height to 1'' (3'' in diameter)	Propagate by seeds Flowers are opulent and appear profusely during the summer
Mentzelia laevicaulis Blazing-star	Sandy deserts	Annual; upright; stems with scales; yellow 5-petaled flowers from February to May; height to 3'	Propagate by seeds
Mirabilis Froebelii Giant four-o'clock	Stony mesas, arroyos and hillsides	Mat-forming annual; very fragrant, large, bright purple, night-blooming flowers; height to 2'	Propagate by seeds
Oenothera deltoides Desert evening primrose	Sandy areas, dunes	Annual; upright; fragrant, white-pink flowers open at sunset; height to 2'	Propagate by seeds
Phacelia crenulata Notch leaf phacelia	Sandy plains, arroyos	Annual; erect; thistlelike leaves; woolly stem and leaves; lavender blossoms with red stamens from spring to fall; height to 2'	Propagate by seeds; easily grown
Salvia columbariae Chia	Not particular as long as well-drained, sunny areas	Annual; erect; opposite, deeply incised, curly leaves; small, deep blue flowers, especially after rains, from spring to fall; height to 20''	Propagate by collected seeds
S. Greggii Autumn sage	Open, dry areas	Perennial; erect herb; much branched; irregular red blossoms from spring to fall; height to 30'	Propagate by seeds

Pacific Forest Region

This forest covers the rugged glaciated mountains and the Pacific Northwest and northern California. Due to the very high rainfall, which can be up to 150 inches annually, the humidity and the generally mild temperature, vegetation is thick, even impenetrable in places. This forest is remarkable for its dense, luxuriant growth as well as for the height of some of its trees. The tallest tree of all, the redwood, and the Douglas fir, which often grows more than 200 feet, are both prominent.

The Pacific Forest covers an area of 65,000 square miles and includes the California Coastal Ranges, the Cascades, the Klamath Ranges, the Pacific Coastal Ranges and the Olympic Mountains. Although there is a great variety of vegetation zones extending from Lower Sonoran grasslands to Alpine shrubs and herbs, this mountainous region will be desirable primarily in terms of its majestic forest.

TREES

Name	Habitat	Growth Characteristics	Notes
Abies amabilis Pacific silver fir	Coastal fog belt and cool interior valleys, rain forests of the Pacific	Dense, spirelike crown; silvery gray, furrowed bark; height to 200'	Handsome specimen, not as beautiful in cultivation as in the wild; needs uniform high moisture
A. procera Noble fir	Deep, moist soils and cool temperatures, 5,000'	Dense, rounded crown; short, rigid branches; reddish; height to 200'	Provides cover, nesting and roosting sites for wildlife
Acer circinatum Vine maple	Logged-over land, under conifers	Branching from base; forms dense thickets; compact size; height to 40'	Propagate by stratified seeds sown in spring
Cornus Nuttallii Mountain dogwood	Shaded areas, coniferous forests at low elevation	Pyramidal with horizontal branching; flowers with white sepals turning pinkish white in spring, possibly blooming again in August to September; beautiful autumn color; height to 40'	Similar to *C. florida* but much taller Considered the most beautiful tree in the U.S.; needs cool temperatures and high moisture Berries provide winter food for wildlife
Fraxinus latifolia Oregon ash	Moist, fertile soils	Narrow crown; straight trunk in good soil, otherwise crooked; height to 75'	Robust and trouble-free

Cornus Nuttallii

TREES (continued)

Name	Habitat	Growth Characteristics	Notes
Larix occidentalis Western larch	Moist mountain slopes	Deciduous conifer; pyramidal with pendulous branches; height to 150'	Requires high moisture and cool temperatures; susceptible to pests and diseases
Picea sitchensis Sitka spruce	Coastal areas in the fog belt, along streams, in low valleys	Loosely pyramidal crown; buttressed trunk; height to 285'	Rapid grower requires high moisture and moderate temperatures Provides roosting and nesting areas, especially blue grouse
Populus trichocarpa Western balsam poplar, black cottonwood	Along streams and in moist areas	Large leaves (woolly, rusty on underside); height to 180'	Propagate by suckers or cuttings, sometimes by seeds; easy to cultivate; grows rapidly
Quercus Garryana Oregon oak	Valleys and slopes, on dry gravel or moist soils	Rounded crown; ascending branches; height to 100'	Propagate by seeds sown in autumn or stratified Attracts quail, red-shafted flickers and thrushes
Thuja plicata Western red cedar	Moist bottomlands, along mountain streams	Densely pyramidal; buttressed trunk; height to 200'	Vigorous, rapid-growing specimen where summers are cool, winters mild and humidity high; disease-free; tolerates extensive pruning Foliage does not turn brown in winter
Tsuga heterophylla Western hemlock	Along the coast in humid mild areas; variety of soils	Evergreen; narrow, pyramidal crown; height to 200'	Rapid grower; tolerates pruning; requires even high moisture Provides excellent winter cover for blue grouse and chickarees

SHRUBS

Name	Habitat	Growth Characteristics	Notes
Holodiscus discolor Creambush, ocean-spray	Sunny, well-drained sites	Deciduous; arching shrub; white flowers in panicles from late June to early July; height to 12'	Propagate by seeds, layering or greenwood cuttings under glass
Kalmiopsis Leachiana Kalmiopsis	Sunny but moist areas with peaty soil	Mat-forming evergreen; rosy purple flowers in late spring; height to 1'	Desirable for rockery
Mahonia Aquifolium Oregon grape, holly grape	Variable, tolerant of sun, shade, dryness, moisture	Evergreen lustrous leaves; yellow flowers in spikes in May; clusters of grapelike fruit; height to 6'	Propagate by seeds, layering or cuttings; easily grown; tolerant of most adverse conditions
Menziesia ferruginea Rustyleaf, mock azalea	Mountainous areas	Deciduous; erect or straggling; alternate with terminal clusters; yellowish/white/pinkish flowers in early summer; height to 2'	Propagate by seeds or division
Physocarpus malvaceus Ninebark	Along streams	Deciduous; spreading shrub; white flowers in dense umbels in late spring; interesting fruit; height to 6'	Propagate by seeds or cuttings
Rhododendron macrophyllum West Coast rhododendron, California rosebay	Mountainous areas	Erect; pale rose flowers in spring; height to 9'	Propagate by seeds
Rubus spectabilis Salmonberry, showy raspberry	Open areas	Upright stems; fragrant, purplish/red flowers in early summer; orange edible fruit; height to 6'	Propagate by seeds, suckers or root cuttings
Salix arctica Arctic willow	Streamsides	Creeping; catkins in spring; height to 1'	Propagate by seeds or cuttings Good ground cover for moist areas

SHRUBS (continued)

Name	Habitat	Growth Characteristics	Notes
Sambucus caerulea Blue elderberry	Along streams	Coarse; compound leaves; edible blue-black fruit with heavy white blooms from June to July; height to 45'	Propagate by seeds or cuttings; vigorous grower
Symphoricarpos albus var. *laevigatus* Snowberry	Dry slopes	Upright with arching branches; spikes of small pink flowers in July; large white berries; height to 6'	Propagate by seeds, cuttings, suckers or division Prone to fungus that discolors fruit
Vaccinium ovatum California huckle-berry	Semishaded areas of good drainage, moist	Evergreen upright shrub; graceful, somewhat arching branches; beautiful shining leaves; waxy white/pink flowers in April; height to 10'	

FORBS

Arnica Chamissonis Meadow arnica	Moist areas at medium and high altitudes	Perennial; erect stem; paired leaves and flowers from June to August; height to 3'	Propagate by division
Boykinia elata Coast boykinia	Woods at medium altitudes with high moisture	Erect with branched stem; terminal clusters of tiny white flowers from June to August; height to 2'	Propagate by seeds or division
Brodiaea coronaria Harvest brodiaea	Dry slopes of coastal ranges, among grass and under trees	Erect, leafless stalk; narrow basal leaves; cluster of lavender flowers from April to July; height to 8''	Propagate by seeds or offsets in sunny dry areas Corms available commercially
Calochortus Lobbii Lobb's mariposa	High altitudes, well-drained meadows	Erect; white cuplike flower from June to August; height to 1'	Propagate by seeds or offsets sown in sunny dry areas
C. Lyallii Lyall's star tulip	East-facing slopes, thin soil, full sun, good drainage	Erect, branching; narrow leaves; white/purple flowers with fringed petals from May to July; height to 2'	Propagate by seeds; slow growing Bulbs sometimes available commercially
Caltha leptosepala White marsh marigold	Along mountain streams, wet mountain marshes	Erect stems with many leaves; flowers with white sepals (no petals) from July to August; height to 1½'	Propagate by seeds or root division; requires plenty of humus and water in winter and spring; sunshine and cool temperatures
Chimaphila Menziesii Little prince's pine	Shaded coniferous woods	Erect with few leaves on stem; white flowers turning pinkish from June to August; height to 8''	Propagate by cuttings; difficult to grow from seeds; requires acid soil and high moisture Tolerates heavy shade of pine woods
Claytonia lanceolata Spring-beauty	High mountain meadows	Corm; erect stem with fleshy lanceolate leaves; white/pink flowers from April to June; height to 6''	Propagate by seeds or tubers; very hardy; requires cool temperatures and moisture; blooms profusely
Dodecatheon alpinum Alpine shooting-star	High altitude, wet meadows with fertile soil	Erect; narrow leaves; cyclamenlike pink flowers from May to August; height to 6''	Propagate by seeds or division; requires good drainage
Erythronium citrinum Adder's-tongue, yellow fawn lily	Shaded woods; neutral soil	Erect stem; spotted basal leaves; nodding, 6-petaled, cream flowers from March to April; height to 1'	Propagate by seeds; slow growing; requires shade and moisture
Heuchera glabra Alpine heuchera	Damp areas along streams, on shaded rock crevices	Panicle of tiny white flowers with reflexed petals from June to August; height to 2'	Propagate by seeds or division; requires good drainage, summer shade

FORBS (continued)

Name	Habitat	Growth Characteristics	Notes
Lewisia pygmaea Dwarf lewisia	High altitudes in well-drained soils	Tiny rosette of leaves; white flowers from May to September; height to 3''	Propagate by seeds or root division in spring; requires well-drained, rocky soil
Mertensia ciliata Bluebells, fringed lungwort	Moist, semishaded areas	Erect; alternate leaves on stem; racemes of drooping dark blue flowers from May to August; height to 3'	Propagate by seeds when ripe; division is difficult Foliage dies down after flowering
Penstemon Davidsonii Lilac beard-tongue	Rocky slopes of high mountains	Mat forming; very showy, purple-violet flowers from June to August; height to 4''	Propagate by seeds or plant division; requires cool, moist areas with good drainage and some sunlight
P. rupicola Crimson beard-tongue	Rocky slopes at high altitudes	Mat forming; dainty ½'' leaves in pairs; 2'' pinkish purple flowers from May to August; height to 4''	Propagate by seeds or plant division in spring; requires excellent drainage
Phlox diffusa Spreading phlox	Open areas; fertile moist soils	Perennial; matting; narrow leaves; pink solitary flower scape from May to July; height to 6''	Propagate by seeds; easy cultivating Plants should be divided every 3 years
Potentilla flabellifolia Potentilla, fan-leaf cinquefoil	Moist meadows about 4,500'	Perennial; multibranched; compound leaves; 5-petaled yellow flower from June to August; height to 1'	Propagate by seeds
Rosa nutkana Nootka rose	Moist areas among conifers	Beautiful delicate pink 5-petaled flowers borne on branch tips from May to July; height to 6'	Propagate by cuttings
Saxifraga Lyallii Lyall's saxifrage	Damp meadows	Basal leaves; cyme of white flowers from July to August; height to 15''	Propagate by seeds or division; requires cool temperatures, moisture and excellent drainage
Silene acaulis Cushion pink, moss campion	High altitudes, rock ledges	Matting, tufted perennial; pink-to-reddish purple flowers with notched petals from June to August; height to 2''	Propagate by seeds, division or cuttings; requires cool temperatures and moisture
Sisyrinchium Douglasii Grass-widow	Meadows, moist woodlands	Erect; narrow leaves; red/pink petals with yellow centers from March to June; height to 1'	Propagate by seeds or division; blooms profusely; available commercially
S. idahoense Western blue-eyed grass	Moist areas, but flexible	Erect; linear leaves; light blue flowers from July to August; height to 16''	Propagate by seeds or division; requires sunny, well-drained area
Trillium petiolatum Round-leaf trillium	Woodlands, open meadows, moist soils	Dark red-purple flower surrounded by 3 bright green circular leaves from April to June; height to 8''	Propagate by seeds or division; requires fertile, moist, partially shaded soils
Viola canadensis Canada violet	Moist areas, typically in shaded woodlands	Long stems; heart-shaped leaves; flowers with white/purple veins from May to July; height to 15''	Propagate by seeds or division; easily grown

California Region

Due mainly to its isolated location, California has the most diverse flora of any ecoregion of the United States.

The mountains and deserts that contribute to this isolation provide an especially good area for developing and nurturing endemic species.

Within state boundaries there are many vegetation habitats—coastal strands and dunes, foothills, mountain peaks, fresh and saltwater lowlands, flats and rolling terrain. Almost every type of climate is represented, from cold-wet, cold-dry to temperate-moist and warm-dry. Rock types include granite, sandstone, limestone and serpentine.

The vegetation of the Sierras, the Coastal Ranges, the foothills and interior valleys are of particular interest to us. The following species include those that are the most prominent, unusual and most useful to the landscape gardener.

TREES

Name	Habitat	Growth Characteristics	Notes
Acer macrophyllum Oregon maple	Shaded canyons and along streams, foothills; moist soil	Broad, rounded crown; height to 90'	Propagate by seeds Provides food for songbirds, game birds and mammals
Arbutus Menziesii Madrona	Logged-over areas, well-drained slopes, sometimes valleys	Evergreen; leathery leaves; crooked trunk; reddish bark; white flowers in panicles; height to 100'	Propagate by seeds, cuttings or layering
Castanopsis chrysophylla Giant chinquapin, western chestnut	Humid coastal valleys	Deciduous; rounded crown; leathery dark green leaves and nuts; ranges from shrub to tall tree; massive trunk; height to 100'	Propagate by seeds or suckers; sprouts freely; not susceptible to blight
Juniperus occidentalis Sierra juniper	Granitic ridges and other windswept peaks to 10,000'	Straight trunk; large branches; height to 40'	Propagate by seeds; easily grown; tolerant of difficult conditions Provides food for mule deer, songbirds and game birds
Libocedrus decurrens Incense cedar	Mountain slopes to 7,000'	Rounded conical crown; tapering trunk; aromatic wood; reddish bark; feathery foliage; large cones; height to 150'	Propagate by seeds or cuttings; easily grown; vigorous; easily transplanted
Pinus attenuata Knob-cone pine	Dry mountain slopes, especially on shallow, sandy soils of the foothills	Uneven, thin-foliaged crown; divided trunk; height to 100'	Propagate by seeds; easily grown Controls erosion Provides food for songbirds, game birds and mammals
P. Balfouriana Foxtail pine	Sterile, rocky soils of mountain slopes to 12,000'	Asymmetrical; somewhat pyramidal crown; stout branches; height to 90' (height varies depending on the soil and elevation)	Propagate by seeds, cuttings or transplanting in spring before new growth Provides food for songbirds
P. Coulteri Coulter pine	Mountainous areas, dry slopes and ridges, 6,000'	Asymmetrical with a loose crown; dark, heavy branches; large cones; height to 90'	Propagate by seeds or cuttings; fast growing; drought resistant Controls erosion
P. Jeffreyi Jeffrey pine	Exposed, dry ridges in the pinyon-sagebrush belt, to 8,000'	Forms pure stands of flat-topped, dense trees; often contorted; conspicuous, fragrant red bark; large, heavy cones; height to 170'	Propagate by seeds or cuttings Attracts game birds and songbirds

*Libocedrus
decurrens*

Camassia Quamash

TREES (continued)

Name	Habitat	Growth Characteristics	Notes
P. Lambertiana Sugar pine	Mountains, slopes, ravines, canyons, to 6,500'	Flat crown; graceful down-sweeping branches; height to 250'	Propagate by seeds, cuttings or transplanting in spring before new growth Prone to white pine blister rust and should not be planted near gooseberries or currants Attracts blue grouse, chickadees, flickers, jays and juncos
P. muricata Bishop pine	Near coast	Dense crown; stiff, gray-green needles; height to 60'	Propagate by seeds or cuttings; not often cultivated; tolerant of high winds Provides food for songbirds, game birds and mammals
Quercus agrifolia California live oak	Valleys, low hills, coastal sand dunes	Rounded crown; short trunk; heavy branches; ranges from shrub to large tree; height to 90'	Propagate by seeds sown in autumn or stratified, by cuttings or layering Provides food and shelter for wildlife
Q. Wislizenii Interior live oak	On variable soils mostly along coast, hills, ravines, chaparral	Rounded crown; spreading branches; evergreen leaves; height to 75'	Propagate by seeds Attracts quail and songbirds, especially vireos and warblers
Sequoiadendron giganteum Giant sequoia	Western slopes to 3,400'	Narrow, open crown; straight trunk; evergreen needles; height to 300'	Propagate by seeds sown in spring or stratified; hardy
Torreya californica California nutmeg	Hillsides, canyons and bottomlands near streams	Evergreen; pyramidal crown (young), open (older); height to 100'	Propagate by seeds sown in spring or stratified over winter or by cuttings; slow growing; difficult to grow from seed but worth trying
Umbellularia californica California bay, California laurel	Rich valleys along streams	Rounded crown; evergreen leaves; ranges from shrub to tree; beautiful autumn color; height to 175'	Vigorous, long-lived

SHRUBS

Name	Habitat	Growth Characteristics	Notes
Arctostaphylos glauca Big-berry manzanita	Chaparral	Erect, treelike; pinkish white flowers in spring; height to 18'	Propagate by seeds, layering, budding or green-wood cuttings under glass
A. Nummularia Fort Bragg manzanita	Mixed evergreen forest, chaparral	Evergreen; erect; spreading branches; pink/white nodding flowers in racemes in spring; height to 1½'	Propagate by seeds, layering or budding

SHRUBS (continued)

Name	Habitat	Growth Characteristics	Notes
Calycanthus occidentalis Sweet shrub	Along streams	Deciduous; spreading; maroon, aromatic flowers in spring; nut-shaped fruit; bright yellow autumn color; height to 10'	Propagate by seeds, layering, suckers or division
Cercis occidentalis California redbud	Canyons and foothills	Small tree or shrub; simple leaves; cerise pealike flowers borne directly on branches in spring; height to 15'	Propagate by seeds sown in spring, by layering or softwood cuttings taken in spring
Garrya elliptica Coast silk-tassel	Chaparral slopes, coastal scrub, lower forest	Evergreen; erect; opposite leaves; brownish flowers from January to March; height to 25'	Propagate by seeds or cuttings of half-ripened wood
Helianthemum scoparium Rush rose	Sunny, well-drained slopes, limestone soil	Deciduous; twiggy; bright yellow flowers in spring; height to 3'	Propagate by seeds, division or green-wood cuttings
Potentilla gracilis Potentilla	Meadows, valleys, hill-sides and woods, moist soils to 8,000'	Deciduous; erect; widely branching; pale yellow to cream-white flowers from May to August; height to 2'	Propagate by seeds or division
Symphoricarpos albus Snowberry, wax-berry	Foothills to 2,000'	Deciduous; variable shape; clusters of white flowers from May to June; height to 3'	Propagate by seeds, cuttings, suckers or division

FORBS

Name	Habitat	Growth Characteristics	Notes
Asarum Hartwegii Hartwegs, wild ginger, asarabacca	Shady woods in moist soil	Deciduous; heart-shaped leaves on hairy stems; brown, 3-petaled flowers from May to June; height to 6''	Propagate by seeds or division
Camassia Quamash Quamash, camas	Wet meadows, along streams, to 8,000'	Perennial; unbranched stem; basal leaves; raceme of bright blue star-like flowers from June to July; height to 2'	Propagate by seeds or bulb offsets
Chlorogalum pomeridianum Soap plant, amole	Open hills and plains, dry areas, deserts	Branched plant with many basal leaves; white flowers open in afternoon in summer; height to 8'	Propagate by seeds or offsets
Clarkia amoena Satin flower	Grassy foothills	Erect stem; alternate narrow leaves; purple, rose, lavender flowers from June to July; interesting fruit; height to 3½'	Propagate by seeds
Clematis lasiantha Chaparral virgin's bower	Hillsides to 2,000'	Vine; white, feathery, 2'' flowers in spring	Propagate by stratified seeds, layering or division
Delphinium decorum Larkspur	Foothills, coastal ranges, Sierra Nevadas to 7,000'	Perennial; erect; deeply incised leaves; spikes of purple flowers in June; height to 1'	Propagate by seeds, division of clumps or by cuttings taken after flowering Vulnerable to disease
Erodium cicutarium Alfilaria, red-stemmed filaree	Hillsides, pastures, waste places	Erect, branched perennial; toothed, opposite leaves; pinkish/purple, 5-petaled flowers bloom inter-mittently throughout the year; corkscrew seed pods; height to 2½'	Propagate by seeds or division
Eschscholzia californica California poppy	Meadows, open places	Annual with erect stem; finely cut leaves; profusion of vibrant, bowl-shaped flowers from February to November; height to 2'	Propagate by seeds

FORBS (continued)

Name	Habitat	Growth Characteristics	Notes
Fritillaria pluriflora Adobe lily, pink fritillary	Foothills	Erect perennial; broad, lance-shaped leaves; pink, 6-petaled flowers from February to April; height to 2'	Propagate by offsets; difficult to find and grow
Gilia tricolor Bird's-eyes	Open grasslands up to 3,000', alkaline soils	Erect; narrow leaves; small blue upright flowers from March to April; height to 6''	Propagate by seeds
Goodyera oblongifolia Giant rattlesnake plantain	Dry/moist deciduous woods	Slender, erect stem; rosette of spotted leaves; loose raceme of large white flowers from July to September; height to 17''	Propagate by seeds or division; difficult
Limnanthes Douglasii Meadow foam	Moist meadows, valleys, open fields near springs	Upright; succulent leaves, deeply notched; blooms from March to April; height to 14''	Propagate by seeds; easily grown; short-lived
Lupinus bicolor Dove lupine	Coastal foothills	Communal species with soft, erect stems; compound leaves; white/blue flowers from March to April; height to 16''	Propagate by seeds
Nemophila menziesii Baby-blue-eyes	Hillsides, valleys in moist soil to 5,000'	Erect; basal branching; blue flowers from February to June; height to 1½'	Propagate by seeds Seeds sown in spring will bloom by summer
Oenothera caespitosa White evening primrose	Arroyos, hillsides	Matting perennial; coarsely toothed leaves; large white flowers in the evening from April to August; height to 6''	Propagate by seeds or division
O. Hookeri Yellow evening primrose	Moist areas to 9,000'	Strong stem; many leaves; flowers bloom in the evening from June to December; height to 5'	Propagate by seeds; easily grown
Papaver californicum Western poppy	On burned-over areas	Annual; erect; finely cut leaves; 4-petaled terminal flower from April to May; height to 2'	Propagate by seeds
Silene californica California Indian pink	Open woods	Perennial; erect; gray-green foliage; scarlet flowers with fringed petals from April to July; height to 1½'	Propagate by seeds, division or cuttings
Trillium chloropetalum Giant trillium	Thickets and woods, shade and moist soil	Perennial; broad, spotted leaves encircling dark flowers from February to May; height to 2'	Propagate by seeds or division Illegal in many places to dig them; available commercially
Veratrum californicum Corn lily, skunk cabbage	Mountainous areas, open places	Erect; parallel-veined leaves; raceme of white flowers from June to August; height to 6'	Propagate by seeds or division
Zauschneria californica California fuchsia	Dry, rocky hillsides to 10,000'	Perennial; erect; narrow leaves; scarlet, trumpet-shaped, 1½'' flowers from summer to fall; height to 20''	Propagate by seeds, division or cuttings
Zigadenus venenosus Death camas	Foothills of lodgepole pine, rocky slopes	Basal leaves; erect racemes of flowers from May to July; height to 3'	Propagate by seeds or division Poisonous to sheep

13

Functional Uses of Plants

While you probably can't wait to get on with the project and decide what plants you're going to put into the ground, take a few minutes to consider practical ways plants can serve you.

You can use plants to improve your environment and to solve specific problems. If, for example, you found an erosion problem when you analyzed your soils, you can use plants to help solve it. Or if you are distressed with the high energy consumption

of your household, you can design your landscape to help reduce it. You can even use vegetation to reduce glare; shade your house; reduce or increase the wind velocity; cool the air; absorb air and noise pollution; and provide lumber, food, natural fertilizers and, in some cases, money.

Any or all of these functions can be incorporated into your landscape plan. In this chapter you will learn how vegetation performs these money-saving tasks and what characteristics the plants needed to do so must have. The lists of plant species suitable for each function will give you an idea of the kinds of plants to use, but they are by no means comprehensive. In some cases, if there is not enough information available about the functional possibilities of native plants, then exotics that are known to perform well are included.

Besides being beautiful, vegetation performs services that can be used to increase your comfort and quality of life. Because recent studies in ecology have led to an increased understanding of the natural forces occurring in plant communities, we can now make maximum use of these natural benefits provided by plants.

Vegetation is one source of almost all necessary nutrients used by living organisms, including people. We know that life requires carbon, hydrogen, oxygen, nitrogen, calcium and many other elements. These elements exist principally in the soil or in the atmosphere for varying periods of time. While animals and people have no real way of freeing and absorbing these molecules into the so-called "building blocks of protein," vegetation does. Moreover, through photosynthesis and respiration, vegetation performs a fundamental role in the cycling of oxygen and carbons without which life would be impossible. The energy of solar radiation not only provides warmth itself, but when it is captured by the chlorophyll of vegetation, it is converted into the food molecules from which all humans and animals absorb energy. All ecosystems run on this energy, and they could not exist without green vegetation. The most obvious, but often overlooked, role of vegetation is its modification of climate, pollution, noise and odors.

Climate Control

Why pay fuel companies for the use of dead plants when you can use live vegetation to heat and cool your house? All fossil fuels—oil, coal and gas—are derived from the decomposition and compression of ancient, long-dead plants. When you burn these fuels, you are burning ancient trapped sunlight. Although a renewable resource, fossil fuels are being consumed at rates far faster than they can be replaced, causing skyrocketing costs and the urgent need for conservation.

Living plants, on the other hand, are abundant and inexpensive, and they have been engaged in the energy business for 2½ billion years. Plants are extremely energy efficient and can accomplish feats that neither modern science nor technology can equal. A single tree can evaporate 100 gallons of water a day and dissipate 230,000 calories of heat. This process is equivalent to the cooling effect of five average room air conditioners running for 20 hours. Furthermore, one beech tree each year consumes carbon dioxide equivalent to that displaced by 800 single-family homes.

When a field is abandoned and returns through stages to forest, each step makes the climate more tolerable for the inhabitants. You can see this by comparing the temperatures of a barren field and a mature forest at different times of the year. In the heat of summer, the forest is cool and comfortable while the field is unbearably hot. Revisit these same landscapes on the coldest day of the year. You will find that the forest temperature is as much as 25° to 35°F. higher. The forest is effectively accomplishing what we've relied upon fossil fuels and mechanical engineers to do—modify the extremes of climate by cooling and warming.

While all of us can't live in a forest, we can use this modifying effect of living plants to increase our comfort and reduce our consumption of fossil fuels. In fact, by landscaping for energy conservation, we can reduce our overall energy needs by up to 40 percent.

Your landscape plan, like plants themselves, must begin with the sun. Its powerful rays strike different places on the earth's surface with different degrees of intensity. The relative intensity of the sun's rays on your property depends on your geographical location—your latitude, the angle of inclination, and the elevations and form of your land. Short of moving, there's not much you can do to change these conditions. But the sun's intensity is further modified by local features in the landscape—vegetation, landforms, water and architectural elements—and these features can be manipulated to take advantage of or alleviate the sun's heat. The significance of this manipulation becomes clear when you consider that the proper locating of one mature shade tree can provide as much cooling as five air conditioners.

In an area like the Northeast, where there are large seasonal variations in temperature, you should try to expose your house to solar radiation during

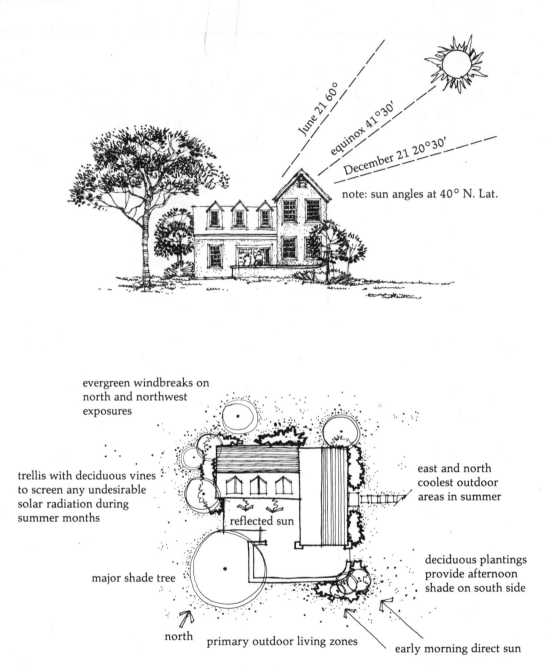

June 21 60°

equinox 41°30'

December 21 20°30'

note: sun angles at 40° N. Lat.

evergreen windbreaks on
north and northwest
exposures

trellis with deciduous vines
to screen any undesirable
solar radiation during
summer months

reflected sun

east and north
coolest outdoor
areas in summer

deciduous plantings
provide afternoon
shade on south side

major shade tree

north

primary outdoor living zones

early morning direct sun

*Wherever a substantial seasonal variation in temperature
occurs, the landscape can perform a valuable service
by helping to moderate the variation—if it is planned
correctly. The key is to use deciduous vegetation
along the southern exposure and evergreen vegetation
along the northwest exposure. The deciduous vegetation
will screen or block the summer sun when you don't
want any more heat than you've got, but won't block
the winter sun when you need all the heat you can
get. The evergreen plantings will buffer the prevailing
northwesterly winds. Knowing the angles of the sun
and distributing plants thoughtfully can allow you to
have sun where and when you want it, and to not
have it where and when you don't want it.*

the cold months and provide dense shade during the summer months. To do this, you will need to look at the analysis of your microclimate, which shows the shaded and exposed areas on your property, the reflective qualities of surface materials, the wind patterns and the effects of precipitation and temperature.

SHADE TREES

The following list includes examples of trees that could be used to provide shade in the different environmental regions. Those that are included are only examples, and there are hundreds of others that can be used. (See charts in Chapter 12 for additional plants.) You will be able to choose many others that are native to your area, simply by observing the shade provided by trees in nature. You may also be able to obtain the degree of shade required by using groupings of different-sized species.

Northern Coniferous Forest
Betula papyrifera — Paper birch
Pinus Strobus — White pine

Eastern Deciduous Forest

Appalachian Oak Forest
Oxydendrum arboreum — Sourwood, sorrel tree
Stewartia ovata — Mountain camellia

Oak-Hickory Forest
Acer saccharum — Sugar maple
Fagus grandifolia — American beech

Coastal Plain
Liquidambar Styraciflua — Sweet gum
Nyssa sylvatica — Pepperidge, sour gum, black gum

Southeastern Mixed Forest
Magnolia grandiflora — Southern magnolia
Ulmus alata — Wahoo elm, winged elm

Subtropic
Coccoloba diversifolia — Pigeon plum, snailseed
Quercus virginiana — Live oak

South-Central Swamp
Nyssa sylvatica — Pepperidge, sour gum, black gum
Taxodium distichum — Bald cypress

Prairie
Celtis occidentalis — Hackberry
Quercus macrocarpa — Bur oak, mossy-cup oak

Rocky Mountain Evergreen Forest
Picea pungens — Colorado spruce, Colorado blue spruce
Pseudotsuga Menziesii — Douglas fir

Great Basin
Acer saccharum subsp. *grandidentatum* — Big-tooth maple
Amelanchier utahensis — Serviceberry

Pacific Forest
Cornus Nuttallii — Mountain dogwood
Quercus Garryana — Oregon oak

California
Heteromeles arbutifolia — Toyon
Quercus Wislizenii — Interior live oak

WINDBREAK PLANTS

If you want to reduce the temperature of the area near your house, you can use a barrier of trees and shrubs to control the wind. You will have to consider the necessary height, width and density of the barrier in reviewing the individual characteristics of the plants and in determining how many you'll need.

Northern Coniferous Forest
Acer rubrum — Red maple
Salix nigra — Black willow

Eastern Deciduous Forest

Appalachian Oak Forest
Cladrastis lutea — Yellowwood
Tsuga caroliniana — Carolina hemlock

Oak-Hickory Forest
Fagus grandifolia — American beech
Quercus palustris — Pin oak, Spanish oak

Coastal Plain
Pinus Taeda—Loblolly pine
Quercus phellos—Willow oak

Southeastern Mixed Forest
Ulmus alata—Wahoo elm, winged elm

Subtropic
Bumelia celastrina—Saffron plum
Coccoloba Uvifera—Sea grape

South-Central Swamp
Acer rubrum var. *Drummondii*—
Drummond red maple
Fraxinus tomentosa—Pumpkin ash

Prairie
Celtis occidentalis—Hackberry
Maclura pomifera—Osage orange

Rocky Mountain Evergreen Forest
Crataegus rivularis—River hawthorn
Pinus flexilis—Limber pine

Great Basin
Juniperus scopulorum—Colorado red cedar,
Rocky Mountain juniper
Populus Fremontii—Fremont cottonwood

Desert
Carnegiea gigantea—Giant saguaro
Yucca brevifolia—Joshua tree

Pacific Forest
Abies amabilis—Pacific silver fir
Populus trichocarpa—Western balsam
poplar, black cottonwood

California
Taxus brevifolia—Western yew
Umbellularia californica—California bay,
California laurel

INSULATING VINES

Vines grown against the walls and roof of your house can provide attractive and effective insulation from both summer heat and winter cold. The following list contains those few vines that are native and useful for landscaping. In many regions there are no appropriate species,

and you may consider using some of the exotics and hybrids that have been successfully grown in your environment.

Southeastern Mixed Forest
Aristolochia tomentosa—Birthwort
Clematis Viorna—Leather flower

South-Central Swamp
Gelsemium sempervirens—Yellow jasmine

Rocky Mountain Evergreen Forest
Lonicera ciliosa—Honeysuckle

California
Clematis ligusticifolia—Western virgin's
bower, Yerba de Chivato
Rosa californica—California wild rose

Erosion Control

Erosion is the natural process that shapes and stabilizes the landscape. While minor erosion can expose rich soils, too much erosion can cause major destruction of soils and landscapes. Wind sweeping over exposed, dry earth lifts the small, lighter particles of soil and carries them away as dust. This is then deposited where it is often a nuisance.

The best way to control wind erosion is by covering any bare soil with vegetation. The four parts of plants that control wind erosion are: dense leaves or needles that create an effective barrier to air movement through the plants; dense branching that controls and slows wind close to the ground; multiple stems and rough bark that decrease the wind velocity as it passes through them; and fibrous roots that grow close to the surface and effectively hold surface soil in place.

Water erosion occurs almost everywhere all the time and is responsible for the loss of valuable soil and the increasing problem of sedimentation in streams. As raindrops hit the exposed earth, particles of soil are dislodged, picked up and carried downslope. Once soil is removed and held in suspension by moving water, it acts as a scouring agent, loosening and removing more soil.

Runoff erosion can be seen in several characteristic forms: sheet, rill and gull. Sheet erosion is the removal of the entire soil layer from

On steep slopes where it can cause severe problems, erosion is best controlled by using several kinds of plants in concert, as here. The shallow, fibrous roots of ground covers, growing intertwined with tree roots that spread along the surface and plunge deep into the subsoil, will hold the soil.

an exposed site. As it continues, softer areas on the surface wash away faster, and small rills, or troughs, carrying water and soil downslope, are formed. As more water and soil flow down the rills, they jam together, become deeper and form gullies, which are difficult to control.

Plants can control and prevent water erosion by means of their leaves, branches and roots. Their leaves and branches intercept raindrops that splash the soil, and their roots hold the soil in place. The plants can absorb excess water either by transpiration or by decomposing and increasing organic material, which increases the soil's capacity to absorb water.

Steeply sloping areas like banks are most subject to severe erosion and need to be vegetated as quickly as possible. On newly graded areas, you may want to use plants that will rapidly spread and hold the soil in place while you establish other, slower-growing species.

EROSION-CONTROL PLANTS

The following plants are examples of those that could be used to control erosion. For the most part, they are quick growing and have dense, fibrous root systems that will effectively hold the soil in place. Here again, you might want to consider some of the introduced species of ground covers that have proven to be successful in your environment.

Northern Coniferous Forest
Pinus Strobus — White pine
Populus tremuloides — Quaking aspen

Eastern Deciduous Forest

Oak-Hickory Forest
Betula nigra — River birch
Rhus typhina — Staghorn sumac

Coastal Plain
Alnus maritima — Seaside alder
Pinus virginiana — Jersey pine

Southeastern Mixed Forest
Rubus trivialis — Southern dewberry

Subtropic
Coccoloba Uvifera — Sea grape
Serenoa repens — Saw palmetto, scrub palmetto

South-Central Swamp
Populus heterophylla — Swamp cottonwood
Typha latifolia — Common cattail

Prairie
Amorpha fruticosa var. *angustifolia* — Bastard indigo
Juniperus Ashei — Ashe juniper, Ozark white cedar

Rocky Mountain Evergreen Forest
Arctostaphylos Uva-ursi — Common bearberry
Juniperus communis — Common juniper

Great Basin
Cercocarpus montanus — Mountain mahogany
Fraxinus anomala — Single-leaf ash

Desert
Peucephyllum Schottii — Desert fir

Pacific Forest
Mahonia Aquifolium — Oregon grape, holly grape
Rubus spectabilis — Salmonberry, showy raspberry

California
Asarum Hartwegii — Hartwegs, wild ginger, asarabacca
Rosa californica — California wild rose

BANK PLANTINGS

Northern Coniferous Forest
Vaccinium angustifolium — Lowbush blueberry
V. Oxycoccos — Small cranberry

Coastal Plain
Quercus phellos — Willow oak
Rhododendron atlanticum — Coast azalea, dwarf azalea
Xanthorhiza simplicissima — Shrub yellow-root

Southeastern Mixed Forest
Rubus trivialis — Southern dewberry

Subtropic
Cassia coluteoides — Senna
Licania michauxii — Gopher apple

Prairie
Salvia coccinea — Scarlet sage
Verbena bipinnatifida — Dakota vervain

Rocky Mountain Evergreen Forest
Arctostaphylos Uva-ursi — Common bearberry
Juniperus communis — Common juniper

Great Basin
Fendlera rupicola — Cliff-fendler bush
Ipomoea leptophylla — Bush moonflower

Desert
Opuntia basilaris — Beaver-tail
Yucca glauca — Soapweed

Pacific Forest
Hulsea algida — Alpine hulsea
Kalmiopsis Leachiana — Kalmiopsis

California
Arctostaphylos Nummularia — Fort Bragg manzanita
Phyllodoce Breweri — Red heather

QUICKLY SPREADING AND REPRODUCING PLANTS

Northern Coniferous Forest
Pinus Strobus — White pine
Populus tremuloides — Quaking aspen

Eastern Deciduous Forest

Oak-Hickory Forest
Impatiens capensis — Jewelweed
Xanthorhiza simplicissima — Shrub yellow-root

Coastal Plain
Pinus Taeda — Loblolly pine
Populus nigra — Black poplar, swamp poplar

Southeastern Mixed Forest
Pinus Taeda — Loblolly pine
Xanthorhiza simplicissima — Shrub yellow-root

Subtropic
Cassia coluteoides — Senna
Rhizophora Mangle — American mangrove

South-Central Swamp
Cyperus esculentus — Nut grass, nut sedge
Polygonum densiflorum — Southern smartweed

Prairie
Allium cernuum — Nodding wild onion
Penstemon arkansanus — Arkansas beard-tongue

Rocky Mountain Evergreen Forest
Erythronium grandiflorum — Avalanche lily
Populus tremuloides — Quaking aspen

Great Basin
Ipomoea leptophylla — Bush moonflower
Populus Fremontii — Fremont cottonwood

Desert
Salvia carduacea — Thistle sage

Pacific Forest
Fraxinus latifolia — Oregon ash
Populus trichocarpa — Western balsam poplar, black cottonwood

California
Libocedrus decurrens — Incense cedar
Rosa californica — California wild rose

QUICK-GROWING PLANTS

Northern Coniferous Forest
Larix laricina — American larch, tamarack
Salix nigra — Black willow

Eastern Deciduous Forest

Appalachian Oak Forest
Magnolia acuminata var. *cordata* — Cucumber tree
Robinia Pseudoacacia — Black locust

Oak-Hickory Forest
Rhus typhina — Staghorn sumac
Viburnum dentatum — Arrowwood

Coastal Plain
Pinus Taeda — Loblolly pine
P. virginiana — Jersey pine

Southeastern Mixed Forest
Ulmus alata — Wahoo elm, winged elm
Xanthorhiza simplicissima — Shrub yellow-root

Subtropic
Cassia coluteoides — Senna
Pinus Elliottii — Slash pine

South-Central Swamp
Gelsemium sempervirens — Yellow jasmine
Polygonum densiflorum — Southern smartweed

Prairie
> *Cornus sericea* — Red-osier dogwood
> *Crataegus Engelmannii* — Hawthorn

Rocky Mountain Evergreen Forest
> *Picea pungens* — Colorado spruce, Colorado blue spruce
> *Populus tremuloides* — Quaking aspen

Great Basin
> *Ipomoea leptophylla* — Bush moonflower
> *Populus Fremontii* — Fremont cottonwood

Desert
> *Opuntia arbuscula* — Bush cholla
> *Salvia Dorrii* — Blue sage

Pacific Forest
> *Populus trichocarpa* — Western balsam poplar, black cottonwood
> *Thuja plicata* — Western red cedar

California
> *Libocedrus decurrens* — Incense cedar
> *Pinus Coulteri* — Coulter pine

Natural Fertilizer

Leaves, and in some cases stems of plants, have a beneficial effect on soil composition and structure. The dead plant material, or litter, that covers the ground in natural landscapes breaks the impact of rain, retards runoff and filters the water into the soil without disturbing the soil structure. During dry weather, the litter reduces surface evaporation, and as the litter decays, it becomes the basis of the humus horizon, which provides mineral elements for plant growth. Humus also provides a sheltered environment for microbiotic life, which breaks down the many kinds of complex substances in the soil. It provides shelter for earthworms, which help to keep the soil granulated. In extremely cold weather, the litter insulates the ground, and in the event of freezing, it tends to honeycomb, allowing early spring rains to soak in. Litter also provides a major source of nutrients for the soil. Some trees like dogwoods have very high nutrient levels, and their leaves decompose rapidly, thus quickly replenishing the soil.

If your soil is nutrient deficient, add some decomposed plant material and stop removing dead plant material. Allow leaf litter and grass clippings to remain on the surface and return their nutrients to the soil. Death and decay are just as natural as life and growth, and if you want to work with the natural system, you must take advantage of the complete cycle.

Pollution Control

Plants can play an important role as natural air filters. They can remove some pollutants from the atmosphere on contact, by sedimentation or by absorption.

Leaf surfaces, especially hairy ones, can trap dust and soot. Atmospheric dust has been reduced by as much as 75 percent with a 200-yard-wide planting. Studies have shown that ragweed pollen was reduced by 80 percent over a distance of approximately 100 yards by a dense evergreen forest. If you live near a source of pollution like a dusty road or a rock quarry, you should plant a dense buffer of hairy-leaved vegetation between yourself and the source.

Plants also control air-polluting gases by introducing oxygen into the atmosphere and diluting the polluted air. Severe pollution, however, may cause damage to the plants. Certain gaseous pollutants — such as sulfur dioxide (from fuel combustion), fluorides (from phosphate fertilizers) and ozone from the atmosphere — can kill vegetation. Some species are more susceptible to pollution damage than others. Plants will vary in their

Once you understand the pollution-moderating effects of plants, you can figure out visually pleasing ways to work them into your landscape to help buffer the infiltration of vexing—or even harmful—dusts, smells and vapors. If, for example, you live along a gravel road, a thickly planted barrier of evergreens can filter the dust thrown up by passing cars from your air. A mix of fragrant shrubs and trees can make your front porch a pleasant place to relax. Similarly, barriers of deciduous and evergreen plants can infilter the pollution of passing cars and trucks, making your yard a healthful place to sun in.

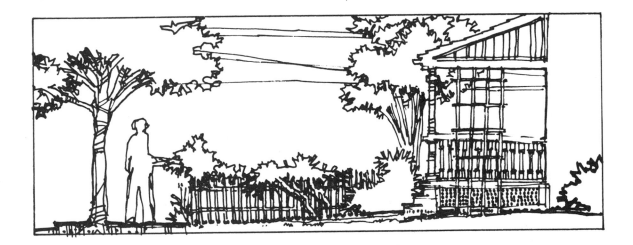

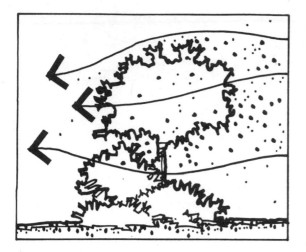

Plants effectively cleanse the air of gaseous and particulate pollutants. They can absorb unpleasant odors, while replacing them with their own pleasant ones. They release oxygen into the atmosphere as a by-product of photosynthesis. As polluted air encounters the oxygen-rich environment surrounding these, it becomes diluted.

resistance to pollution depending on their genetic makeup as well as their age, the distance from the source of pollution, and the concentration and duration of exposure. If you have problems with unexplained loss of foliage, you should check for a nearby source of pollution.

In addition to absorbing and metabolizing unpleasant odors, plants provide their own pleasant odors. Aromatic plants have long been used for their delightful and stimulating fragrance. But they can also absorb less unobtrusive odors and deodorize the smell with their own scents.

POLLUTION-TOLERANT PLANTS

The following plants include those that are tolerant of or resistant to certain pollutants. In general, they will survive higher-than-normal concentrations of the polluting agent that is mentioned. For information on pollutants that are not mentioned, check with your county extension agent or the United States Department of Agriculture.

Northern Coniferous Forest

Abies balsamea—Balsam fir (tolerant of ozone and hydrogen chloride; moderately resistant to sulfur dioxide)

Eastern Deciduous Forest

Oak-Hickory Forest

Acer saccharum—Sugar maple (tolerant of ozone and sulfur dioxide)

Cornus florida—Flowering dogwood (tolerant of ozone, peroxyacetyl nitrate [PAN] and sulfur dioxide)

Coastal Plain

Liquidambar Styraciflua—Sweet gum (moderately resistant to 2-4-D and sulfur dioxide; tolerant of PAN)

Nyssa sylvatica—Pepperidge, sour gum, black gum (moderately resistant to chlorine; tolerant of ozone and sulfur dioxide)

Southeastern Mixed Forest

Magnolia grandiflora—Southern magnolia (tolerant of chlorine)

Quercus spp.—Oaks (tolerant of hydrogen chloride)

Subtropic

Pinus Elliottii—Slash pine (moderately resistant to ozone)

Quercus virginiana—Live oak (tolerant of sulfur dioxide)

South-Central Swamp

Acer rubrum var. *Drummondii*—Drummond red maple (tolerant of sulfur dioxide, ozone and hydrogen chloride)

Nyssa sylvatica—Pepperidge, sour gum, black gum (moderately tolerant of chlorine and ozone)

Prairie

Platanus occidentalis—Sycamore, buttonwood, American plane (resistant to fluoride)

Populus deltoides—Eastern cottonwood (resistant to sulfur dioxide)

Rocky Mountain Evergreen Forest

Picea pungens—Colorado spruce, Colorado blue spruce (tolerant of ozone and PAN; moderately resistant to 2-4-D)

Pseudotsuga Menziesii—Douglas fir (tolerant of ozone and PAN; moderately resistant to sulfur dioxide)

Great Basin

Juniperus spp.—Junipers (tolerant of hydrogen chloride and sulfur dioxide)

Pinus edulis—Pinyon nut pine (tolerant of ozone)

Pacific Forest

Pseudotsuga Menziesii—Douglas fir (tolerant of ozone and PAN)

Thuja plicata—Western red cedar (tolerant of sulfur dioxide, ozone and hydrogen chloride)

California

Juniperus spp.—Junipers (tolerant of hydrogen fluoride and sulfur dioxide)

Pinus Sabiniana—Digger pine (tolerant of ozone)

AROMATIC PLANTS

The following plants produce their own pleasant odors, which can often effectively mask another unpleasant odor. Depending on the severity of the offending smell, you may need to plant a larger grouping of the aromatic species in order to reodorize the area.

Northern Coniferous Forest

Thuja occidentalis—American arborvitae

Tsuga caroliniana—Carolina hemlock

Eastern Deciduous Forest

Appalachian Oak Forest

Chionanthus virginicus—Old-man's-beard, fringe tree

Rhododendron arborescens—Smooth azalea, sweet azalea

Oak-Hickory Forest

Epigaea repens—Trailing arbutus

Rhododendron prinophyllum—Early azalea

Coastal Plain

Comptonia peregrina—Sweet fern

Myrica heterophylla—Wax myrtle

Southeastern Mixed Forest

Magnolia grandiflora—Southern magnolia

Osmanthus americanus—Devilwood

Subtropic

Lantana Camara—Yellow sage

Persea Borbonia—Red bay

South-Central Swamp

Itea virginica—Sweetspire

Nymphaea odorata—Fragrant white water lily

Prairie

Filipendula rubra—Queen-of-the-prairie

Salvia coccinea—Scarlet sage

Rocky Mountain Evergreen Forest

Lonicera ciliosa—Honeysuckle

Pseudotsuga Menziesii—Douglas fir

Great Basin

Ceanothus Greggii—Redroot desert ceanothus

Philadelphus microphyllus—Mock orange

Desert

Aloysia Wrightii—Lippa

Yucca glauca—Soapweed

Pacific Forest

Rubus spectabilis—Salmonberry, showy raspberry

California

Rhododendron occidentale—Western azalea

Ceanothus thyrsiflorus—Blueblossom

Noise Control

Plants can also act as noise filters. Outdoor sounds are usually deflected, reflected, refracted or absorbed by plants or landforms and reduced before they reach the receiver.

Temperature, humidity and, most importantly, wind have a definite effect on noise. Noise levels when measured upwind may exceed those measured downwind by as much as 25 to 30 decibels. Sound can be deflected by introducing an element that causes a noise to be bounced away from the hearer into another area. Reflection causes the sound to be reflected toward its source. Refraction occurs when acoustical energy is diffused or dispersed by striking a rough surface. Sound is also dispersed by turbulence and gusty winds, and sound shadows may be produced upwind of noise sources. Absorption takes place when an element receives the sound waves and traps or absorbs them, converting the sounds into other energy forms and, ultimately, heat.

Plant structure, especially vertical density, is the key to noise abatement. Wide belts of tall, dense trees are the most effective and have been shown to reduce sound levels by 4 to 8 decibels. This screening effect is most pronounced when trees and shrubs are combined with other soft surfaces, such as ground cover, instead of a hard, paved surface. Depending on the kind of noise, loudness may be reduced by 50 percent or more.

Vegetation is most effective in reducing irritating, high-frequency noises. Some plantings 25 to 50 feet wide, while reducing noise at higher frequencies by 10 to 20 decibels, are much less effective in reducing noise of lower frequencies. The lowest frequencies are the most difficult to eliminate and are not affected by plantings. Fortunately, they are the least annoying. Plantings of a single species are not as effective as mixed plantings, which will muffle a greater variety of noises.

In addition to controlling sounds, plants, in a sense, make their own sounds. The wind rustling through tree leaves helps to mask offensive noises. Plants also attract wildlife, such as birds and squirrels, and their busy noises help divert your attention from unwanted sounds.

Hedges and other narrow plantings are relatively ineffective in controlling noise, and noise buffers should be at least 25 feet wide. The height is also critical, since sound will travel over the top of a low barrier.

Highway noise can be greatly reduced by combining plants with slopes or earth mounds that rise above the edges of the highway. The most effective way to screen highway noise is to plant buffers of both trees and shrubs, 25 to 35 feet in width. If you use species that will help to control pollution, you can get double value from your efforts.

NOISE-CONTROL PLANTS

The following list includes examples of species that can be used to control noise. They should be used in combination with other plants in barriers that are lower toward the source and higher toward the hearer. This will direct the unwanted noise upward, away from the hearer.

Northern Coniferous Forest
> *Abies balsamea* — Balsam fir
> *Pinus Strobus* — White pine

Eastern Deciduous Forest
> **Oak-Hickory Forest**
> *Abies Fraseri* — Southern balsam fir
> *Quercus palustris* — Pin oak, Spanish oak

Coastal Plain
> *Pinus palustris* — Longleaf pine, southern yellow pine
> *P. Taeda* — Loblolly pine

Southeastern Mixed Forest
> *Pinus echinata* — Shortleaf pine
> *P. Taeda* — Loblolly pine

Subtropic
> *Casasia Clusiifolia* — 7-year apple
> *Pinus Elliottii* — Slash pine

South-Central Swamp
> *Erianthus giganteus* — Plume grass
> *Panicum virgatum* — Switch-grass, panic grass

Prairie
> *Juniperus Ashei* — Ashe juniper, Ozark white cedar

Rocky Mountain Evergreen Forest
> *Juniperus communis* — Common juniper
> *Phlox multiflora* — Phlox

Great Basin
> *Juniperus monosperma* — One-seeded juniper
> *J. scopulorum* — Colorado red cedar, Rocky Mountain juniper

Pacific Forest
> *Abies amabilis* — Pacific silver fir
> *Picea sitchensis* — Sitka spruce

California
> *Juniperus occidentalis* — Sierra juniper
> *Taxus brevifolia* — Western yew

Level Section

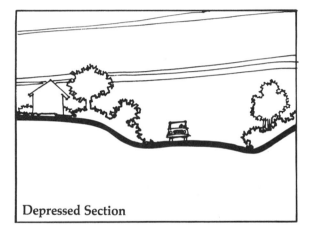

Depressed Section

Studies of highway noise suggest that plant barriers are very effective in buffering and deflecting highway sounds. The optimum width of such a barrier is 25 to 35 feet. It should include both trees and shrubs. The most effective barriers are planted in conjunction with landforms that either depress or elevate the noise source. If there is no change in grade, the plantings should be arranged to channel the noise up and away. Thus, ground-hugging plants should be closest to the sound source, taller ones a bit farther away and towering trees should be the final perimeter.

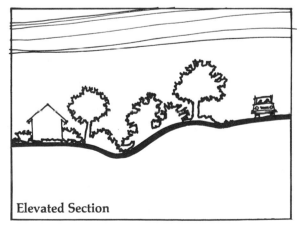

Elevated Section

Edible Ornamentals

In these days of rising food costs, you might look again at those flowering trees or shrubs surrounding your home. Why not grow equally attractive species that provide nutritious, tasty and unusual food? Over the past few decades, considerable effort has been spent, not to increase the food yield of crab apple, honey locusts and other fruit-bearing trees, but to develop sterile varieties that spare us the trouble of gathering a front-yard harvest.

Besides obvious favorites like apple, peach and cherry, there are many lesser-known but equally attractive and productive food-producing plants.

The following lists contain species, both native and exotic, that can provide food as well as beauty. In many cases, they will require higher maintenance than a nonfruiting ornamental, but the bonus to your diet (and grocery bill) will make any extra work worthwhile.

EDIBLE NATIVE PLANTS

Northern Coniferous Forest

Gaylussacia baccata — Black huckleberry (fruit)

Vaccinium angustifolium — Lowbush blueberry (fruit)

Eastern Deciduous Forest

Oak-Hickory Forest

Juglans nigra — Black walnut (nuts)

Rubus flagellaris — American dewberry (fruit)

Coastal Plain

Amelanchier obovalis — Coastal Juneberry, shadbush (fruit)

Southeastern Mixed Forest

Asimina triloba — Pawpaw (fruit)

Rubus trivialis — Southern dewberry (fruit)

Subtropic

Annona glabra — Pond apple (fruit)

Coccoloba Uvifera — Sea grape (fruit)

South-Central Swamp

Nelumbo lutea — American lotus (tuberous roots and seeds)

Typha latifolia — Common cattail (young shoots and stems, root stalks and down of flower heads)

Prairie

Carya illinoinensis — Pecan (nuts)

Prunus angustifolia — Chickasaw plum (fruit)

Rocky Mountain Evergreen Forest

Fragaria vesca — Strawberry (fruit)

Gaylussacia baccata — Black huckleberry (fruit)

Great Basin

Pinus edulis — Pinyon nut pine (nuts)

P. monophylla — Single-leaf pinyon (nuts)

Desert

Carnegiea gigantea — Giant saguaro (fruit)

Olneya Tesota — Ironwood (seeds)

California

Camassia Quamash — Quamash, camas (bulb)

Vaccinium occidentalis — Western blueberry (fruit)

TREES FOR NUT AND SEED PRODUCTION

Carya illinoinensis — Pecan

C. laciniosa — Shellbark hickory

C. ovata — Shagbark hickory

Castanea mollissima — Chinese chestnut

C. pumila — Chinquapin

Corylus americana — Hazelnut

Fagus grandifolia — Beech

Gleditsia triacanthos — Honey locust

Juglans cinerea — Butternut

J. nigra — Black walnut

J. regia — Carpathian walnut

Pinus edulis — Pinyon pine

P. Sabiniana — Digger pine

Quercus alba — White oak

Q. bicolor — Swamp white oak

Q. Michauxii — Swamp chestnut oak

Q. prinus — Chestnut oak

TREES FOR FRUIT PRODUCTION

Amelanchier canadensis — Serviceberry
Asimina triloba — Pawpaw
Celtis occidentalis — Hackberry
Cornus mas — Cornelian cherry
Diospyros virginiana — Persimmon
Malus coronaria — Crab apple
Morus alba — White mulberry
M. nigra — Black mulberry
M. rubra — Red mulberry
Prunus alleghaniensis — Alleghany plum
P. cerasifera — Cherry plum
P. Cerasus — Sour cherry
P. pensylvanica — Pin cherry
P. serotina — Black cherry
P. virginiana — Chokecherry
Sorbus americana — American mountain ash
Viburnum prunifolium — Black haw
Ziziphus Jujuba — Chinese jujube

SHRUBS FOR FRUIT PRODUCTION

Arctostaphylos Uva-ursi — Common
  bearberry
Cornus canadensis — Bunchberry
Cydonia spp. — Quince
Gaultheria hispidula — Creeping snowberry
Gaylussacia spp. — Huckleberry
Opuntia spp. — Prickly pear
Physalis pruinosa — Ground cherry
Prunus maritima — Beach plum
Ribes spp. — Currant, gooseberry

Rubus spp. — Blackberry, raspberry
Sambucus canadensis — Elderberry
Shepherdia argentea — Buffalo berry
Vaccinium spp. — Blueberry
V. macrocarpon — American
  cranberry
Viburnum Lentago — Sweet viburnum
V. trilobum — Highbush cranberry

TREES FOR SUGARS, DRINKS OR SEASONING

Acer saccharum — Sugar maple
Betula spp. — Birch
Ptelea trifoliata — Hop tree
Rhus glabra — Smooth sumac
R. typhina — Staghorn sumac
Sassafras albidum — Sassafras
Tilia americana — Basswood

SHRUBS FOR MISCELLANEOUS EDIBLE USES

Calycanthus floridus — Sweet shrub
Ceanothus americanus — New Jersey tea
Comptonia peregrina — Sweet fern
Gaultheria procumbens — Teaberry
Hamamelis virginiana — Witch hazel
Ilex glabra — Inkberry
I. vomitoria — Yaupon
Lindera Benzoin — Spicebush
Myrica pensylvanica — Bayberry
Rosa rugosa — Rose

14

Aesthetic Uses of Plants

In doing your site analysis, you examined the appearance of your landscape and determined what was good and bad about the way it now looks. As you design your natural landscape, you will need to return to this evaluation to make sure you are solving all of the existing visual problems. You will also need to be sure that your new plantings are attractive as well as functional. By using native plants in their proper habitats, you will be able to achieve the delicate balance of form, color and texture that often escapes the amateur landscape designer. Because your design must also work for your unique property and your particular family, you will need to make sure that screening is provided where needed, good views are enhanced and spaces are defined. Here is where you learn how to do it.

Nature is the best, and least expensive, landscape designer. In nature, abstractions like color, texture, form and line are worked out by the very best design principles. Whereas design judgments are often arbitrary and subject to personal opinion, the forms and beauty in nature are the result of life-sustaining functions. The leaves of a tree are arranged in various patterns, not to provide us with shade or graceful form, but to get the amount of sunlight they require. And the flowering species that occur at the edge of forests are there, not so we can see them, but because they too need the sunlight that's not available in the dark forest.

Such simple design rules as placing high things in back and low items in front, planting in masses, giving trees and shrubs room to grow, screening undesirable views and framing beautiful ones are basic to good planting, says landscape architect Tom Shively. More detailed suggestions are hard to give specifically; much more useful is observation on your part. Look at how plants grow in nature: the massing of different textures in marshes; the grouping of soft, billowy forms in abandoned fields; the complex face of the edge of a woods; the specific microenvironment of each group of flowers and ferns in the woods. Each kind of plant has its own favorite type of place to grow; if you carefully study what it is. before you in nature and try to reproduce the same effects, you can achieve real success.

Much of our visual experience of the landscape is spatial, and it is this aspect that can be manipulated to create a design that works for you. The spaces formed by vegetation are one of the most conspicuous aspects of natural landscapes. Plants are able to form walls, ceilings or floors in the landscape. They're able to articulate, define,

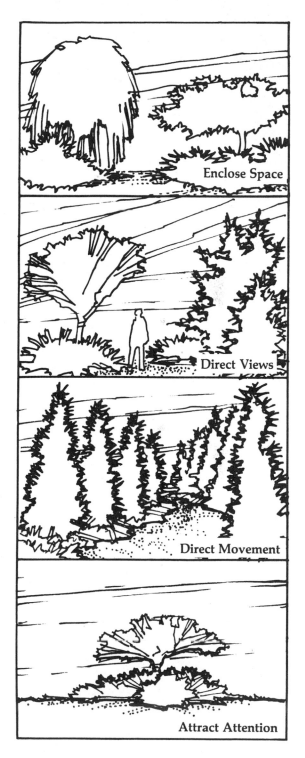

Plants can perform all sorts of practical visual effects. They can be used to create spaces, either by setting off a perimeter or by enclosing space underfoot and overhead as well. Plants can be chosen and placed to direct movement and sight. You can even attract attention with plants. Every ecological region has plants that can be manipulated in size or form to create the visual effects you desire.

Hedge

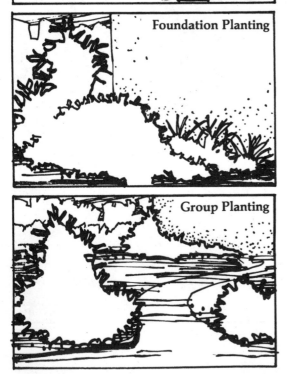

Windbreak

Foundation Planting

Group Planting

Plants in the landscape serve aesthetic and functional purposes, often simultaneously. A hedge, for example, can be attractive and at the same time can define a boundary or enclose a space and can screen out prying eyes or an unattractive view. A windbreak can do all of the same things, yet can present a different appearance than a hedge. Foundation plantings, group plantings, and specimen plants all have legitimate places in a natural landscape, despite the bad reputation they've gained through the mishandling of them so common in contemporary landscaping. Foundation and group plantings can both define elements in the landscape, such as pathways and entranceways, and can help integrate man-made objects with the landscape. When choosing plants for such uses, you must study plant associations that exist in truly natural settings, rather than select plants, then prune or otherwise force them to serve your purposes.

Specimen Plant

enclose or limit exterior space, either by themselves or in conjunction with other physical components of the landscape, such as ponds or rock outcrops.

Plants are often treated as sculptural elements with individual and seasonally changing beauty, particularly when they stand alone as specimens. But series of single plants growing together may form a nearly solid visual barrier, and it is the whole, rather than the individual specimen, that creates the space and form. Plants can control both the size and quality of exterior space, and you must consider this when locating plants on your property.

Plant walls can be formed by narrow hedges or wider border plantings. Ceilings can be created by large canopy trees or overhead vines. Floors, too, can be defined by a change in texture, such as paving adjacent to ground cover or grass. The following information describes how to use plants to achieve the visual effects you desire.

Screening and Privacy Control

Plants can be used to screen undesired views and to create a sense of privacy. While fences or walls can perform the same functions, plants are more attractive and less rigid. Go back to the evaluation you made, in which you determined what needed to be screened in your landscape. Now decide where the screen is needed; how dense it should be; whether the viewer is stationary or mobile; at what season the view is most unsightly; the viewer's angle of approach to the unpleasant view; and whether he or she can be directed to an alternative view in addition to or instead of screening. After making these decisions you can select the height, width and extent of plant material you will need. In general, effective screening and development of privacy require plantings that reach 6 feet or more in height. If year-round screening is important, evergreens should be used.

In addition to screening unattractive views, plants can be used to direct your eye to beautiful ones. You can do this by placing plants so they

Within the larger vocabulary of the natural landscape, you can choose and use plants, individually or in combination, to achieve your aims. In each of the top three situations, a single element has been derived from the natural planting, on the bottom, and planted in such a way as to perform a specific function.

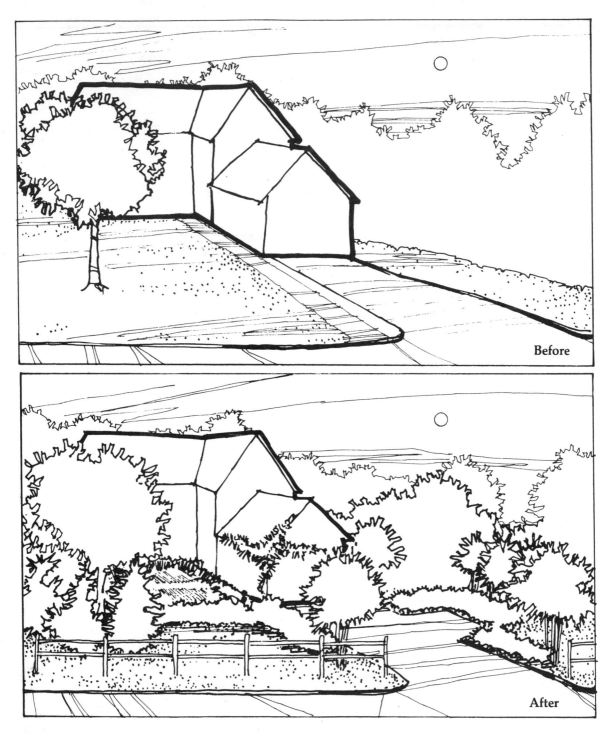

Before

After

Visual screens and barriers were created around the front of the suburban property in the landscape plan developed for it (see Chapter 11). In the "before" sketch, the house can be seen to be an awkward part of the landscape. After new plants are established, the house is seen as integral to the landscape. The plantings frame views of the house and direct movement to desired locations.

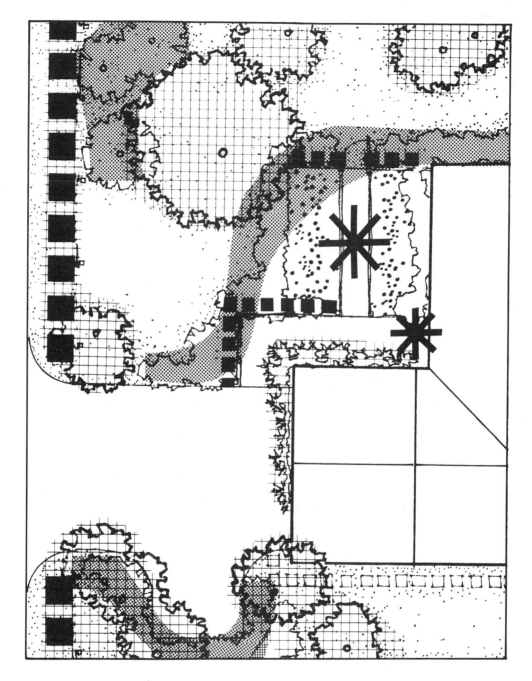

The plan view casts the planting plan (from Chapter 11) in a different light. The lines of dark blocks denote barriers, the sweeps of shading denote buffers and the crosshatching denotes screens. Two focal points of the landscape—the flower and herb garden and the front entrance of the house—are marked with asterisks. In developing your own landscaping plan, you can use such symbols to mark on a base map where you need screens and barriers, then find plants that will fit your needs.

reveal an outstanding view gradually as one moves through the landscape, or it may be done by framing or restricting the view with plants.

In general, it is better to frame a view so that it is seen through an opening from a desirable location. This creates greater richness and a more exciting experience than a fully revealed view, which can quickly become boring and commonplace.

PLANTS FOR SCREENING

Northern Coniferous Forest
Picea rubens—Red spruce
Pinus Strobus—White pine

Eastern Deciduous Forest

Appalachian Oak Forest
Abies Fraseri—Southern balsam fir
Tsuga caroliniana—Carolina hemlock

Oak-Hickory Forest
Ostrya virginiana—American hop hornbeam
Rhus copallina—Shining sumac

Coastal Plain
Pinus rigida—Pitch pine
Rhododendron viscosum—White swamp azalea

Southeastern Mixed Forest
Ilex Cassine—Dahoon, cassina
Ulmus alata—Wahoo elm, winged elm

Subtropic
Coccoloba diversifolia—Pigeon plum, snailseed
C. Uvifera—Sea grape
Forestiera acuminata—Swamp privet

South-Central Swamp
Crataegus viridis—Green hawthorn

Prairie
Juniperus Ashei—Ashe juniper, Ozark white cedar
Prunus Munsoniana—Wild-goose plum

Rocky Mountain Evergreen Forest
Picea pungens—Colorado spruce, Colorado blue spruce
Sambucus pubens—American red elderberry

Great Basin
Juniperus monosperma—One-seeded juniper
J. scopulorum—Colorado red cedar, Rocky Mountain juniper

Desert
Olneya Tesota—Ironwood
Yucca brevifolia—Joshua tree

Pacific Forest
Acer circinatum—Vine maple
Picea sitchensis—Sitka spruce

California
Juniperus occidentalis—Sierra juniper
Pinus Coulteri—Coulter pine

Circulation

Plants can effectively control the movements of people and animals. This can be done by visually implying a barrier or by actually providing an impenetrable object. Thick, solid plantings of 6 feet or more will serve for both physical and visual control. Using plants with thorns, such as roses or blackberries, planted closely together will be just as effective as a fence in stopping movement.

PLANTS FOR BARRIERS

Eastern Deciduous Forest
Robinia hispida—Rose acacia, bristly locust
Rubus flagellaris—American dewberry

Coastal Plain
Zanthoxylum clava-Herculis—Hercules'-club

Southeastern Mixed Forest
Rubus trivialis—Southern dewberry

Subtropic
Lycium carolinianum—Box thorn, Christmas berry
Pithecellobium Unguis-cati—Cat's-claw, black bead

South-Central Swamp
Crataegus viridis—Green hawthorn
Gleditsia aquatica—Water locust, swamp locust

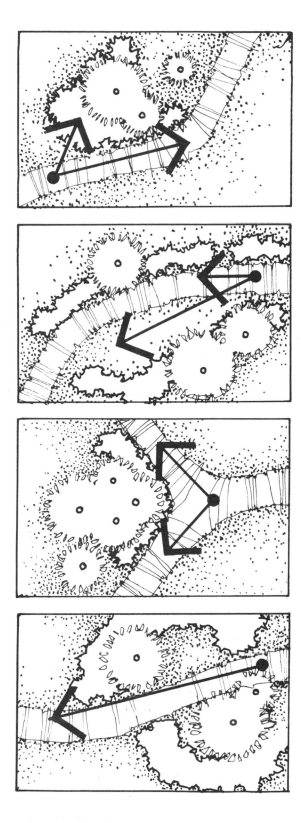

While a straight line may be the shortest distance between two points, it is not necessarily the most pleasant way to get somewhere. But unless there is an obvious reason for a meandering or circuitous walk, the path may be bypassed in favor of a more direct route.

In the situation at top, any effort to take a shortcut to the left is stopped by a barrier of plants. In the next situation, there is nothing to inhibit the taking of a shortcut below the path; thus a walker is likely to take the shorter route, in time wearing a path in the ground cover. The third drawing illustrates an effective split in a path, allowing a walker to go either way, but definitely not straight ahead. The path will be followed in the final situation simply because there's no way to shortcut the relatively straight path.

Prairie
> *Bumelia lanuginosa* — Chittamwood, false buckthorn
> *Maclura pomifera* — Osage orange

Rocky Mountain Evergreen Forest
> *Crataegus rivularis* — River hawthorn
> *Juniperus communis* — Common juniper

Great Basin
> *Echinocereus viridiflorus* — Green pitaya
> *Juniperus scopulorum* — Colorado red cedar, Rocky Mountain juniper

Desert
> *Holacantha Emoryi* — Crucifixion thorn
> *Yucca aloifolia* — Spanish-bayonet

Pacific Forest
> *Rubus spectabilis* — Salmonberry, showy raspberry

California
> *Rosa californica* — California wild rose

Flowering Trees

Although the flowering period for most plants is very brief, it can be spectacular. The delicate white flowers of the dogwood and the early spring blooms of the red maple can provide a dramatic lift for winter-wearied spirits.

When you choose a plant, you should always consider the color of its flowers, but never let that be the sole determinant of your choice. There is much longer lasting color in the foliage, bark and fruit, and this may be even more dramatic than that of the short-lived flowers.

FLOWERING TREES

Northern Coniferous Forest
Acer rubrum — Red maple (red)
Sorbus americana — American mountain ash (white)

Eastern Deciduous Forest

Appalachian Oak Forest
Halesia carolina — Silver-bell, silver-bell tree (white with pink, early spring)
Stewartia ovata — Mountain camellia (white, July)

Oak-Hickory Forest
Cornus florida — Flowering dogwood (white, early spring)
Liriodendron Tulipifera — Tulip tree, tulip poplar (white, June)

Coastal Plain
Magnolia virginiana — Sweet bay (white, June–July)

Southeastern Mixed Forest
Cotinus obovatus — American smoke tree (purple-brown, early summer)
Magnolia grandiflora — Southern magnolia (white, June–July)

Subtropic
Erythrina herbacea — Cardinal-spear (red, March)
Piscidia piscipula — Jamaica dogwood (white)

South-Central Swamp
Acer rubrum var. *Drummondii* — Drummond red maple (red)
Gleditsia aquatica — Water locust, swamp locust (white)

Prairie
Cercis canadensis — Eastern redbud (pink, April–May)
Cotinus Coggygria — Smoke tree (purple-brown, spring)

Plains
Cephalanthus occidentalis — Buttonbush (white, July)
Itea virginica — Sweetspire (white, June–July)

Great Basin
Amelanchier utahensis — Serviceberry (pinkish white, spring)

Desert
Carnegiea gigantea — Giant saguaro (white, spring)
Dalea spinosa — Smoke tree (blue)

Pacific Forest
Cornus Nuttallii — Mountain dogwood (white, spring, August–September)

California
Arbutus Menziesii — Madrona (white, May)
Heteromeles arbutifolia — Toyon (white, June–July)

Form

Form is less of a concern in natural landscaping than it is in traditional formal plantings. In the common landscape design where foundations are decorated with pyramidal, columnar or rounded plants, forms can be an unnatural, unattractive and high-maintenance obsession. Most of your plantings in a natural landscape will occur as groups of different species, each with its own form, but together creating a diversified, rich and interesting appearance.

If you intend to plant a tree or shrub where it will stand alone and be seen as an individual specimen, then you should know what general shape it has.

FORM PLANTS

Northern Coniferous Forest
drooping
Sorbus americana — American mountain ash
irregular
Pinus Banksiana — Jack pine
Salix nigra — Black willow

Cereus giganteus
(columnar)

Torreya californica
(pyramidal)

Bursera microphylla
(irregular)

Abies procera
(rounded)

Pinus Balfouriana
(horizontal)

Pinus edulis
(rounded)

Acer saccharum
(rounded)

Magnolia acuminata
(pyramidal)

Cornus florida
(irregular)

Pinus rigida
(irregular)

Halesia carolina
(rounded)

Ulmus crassifolia
(drooping)

*Form is important primarily with specimen plantings.
Any of these trees would be a marvelous specimen,
calling attention to itself.*

pyramidal
>   *Abies balsamea* — Balsam fir
>   *Picea rubens* — Red spruce
rounded
>   *Acer rubrum* — Red maple

Eastern Deciduous Forest

Appalachian Oak Forest

pyramidal
>   *Abies Fraseri* — Southern balsam fir
>   *Magnolia acuminata* — Cucumber tree
rounded
>   *Halesia carolina* — Silver-bell, silver-bell tree
>   *Styrax grandifolius* — Snowbell, storax

Oak-Hickory Forest

irregular
>   *Betula nigra* — River birch
>   *Cornus florida* — Flowering dogwood
pyramidal
>   *Liriodendron Tulipifera* — Tulip tree, tulip poplar
rounded
>   *Acer saccharum* — Sugar maple
>   *Carpinus caroliniana* — American hornbeam

Coastal Plain

irregular
>   *Magnolia virginiana* — Sweet bay
>   *Pinus rigida* — Pitch pine
pyramidal
>   *Quercus phellos* — Willow oak
>   *Taxodium distichum* — Bald cypress

Southeastern Mixed Forest

rounded
>   *Crataegus Marshallii* — Marshall's hawthorn
>   *Quercus falcata* — Spanish red oak

Subtropic

irregular
>   *Piscidia piscipula* — Jamaica dogwood
>   *Zanthoxylum Fagara* — Wild lime

rounded
>   *Coccoloba diversifolia* — Pigeon plum, snailseed
>   *Sideroxylon foetidissimum* — Mastic

South-Central Swamp

irregular
>   *Populus heterophylla* — Swamp cottonwood
pyramidal
>   *Quercus Nuttallii* — Nuttall oak
>   *Taxodium distichum* — Bald cypress

Prairie

drooping
>   *Cotinus Coggygria* — Smoke tree
>   *Ulmus crassifolia* — Cedar elm
irregular
>   *Maclura pomifera* — Osage orange
>   *Plantanus occidentalis* — Sycamore, buttonwood, American plane
rounded
>   *Celtis occidentalis* — Hackberry

Rocky Mountain Evergreen Forest

pyramidal
>   *Pinus flexilis* — Limber pine
>   *Pseudotsuga Menziesii* — Douglas fir

Great Basin

rounded
>   *Acer saccharum* subsp. *grandidentatum* — Big-tooth maple
>   *Pinus edulis* — Pinyon nut pine

Desert

columnar
>   *Carnegiea gigantea* — Giant saguaro
>   *Lemaireocereus Thurberi* — Oregon-pipe cactus
irregular
>   *Bursera microphylla* — Elephant tree
rounded
>   *Cercidium floridum* — Blue palo verde

Pacific Forest
    pyramidal
        Larix occidentalis—Western larch
        Thuja plicata—Western red cedar
    rounded
        Abies procera—Noble fir

California
    horizontal
        Pinus Balfouriana—Foxtail pine

irregular
    Pinus Coulteri—Coulter pine
    P. Sabiniana—Digger pine
pyramidal
    Pinus muricata—Bishop pine
    Torreya californica—California nutmeg
rounded
    Juniperus occidentalis—Sierra juniper
    Taxus brevifolia—Western yew

SECTION III
Landscape Construction

15

Working with the Earth

Shovel in hand, you are at last ready to start landscaping. You may have started your project months ago, but only after you've studied your property, your desires and your capabilities, and only after you've plotted out on paper exactly what you are going to do, are you ready to turn that first spadeful of earth. Your site plan should

be done, your planting plan as well, and your phasing plan should not be far from hand.

In many situations—perhaps in most—the construction work is minimal. If you are in one of these situations, skim right on through to Section 4.

But perhaps your plan requires you to push

the earth a bit, lay drives or paths, build a patio, put up a privacy fence. Much of this work should be tackled before you do planting. No sense in risking tender new plants. If this is your situation, read on, for the following chapters will tell you the basics of landscape construction, from elementary earth moving, to the basics of paving, to the fundamentals of building privacy fences.

The exact sequence in which you'll work should be established by your phasing plan, and in preparing this plan, you should have given considerable thought to the best approach. Most likely, you'll be reading this before even beginning your site analysis. But if you are ready to build and plant but haven't read through the remaining sections of *Nature's Design*, now's a good time to do it. Then reevaluate your plans; what you learn may prompt you to change them.

Usually, any earth-moving work is done first, followed by interrelated construction and planting projects. Earth moving can be a lot of work, and it shouldn't be done without very good reason. If your landscaping plan is truly natural, you'll be doing as little as possible to alter nature's original design for your property. Occasionally there's no way around it. You want a relatively flat area beside the house for outdoor activities. You have a drainage problem. You want a pond. So you do some earth moving.

In planning any earth moving, consider the ramifications of what you are going to do. Be sure that in solving one problem—if indeed it's a problem you are trying to solve—you are not creating another. Be sure, too, that the problem is really a problem; maybe you should plant a bog garden rather than grade a hollow to drain it.

Grading

Grading, which is the moving of earth, is generally done to provide slopes for drainage and to create level areas for construction of outdoor terraces or walks. It may also be done for more specialized purposes—to control erosion, excavate pools, build protective berms or ridges, or to improve the appearance of the land. Grading is done with a wide range of tools, from the basic pick, shovel and rake, through all sizes of tractors and bulldozers, to giant power shovels, carryalls and prime movers. Unless you are a proficient

operator of heavy equipment or are willing to pay the price of hiring one, you will need to confine your grading projects to the pick and shovel scale.

GRADING ORDINANCES

City and township ordinances have been established in many places to control grading operations. These are essential because building foundations that are close together may be endangered by reckless undercutting, or roadways may be obstructed by washed-out slopes. You may be required to submit plans and specifications, secure a permit and allow regular inspection of all grading operations except excavations less than 5 feet deep or fills less than 3 feet high requiring less than 5 cubic yards of soil.

The ordinance may establish maximum cut-and-fill slopes and drainage controls and often contains an important section titled "Compaction of Fills." This regulates all fills intended to support buildings or structures and requires that they be compacted to a minimum of 90 percent. Compaction of fill for other purposes may not be required except where necessary to prevent saturation, slipping or erosion. The percentage of compaction required always depends upon the particular circumstances and type of fill.

Compaction techniques should be done under the supervision of a licensed engineer because it usually involves placing fill in thin layers, each with a specified moisture content. It requires heavy equipment, such as a sheepsfoot roller, which must be applied for the proper length of time. Deviations from the standards may be permitted if overseen by a licensed civil engineer.

Although not necessarily pointed out in a grading ordinance, the legal rights of others may be affected by any grading you do.

Utilities are likely to come after you with an expensive lawyer if you uproot a buried cable or pipe. Such lines are covered in easements listed on deeds. Check your deed, and if there's any doubt, contact utilities operating in your area. (You *should* have located these lines on your base map, way back when.) The company will undoubtedly help you and safeguard its rights and property by staking out the right-of-way for you.

If you are unhindered by utility *companies*, don't overlook your *own* utilities: your well and your septic tank. These, again, should be on your base map, but double-check before unleashing a bulldozer.

Next, check your plans to ensure that you aren't going to be diverting runoff onto a neighbor's land or onto a road. Don't expect to get away with flooding a neighbor's yard or the community's road to eliminate a wet spot in your yard. If your solution presents a sufficiently egregious problem for someone else, you can expect to have a new problem, probably legal.

If you have doubts about your grading plans, get professional advice—from municipal officials, soil conservation service advisors or a professional engineer.

CUT AND FILL

There are two kinds of grading operations—cutting, which is the removal of soil, and filling, which is the addition of soil. Soils and earthwork techniques vary throughout the country, but certain principles are basic to all regions. Because soil consists of small particles that do not normally stick together, it is difficult to create a very steep slope. The degree of possible slope is based on the angle of repose of the material that you are grading. Sand has the lowest angle of repose and rock the highest. Most soils fall between them. Normal maximum angles for ordinary soil are 1 vertical foot to 1 horizontal foot (1:1) for cut slopes, and 1 vertical foot to 2 horizontal feet (1:2) for filled slopes. Any buildings or outdoor structures, such as pools, should be based on undisturbed subsoil and not on fill, which may shift enough to crack foundations. If a slope steeper than 1:1 or 1:2 is required, it can be held up with a retaining wall or other structural assistance.

A newly cut or filled slope will not remain smooth and stable without controlling the runoff of surface water. Water running over the slope from above will erode and wash the soil away. This surface water can be diverted from the top of the slope with berms or ditches that parallel the slope and channel the runoff to lower ground. After you have graded the slopes and established drainage controls, you must cover the bare ground surfaces as quickly as possible. This will protect the surface from the direct impact of rain and wind and also minimize the slow decomposition

and crumbling that occurs on exposed soil. If you want to establish ground covers on newly graded slopes, plant them close together to provide immediate protection.

Changing existing grades always disturbs the natural relationship between topsoil, subsoil and bedrock. This can be avoided by stripping all existing topsoil from areas that are to be graded, built over or paved and stockpiling it to be used later. At least 6 to 12 inches of topsoil should be removed, and the grading should allow for this depth of soil to be replaced after the rough grades are made. It takes several hundred years to build a layer of good, natural topsoil, and too often it is buried under tons of subsoil and rubbish where it can't be recovered. The few dollars saved in grading costs will be spent to haul in new topsoil.

DO-IT-YOURSELF GRADING

With a pick and a shovel and a wheelbarrow, you can do a great deal of earth moving yourself. Don't be unnecessarily intimidated by a task, either because you can't figure out how to measure and thus control the grade, or because the amount of earth to be moved seems monumental. Most anyone should be able to master the simple yet effective techniques necessary to measure grade. And if you will but allow yourself the time and apply yourself diligently, veritable mountains of earth can be moved with a shovel and wheelbarrow.

Nevertheless, use good judgment. Tackle the jobs you can manage yourself and hire out those you have any hesitation about handling. Get an estimate from a contractor, and you may find yourself tackling those jobs you first hesitated on.

ROUGH GRADING

The classic cut-and-fill project is one in which you dig into a slope, creating a cliff bounding as many as three sides of the bottom of the excavation. The material excavated is simply pushed over the edge of the cut, down the slope, broadening the excavation bottom. What's removed from the cut is used as fill, in other words. Depending upon the size of the excavation, this sort of project is quite easily handled with pick and shovel. Just remember to strip the topsoil first from both the area to be filled and the area to be cut.

A lot of earth can be moved with simple hand tools, your personal energy and time. The tool of choice for breaking up soil in making a cut is the mattock, a double-ended pick with one pointed blade and one broad, flat blade. Swinging a mattock is good exercise. Use a long-handled spade when you need a shovel. One with a flat-edged blade won't

work as well. A substantial contractor's wheelbarrow with a deep, commodious tub is best for hauling waste from cut to fill. Compacting can be done using a standard lawn roller, with a rented hand or power tamper, or with a homemade tamper, made from plywood and a length of 2 × 2. Spread the fill in layers and compact each layer.

Use a spade—that is, a long-handled shovel with a pointed blade—for scooping up the soil. Use a mattock, a pick that has a pointed blade and a flat blade, for loosening the soil. Depending upon the situation, a tiller might be used to loosen the soil.

As you build up the fill, tamp it. Spread about 6 inches of soil, then compact it with a heavy roller or, better, with a rented manual or power tamper. Spread more soil and compact that. More soil, more tamping. As noted, this compaction process is particularly important if you plan to build anything over the fill, whether it's a shed or only a sidewalk. If time isn't a factor, give nature a few months to really settle the fill before you construct anything on it.

Even if you are cutting only, or filling only, the general methods remain the same.

Sometimes disposing of material removed from a cut can be a problem. Try working it into your property's terrain. If, for example, you're excavating for a pond, consider building a low ridge along one side of the pond. Or use the material to create drainage swales.

Likewise, getting clean fill can be a problem. Avoid fill that's laden with foreign objects, particularly building materials, unless it will be deeply buried. Large stones, pieces of brick and concrete block, or scraps of wood or plasterboard will make planting more arduous than it need be. And soil that's been polluted with cement, lime or plaster, or with how-do-you-know-what chemicals, domestic or industrial, won't support healthy plants and may even be harmful to you. You're working on a natural landscape here, so keep that in mind when you hunt around for fill.

(The caveat against foreign objects in fill, by the way, should be borne in mind if you are building and as you do any landscape construction project. Clean up after yourself or your builder. Don't figure on covering building refuse with a few inches of topsoil and being able to forget it.)

If at all possible, try to get fill that's similar to the soil in your area. You may create a wet spot if you use impermeable fill. On the other hand, you may create a dry spot if you use fill that drains markedly faster than surrounding soils. This probably would only be a problem in protracted dry spells.

FINISH GRADING

The classic cut-and-fill situation doesn't present any particular problems other than laborious work. It is clear-cut and lacks subtleties. You just pick and shovel your way until the ground looks pretty much the way you want it. When you get the ground underfoot roughly level (or roughly to the slope you want), you've completed the rough grading.

But it is unlikely that you want the ground underfoot absolutely level, and it is a surety that you don't want a subtle slope in the wrong direction. You'll get puddles or runoff collecting in the wrong spots—your basement, the patio, where you park the car. You may have to do finish grading. Here's where the measuring comes in.

A rough level of accuracy can be achieved using the home surveying technique explained in Chapter 3. This approach will help you establish how close you are to a desired slope, but it may not do for determining that an area slopes ever-so-gently away from the house.

To establish the degree of such subtle changes, use stakes and string and a line level, which is a tiny spirit level that can be suspended on a string. Start in the spot that is at the proper level or elevation; drive a stake there. Walk to the opposite end of the area and drive a stake there. Run a string between the stakes and level it up, using the line level. If the ground surface parallels the string, the ground is level.

If you want to establish a slight grade, calculate how much lower one end of the area should be than the other in terms of vertical drop. For example, if you want the drop to be 2 inches for every 10 feet of run, and the area is 15 feet wide, then the lower end should be 3 inches below the upper end. At the lower stake, measure down 3 inches from the string, mark the spot, then retie the string.

For a broad area, you will probably need to set up a gridwork of strings to help you establish the grade. First, set up parallel strings 5 to 10 feet apart, running from one end of the area to the other. Then establish the cross grade with rows of strings at right angles to the first set. Leave enough room between the strings and the ground to use a shovel or rake without getting tangled up. If the ground is so uneven at the start that the strings

Finished grade is established by calculating the desired deviation from a level plane, then setting up means to monitor that deviation. In your situation, tie string between two stakes, using a line level to ensure that the string is level. Tie the string high enough on the stakes so that you'll be able to work a rake beneath it. Establish the slope by measuring down the low-end stake (or up the high-end stake) the amount the ground must slope, mark the spot, then retie the string. In most situations, you'll need several strings to guide your work. You may find it worthwhile to set up a gridwork of strings to help you monitor a compound slope. In doing the grading, work immediately under the strings first, creating a uniform distance between string and ground, even if it means making substantial cuts or building distinct ridges. Then cut or fill the intervening areas. Of course, the more lines you string, the more lines there'll be to tangle up in your shovel, rake and feet.

lay across the ground, make little cuts for them to run through. Then, once the grid is set, continue cutting the surrounding ground until you've got the grade you want.

These basic techniques should see you through most grading projects. But there are still things to know about working with the earth. All, in one way or another, involve grading, and all will be covered in the following pages.

Drainage

If you have drainage problems, they may be caused by the type of soil or by excess filling or disturbance of the soil during construction. Whether or not you can solve the problem yourself depends on the type of drainage system you need, surface or subsurface; on your soil conditions; and on your physiography.

In general, it is easier to improve surface drainage than to install subsurface drainage systems. If you need to improve the subsurface drainage, a tile system may be the answer. Preferably, this should be done before you finish the grading or start the planting, but after heavy construction has been completed. It should be installed in conjunction with a proper surface drainage system. You should consult the Soil Conservation Service; its experts can make recommendations about drainage systems for your soil type and physiography.

SURFACE DRAINAGE

Surface drainage, which is the removal of water over the surface of the soil, is accomplished by grading and is less complicated and often eliminates the need for installing a subsurface system. However, good surface drainage should exist even if an underground system is also used. If you don't have drainage problems, it is still to your advantage to understand the principles and methods of surface drainage to ensure that your landscaping plans don't destroy an existing system.

Surface drainage is based on the very simple fact that water flows downhill and that the more confined the area and the smoother the surface, the faster the flow will be. On areas where there is no penetration of water into the soil, such as roofs, nonporous patios, walks or driveways, there will be a lot of runoff, which must be directed to a suitable area.

All building roofs should have gutters and downspouts that drain into a dry well or carry the water to central collecting points. Without gutters, the water from rainfall rushes off the roof onto the soil surface with great force, creating compaction and eventual problems for any plantings. Although it is common practice to plant rows of woody plants under a roof line, these plants have a difficult enough time surviving the water falling directly on them, let alone the wet compacted soil or the ice that forms on them in the winter. The runoff from the downspout should, if not connected to a dry well or storm sewer, be directed to a larger planted area that permits a flow of water away from the building. This is often accomplished by a concrete gutter, but a more aesthetic method is a narrow swale, or sod waterway, which gradually becomes larger. Another, more creative, way of using this waterlogged area is to locate rocks where they can take the impact of the falling water and to plant water-loving species that will enjoy and absorb the excess moisture.

Drainage from large paved areas, such as an extensive nonporous parking area or a nearby road, can best be accomplished by the installation of a storm-sewer system at the time of construction. An adequate gutter system can move the water to storm-sewer collection points and prevent it from flowing into nearby planted areas. If there are no gutters and curbs, not only is the nearby soil forced to handle excess water, but in northern climates the salt used to melt the snow and ice will be carried to them also. Smaller paved areas, such as patios or walks, cause fewer problems but should, nevertheless, be adequately drained. That means ensuring that they slope in the direction you wish the water to go (away from the house) and, if possible, providing a porous surface with adequate underdrainage.

Surface drainage techniques for planted areas are relatively simple but must be consciously designed. Unwanted depressions or low pockets should be eliminated, and the grade should always be made lower in the direction away from structures and paved areas. Water should flow to a central surface drainage system, such as a swale, to surface inlets of a subsurface drainage system or dry well, or to a street or public storm sewer. It should never be carelessly directed off your land, as

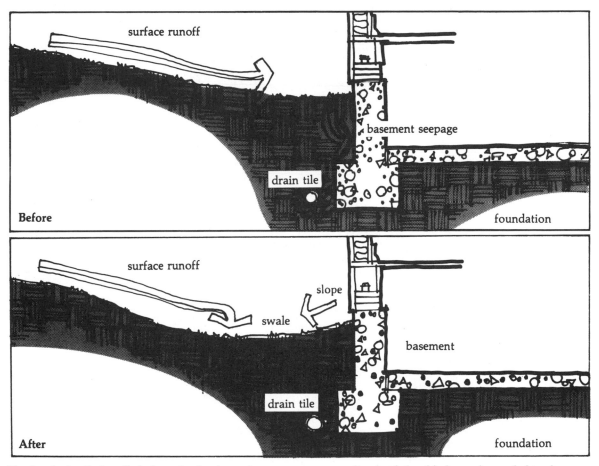

Having drain tile installed along the footings of a building is not in itself a guarantee that surface runoff will not seep into the building's basement. The surrounding land should always be graded to slope away from the foundation.

directing water onto your neighbor's property is not ethical and, in most cases, is not legal.

CREATING A SWALE

Swales are really shallow drainage ditches. When properly shaped, they are barely visible. A swale must have enough slope to carry water to a collection ditch but not so much that it acts as a flume. The layout of a system of swales will depend on the existing physiography and on the amount of water to be drained. The amount of water to be drained also influences the size of each swale. By using your contour map and your analysis of the existing drainage conditions, you can see where you need swales to redirect surface water.

Once you've mapped the swale (or swale system) on paper, map it exactly where it will be. Use strings and stakes or some lime to mark its position.

Digging the swale is simply a matter of excavating a trench the width and depth of a shovel's blade, mounding the soil removed along the downhill side of the trench, then shaping the cross section of trench and soil heap into a gentle hollow and berm. There are no hard and fast rules on the specific dimensions of a swale. Generally, the steeper the slope, the deeper the swale; and the greater the drainage area, the wider the swale. You may have to depend upon your own experience with the volume of runoff you are trying to redirect.

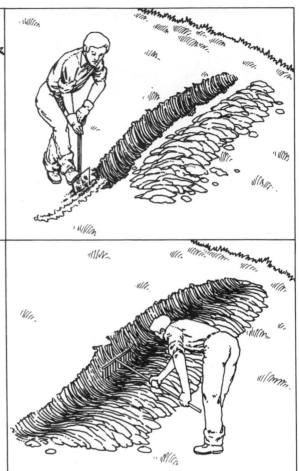

Marking the course it is to follow is the first step in creating a drainage swale. A good way to do this is with lime. Scoop some into a small paper bag, then dust it from the bag along the swale's path. Remove sod and set aside topsoil. Then dig a shallow trench that will be the swale's basin, turning the soil onto the downhill side. Since a swale should be a gentle, attractive depression, rather than a ditch, use a rake to contour the waste soil and the trench. Relay the sod to forestall erosion.

To avoid erosion and to prevent the transformation of your new swale into a raw gutter, sod the swale as promptly as possible. If sod is beyond your means, seed it and mulch it well.

SUBSURFACE DRAINAGE

If your drainage problems really are problems, and if simple surface drainage systems won't solve them, you have to consider subsurface systems. The conventional subsurface system is a network of drain tiles, carefully engineered and installed to drain water from the soil and quickly direct it to a stream, catch basin or storm sewer. Such systems are best designed and installed by professionals. It's unlikely that you'll need much of such a system if you are creating a truly natural landscape.

There are two home-brewed variations of the tile system, however, that you can excavate yourself if the area to be drained isn't too big. One is a French drain, the other a dry well. Both involve filling an excavation with crushed stone, in one to provide a permeable passageway for water through otherwise impermeable soil, in the other to provide a subsurface catch basin.

A French drain is simply a trench that has sufficient pitch to naturally redirect water from where you don't want it to where you do want it. The key is to keep the bottom of the trench as evenly sloped as possible, so that water will flow through it, rather than collect in depressions.

Here again, you must calculate the degree of slope you want or need, then work with stakes and strings to measure the slope of the trench as

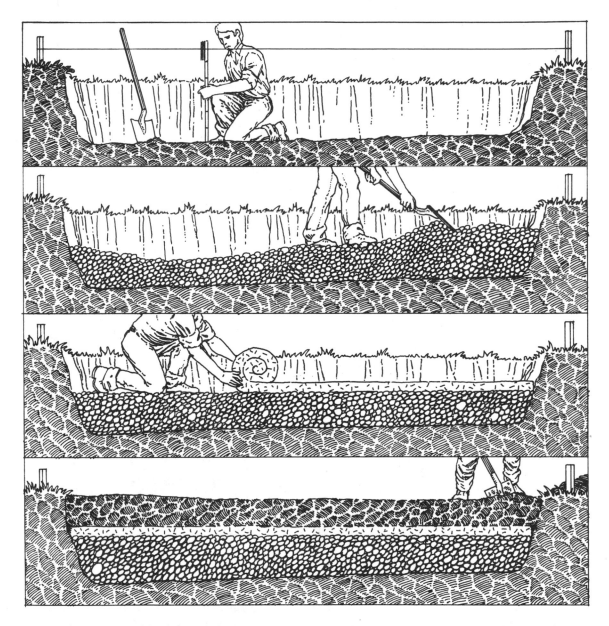

A French drain is created by digging a ditch, partially filling it with crushed stone, then backfilling with earth. Dig the ditch to the desired depth, monitoring the contour of the bottom by measuring from a level line strung at the excavation's edge. Fill the trench to within a foot of the surface with crushed stone. Then

cover the stones with batts of unbacked fiberglass insulation and backfill. A dry well is made in much the same way, though the excavation is a pit, rather than a trench. Dry wells often have French drains leading away from them.

you excavate. In plotting your French drain, follow the topography. While it is conceivable that you could get water to flow counter to the contour of the ground using a French drain (and certainly

using drain tile), there's no point to making more work for yourself. You could end up having to dig quite a trench.

After the trench is dug—make it 2 to 3 feet

deep—pour in crushed stone, about a 1–foot layer. Lay batts of unbacked fiberglass insulation on the stones, not to insulate them, but to prevent soil particles from filtering into the pore spaces, thus plugging up your drainageway. Backfill over the insulation.

A dry well is constructed in the same way. It is, however, a pit rather than a trench that you dig. And it is advisable to put batts of insulation around the sides of the pit before filling it with crushed stone.

Retaining Walls

The need for a retaining wall occasionally arises in connection with grading. If a slope is too steep for planting or stability, a properly constructed wall can keep the soil from eroding and provide more useful, level areas.

Because retaining walls must support a great deal of weight and accommodate drainage from the slope, they have to be carefully designed and constructed. In many places, building regulations govern the construction of retaining walls. A permit must be obtained, and the construction monitored by a building inspector. This shouldn't intimidate you. Rather, the regulations should help you with the design, and, if you approach the inspector in person and in the proper spirit, he can be a source of information and guidance rather than a source of aggravation and extra work.

A low wall, such as that required to retain a gentle slope, is easily constructed by a beginner. But if the wall is going to be more than 4 feet high, the advice of a professional may well be in order. You may want an engineer to design the wall so you can build it.

The materials you use and the method of construction should be determined by the intended use of the wall, your skills, your finances and the character of your landscape. A concrete-block wall may hold up a bank, but it definitely will be a jarring intrusion in a natural landscape. The wall could just as easily be constructed of stone, brick, adobe, railroad ties or some other material and be more in harmony with your landscape.

RAILROAD-TIE WALL

Railroad-tie retaining walls are seen more and more these days. They are relatively easy to build,

Layout and excavation are the first steps in building a retaining wall of railroad ties. Where a bank is to be cut into an existing slope, a significant excavation will have to be done before layout can start. Where a wall will be erected on an existing slope and a bank created by backfilling behind the wall, the layout can be done first. Layout is most easily done by marking the ends and the exposed face with stakes and string. Excavate a trench about 6 inches deep to set the first course of ties in. The first course of ties, set in the trench, should be level end to end, but should tip very slightly into the slope. Subsequent courses should in their turns be set ¼ inch back from the edge of the preceding course. Set the first tie, and adjust the ¼-inch front-to-back pitch with a ruler and level.

The ties may have to be cut to length and must have holes drilled in them for rebar pins that will hold them in place. Use a chain saw to cut the ties and a ½-inch power drill with an electrician's auger to drill the pilot holes. When drilling holes in the first course ties, prop one tie up on another so the drill bit doesn't dig into the ground, dulling it. Pilot holes must be drilled in subsequent courses after the ties are in place. Drive the pins with a sledge hammer. After the second course is secure, excavate for the deadmen, placing them 6 to 8 feet apart, and for the lateral drainage system. Fill the drainage excavation with crushed stone, lay the drain tiles, cover them with more stone, then set the deadmen in place. Position

the crossplates and pin them in place, then set the connecting ties in place and pin them.

From this point on, completion of the wall is routine. Cut each tie to length, set it in place, ¼ inch back from the edge of the tie it rests on, drill deep holes for the rebar pins, then drive the pins in place. Similarly, end walls should be built up on the deadmen at each end of the main wall. The end ties can be secured to the wall by pins driven at right angles into the wall. The backfilling can proceed as the wall rises, or be done at one time after the wall is completed. Remember to form a lateral drainage swale behind the wall, and plant the bank as promptly as possible to prevent soil erosion.

the materials are readily available and they look good in a natural setting. These reasons are all particularly pertinent to the do-it-yourselfer creating a natural landscape.

In building a railroad-tie wall, as in building any retaining wall, the first steps are to lay out the wall and to acquire your materials. Obviously, when you will be purchasing materials, you want to be able to estimate accurately what you'll need, so you don't either overbuy or underbuy. Knowing the size of the wall, in length and height, is important in doing the estimating. Lay out the wall in place, to be sure the calculations you've done on paper actually hold.

The timbers you'll use commonly are sold in 8-foot lengths of 6 × 6 and 6 × 8. Real railroad ties are pickled in creosote, which makes them rot resistant but also hard on the hands—use gloves—and hard on plants. Most lumber dealers and garden centers will have landscaping ties, which are the same as railroad ties but for the preservative (and consequently the color).

As you build, you'll pin the timbers first to the ground, then to each other, using lengths of the reinforcing bars used in concrete work, commonly called rebar. The ⅜-inch size is what you need. You should use three pins for each timber, with the pins for the bottom course being at least 36 inches long and the pins for subsequent courses at least 12 inches long.

As the courses are built up, offset each course toward the cut by at least ¼ inch, so the wall leans into the hill. This will help the wall resist the pressure of the mass of soil. You should also incorporate an arrangement called a deadman at each end of the wall and every 6 to 8 feet in between. The idea is to bury an anchor deep in the hillside to help secure the base of the wall. Thus, a 2- to 3-foot piece of tie, called a crossplate, is located 8 feet from the wall and parallel to it; it is connected to the wall by an 8-foot tie.

All these timbers and the necessary rebar pins have to be figured into the bill for materials for your wall.

You will need some tools that aren't always a part of the home handyman's collection. The first is a chain saw, used to cut the ties. You can *try* cutting them by hand, but the exercise gets old quickly, and it will definitely slow your progress. To drill the pilot holes for the rebar pins, you need a *heavy-duty* ½-inch electric drill equipped with a ⅜-inch electrician's auger bit, which is 18 inches long. You'll need a sledgehammer to drive the pins. You should be able to rent these tools.

BUILDING THE WALL

The first course of your railroad-tie retaining wall should be laid about 6 inches in the ground. So, after laying out the wall, dig a trench about 6 inches deep. The bottom of the trench must be level, so if you are working with a complex slope, your trench may be more than 6 inches deep in places; it must be that deep at the shallowest point. If your soil is impermeable, so that drainage is a problem, you may find it advisable to excavate deeper and add 6 inches or so of crushed stone in the bottom of the trench. In any case, no footer is necessary, nor is it necessary to begin below the frost line.

Drill three holes through each tie to be used in the first course, one in the center and one about 6 inches from each end. Don't drill through the tie and into the ground, as this will dull the bit; prop the tie on another.

Lay these ties in the trench, butting the ends together, and leveling them from end to end. From front edge to back edge, however, the ties should have a ¼-inch pitch. Use a level and ruler to establish this pitch. Cut lengths of rebar and pin the ties in place.

Add the second course. The front edge of the ties making up this course should be ¼ inch back from the front edge of the first-course ties. Rather than butting the ends tightly together, leave a gap between them to allow for drainage. Stagger the joints from course to course. Carefully drill three holes through each of these ties and on into the first-course ties; don't drill all the way through the first-course ties too, though, or the bit will suffer. Cut rebar pins and drive them in place.

You are ready, now, to excavate for behind-the-wall drainage and for the deadmen. The drainage trench is created by simply widening the trench in which the first course of ties rests, then backfilling with crushed stone. Lay either 4-inch ceramic drain tiles or perforated plastic drain pipe atop the stone, a couple of inches from the second-course ties. Cover joints between tiles or lengths of pipe with tar paper or batts of unbacked fiberglass insulation, then cover the tile or pipe with more crushed stone.

Mark the position of each deadman's crossplate and ready a trench for it, if necessary. Cut the crossplates, drill a couple of holes for rebar pins in each, position them and pin them in place. Then add a tie connecting the low wall to the crossplate and pin it to both.

The internal deadmen are now complete, but the end ones will be the foundations for end walls.

The erection of the wall to whatever height you've planned follows routinely from this point. Each new course is pulled back ¼ inch toward the hillside. Butt the ties tightly together. Each tie is pinned in three places to the ties beneath it. The end-wall ties, joining the main wall at right angles, are pinned not only to the tie beneath but also at right angles to the end of the adjacent tie.

You can backfill as you build, or wait until the wall is complete. Just remember to backfill in layers and tamp each layer.

STONE WALLS

Stone is probably the most overlooked building material available today. It's strong, extremely attractive, usually almost cost-free and, best of all, it's easy to work with. All you need to build with stone is time, determination and stone. You don't even need mortar.

The art of stonemasonry is usually shrouded in mystery, for the stonemason is a person who literally builds structures out of the bare earth. Stonemasonry need not be thought of as some sort of archaic art; it's a basic construction method, easily adaptable to those with limited experience or ability. Because of the very nature of stonework, there is room for error. All you need worry about is that the face of your wall remains plumb.

There may be abandoned or ruined stone buildings in your area. Seek out the owner and bargain. Construction crews often consider the stones they have to excavate a nuisance. Offer to take them off their hands. Abandoned quarries seldom are picked clean, so check at the bottom of slopes for usable rubble.

If you have to buy stone from a working quarry, keep in mind that unless the quarry is close to your home, hauling costs may exceed the cost of the stone itself.

When buying stone, you will order by the cubic yard. Measure the length of your wall in feet, and multiply by the height and width. Divide this total by 27 to get the cubic yards needed. Add 5 percent or so for waste.

Once you have the stones at the building site, you must sort them. A word on stone-handling safety is in order. Regardless of your age, remember that the age of a stone wall is measured in decades, so if you become fatigued while working, it is of no consequence at all should you decide to leave the next stone for tomorrow. Unless you are used to this heavy labor, your body will do only so much work at first, but each day your strength will build.

Remember that the way to lift is by making your legs do the work, not your back. Always keep the stone close to your body. Always be careful of your footing. It is also worthwhile to purchase tough-skinned mason's gloves.

Separate your pile of rocks. In one pile, put the flattest, squarest, and most regular pieces. These will be needed for ends, corners and top. Put long stones whose length is equal to the wall's width in another pile. These will be the "tie" stones. Also, make a pile of small, wedge-shaped stones.

From time to time, you may have to cut stones. This is done with a chisel and sledgehammer. To cut a slab, score a groove about ½ inch deep where the stone is to be cut. Make the cut by one of three methods: lift one end of the slab and strike along the groove with a hand sledge; lay the slab on a bed of sand and strike along the groove with the sledge; or place an angle iron beneath the slab and strike it from the top with the sledge.

Although you can use mortar to bind the stones together, cultures all around the world have built walls without mortar. Here in North America, it is mostly a rural tradition, but a well-laid drywall will beautify a garden or home landscape anywhere.

DRYWALL CONSTRUCTION

The first step in the actual construction is to lay out the wall. Stake the two front corners, and then the back two corners.

The width of a drywall is not altogether arbitrary. For a wall 3 feet or less in height, the minimum width is 24 inches. For each 6 inches

Use your head when handling stones. Never lift more than you must. Roll stones along the ground or up ramps made of strong planks. Cut pipe or 1-inch dowel into 1- or 2-foot lengths and use them as rollers in moving stones that are too large to tumble end over end. And don't be reluctant to enlist help.

higher than 3 feet, add 4 inches to the bottom width. A real journeyman wall builder lays up low- and medium-height walls with both faces plumb. The taller the wall, the stronger the argument for building it with a bit of taper, or batter. A good guideline is that the top should be one-fifth narrower than the bottom.

When these planning steps are complete, prepare your foundation. Walls 3 feet high and less generally can be built right on the ground, without any digging besides leveling a strip equal in size to the wall's bottom dimensions. As time passes, the bottom course of stones will settle into the ground anyway. For taller walls, it will be a stronger construction if you dig down a foot or so and flatten the bottom of the trench.

The first layer of stone must be a sound, level base. Instead of using valuable slablike rocks below ground, you can achieve the same effect by digging holes to fit rocks with only one flat face so the flat face is up. These faces need not be exactly level but should dip slightly toward the inside of the wall. This will turn the force of gravity in your favor by having all the pieces of the wall pull inward. Place all the stones that are below ground level a few inches apart, and fill in the spaces with smaller rocks and gravel for drainage purposes.

With a retaining wall, of course, you must provide for drainage from behind the wall. The nature of drywall construction is such that there is some allowance for water to weep through the gaps between stones. But you should also provide for lateral drainage along the base of the wall, just as you do with railroad-tie construction. Along the back of the wall, excavate a shallow trench, then fill it with crushed stone. Lay 4-inch ceramic drain tile or perforated plastic drain pipe on the stone, covering the joints between tiles or pipes with tar paper or batts of unbacked fiberglass insulation, then covering the entire run with more crushed stone. As the wall is laid up and as you backfill, this drainage system will be buried in the hillside.

For the first above-ground course, use the biggest rocks you have so you don't have to lift them off the ground. At this point, you will begin to apply the basic principle in drywall construction: One over two, two over one. This is exactly the way a brick wall is laid, and it provides that

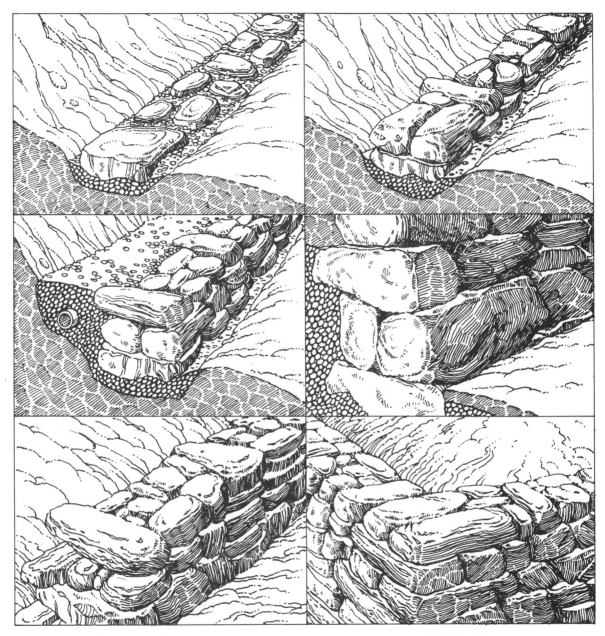

A stone drywall can be bedded on the ground or in 5 to 6 inches of sand spread in a 6- to 10-inch-deep excavation. All the huge, irregular rocks should be used, if possible, in the first course. Throughout the wall's construction, tie stones, which are large enough to extend from one face of the wall to the other, should be laid every few feet. There should be tie stones at the ends of the wall in every other course. Start the first course with tie stones at the ends. Use gravel to fill between stones in the first course to help drainage. Lay up the next course, starting the one-over-two pattern that characterizes stone and masonry work. Use odd and irregular stones in the center of the wall as much as possible, and try to angle the stones toward the center. After the first two or three courses are finished, install a lateral drainage system behind the wall, then start backfilling. From this point on, alternate from stonework to backfilling. The thickness of the wall should increase as the wall rises, with the additional thickness being taken up on the inside; the exposed face should have slight batter.

there be no vertical fissure where the wall can separate. So, position your stones so that the one going on top always covers the space between at least two stones beneath it.

Check the stones with a level as you go. If a rock wobbles, see if you can knock off a knob or point to make it fit more solidly. If not, use the small, wedge-shaped stones to shim it up. These shims should always be placed toward the inside of the wall, pointed end out. If they are placed near the outside, they tend to work themselves out.

As you work, place your stones with the flattest sides as top and bottom. The next flattest side, or the next largest flat dimension, should go toward the outside.

If you have a lot of round or irregular stones, start each course by placing the worst stones down the middle of the wall, placing and shimming them so they do not wobble. Then, place rocks with at least one flat side along the sides. In this type of arrangement, each stone should touch five others: rocks to each side, two rocks beneath, and at least one core stone. If you are short of stones, you can also use this arrangement to fill the core of the wall with rubble.

On any wall, you must place tie stones every 6 to 8 feet. A tie stone runs across the wall, its longest dimension perpendicular to the line of the wall. In such a manner, these rocks tie one face of the wall to the other, and add to its transverse strength.

Ends and corners demand special attention, and you'll have to use your best rocks for them. The biggest, flattest rocks, and any rocks with square ends, should go on the ends. Ends should use as many long rocks as possible to tie the end into the wall, and the end must also use tie rocks on every other course.

MORTARED STONE CONSTRUCTION

You may, just now, be thinking of all the mortared stone walls you've seen. The truth is that you *can* mortar the stones together, but all you'd really be doing is making more work and expense for yourself.

To build a sound mortared stone wall, you should dig down below the frost line and start there. You should pour a concrete footing first. Then you should follow all the procedures you would for building a drywall. But you must mix mortar, with all that entails: cement, lime, sand and water, a mixing tub and hoe, trowels and a striking tool, plus lots of cleanup.

Only you can decide whether or not the reward offered by the mortared stone wall will make the effort and extra expense of constructing it worthwhile.

The specifics of doing the work lie between laying up a drywall and laying up a brick wall. Information on pouring the footing and mixing mortar are covered in the following section, "Masonry Walls."

Once the foundation is started, you build from the corners first, and fill in the middle. For the bottom layer of stone, a layer of mortar up to 2 inches thick should be spread, and stones laid in this. Each stone in the entire wall should always be laid on its broadest face. With a layer of stone in place, smaller stones should be used to fill in the gaps behind the face of the wall, both to add strength and to save mortar.

To lay the second layer of stone, spread mortar about 2 inches thick along an area 4 to 5 feet long. Place stones so that they intercept joints between stones below. This will greatly add to the strength of the wall, as there will be no channels of mortar running straight for any distance. For beginners, it is better to find a stone to fit an area than to shape a stone to fit.

When you are laying up a wall, run a string from one corner to the other, directly along the face of the wall. As you prepare to put a stone in place, look over the top of the wall, down the string and the face of the wall, line up the face of the new stone with this plane, and gently rest it on the bed of mortar, gently pushing it down to ensure good contact. If a stone must be moved after it has been set in the mortar bed, it should be lifted out entirely and reset to ensure a good bond.

With the front stones in place, the back of the wall may be filled with a cheaper class of masonry or poured concrete known as backing, to save cost. Every few feet you should place a stone that runs entirely through the width of the wall, to tie the different layers together and to add strength.

Due to the weight of the stones, you should not add more than about 2 feet in height to the wall at a time. Allow the mortar to dry completely before adding another layer.

MASONRY WALLS

Building a masonry retaining wall presents more toil than either of the mortarless alternatives already presented. But if your plans call for one, you can build it yourself.

The first step, of course, is to calculate how much of each material you'll need, purchase it and get it delivered to the site. You'll need your masonry units, be they bricks, blocks or both. You'll need builder's sand, hydrated lime (not agricultural lime), Portland cement and, if you will be mixing the concrete for the footing yourself, gravel. Estimating the quantities of ingredients needed for mortar and concrete can be tricky, but you should be able to get some assistance from the people at the building-supply company. Read over the section on mortar that follows and the information on mixing concrete in the next chapter, so you'll be able to hold up your end of the discussion. Don't buy bags of mixed dry ingredients: they are far too expensive for the quantities you'll be needing.

BRICKS AND BLOCKS

Brick walls can be made of single, double or triple thickness, and there are a variety of ways of arranging or bonding the bricks. For a retaining wall, you should use at least a double thickness of brick. A single thickness won't be strong enough.

You can use blocks, though the wall won't be terribly attractive. Blocks are used a great deal in construction these days for two very practical reasons. One is that they are significantly less expensive than bricks. The other is that a block wall goes up a lot faster than a brick wall because the structural units are larger. You can compromise on your materials by building a brick-veneered block wall. In this situation, you build a block wall, then lay up bricks against the blocks, making the wall thicker and more attractive. For a retaining wall, this isn't a bad approach.

Additional strength can be gained with a block wall by pouring concrete into the cores of the blocks after the wall is laid up. The strength can be bolstered further by imbedding reinforcing bars in the footer so that they project vertically out of the concrete about 10 inches. These bars will fit into the cores of the first two courses of block. When the cores are filled with concrete, all the elements of the wall—footer, blocks and concrete—will be securely bonded together.

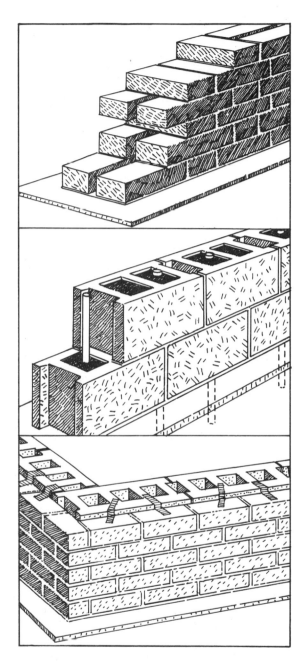

Masonry retaining walls can be constructed of brick (top), block (center) or brick and block (bottom). Brick walls should be at least two bricks thick. Though not necessary, a block wall can be strengthened by installing rebars in the footing that extend into the block cores, then filling the cores with concrete. If you plan to veneer a block wall with brick, be sure to use wall ties in the mortar joints to bond the two materials together.

Full-size blocks weigh about 30 pounds each, and the standard size is 8 inches wide, 8 inches high and 16 inches long. Actually, the dimensions are 7⅝ inches by 7⅝ inches by 15⅝ inches; the nominal dimensions allow for half the ¾-inch mortar joint that you would have between blocks in a finished wall. Specialized blocks are available for corners and solid top courses. Also available are 4-inch-wide blocks, ordinarily used for interior partitions in buildings, but which you could use for a veneered wall.

There is a wide variety of bricks available, differing not only in texture and color, but also in grade. While finish and color are matters of personal taste, the grade of the brick you choose should depend upon the job it is to do.

Severe-weathering bricks (SW) are for use where the bricks are in contact with the ground, as they will be in the retaining wall you are planning. Medium-weathering bricks (MW) are for use where they will be subjected to freezes but will not come into contact with the ground. If the bricks will be used in a veneer over a block retaining wall, you could get by with MW bricks. Stay away from no-weathering bricks (NW), as these are designed for interior work.

Most bricks measure 8 inches by 2¼ inches by 3¾ inches. When calculating the number of bricks needed, however, use nominal dimensions that take into account a ½-inch mortar joint. Thus, you would work with 8½ inches by 2¾ inches by 3¾ inches.

The pattern of bricks and half-bricks, placed as headers or as stretchers, is called the bond. The simplest, and in the United States by far the most common, is the running bond. It has all bricks laid as stretchers, except at ends and corners. Ends use half bricks set as headers. A stronger bond, because it has more transverse strength, is the American bond, in which every sixth course is a header course. This is a good bond to use in a double-thickness retaining wall.

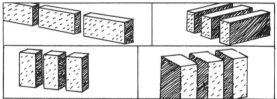

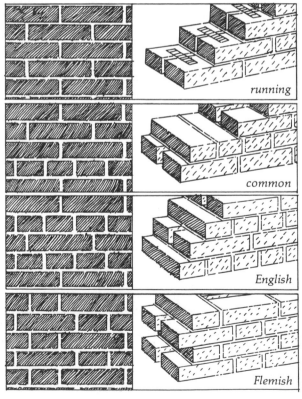

running

common

English

Flemish

The nomenclature of the brick has the tops and bottoms called beds, the sides called stretchers and the ends called headers. Bricks can be laid on any of their faces in various combinations called bonds. The running bond may be the most familiar, with the bricks set in stretcher courses—on their beds with their stretchers exposed—in a one-over-two pattern. The common, English and Flemish bonds are all ideally suited to double-thickness construction, since the header bricks—those laid on their beds with their headers exposed—tie the two layers together. Row-lock courses, in which the bricks are set on their stretchers, and soldier and sailor courses, in which the bricks are set on their headers, generally serve decorative rather than structural purposes, though a row-lock header course is a good way to complete a double-thickness retaining wall.

Note that in double-thickness, 8-inch-wide walls, the stretcher courses are laid side by side, so the wall is two bricks thick. Obviously, you'll leave a ½-inch gap between the adjacent stretcher courses to compensate for the greater length of a single brick over the combined width of two bricks. But you'll find, as you lay up the bricks, that your fingers need that ½-inch gap. You'll find yourself leaving it if you build a brick veneer against a block wall.

MORTAR

Neither bricks nor blocks are bonded together with concrete. You use mortar, which is a mixture of Portland cement, hydrated lime, sand and water. Dyes are available if you dislike the gray-white color of plain mortar; inquire where you buy your bricks and mortar ingredients. You can buy mortar cement, which is ordinary Portland cement to which hydrated lime has been added; the use of this cement obviates the need for lime.

To mix mortar, combine 1 part cement, 3 parts sand and ¼ part hydrated lime with water. This is the optimum mix and is the one you'd get using mortar cement. (When using mortar cement, incidentally, mix 1 part of it with 3 parts of sand.) If you do use more lime, you should also use more sand. Don't add more cement, though. You can go as far as to combine 1 part cement with 2 parts lime and 9 parts sand, but you won't get a very strong finished product.

You can do the mixing with a cement mixer, but if you are working alone, as opposed to working with a whole crew of experienced bricklayers, it's probably more efficient to mix small batches of mortar by hand. Use a wheelbarrow or a metal trough especially made for the job to mix in. A regular hoe will do for mixing, but a special mason's hoe, which has a couple of holes drilled in the blade is better. Use an old bucket for measuring out the ingredients. A flat-bladed shovel is useful for shoveling cement and sand into the bucket and for shoveling mortar onto your mortar board. Keep your tools hosed off; the mortar will dry on them surprisingly quickly, and, once dried, it won't come off. They don't need cement overshoes.

Mix your dry ingredients first. Then slowly add water. It is too easy to overdo the water, giving you soup, rather than what masons call mud. For block work, you want fairly dry, sticky mortar, while for brick work, the mortar can be wetter. But in no case do you want a runny mix. So mix the dry ingredients, then add a little water at a time, while mixing, until you have the consistency you desire.

If you do go too far, you can always add more sand, cement and lime to soak up the excess moisture and, in the bargain, give you a larger batch.

Be somewhat reserved about the size of the first batch you mix. Experience will demonstrate how far a modest batch will go and how long it takes to use it up. You *can* revive a batch that's drying by working in a little water, but if you find yourself doing this routinely, you probably ought to cut back on the amount you are mixing in the first place.

TOOLS

Tools needed start with the aforementioned mixing equipment. To apply the mortar, you will use a trowel. Choose one with a substantial wooden handle, since you will use the end of it to tap the bricks or blocks into alignment on the mortar bed. Some masons twist a rubber crutch tip on the handle to extend the life of the tool. If you use the metal trowel blade, the blocks or bricks could crack.

Perhaps the most important tool is the mason's level. It is used to check both horizontal level and vertical plumb. Most masons equip themselves with two levels, one an 18-inch level for aligning individual bricks or blocks, the other a 4-footer for checking several bricks or several courses at a time.

To go with the levels, you'll need string and line blocks. You start laying up a wall at the corners (or ends), building up courses with a diminishing number of bricks in each. A level is used here to get the corners square and plumb. Then a string is stretched from one corner to the other, lined up with the front top edge of the first course. The space between the corners is then filled in, using the string rather than a level to check the alignment. The line blocks hook over the end bricks and the tension on the string holds them in place. As one course is completed, it's easy to move the blocks and string up to the next, one end at a time.

A mason's rule could also be handy, although you can cobble up a storyboard to use instead. A mason's rule looks, at first glance, like an ordinary folding rule, and it does have standard inch and foot increments marked on one side. But the other side has standard brick and block and mortar-joint spacings marked on it. With it, you can quickly tell if you are laying down mortar joints of a consistent thickness. And that's harder to do than you might imagine. If you don't want to spend the money for this rule, then use a regular ruler to mark the brick and mortar spacings on a board, making it a storyboard. For a retaining wall, you most likely won't need a long one.

You'll need a jointer, or striking tool, and a dust brush. The jointer is used to finish off the mortar joints so they are uniform in appearance and shed water. This is sometimes called striking off the joint, hence the name striking tool. The brush you'll use to dust the sandy mortar particles off the wall as you strike off the joints.

A mason's hammer, or brick hammer, and a brick chisel are tools you may want to invest in, though you could get by without them, depending on the job. First of all, it is possible that you won't need to cut any bricks or blocks to do your job. Or it's possible that you could use a claw or ball pein hammer, if you already own one, to break the few bricks you have to cut for your job. If you cradle a brick in one hand and give it a sharp rap in the center with a hammer, it will break just about in half. If the rough edges can be concealed in a mortar joint, and they usually can, there's no need for further chiseling. You can use the edge of the trowel to whack off ragged edges.

Finally, you'll need something to hold your mortar as you work. Perhaps you can work right out of the wheelbarrow you use to mix the mud. A square piece of exterior plywood can be set on sawhorses or blocks. Or you can buy a mud pan, made specifically for the purpose.

You've got your tools and materials, and you are ready to go. In sequence, you'll excavate for and pour the footing, build the wall, install the drainage system behind the wall, then backfill. So the next step is to prepare the footing.

FOOTINGS

Concrete footings are a preliminary and important step. They must always be set below the frost line so they can protect the structures built upon them from frost-heaving damage. Many specifics on how deep, how wide, how thick, and other details about the footings for your area are spelled out in local building codes.

As a rule of thumb, the thickness of a footing should be twice the width of the wall or other structure it is supporting. The footing should be twice the width of the wall it supports. However, if it is supporting a retaining wall, which in this case it is, increase the width by at least one-third.

Part of your preplanning also should include determining if a particular location and type of reinforcement is required by any local codes. Usually, a minimum of three horizontal rods are placed in the lower third of the footing's thickness. Also, some walls require vertical reinforcing bars, which actually must be anchored in the footing. Usually, they are placed no closer than 24 inches.

Finally, under the category of preplanning, determine the necessary depth of footings. The object is to set the footing below the frost line. In Bangor, Maine, for instance, the depth is 48 inches. In Tampa, Florida, which has no real frost line, it is 6 inches. The excavation for footings thus can be a major task.

Use the walls of the excavation as the form for the footing. Excavate first for the wall, creating a trench that's wide enough to work in. Then dig a second trench, positioning it exactly where you want the footing, and digging it only as wide and as deep as the footer is to be. Put a layer of sand or crushed stone in the bottom of this trench, then pour the concrete.

LAYING UP THE WALL

When the footer has cured, you are ready to lay up the wall.

Make a dry run of the first course. Lay out the corners or ends first, working *without* mortar. Then place all the stretcher blocks or bricks along the footing, leaving a ⅜-inch gap between them for mortar.

Set up a string to mark the top edge of this course. Drive a couple of stakes into the ground at each end of the wall, and run a string from one to the other, positioning the stakes and the string so that when you line up the bricks or blocks with the string, they will be straight and level. Then remove

A footing is a monolithic concrete structure, set below the frost line, upon which a wall is built. It can be a very easy concrete project, since it needs no elaborate forms and no elaborate finishing. To lay out the footer is to also lay out the wall and the necessary excavations for both. Set up batter boards at each end of the site for the wall, with a nail in each marking the position of excavation, footing or wall. Strings can be run between nails or taken down as the needs of the work dictate. After the various boundaries are set, dig a broad ditch to the depth of the top of the footer. You'll have to work in this trench to lay brick or block on the footer, so make it roomy enough. Then dig a trench for the footer, making it just as wide and deep as the footer is to be. Pour in the concrete, lay in rebar, top off the pour and screed. The surface should be level, but it need not be floated or troweled.

the bricks or blocks and stand them along the footer.

Spread a thin layer of mortar on the footer beneath the strings. You start working at the corners or ends. Use the thin mortar bed for marking guidelines for the first course of bricks. Use a plumb bob or hold the level next to the guide string to mark a spot directly below it in the mortar. Locate similar points about 2 feet away and connect the two with a straightedge. Then you can remove the strings.

Lay about ½ inch of the mortar from the corner down the wall line, but be careful not to cover the lines in your first mortar. Place the first brick in the mortar against the line. Check it for

horizontal level, both lengthwise and crosswise. Take the next brick and smear mortar on one end with your trowel. A bricklayer will do this, then with three more flicks of his trowel, shape the mortar into a tidy, four-sided pyramid, in a process called buttering. Push the buttered end of the brick against the first brick, carefully squeezing the vertical mortar joint down to ½ inch, then settle the brick into the mortar bed. Check the level and alignment with the level. Repeat the process for a half dozen bricks or so.

Go back to the end and start the second course. Remember to follow your plans to achieve the desired bond. Check frequently with your level to ensure that this new course is level and

BUILDING A BRICK WALL

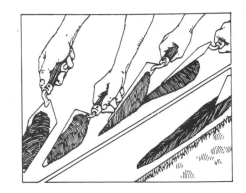

Before mixing mortar and starting to lay bricks, do a dry run. Snap a chalk line along the footer to delineate where the wall will be. Set out bricks along the line, leaving a mortar-joint's space between bricks, and mark the ends of the wall on the footer. You may want to adjust dimensions slightly at this point to avoid having to cut bricks. Now mix some mud and set to bricklaying.

The first skill to master is throwing the mud, which is what masons call the process of spreading mortar. Scoop up a trowelful of mortar and spread it along the footer by twisting your wrist as you pull your outstretched arm toward you along the footer. Drag the point of the trowel down the center of the mortar, creating a furrow. If it doesn't look right, scrape it up and try again. It's a skill that's honed by practice.

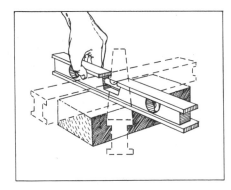

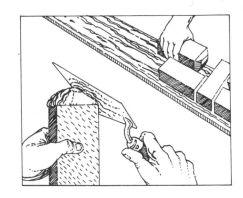

Set the first brick in place, right at the end of the wall. Press it into the mortar, until you judge the mortar joint to be ¾ to ½ inch. Use the trowel to scoop up the mortar that's squeezed out. Level the brick, not only from end to end, but from side to side and diagonally from corner to corner. Subsequent bricks in this course will be leveled in concert with this brick, so get it right.

Subsequent bricks in the course must be buttered, another skill to master. Hold the brick, header up, and smear some mortar on the header with the trowel. Three more flicks with the trowel should leave you with a modest pyramid of mortar on the header. The brick is then ready to be set in the mortar bed, against the first brick.

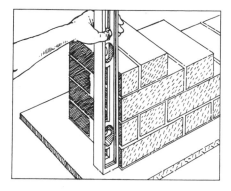

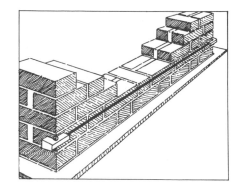

Lay five or six bricks in the first course, then start on the second course. You'll be able to run this course one brick less. Then lay up the third and fourth courses. As you lay the bricks, use the level to align the stretchers of all the bricks in a course, and to check that the wall is plumb. When you reach the one-brick course, head for the other end of the wall and repeat the process there. Then use line blocks to fill in between the ends.

Line blocks support a line strung from end (or corner) to end of the wall. Each block hooks around the end of a brick, and the tension on the line holds them in place. The string is aligned with the leading edge of the first course of bricks. By laying the bricks up to the string, you can fill in between the ends without resorting to the level. When one course is done, you move the string up and complete the next course. And so on.

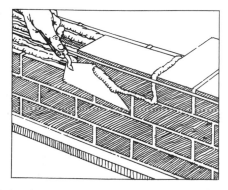

As each brick is set into place, mortar will squeeze from the bed beneath it. You should, at the same time you set the brick with your hand, sweep the trowel along the joint, scooping up the excess mortar and returning it to the mortar pan. This is not only good economy, it saves a lot of cleanup later.

Every so often, you should stop bricklaying and strike off the mortar joints with a jointing tool. The proper finish can't be achieved if the mortar has been allowed to dry too much, and experience will teach you how often you must perform this task. You should be able to pick up bits of mortar with the jointing tool to press into voids in the mortar joints. After the joints are struck, brush off the wall with a dustbrush. This too will save cleanup work later.

The wall is erected through the process of building up the ends, then filling in, building up the ends, then filling in. Ultimately, the wall will be completed and ready for a cap of some kind. You may want to pour concrete capstones, but if the wall is no more than a double thickness of brick, you can top off the wall with a rowlock header course.

plumb, and use your storyboard to keep the mortar joints uniform. You can add several more courses, each course being a half-brick shorter than the previous one, giving one end of your work a stepped appearance. Your last course should be only one brick long. Repeat the entire process at the other end of the wall.

String a line between the two ends using line blocks, and begin filling in the courses between them. Line up the bricks with the string. When you get to the last brick in each course, butter both ends and ease it into place.

As you work, use the trowel to scrape excess mortar from the mortar joints. If you do it properly, you'll be pressing the brick into the mortar bed and cleaning up the squeeze-out at the same time. The little gobs can be tossed back into the mortar pan. Try to avoid smearing the faces of the bricks with mortar, since it is very difficult to clean off. And you do want your wall to have a clean appearance eventually.

Periodically, you should strike off the mortar joints. You don't have to do this immediately after each brick is laid, but you should stop every few courses to do it. Just slide the broad face of the striking tool along the joint, giving it a concave shape. If you've got little pockets in your joints that need more mortar, hold a trowel with a bit of mortar on it by the pocket and use the jointer to push the mortar off the trowel and into the pocket.

After the joints are finished off, use the dust brush to clean the wall.

The final cleanup is done after the wall is completed and the joints have cured. Get a small bottle of muriatic acid at the building-supply company, and mix a very dilute solution according to the directions on the bottle, usually an ounce or two in a bucket of water. Wash the wall with the solution, using a stiff brush. For hard-to-clean spots, a scrap of brick can be used, though you don't want to deface the wall by scratching up the bricks. Wear rubber gloves for this job, and don't splash the acid solution around. It may be dilute, but it is still acid, and it can still burn.

Protecting Existing Plants

Earth moving can be dangerous to plants. Particularly where earth-moving machinery is called into action, plants can be scraped, broken, crushed or uprooted, but even a careless pick swinger or wheelbarrow pusher can injure plants. Moreover, regrading can often present special dangers for trees, either by exposing their roots or by burying their roots too deeply.

Consequently, if your landscaping plan calls for the preservation of existing plants, and at the same time requires grading, drainage work or other construction projects, you've got to take some precautions.

First of all, if you've got to make use of earth-moving equipment—bulldozers, backhoes, what have you—make sure you and the operator are on the same wavelength regarding the value you place on the trees and shrubs that are to be preserved. If possible, fence off areas that are not to be encroached upon. If that's not possible, discuss the matter not only with the contractor, but with the machine operator. Try to be an on-the-spot observer, and if you don't think the work is going well, don't be reluctant to speak up.

If you are doing work yourself with pick and shovel, you are in control. You shouldn't gouge or uproot plants accidentally, although it is possible to do. Avoid cutting too many roots when trenching or cutting. Think about where you are routing paths or swales. Don't run a heavily laden wheelbarrow over tree roots again and again; vary your passage if you can't avoid the roots altogether. Don't store mounds of materials—gravel or bricks or boards—on those roots, either. Again, try to fence off the preservation area from the *immediate* work area.

These cautions, however, are largely common sense. What you might overlook is the sensitivity of trees, especially, to grading that exposes or buries roots. What you might not realize is that you *can* save that terrific tree that you figured you'd lose in the grading.

CUTTING AROUND TREES

Ordinarily, cutting at a spot occupied by tree roots would remove the roots, thus killing, or at least severely injuring, the tree. You can save the tree if you are willing and able to compromise the cutting and build a retaining wall around the specific area containing the tree roots.

Doubtless, the value you place on the tree will dictate whether or not the grading plans can be altered to allow for a hummock harboring a

The grade around a tree can be lowered only if the roots of the tree are protected. This is done by maintaining the grade within the circumference of the drip line. Using lime, mark the drip line on the ground. Do the grading, but don't cut within the drip line. When the excavation is completed, build a retaining wall around the tree at the drip line.

tree. And your building skill will determine whether or not you can construct a retaining wall to gird the hummock.

Here's how to do it.

Start by marking the tree's drip line on the ground. Use stakes and string or a trail of lime; this will mark the perimeter of the cut. Some people have successfully tightened that perimeter by one-third by combining root pruning and branch pruning. If you've never done it before, you probably will want to avoid risking the tree.

After the regrading is roughly done, construct the retaining wall, just as you would any other retaining wall. In backfilling, use compost or a mixture of topsoil and peat, rather than subsoil. As you would in any backfilling operation, be sure to put down the soil in shallow layers, compacting each layer.

FILLING OVER TREE ROOTS

Adding fill changes the oxygen content of the soil that was already in place and, in some situations,

can raise the water table. Both of these results can be deleterious to existing trees. Consequently, you have to take special precautions in filling over tree roots. You need to construct a tree well and drain system if more than 8 inches of fill are to be added.

Start by stripping the sod from around the tree, extending the stripped area several feet beyond the tree's drip line. Spread compost or other organic fertilizer over the area, loosening the soil and working the amendment into the top 2 or 3 inches. Be careful not to sever or nick the tree roots while doing this.

Next, assemble the drain system. It will look like a wagon wheel, with the tree as the hub. Use clay drain tiles or perforated plastic drain pipes, positioning the holes down. The spokes of the system should extend beyond the drip lines; you should have four to six of them. In most cases, the pipes can be laid on the original grade, but you should have at least ⅛ inch drop per foot of run *away* from the tree trunk. The ends of the pipes should be 6 inches to a foot from the trunk; an older, slow-growing tree can be crowded a bit.

Install tiles or pipes around the perimeter of your system, connecting the spokes. Vertical breathers are the last elements of the system to be added. Place one at each intersection between spoke and rim. A line should next be extended from the system's lowest point to a storm sewer or a dry well.

As you lay the tiles or pipes, butt the ends of the pieces together, then lay a piece of tar paper or unbacked fiberglass insulation over the joint. Then heap crushed stone over it. You need not cement the pieces together. After the whole system is laid out, spread crushed stone over all the spokes and the rim, to a depth of 8 to 12 inches.

The last step before filling over the sytem is to construct a retaining wall around the tree trunk, to hold the fill away from the trunk, creating a tree well. It is a good place for a stone wall laid up without mortar. An interesting and easy-to-deal-with approach is to use concrete blocks, laid down as the fill is built up, forming a funnel-shaped well. The cores should more or less face the trunk and be packed with soil. Very little of the blocks, which aren't attractive by any stretch of the imagination, shows, and you can plant a ground cover that extends right down into the well.

In any case, the fill is put down only after the drain system is in place and the retaining wall has been started (or finished). As with all fill operations, the fill should be put down in layers and compacted.

You don't, of course, have to be encircling the tree for either approach to work. If you are cutting or filling at one side of a tree, you have only to build half or a quarter of either system to work. You do, however, have to do the preservation work *before* you do the grading. Once the tree shows the symptoms of root injury, it is too late to go back. So plan ahead.

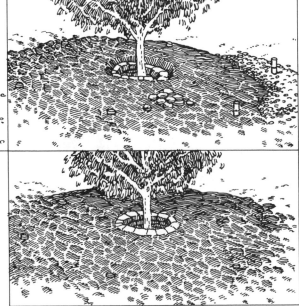

The grade around a tree can be raised only if air and drainage are provided around the roots and a well is created for the trunk. The air and drainage are provided by a standard clay or perforated plastic drain system, laid out in a spoked-wheel pattern, with a vertical breather extending to the ultimate soil surface at each spot where spoke and rim join. As the fill is spread over the system and tamped, a retaining wall must be built to maintain an air space around the trunk.

16

Paving

Paving may be the major portion of the construction work you do in your landscaping project. You may need or want to construct walks, a
driveway or a patio.

   If you do, here you'll find out how. The
general principles are the same, whether you are
constructing a broad driveway or a narrow path
through the woods. There are a lot of different

materials to choose from. You can choose one for
your entire project, or you can select different
materials for different parts of your project.

Planning

Your paving project should begin with design considerations. You have the walks or the drive laid out

in your landscape plan, but now you've got to weigh that design in light of construction possibilities, choices of materials, and economic realities.

WALKS

Plan your walks so that they provide a visual, as well as physical, link between elements in your landscape. While the shortest distance between two points may not be the most attractive, curved walks that have no apparent reason for curving are even less attractive.

If your house is close to the street, where visitors park, a decent walk to the entrance is often the best. But if the house sits back from the road or if you live in the country, you may need, not a walk to the street, but a guest parking area that directs visitors to the front door.

Use as few walks in addition to the entrance as possible, to avoid cutting up areas where it isn't necessary. Secondary walks designed to ramble through the garden or to lead to a vista or patio need not be paved, since they will be used only in fair weather. Stepping stones, gravel and grass are frequently more attractive and are cooler and more inviting in summer, while walks leading to the patio are often best paved in the same material as the terrace itself.

STEPS

Where a walk leads from one level to another, the usual practice is to install steps at the slope, though ramps may be used if the slope is not too steep, or where it is necessary to wheel conveyances from one level to another.

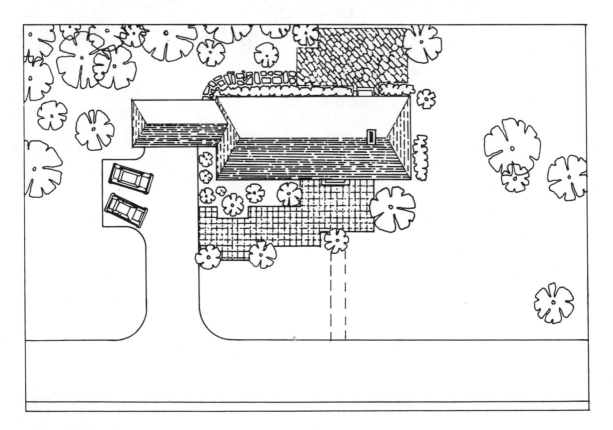

To locate a walk, you first must decide where it must go to and from. In this case, because there is no on-street parking, there is no need for the traditional door-to-curb path. The front entrance is made more inviting by widening the path and using a paving material that unites the house with the landscape. In many cases, a path worn into the ground can tell you where there's a need for a walk. Here, stepping stones are used to make a secondary path for the much-used route from the garage to the patio.

The steepest steps used in gardens are usually proportioned to rise no more than 6 inches per foot of run. Although this is the minimum rise used for indoor steps, outdoors they are more comfortable when they are gradual. All the steps and all the risers in one flight of steps should be the same size, and you should avoid steep, narrow steps unless they are absolutely necessary.

The steps should blend with their surroundings. The materials should be the same as those used for the walk, or the same material may be used for the rise and soil used for the tread. The edging will determine the attention drawn to the steps—edges may be overgrown with plants, making them almost invisible, or they may be clear and bare, making them a strong design feature.

Steps, as well as walks, must be in scale with the surroundings and must serve their particular use. People in motion outdoors require more space than they do when moving inside the house. Two people can walk side by side on a 4-foot-wide garden path, but a 5-foot-wide one gives them freedom to stroll and raise their eyes from the path. The width of gates, passageways and openings should be determined by the size of the equipment to be carried through.

The width of your walks should be governed by the kind of traffic they'll bear. The main entranceway should be wide enough for two abreast, meaning 4 feet or more. Solitary paths through a prairie or woodland need be only a couple of feet wide. A conduit for walkers, pedalers or those pushing a wheelbarrow should be wider than a solitary path, narrower than an entranceway.

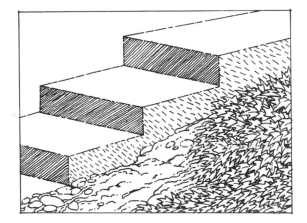

The best riser-to-thread relationship for outdoor steps is 6 inches to 15 inches. You can use other dimensions, depending upon the materials, but keep in mind that outdoor dimensions are always at a larger scale than those indoors.

DRIVEWAYS

The appearance of many landscapes is spoiled by poorly designed and maintained driveways. Parking areas and turnabouts should be provided when necessary, but they should never dominate the scene.

Place the driveway on the service side of the house for convenience to the side entrance or kitchen doorway. All services to the house and grounds, including fuel delivery, should be on the same side if possible. Space permitting, the driveway should not be closer than 8 feet to the side of the house, and it should be direct with ample turning space. Try not to have a driveway that goes around the house; a circular driveway takes up a lot of space.

Although a driveway is often best constructed by an expert, you should carefully consider its location and material. Long driveways or large parking areas take up a lot of space and can cause major changes in the natural drainage patterns. Whenever possible, you should use a porous paving material. If you *must* use a nonporous surface, provide for drainage along the edges.

Although asphalt and concrete are commonly used for driveways, they are by no means the most attractive materials. Gravel is an improvement, but better still are cobblestones, heavy-duty pavers or stabilized soil. Whatever the finished material, make sure the driveway is of all-weather construction with a thick foundation.

TERRACES

The garden area that you will probably use most is the terrace or patio where you can relax and entertain. Since tables and chairs will be placed there, a terrace should be relatively level. It should directly connect with the living room, kitchen or any other room where there are related activities. But this doesn't mean that the terrace must be built against the house. You may get more enjoyment from being out in the garden, and you may get a better summer breeze. By connecting the house and the terrace with a paved path, you can make the walk to the terrace pleasant and convenient. If you provide shade for all or part of the terrace, it will get more use on hot, sunny summer days.

Be sure that the terrace is in scale with the rest

Driveways are an important, functional part of the landscape. They should be as direct a route as possible from street to garage or house, and they

should be wide enough to accommodate the average automobile. All curves should be appropriately radiused to allow easy maneuvering.

of the landscape and will accommodate your desired activities. By leaving generous open spaces for planting, you can make any paved area seem to cover a much larger area and achieve the feeling of a bigger terrace.

MATERIALS CONSIDERATIONS

There are several points to consider in choosing a paving material. Although you will probably find that no one type meets all of your needs, you should make sure that the color, texture and pattern blend well with your landscape and with the materials of your home. Is the look formal or rustic? And is the size of the individual paved areas in scale with the other elements in your landscape?

The texture, too, must be suitable for the intended use of the paving. While cobblestones set high are attractive and durable, they are uncomfortable to walk on, and the unwary can trip on them. Smooth-textured concrete, on the other hand, can be slippery when wet or freezing.

Consider also how readily paving will show dirt and dust, and how easily it stains. Can you sweep or hose the surface to remove debris? How will the paving stand up under your use and your climatic conditions? Is it subject to cracking or disintegration? How much skill and effort are needed to lay the material? Are you up to it, or can you afford a skilled laborer? The material you choose should be suited to its purpose, pleasing to the eye and priced within your budget.

Regardless of the type of paving you choose, you will almost always have to prepare a foundation or subbase, which will play a role in the ultimate appearance and durability of the finished paving. This foundation must assure adequate drainage and help to provide a stable, level bed.

In some cases, a sand base will be adequate, and the paving slabs can be set in the bed with or without mortar. Usually, however, the sand should be underlain by at least 3 inches of coarse gravel (and in some cases up to 9 inches) to provide better drainage and greater stability.

DRAINAGE

If drainage is a problem, you may need to install 3- to 4-inch drain tiles under the center or around the edge of the paved area.

Whether or not you use drain tiles, you will have to slope the surface of the paved area a minimum of 1 percent to ensure adequate surface drainage. Paving that has a slope up to 3 percent (3-foot drop per 100 feet) looks flat to most people, but slopes beyond 4 to 5 percent are too slanted for use in terraces, although walks and drives may go up to 10 to 12 percent.

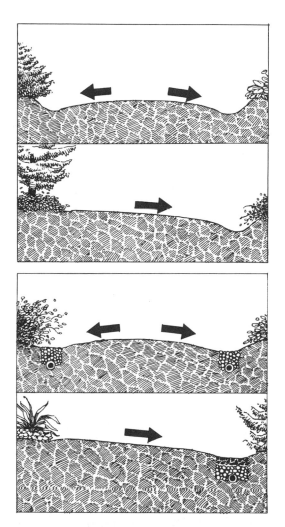

Surface drainage is almost always easier to create than subsurface drainage. The surface of a driveway can be drained in two ways. It can be crowned, with either swales or subsurface drains along each side, or it can be graded with a slight pitch to one side, with a swale or subsurface drain along only one side. These two approaches will work, regardless of the length of the drive or the material used to pave the drive.

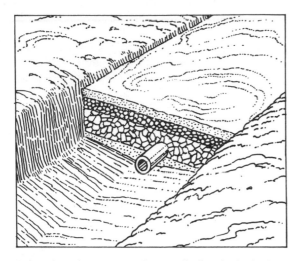

Subsurface drainage can be installed in the bed of a paved walk. It is particularly suitable for porous or semiporous paving materials, such as loose aggregates or the various pavers that can be bedded in sand. You must excavate more deeply than you ordinarily would, grading the bottom of the excavation so it slopes from the sides to the centerline. Spread a layer of sand, then lay the drain tiles or pipe. Cover the line with crushed stone, then spread more sand for the paving's foundations.

Paved surfaces can be drained as a flat sheet so that water runs off all along the low end, or they can be high in the middle, allowing water to run off from all sides.

Lay 3- or 4-inch-diameter drain tiles about 1 foot deep. Cover joints loosely with tar paper to keep soil out of the pipe, and backfill the trench around the pipe with gravel. Run the tile lines to a natural swale, stream, storm drain or nearby dry well. The line should drop at least 1 foot in 100.

Read or reread the previous chapter's information on drainage, then plan your work. Using stakes and string, lay out the area to be paved, making sure that you've got the proper slopes in the proper places. From your stakes and string, you must be able to gauge the surface level of the finished paving, as well as the necessary depth of excavation.

Excavate a foot deep, and shape the bottom of the trench so it slopes slightly toward the centerline, which is where the drain tiles or pipe will be laid. Lay the tiles, as described in the previous chapter. Cover the joints, then add about

a 6-inch layer of crushed stone to the trench. Backfill to the appropriate level for the paving, and begin that work.

UTILITIES

Plan and install utility lines before you begin paving. Plan for sanitary sewers, storm drains, tile lines, water pipes, gas lines and electrical conduits. This will save time and money and will eliminate the need to dig up pavement for a utility line later.

Layout

The first key task in any paving project is layout. This is a matter of delineating the boundaries of the area to be paved. Carried through to its conclusion, it involves monitoring the depth of necessary excavations and spreading of base layers of crushed stone or sand.

The principal tools for layout are stakes and string, a line level and a tape, a long one if the area to be laid out is large. Read or reread the section on do-it-yourself grading in the preceding chapter. Here you'll learn the basics of establishing the grade, which is important if you want your walks or patio to drain properly.

Lay out the perimeter of the excavation first. For a patio, establish either the length or the width first. Set up parallel strings marking each end of the patio. The stakes between which the strings are suspended should be well outside the excavation area; the string should be 2 to 4 feet longer than the length of the side.

Then establish the other dimension. Make sure these sides are parallel and at right angles to the first sides. Again, the stakes should be driven into the ground well outside the excavation area. Make sure that excavation won't dislodge the stakes.

With the boundaries set, you should next adjust the vertical alignment of the strings, so that you have some reference point from which to work in establishing the rough grade of the excavation bottom.

When you dig, excavate enough room to work easily and efficiently with forms or header boards. This means you should dig a foot beyond the perimeter of the area to be paved, hence the need to have the stakes well back from the perimeter.

How deeply you dig and what sort of forms and base you construct depend upon the kind of material you chose for your paving. For loose aggregates, the excavation need not be deep at all, but for a 4- or 5-inch-thick concrete slab, you've got to dig down about 10 inches to allow for the gravel base.

You'll use the same principles in setting up forms as you did in layout. The forms—or headers—should be plumb, level or set at a controlled pitch, and set at the proper elevation, so that it only sets below or above ground level if that's what you've designed it to do.

Drive stakes well into the ground, making sure that their tops align with the grade you want to establish. If you will eventually be removing the forms, be sure to compensate for the thickness of the form itself in positioning the stakes along the perimeter.

Using duplex nails, which have two heads and are sometimes called scaffolding nails because they are made for temporary construction like forms and scaffolds, nail through the stakes into

Forms, whether temporary ones for concrete work or permanent headers for a brick patio or a gravel path, are built in the same general way. Start by driving 2 × 2 stakes into the ground to support the form boards, placing them 3 to 4 feet apart. The length of the stakes depends upon the strength necessary: are the forms to contain wet concrete or merely bound a space? Using string, a line level and a rule, mark the top of each stake so you can properly align the form boards. You must account for the depth of the paving's foundation, the thickness of the paving, and

any grade deviation necessary for drainage. Hold the form board against the stakes and nail through the stakes into the boards. If the forms are to be temporary, use duplex nails here. If the forms are permanent, saw off the tops of the stakes at an angle, both to promote drainage from the stake top and to help conceal the stakes. Concrete forms should be further braced with additional stakes driven into the ground at an angle and nailed to the upright stakes and the form boards.

the form boards. Try not to knock the stakes out of alignment as you nail the forms into place. Holding a hand sledge or a large rock behind the form board when nailing is sometimes helpful.

If the forms will be used for concrete work, they should be braced. And if you did knock the forms out of alignment, the braces can often be used to rectify this.

With the excavation completed and any necessary forms set up, you are ready to proceed according to the dictates of the materials you are going to use.

Loose Aggregates

As you investigate the various kinds of paving you can use in your natural landscape, consider the lowest cost and most easily applied first: loose aggregates. Loose aggregates are materials that range from wood chips to the most familiar, crushed stone (often called gravel). These materials usually present a neat and attractive appearance, but equally important to you, they give a more natural feeling than most paving.

The loose aggregates are porous and allow the natural drainage patterns to prevail, providing water to nearby plant roots and for the recharge of groundwater, instead of increasing runoff.

There are disadvantages, however, that you should think about. Loose aggregates can be uncomfortable to walk on and very difficult to wheel anything across. Regular rolling is necessary to keep the surface compacted. Containment around the edges is important in some situations.

CRUSHED STONE

Crushed stone is surely the most familiar of the loose aggregates. It's available everywhere, since it's a staple of the building industry. It's an essential ingredient of concrete and a base for roads and highways. Uniform sizes, from ¼ inch up to 2 or 3 inches in size, can be purchased. Unscreened gravel, perhaps the least costly and best suited for your application, has stones of varying sizes and includes lots of rock dust.

Crushed stone provides a durable surface for walks and drives and even in some situations for terraces. It should be renewed from time to time. It stands up best when applied over bedrock, but solid earth is a satisfactory base. In any situation, a crushed rock surface will dry quickly.

For best results, lay down the stones in layers, dampening and rolling each layer before putting down the next. You'll need ⅔ of a cubic yard of crushed stone to cover a 100-square-foot area to a depth of 2 inches.

SPECIALTY ROCKS

Every area has some specialty rock used as a loose aggregate. Often these are simply colored rocks, which derive their colors naturally or through the use of dyes. Presumably, you'll stick to natural colors in a natural landscape.

Dolomite is a limestone that is remarkably white. It can be attractive when used sparingly, but as is the case with anything white, it is tough to keep clean. Muddy feet or tires will quickly ruin its special character. It is a good idea to lay plastic sheets on the ground before spreading dolomite to prevent the earth from staining it. Dolomite is not expensive.

Redrock is a rocky clay that compacts solidly when dampened and rolled. This characteristic makes it a dandy base for other aggregates, but it also makes redrock a good surface material in natural settings. In time, the surface will break down and become quite dusty. When this happens, it can either be renewed or covered over with another aggregate.

Riverstone is very popular for landscaping in many areas. It is simply small, rounded pebbles, such as you'd find in a stream bottom. If this material is particularly appropriate for your region, you may want to use it for walks, though it may be a bit expensive for covering a drive.

WOOD CHIPS

Wood chips are both the most easily used and the least satisfactory of the loose aggregates. And many, in fact, would question calling them an aggregate.

Nevertheless, wood chips are worthy of consideration in a natural landscape. They make soft, springy paths and are particularly appropriate for woodland paths. In a more domesticated setting, you may want to install headers to confine them to terrace or path areas.

Sawmills and tree-pruning operations generate wood chips as a by-product. If you don't live near a sawmill, contact landscapers or utilities.

The latter are often glad to be rid of chips generated when crews prune around power lines.

Simply mark your paths and spread layers of chips. Renew them as experience dictates, annually in some areas, less frequently in others.

Brick

Brick is a very versatile and easily laid paving material. It is available in a wide variety of colors, textures and shapes, and under most conditions, it will provide a solid and durable surface. Because bricks are compact in size, they are excellent for making gradual changes of direction or level, and they can be laid in many attractive patterns. Rough textured and porous, bricks absorb water and provide a cool surface that reduces glare and gives good traction.

Finish and color are matters of personal taste, but the grade of brick depends on the job it is to do. General information on bricks can be found in the retaining walls section of the preceding chapter. You can use common bricks for paving, but there are special bricks made for paving called pavers. Pavers are harder and more resistant to abrasion than regular bricks. Usually they are of slightly different dimensions than common bricks, such that the width of the paver is half the length, an important consideration if you want to lay the bricks in anything other than a running bond.

A paver is a special brick made for paving. Its most obvious attribute is its size, which is such as to allow it and its brethren to be butted together without mortar joints in a variety of attractive patterns. Common building bricks are ½ inch too long to allow this. Building bricks can, however, be used for paving if you incorporate ½-inch joints filled with mortar, sand or some other material.

As mentioned, bricks can be laid in a variety of attractive patterns. Some patterns tend to direct the eye to emphasize the features of the brick. Others can only be laid in large areas; otherwise they look too busy. Basket-weave patterns, which have sets of two or three bricks placed in alternating directions to suggest weaving, are a popular choice. Herringbone patterns require some brick cutting, but the results are attractive. Walks and patios can also be laid in the running bond so widely used in walls. You can set bricks flat or on edge.

Materials like stone, railroad ties, boards or gravel can be used with brick to add variety and contrast. An attractive walk can be made by combining bricks with concrete paving blocks, slates or cobblestone. For example, start by laying the bricks down the middle of the path, spacing them about ¼ inch apart. Then lay the blocks or stones along both sides of the bricks.

THE CROWNED BED

This foundation will support any walk, but it's particularly good for a brick walk.

Ordinarily, you have two choices for providing surface drainage of the walk's surface. One way is to grade the sand bed so that one edge is higher than the other; the water simply runs off the lower side of the walk. Or, you can build a crowned bed so water runs off both sides. This is actually easier to do than the first option. (In either case, of course, the walk should be sloped so that water runs away from the house or any other buildings.)

The first step in creating a crowned bed is to calculate the dimensions of the crown. You want each side to be ⅛ inch lower than the crown for each foot of width. Thus, a 4-foot-wide walk will have ½ inch of drop on each side.

Build a wooden template to accurately shape the sand. Start with a piece of 1 × 2 as long as the walk is wide. On each end, glue a block of wood equal in thickness to the drop you want. Scraps of plywood are useful here, since you'll doubtlessly be dealing with thicknesses of ⅜ to ½ inch. Cut a piece of ¼-inch plywood slightly longer than the 1 × 2. Position the plywood along the 1 × 2, with the ends resting on the blocks glued to the 1 × 2. Squeeze the plywood to the 1 × 2 at

A crowned bed for a brick or stone walk is created by shaping the sand bed with a template fabricated for the job. On a wide walk, two people, one on each side of the walk, are better able to screed the sand than one person. Be sure to monitor the work so the proper grade is maintained from one end of the walk to the other.

dead center and nail the two pieces together. Then nail the plywood to the blocks.

Spread a 4- to 5-inch layer of sand in the excavation for the walk. Press the template, curved face down, onto the sand and draw it along to form the crowned bed. Avoid disturbing the bed as you work, difficult as that may seem. Once the sand bed has been shaped, the bricks can be laid.

USING HEADERS

If you are going to use wooden headers, that is, permanently installed boards to define the edges of the walk or patio, you can use them as a guide for leveling the sand bed.

Use boards on the order of 1 × 4s for the headers. Redwood or cedar or cypress will be the most durable woods to use, but in any case, the headers should be treated with a wood preservative. Install the headers as you would forms, but use galvanized common nails rather than duplex nails, and shorten or bevel the stakes so they don't show. They should be set to the appropriate depth and have the appropriate slope. Nail them together at the corners.

Cut a board for striking off the sand bed and leveling the bricks. It should be about 12 inches longer than the shortest dimension of the area to be bricked. In each end, cut a notch about ½ inch less than the depth of a brick and 6 inches wide.

To strike off the sand, set the board over the headers, notches down, and with the aid of a helper, slide it back and forth along the headers. Thus, you'll be able to create a nice, level sand bed.

By making the notches slightly smaller than a brick's depth, you are allowing for a modest amount of settling. Otherwise, the headers would eventually come to be higher than the brick surface. If that's the effect you want, of course, you can adjust the size of the notches accordingly.

If your plan calls for the use of bricks or stone slabs as headers, you won't need header boards.

This will make striking off the sand bed a bit more tricky, since you won't have solid guides to work with. But you will have to strike off the sand, establishing the appropriate depth and slope.

Then, around the perimeter of the area to be bricked, dig a narrow trench for the header bricks. These you'll set on end, either perpendicularly or at an angle. Set the headers in place, one by one, tamping soil against them on the outside and sand against them on the inside. Follow the strings you set up to guide the excavation, and be sure these headers are set at the proper depth. Use a level to ensure that they are level and plumb.

To set these bricks more permanently, bed them in mortar. This is more work all around. The trench for them should be dug a bit deeper and backfilled with a layer of crushed stone. Mix a batch of mortar, following the directions in the retaining walls section of the preceding chapter. Then trowel mortar onto the stones and set the bricks. If you want mortar joints between bricks,

Successfully setting a soldier course of bricks to serve as headers for a patio or walk is largely a matter of careful excavation. After completing the basic excavation for the area to be paved, use a garden trowel to dig a trench around the perimeter of the area. Make the trench close to 4½ inches deep, and wide enough for a brick. Keep the sides of the trench as nearly vertical as you can. Set the bricks in place, checking them with a level, and tamp earth against their outer faces. If you get the trench too deep, use sand to backfill.

you'll have to butter up the bricks as you go. Again, use a level to ensure that each brick is level and plumb.

Even if you intend to have no headers at all, neither boards nor bricks nor stones, you can, and probably should, set up forms to ease the work of striking off the sand bed and setting the paving bricks. Allow yourself enough working room to be able to pull up the headers when the bricklaying is done. Backfill against the bricks.

LAYING THE BRICKS

Once the headers are set up, laying the remaining bricks is simple work. It should be done as methodically as possible.

First, settle the sand bed by wetting it and tamping it. After the sand has dried, start laying the bricks. Simply start in one corner and work out, setting the bricks in place in accordance with the pattern you've picked. If you are using true

Headers are excellent guides to use in screeding a sand bed for a brick or stone patio or walk. Some elementary carpentry work on a length of 1 × 4 or 1 × 6 will yield a simple but effective device for screeding the sand bed to the proper elevation and leveling the bricks or other pavers.

Bricks can be laid on a screeded sand bed almost as quickly and easily as you can set them out. If you are working with wooden or brick headers, start in a corner and set the bricks out in your chosen pattern. Level the bricks with a level or long straightedge, using a mallet to more deeply set those few that are too high. Lift out the bricks that settle too much and add more sand beneath them. After all the bricks are laid, spread dry sand over them and sweep it back and forth over the surface, letting it settle into the joints. Hose the surface to settle the work. After it dries, repeat the sweeping of sand and the hosing, doing it again and again until the joints seem adequately filled with sand.

pavers, you can butt the bricks together. If you want any kind of joint, allow space for it.

Each brick should be tamped into place and leveled. As a practical matter, you probably will not use a level on each and every brick. Rather, you'll use the headers and the board you use to strike off to level the bricks in aggregate. If you've deliberately set the headers below the level of the bricks, tack blocks on the ends of the striking-off board to compensate. Set the board on the headers and sight beneath it to determine if the bricks are level.

Wet down the bricks once they are all in place to help settle them.

If you've chosen to have a joint between bricks, dump sand or a sand and cement mix on the bricks—*before wetting them*—and sweep it into the joints. Then wet the bricks. You will have to add more sand to the joints in a repetition of the initial process. Adding cement to the sand will give you a mortarlike joint.

Just as you may have mortared your header bricks in place, so too can you mortar the other bricks in place. You'll have to allow for the bed of mortar in striking off the sand. But once that's done, it's a matter of mixing mortar, spreading a mortar bed an area at a time and laying the bricks. Laying in mortar will necessitate leveling the bricks with a level, since you won't be dealing with a bed of uniform thickness.

Moreover, laying the bricks with a mortar joint means you'll either have to butter each brick as it's laid, or you'll have to try to maintain a uniform spacing of the bricks, then grout them later. Either approach can be tricky for a novice.

Stone

Natural stone slabs are one of the most durable and attractive paving materials you can use. Because it is a material found in nature, it looks appropriate in almost any landscape. It is one of the best paving materials for laying directly on the soil or on a bed of sand because its weight is enough to ensure stability. While it is long lasting and relatively easy to lay, it is an expensive material in some areas, especially if newly quarried.

The most commonly available paving stone is flagstone, which is cut from any stone that splits into flat pieces, such as sandstone or slate. Flagstones are available in irregular or rectangular shapes and range in thickness from ½ to 2 inches. Uneven chunks of natural stone, gathered from a field or left over from quarrying, can make a rustic and attractive, although uneven, surface. Bluestone, granite and marble are expensive but beautiful, and they work well in a formal setting. Large irregular pieces of stone require care in laying, as they look best when fitted together like a jigsaw puzzle. With both irregular and rectangular stone, it is a good idea to arrange the pattern before fixing the stones.

Stones laid on soil should be at least 2 inches thick to ensure stability and strength. Fill the joints between the stones with soil and plants. To lay the stones on soil, simply dig to a depth slightly less than the thickness of the stones and fit them into place.

For a more stable surface, set up headers and put down a 2-inch-thick sand bed. For even more stability, lay 4 to 6 inches of crushed stone beneath the sand. When filling in the joints, use a mortar mix instead of sand or soil.

The final grade should be evenly sloping for proper drainage. Lay the stones in place, and after establishing the pattern, tamp them in place with a mallet so they don't wobble when walked on. Fill the joints with sand, soil, or sand mix.

Try to work with the natural size and shape of the stones, as cutting is difficult. If you have to cut some, you can do it with a broad cold chisel, a hand sledge and a 2 × 4. Mark where you want to make the cut by making a ⅛- to ¼-inch groove with the hammer and chisel. Place the stone on the 2 × 4, holding the chisel in the groove at the middle of the stone, and hit it sharply.

Concrete

Although concrete can be harsh, glaring and cold, it can also be used with delicacy and imagination. Because of its wide range of colors and textures, it has a great variety of uses. Since it is a plastic material, concrete can be made to take almost any form. Add to this its fairly low cost and its relative ease of handling, and you can see why it is used so frequently in residential designs.

Concrete is a durable material. However, if not properly mixed and handled, it can crack and buckle, and the surface can flake and break up. Because it sets quickly, it must be handled with speed, and single blocks must be completed in one pour, not stretched out over several days. However, a large job can by design be broken into a grid-work of small blocks that can be poured one or two at a time to spread out the work.

INGREDIENTS

In almost all cases, your concrete mixture will begin with Portland cement. It comes in standard 1-cubic-foot bags weighing 94 pounds. It must be kept dry because it absorbs moisture readily, and when it does, it lumps up. If there are lumps that do not crush easily between your fingers, the cement has been ruined.

When you add water to cement, it forms a paste that binds the aggregates—sand and gravel—into concrete.

The sand must be clean, for if it is not, the concrete will not bind. Do not use seashore sand. Mortar sand is another, finer, variety, and it should not be used for mixing concrete.

When buying gravel, you can specify the maximum size you want, or you can order what is known as "bank run," or unscreened gravel, which includes gravel of all sizes and some rock dust.

Obviously, the water you use must be clean. It should not contain any oil or organic waste. Potable tap water is fine. Seawater should not be used.

Before you order your materials, you will have to determine the proper mix for your job. Generally speaking, the more wear and weathering the concrete must endure, the greater the percentage of cement you will use. (Consult the accompanying chart.)

Concrete Mix

Here are recommended proportions for common home projects.

	Cement	Sand	Gravel
Floor	1	2	3
Sidewalk (light traffic)	1	2	4
Sidewalk (heavy traffic)	1	1½	3
Driveway	1	2½	3½
Stairs	1	2	4
Footings	1	2	4

To estimate how much concrete your job calls for, first compute the area you are covering. Multiply this by its thickness, which will give you a figure in cubic feet. To get cubic yards, divide this figure by 27, for the 27 cubic feet in each cubic yard.

MIXING CONCRETE

Mix your concrete only after all your forms and other equipment are ready and in place. If you are using only a few cubic yards of concrete, it can be mixed by hand. For bigger jobs, you may want to consider having ready-mixed concrete delivered.

A wheelbarrow is ideal for mixing small batches of concrete. You also can use a washtub or a mixing trough, or mix on a piece of plywood or a concrete floor. A hoe or square-ended shovel is the best mixing tool. You may be a bit disappointed at how little you can actually mix in these containers, so if you will be pouring a walk or patio, plan to rent a small mixer.

When it comes right down to mixing your ingredients, just keep the proportions and the relative consistency of the product you want in mind. The chart reflects the proportions to use: one quantity of cement to two like quantities of sand and three like quantities of gravel. You can use a can or bucket to measure your quantities. Or even measure in shovelfuls.

First, mix the cement, sand and gravel. They must be thoroughly blended and should have a uniform color, showing neither light nor dark streaks.

Add the water, little by little, until the entire mixture is evenly moist. To test the blend, draw the back of the shovel over the concrete in a poking motion to create a series of ridges. If the mix is too wet, the ridges will sink back into the pile. If it is too dry, the ridges will be indistinct.

If your mixture is too wet, add small amounts of cement, sand and gravel in the same proportions you used in the original mix. If it is too dry, sprinkle only small amounts of water across the heap.

If you use a mixer, first measure the ingredients to the proportions you need. With the mixer stopped, load in the gravel and some water.

Start the mixer, and while it is running, add the sand, cement and more water. Keep the mixer running for at least three minutes, or until the mixture is of uniform color. Add water a little at a time until you get a mix of the right consistency. Use the concrete as quickly as possible.

When you get done working with concrete, clean up everything. Once the concrete hardens on tools, it's all but impossible to get it off. A stiff fiber brush is a big help in cleaning up, and unless you're looking forward to swinging a 200-pound shovel someday, what little time it takes is worth the trouble. A good hard stream of water will do a pretty good job on the mixer, but throw 5 or 6 shovelfuls of gravel in, add water until it's really sloppy, and just let it thrash around for a while. Then rinse it out with the hose until the water runs clean.

TOOLS

Working with concrete requires some special tools.

Striking off, or screeding, is one of the first smoothing operations. It can be performed with a 2×4 cut a few inches longer than your job is wide. This job is best done by two people, though one person could handle a narrow walk.

Unless you are a creative wood and sheet-metal worker, you'll probably have to buy or rent the other tools you'll need. These incude a wooden float or leveling trowel; a bullfloat, which is a large float with a long, broomlike handle; an edging trowel or edger; a finishing trowel; and a mason's trowel.

You'll also need a shovel or two, a hoe, perhaps a rake, and, of course, a hammer and saw for setting up forms. Depending upon the type of reinforcing you use, you may need a hacksaw or wire cutters.

Kneeboards are useful for distributing your weight over a broad area of the concrete and are used in floating and troweling broad expanses of concrete. Use 1- or 2-foot-square pieces of plywood.

STEP-BY-STEP PROCEDURES

With any concrete project, some careful planning is necessary.

First, develop your specifications. Measure the area to be paved or the volume of the form to be filled, and compute how much material you will need.

You will need forms. If you are pouring a slab, you must construct a form to run around the perimeter.

Forms can be constructed of common boards or dimension lumber. The very best forms are constructed of green wood (wood that hasn't been dried). If you will be buying wood specifically to build your forms and you can buy directly from a sawmill, by all means buy and use green lumber. It'll be less expensive, too.

In constructing forms, consider the weight of the concrete. For a sidewalk, 1-inch stock will be adequate. For a large patio or wall, you may decide the extra strength of 2-inch stock advisable. In any case, stake and brace the forms securely. Trying to repair a broken or uprooted form while your concrete sets will age you quickly. As an aid to easy disassembly, use duplex nails in constructing forms.

Consider reinforcement. For a walk or patio you probably won't need it. But for a driveway you probably will.

There are two types of reinforcement: wire mesh and steel rods. There are specific products marketed for reinforcing concrete, but you can improvise, using pipes, rods, flat and angle iron, wire and various types of woven wire fencing.

The purpose of the reinforcement is to prevent the loads that the concrete will be subjected to from pulling it apart. Ordinarily, the reinforcement is located in the center of the concrete mass, either by pulling it from the bottom to the center with a rake after the concrete has been poured, or by pouring about half the concrete, laying the reinforcement in place and pouring the remainder of the concrete.

In any case, the reinforcement material should be clean and rust-free. You don't want anything to prevent a good bond between the reinforcement and the concrete.

THE FOUNDATION

A firm foundation will immeasurably lengthen the life of any concrete slab, small or large. It will provide the support and ensure the drainage it needs. And the foundation necessary will depend on the soil conditions and the use you'll put the concrete slab to.

BUILDING A CONCRETE WALK

Crushed stone should be used as the foundation for any in-ground concrete work. After the excavation is dug and the forms set up, spread a 3- to 6-inch layer of stone in the bottom, screeding the stone as you would sand for brick or stone paving. A walk can and should be divided into blocks using an asphaltic expansion-joint material. Cut strips of the material to fit between the form boards and nail it in place.

Once the pour is started, it should be continued until the slab is completed. Since hauling wet concrete is no easy task, try to position your mixer close to the forms. Use a shovel to spread the concrete. Work the concrete with the blade of the shovel to break up air pockets.

After the entire foundation is covered with concrete, lay reinforcement in place. You can use specially made reinforcing bars or screen, or you can use large-mesh fencing. Complete the pour, covering the reinforcing so that it is about in the center of the

slab. Screed the slab using an expendable length of 2 × 4. This works best if two people man the screed. Rest the screed on the top of the forms and work it back and forth in a sawing motion as you drag it along the slab, leveling off the concrete surface.

Finishing the slab proceeds in two stages. The surface is floated as soon as the screeding is done. Use a wooden tool called a float, or, for large areas like a patio or drive, a darby, to smooth the surface and force the aggregate down into the slab, away from the surface. As the excess water rises to the surface, stop floating and take a break. An hour or more later, after the water has evaporated, trowel the surface to its finished texture with a steel trowel and finish the edges with an edger. If the forms are eventually to be removed, use a bricklayer's trowel to cut the slab from the form boards. A large slab should have expansion joints cut into it with a tool made for the purpose. At this point, the concrete will support your weight, but use concrete kneeboards to distribute it over a wider area if you must venture onto the slab for troweling.

The concrete should cure for a week. In the old days, burlap or straw was spread on the concrete and sprinkled daily during the curing period. Now, as often as not, plastic is laid over the slab and the edges weighted down. The plastic keeps the humidity high around the concrete, preventing it from drying out too quickly. The forms can be stripped from the work before or after curing. The forms will part from the concrete most easily if they were made of green lumber or if they were coated with old crankcase oil before the pour.

You will need a crushed stone base on any filled soil. The soil should be rolled or tamped and topped with at least 6 inches of stone.

On clay or any other poorly drained soil, use about 2 inches of stone.

On sandy or other well-drained soil, a stone base won't be needed.

When excavating for your concrete slab, be sure to make allowance for the thickness of whatever base is required.

After all these preparations are completed, set up your forms.

Oil the surfaces of all the form boards where they will touch the concrete, to avoid sticking. You can use used crankcase oil, which you usually can get free at a garage or gas station.

THE POUR

Mix the concrete and pour it into the forms as quickly as possible. Work quickly but carefully, placing the concrete as accurately as you can with a shovel or hoe, leaving it about an inch above the top of the form. Knead the concrete with the shovel blade to work out air pockets.

Strike off the concrete using the strike-off board. The board rests on the top of the forms. Your object is to skim off the excess concrete so the surface is flush with the top of the form boards.

Next you bullfloat the concrete. Hold the surface of the bullfloat level, and work it as if you were using a sponge mop. This step will level bumps and fill holes, pushing pieces of gravel below the surface.

After bullfloating, you must wait as the water rises to the surface and evaporates. The amount of time it takes can range from one hour to eight hours.

FINISHING

Check the concrete periodically. After the sheen of water has disappeared, run a trowel along the edges of the forms. If the concrete has set enough to hold the shape of the trowel, you can proceed with the floating. This further smooths the surface. Work the float flat on the concrete, in wide, arc motions. But *don't press too hard*. It is hard to erase gouges made at this point.

Troweling isn't necessary. But it will increase the smoothness of the surface and make it more dense. The first troweling is done immediately after floating. Hold the trowel flat against the concrete. The second troweling should be done later, when your hand leaves only a slight impression in the concrete. For a skid-resistant surface, use a stiff-bristled brush on the concrete after the last troweling.

CURING

The concrete should be cured for five to seven days, depending on the weather. The object is for the concrete to dry slowly, so you must keep it moist by covering it with plastic sheets or damp burlap or straw and sprinkling it periodically.

After several days of curing, the forms can be removed. But for best results, allow your concrete to cure several days after removing the forms and before subjecting it to use.

PAVING BLOCKS

Cast paving blocks are useful for making your own patio or garden walk. They are fairly easy to make in basic square, rectangular, triangular or round shapes. For more decorative blocks, texture and design can be added with pebble- and sand-casting techniques.

The basic slabs can be made 2 to 4 inches thick. Choose form boards, therefore, that match the thickness you desire.

One technique for making the blocks is to pour a slab and cut it into blocks. A simple perimeter form several feet in each dimension is constructed. Nail your side pieces to each other, and reinforce the corners or other joints with 2 × 2 or similar stock stakes, about 8 inches long. They should be driven into the ground so they are flush with the top of the form. Your form should be placed in a smooth, level place. Allow ½ inch below the bottom of the form to lay a layer of sand. Smooth the sand, and it will make the finished slabs easier to lift.

A variation is to cast your blocks in individual forms. You can construct these from 1 × 2s or 2 × 4s to give the size blocks you want.

Hinge three corners using either one or two butt hinges fastened with 1-inch #8 screws to the face of one board and the end of the adjoining board. You also could use strap hinges screwed to both faces, with the ends of each board cut on a 45-degree angle for the necessary interior joint.

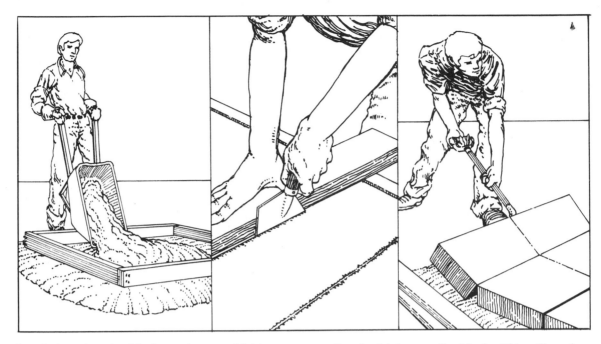

Rough-shaped paving blocks can be poured fairly easily without the use of scores of small forms. Nail together a large form and set it on top of a sand bed. Pour in concrete, screed it and float it. As the concrete sets, use your trowel and a stout straightedge to slice the slab into smaller blocks. This will not be as easy as slicing a cake, but it can be done. At the same time, cut the slab from the form with the trowel. After the concrete sets, strip away the form and break the slab into blocks.

No matter what type of hinges you use, install a hasp instead of a hinge on the fourth corner to close the form while casting.

To pour paving blocks or flagstones, start by setting the form in place and oiling the inside faces. Lay and smooth the sand bed. Mix the concrete and pour it into the forms. Using the strike-off board, bring the concrete even with the top of the forms.

After about four hours, cut the concrete into the size blocks you want. Use a strike-off board as a straightedge, and cut all the way through the concrete with the tip of a trowel. It may appear that the cuts close back up, but as you will see later, they have not done so.

After two or three days, remove the form boards. You will be able to lift the blocks by sliding the tip of a spade under them. Note how they crack apart where you made the cuts earlier.

Stand the blocks on edge for two to three weeks for complete curing. Cover them with moist sacks and protect from direct sun and freezing.

With a single block form, the procedure is the same, except that you do not make any cuts. Remove the form after four days and stand the blocks on edge to cure.

Soil Cement

You can mix Portland cement right into the soil for a hard, dry surface, suitable for secondary paths, service areas and even driveways that don't have heavy loads.

Loam and sandy soils harden best with this method, and they should be free of grass, twigs and trash. You will need to use headers to prevent the edges from crumbling.

Loosen the soil to a depth of 6 inches by hand or with a tiller. Mix cement evenly into the soil at a rate of 1 cubic foot of cement to every 9 cubic feet of soil. A path 5 inches wide, 18 inches long and 6 inches deep contains 45 cubic feet of soil and will need five bags of cement. Spray the soil surface lightly until it no longer absorbs water. When dry, roll to compact the soil.

Wood Paving

Wood paving can be beautiful, but it also has serious drawbacks. One of the best reasons for using wood is its appropriateness in the garden. A wood surface provides an effective link between man-made and natural elements. Unless it is brightly painted, it will never clash with the landscape or the architecture.

Wood is a marvelous accent material when used with other paving materials. Wide edgings or headers made of heavy timbers or railroad ties are popular. Wooden rounds can add variety to a loose gravel surface or break up an expansive surface of concrete or brick.

Impermanence is the critical drawback of wood paving. Nowhere will wood paving set into the ground endure more than a decade, and in humid climates, its life span can be cut to only two or three years. The wood will soak up moisture and be prey to cellulose-consuming bacteria, fungi and insects.

There are simply dozens and dozens of wood species available in the world, all with varying degrees of in-ground longevity. If you've got to buy from the usual sources—building suppliers or landscaping centers—stick to redwood, cedar and cypress. These are the most rot-resistant woods, and they are available across the country, though at a price. If you have access to a supply of some other wood and it won't cost a great deal, you may want to use it despite its limited potential life.

Regardless of the wood, the heartwood, which is the core of the log, is more resistant to decay. This wood is invariably darker than the sapwood, which is the outer ring of wood in the log. Because of the special sawing techniques that must be used to extract heartwood boards, such boards are particularly expensive. But again, you may judge the durability of this wood to be worth the premium.

Treat the wood you use for paving with some sort of wood preservative. Many preservatives will harm plants, but that may not be as signifi-

Wooden pavers can be cut from landscaping ties, logs or other wooden timbers. Use a chain saw and try to make the blocks of uniform thickness. The blocks are just like bricks or flagstones. Before laying the blocks, spread a sheet of plastic over the sand bed. Punch a pattern of holes in the plastic, one per square foot, for drainage. Set the blocks in place and sweep sand into the spaces between blocks. Gravel or other loose aggregates could be used around the blocks instead of sand.

cant a consideration here. Creosote, perhaps the most familiar preservative, will stain any wood an oily brown and imbue it with its characteristic stink. But it's a good and relatively inexpensive substance. If the color of the wood is important to you, use a compound that won't color the wood. There are several that fit the bill.

Although you can pave an area with railroad or landscaping ties, the most popular approach is to pave with end-grain blocks or rounds. These should be set in a sand bed, just as bricks or stones are. Fill the gaps between the individual blocks or rounds with sand or gravel. Take some time to experiment with layouts. Depending upon the uniformity of the material, you may be able to develop a pattern, but more likely, you'll have a random spread. The randomness need not be haphazard, however.

If ground moisture is a concern, you can spread sheets of plastic over the sand bed before laying the blocks or rounds. Punch drainage holes in the plastic, one hole per square foot. These will allow precipitation to percolate away but will limit the amount of ground moisture that's taken up.

Finally, you can set wood blocks into mortar for a firmer bedding. Given the impermanence of the material, it probably isn't a good thing to do.

Steps

Steps can be constructed using any of the preceding materials, though steps using loose aggregates would also have to incorporate some sort of monolithic riser. In a nutshell, building steps in the landscape involves excavating steps into the hillside, then laying down paving. Good drainage is vital if the steps are to be long lasting.

Building steps is not the easiest landscape construction project you could undertake, though an aggregation of three or four steps shouldn't be too difficult to build.

If you do detailed sketches of no other phase of construction, do them for this. A scaled drawing of the steps will help you calculate the excavation that's necessary. And the excavation that's necessary may be a real challenge to your surveying skills. You'll want to have reference points on paper to help you monitor the work.

As with other paving projects, the first step is layout. You must first measure the aggregate rise

and the total run, then divide it into a number of steps and a step size (height of riser and width of tread). Recall that the most appropriate maximum rise is 6 inches per foot of run. If you discover that you are going to have long, steep steps, you should look for alternative routes or plan to do a lot of digging.

To measure the rise and run, take up your stakes and string, line level, spirit level and tape measure. Drive a short stake into the ground at the crest of the hill. Tie the string to it, hang the line level on the string and extend it out over the slope. Standing at the base of the hill, hold the string up so it is level and measure from the string to the

The number of steps needed in an outdoor stairway can be calculated from the total run and total rise. The run and rise can be measured using a simple stake-and-string setup. Drive a short stake into the ground at the top of the proposed stairway and a tall stake at the bottom. String a level line between the stakes. The length of the line is the run, and the distance from ground to string along the tall stake is the rise.

ground. Cut a stake long enough to be driven into the ground and still extend up above the level string. Drive the stake into the ground, making sure it is plumb. Tie the string to the stake. Record on your sketch plan the total rise, which is the distance from the ground to the string, and the total run, which is the distance from stake to stake.

Work out how many steps you'll need and how big each will be. Sketch a cross section of the hillside, then superimpose the design of the steps on it. Sketch in the dimensions of the materials you plan to use, allow for a gravel foundation, if necessary, and calculate the dimensions of the necessary excavation.

Then break out the pick and shovel and start digging.

If you use ties for the risers (and tread), pin each step with at least two rebar pins, as in constructing a retaining wall of ties. Brick risers should be set in a mortar bed. If you use stone risers, you may be able to set them deeply enough in the earth to obviate the need for mortar. In any case, the general techniques for paving the steps are the same as those for paving a walk.

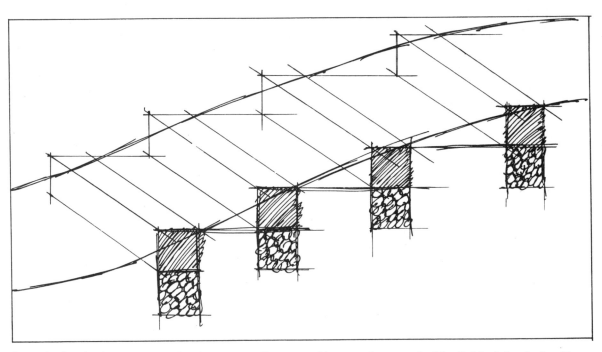

A simple sketch of your proposed stairway can tell you a lot. Do a cross section by drawing the contour of the slope, then superimposing the steps on the contour. If you use graph paper, you should be better able to work to a scale. The finished sketch should give you an idea of what the necessary excavation should look like, where each part of it will be and so on.

17

Privacy Fences

Wherever they can be used, live plants make the best fence for a garden. Trees and shrubs will permit air to pass through but still diminish the force of the wind. They are more effective in screening dirt and noise than fences or walls. However, walls or fences give you an immediate barrier that might take years to achieve with plants. Or you may want them as a background for plants, each emphasizing the beauty of the other.

The height of an enclosing structure is very important. If the purpose of the fence is to ensure privacy, it must be tall enough so that passersby cannot see over it and neighboring houses are screened. Unless the garden is much lower than the road, a moderate 3- or 4-foot wall or hedge is

285

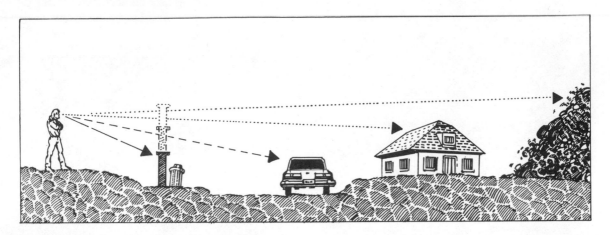

The height a privacy fence or screen must be to be effective depends upon the object or view that needs to be screened and its distance from the viewer. It is easy enough to figure out how high the fence must be to screen objects and views from your own view, but somewhat trickier to determine how to screen yourself from the view of others.

all that is needed for privacy. In some places, zoning laws prohibit building walls higher than 6 feet. However, within setback lines, the fences may be built as high as desired.

If the barrier is intended to screen an outdoor living area from the windows of a neighboring house, it may be necessary to roof the area, either with an awning or trellis, or with trees. If trees with dense foliage are planted close enough, they may act as a natural shield and at the same time provide shade.

A barrier may be low and airy or even transparent if you only intend to define the edge of a garden area. If the living area overlooks a fine panorama, a nominal boundary may be all that is needed on the side toward the view. This might be a low wall, an open fence or even a water feature, such as a pool or stream. In this case, the enclosure would be formed by the bank of the stream and would provide a ground-level barrier.

When an enclosure is intended to act as a barrier to movement but not to vision, it must be somewhat higher. A 4-foot hedge or fence can screen out surrounding ground-level objects, but the eye can travel over its top to distant views. Small children and pets may be confined by medium-sized barriers without limit to vision. Besides the old-fashioned picket fence, there are many new materials being used for transparent or translucent screens. Among these are louvered fences, pierced panel screens and trellised and latticed fences.

Planning

Some planning should precede any fence building you do.

For a fence around a garden, yard, patio or swimming pool, start by placing stakes at the corners and where your gates will be. Measure all the sides as accurately as you can. To determine how many posts you need, start with one for each corner and a pair for each gate. For the spaces between, figure on one post every 5 to 8 feet, depending on how the space divides up.

BOUNDARIES AND LEGAL MATTERS

When your fence is on your property line, its placement is very important. The most care must be taken if your home is close to neighbors, in a city or suburban setting. In rural areas, you probably will not have as many neighbor problems.

The point is, if you erect a fence on your neighbor's property, it comes under his or her control, or at best, it can become the topic of a legal fight. Unless you are a lawyer yourself, such confrontations are best avoided.

If you are fencing a backyard or garden along the boundary line, you may want to ask your neighbor to split the cost and labor. If you do, it may be a good idea to add a clause to both deeds spelling out your agreement, should the fence need repairs after the property changes hands.

ECONOMICS

The truth about any fence building is that costs may be the most important factor in deciding what you build. If you can locate used material, you can keep costs down. But beware of combining worn material with new. If your posts have only 10 years of life left, it will not matter if your boards have 50 years.

It is difficult to advise specifically on what fencing materials cost. They vary from place to place and from year to year. Lay out your fence, inventory the number of posts and the amount of lumber you will need, and do some comparison shopping. But in more than a few cases, you will have settled on the exact fence materials you want or need before you consider the cost.

DESIGN AND LAYOUT

Fences designed to block the view of neighbors or passersby are called privacy fences. They usually are built around relatively small areas, such as a backyard, patio, sun deck, or swimming pool.

There are several types of wooden privacy fences. To serve their function, they must be of fairly solid construction, which raises two planning problems—frost and wind.

The problem of frost is that it flows downhill, like water. A solid fence placed at the bottom of a hill faces the biggest threat of damage from frost heaves. Any post in that position should be planted extra deep in concrete.

A solid fence is not the best protection against wind. Actually, it not only must be constructed extra strongly to resist wind pressure, but it can aggravate wind conditions on one side of the fence. An eddy is formed on the lee side of the fence, creating a low pressure area close to the ground. This causes wind blowing over the top of the fence to swoop down to ground level.

Wind-tunnel tests have shown that three designs seem to be the most protective—down-canted, horizontal louvers; vertical boards with spaces between them; or baffle panels mounted atop the fence leaning at a 45-degree angle to the inside.

While most wire, rail and other fences can be

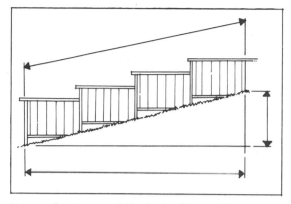

Privacy fencing on a hillside should not follow the contour. Rather, each panel should be level and, when combined with other panels, should form a step pattern. You have to use stakes and string to measure the rise and the run of the slope, as in working with steps (see Chapter 16). Divide the run into 8-foot-or-less post placement units, then divide the number of between-post gaps you have into the diagonal distance so you know where to place the posts on the hillside. To calculate the proper length for each post, you have to add the rise of the slope between posts to the height of the fence, so further stake and string measures of smaller rise and run distances may be necessary.

built to follow the contour of hilly land, the privacy-style fences are best built in terraces or steps. This requires careful planning. Measure the horizontal distance from the top to the bottom of the hill and the vertical drop. Measure the diagonal distance along the slope and lay out this triangle on graph paper. If you know the height and spacing of your posts, you can work out the placement of the horizontal pieces to give a regular step pattern.

Construction Principles

There are some features of construction that are common to many types of fences. The most important of these probably is the post.

SETTING POSTS

Unless you have very many holes to dig, you probably can do the job by hand. Digging tools come in two styles, the auger and the clamshell digger. If your soil is rocky, the clamshell is more suitable to the job. An auger makes a neater hole and is best suited for deeper holes.

A rule of thumb is for the holes to be one-third as deep as the post is long, usually about 24 to 30 inches. At the bottom of the hole, before you put in the post or anything else, put in a few inches of stones to allow water to drain away from the post. Alternate layers of soil and stones, tamping down firmly every few inches. Recheck the plumb of your post as you go along.

You can make the post stronger by putting brick-sized rocks in the hole, or by attaching horizontal wooden cleats (10-inch pieces of 1×2 are suitable).

Setting the posts in concrete will make for a strong, more permanent set. Mix your concrete on the dry side, because the mixture will absorb moisture from the soil. A mixture of one part cement, two parts sand, and three parts gravel is about right.

Make sure the post extends below the concrete. If not, the post will be enclosed by a water-catching concrete cup, and it will rot more quickly.

When you pour the concrete, mound it around the post so rainwater will run away. You can make a watertight expansion seal for your posts by first cutting old shingles to fit along the sides of the post. When the concrete dries, pull the shingles out and fill the spaces with tar.

BUILDING THE FENCES

Wooden privacy fences begin with a basic frame. In most cases, 4×4 posts, 8 or 9 feet long, will do the job.

You will need at least two horizontal rails, one at the top and one at the bottom. The bottom should be 4 or 5 inches off the ground, and the top can be either a like distance from the top of the posts, or mounted atop the posts. Use 2×4s for these rails.

Depending on your carpentry skills, you can choose from a variety of joints for the rails. The simplest is to toenail the 2×4s to the posts, but this is also the weakest method, so you should at least reinforce with a 2×2 or similar-sized block under the rail. Other joint methods include dado, and mortise and tenon.

For any wooden fence, it is definitely worthwhile to spend the little extra money for aluminum or galvanized nails instead of common steel. Any joint held by a rusted nail is weakened, and the rusty nails can leave stains.

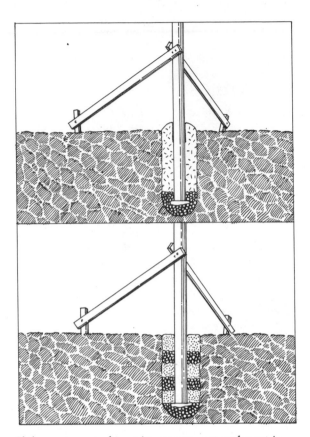

If the posts are to be set in concrete, set each post in place and nail temporary braces to it to hold it plumb while you do all the concrete work. Add more crushed stone to the hole, so the post will project through the concrete. Pour in the concrete and, after it has set, remove the braces. Don't neglect to cure this concrete. The initial task—setting and bracing the posts—is the same when posts are to be set in tamped earth. When backfilling, mix layers of earth and crushed stone. Use a pipe with a cap on the end to compact each layer.

VERTICAL BOARD FENCE

The simplest construction is to nail vertical planks to the rails. The most popular-sized planks are 1-inch board, using either random widths or 6- or 8-inch widths. They can be butted together for a really peep-proof enclosure. Or, you can leave space between the planks in the style of a picket fence. Another alternative, to give both airiness and privacy, is to nail planks to both sides of the rails, placing them so the boards on one side are opposite the spaces on the other side.

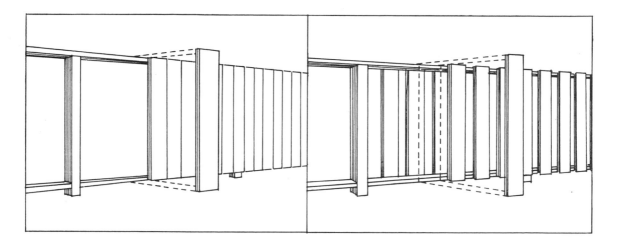

A vertical board fence is constructed by nailing boards of uniform or random widths to 2 × 4 rails toenailed in place between posts.

Materials for One 8-Foot Section of Board-on-Board Fence

WOOD

    2 pcs. 4 × 4 × 8' (posts)

    2 pcs. 2 × 4 × 8'   or   Top rail: 1 pc. 2 × 4 × 8'

                                             Bottom rail: 1 pc. 2 × 4 × 92½"

    8 pcs. 1 × 8 × 12'   or   Vertical boards: 16 pcs. 1 × 8 × 6'

HARDWARE

    Galvanized 8d nails

    Galvanized 12d nails

Materials for One 8-Foot Section of Vertical Board Fence

WOOD

    2 pcs. 4 × 4 × 8' (posts)

    2 pcs. 2 × 4 × 8'   or   Top rail: 1 pc. 2 × 4 × 8'

                                             Bottom rail: 1 pc. 2 × 4 × 92½"

    9 pcs. 1 × 6 × 12'   or   Vertical boards: 18 pcs. 1 × 6 × 6'

HARDWARE

    Galvanized 8d nails

    Galvanized 12d nails

LOUVERED FENCE

For a louvered fence, plan on your 1 × 6 board fitting between the two rails. To space the planks evenly and on a regular angle, you should make spacer blocks. Cut a 1-inch strip at a 45-degree angle every 3 inches. Nail the pieces along both the top and bottom rails. It will be easiest to put on the first pair of spacer blocks, one at the top and one at the bottom, then the first louver, and so on.

You can set horizontal louvers in the same manner, with the spacers mounted on the vertical posts. You may want to use lighter wood for horizontal louvers, perhaps ½-inch instead of 1-inch stock.

There are disadvantages to louver fences. Because the louvers overlap, you will need more wood per running foot of fence than for other types of fence. Also, unless you use top-grade, kiln-dried lumber, vertical louvers may twist and horizontal louvers may sag after they have been exposed to the weather for a few months.

BASKET-WEAVE FENCE

Basket-weave fences are popular because they are attractive and do not require much heavy lumber.

A vertical weave is easy to make. Use 4-inch by ¼-inch strips of any length for the slats. For the horizontal spacers, use pieces about 1½ inches by 1 inch and the length you need to go from post to post. Toenail or dado the spacers to the posts.

Paint or treat with preservative all the wood pieces before you assemble the fence. Basket-weave fences are very hard to paint when they are assembled.

Slide the slats down from the top, weaving them alternately front and back around the spacers. A wooden mallet or block of wood will be useful to tap the slats into place and also to tap them sideways to butt against the other slats.

A horizontal weave fence can be made by nailing each end of the slats to the posts and weaving the spacers through. A better method is to build the panels before mounting them on the

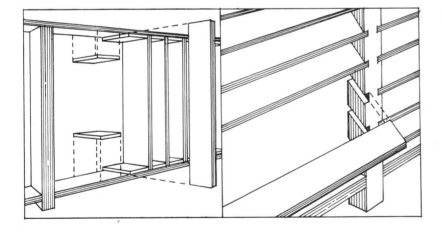

A louvered fence is easily made by setting boards vertically between the rails or horizontally between the posts. To secure the boards at the proper 45-degree angle to the plane of the fence, you can cut dados in rails or posts, or you can cut angled spacers from 1 × 4 boards.

Materials for One 8-Foot Section of Vertical Louvered Fence

WOOD

2 pcs. 4 × 4 × 8' (posts)		
2 pcs. 2 × 4 × 8'	or	Top rail: 1 pc. 2 × 4 × 8'
		Bottom rail: 1 pc. 2 × 4 × 92½''
11 pcs. 1 × 6 × 10'	or	Louvers: 22 pcs. 1 × 6 × 5'
1 pc. 1 × 4 × 10'	or	Spacers: 22 pcs. 1 × 4 × 5''

HARDWARE

Galvanized 8d nails
Galvanized 12d nails

To make the vertical basket-weave fence, first nail the 2 × 4 top and bottom rails in place, then toenail 2 × 2 spacers in place. The vertical slats will be secured between two 1 × 1 stops nailed to the rails. Nail both stops to the bottom rail, but only one to the top rail. Weave the slats into place, forcing their ends between the stops on the bottom rail. After all are in place, add the second stop to the top rail.

posts. To do this, make a panel-weaving tool. It requires two lengths of 2 × 4, 15 inches longer than the width of the panels you want; four 8-inch pieces of 1 × 4; and about 3 feet of 1 × 2 stock.

Nail the 1 × 2 × 3-inch jaw blocks along one of the 2 × 4 pieces. Space them apart exactly twice the width of the planks you are using in your weave. (If your planks are 4 inches wide, space the blocks 8 inches from center to center.)

At both ends of this 2 × 4 beam, nail two 1 × 4 end pieces, one on each side.

Using the other 2 × 4 beam, nail similar jaw blocks at the same interval as on the other beam, but stagger them so they are opposite the spaces on the other beam.

Place the second beam between the upright pieces of the first beam and adjust the jaw blocks so they mesh. Drill a hole through the two end pieces and the upper 2 × 4 and insert a bolt, large nail or dowel for a hinge.

To use the tool, lay the 4-inch by ¼-inch slats side by side on the ground, butting but not overlapping. To make the end frames, use two 1-inch-square pieces, as long as your panel is high. Put one beneath, and one on top of the planks, and nail together.

Slide the started panel, joined end first, onto the jaw blocks of the weaving frame. While the lower blocks push up on every other slat, close the frame so the upper blocks push down on the alternate blocks.

At this point it will be easy to weave a spacer through the slats. Then slide the panel about 18 inches along the frame, and adjust it so the slats

that were pushed down before are now pushed up, and vice versa.

Continue this to the end of the slats. Then finish the panel by sandwiching that end between two more 1-inch-square strips. You may also want to nail a 1-inch-square framing strip along the top of the panel, nailing it from behind before fastening the panel to the posts using 10d nails.

Gates

Almost any fence you build will need a gate or other passageway. Gates in fences around a garden or yard need only be big enough to admit people. If there is any need to get in with a garden cart or mower, 4 feet is a good minimum width.

A gate for any of the fences can be made simply by building a 2 × 4 frame of the appropriate dimensions and installing boards or louvers or a basket-weave panel to match the fence.

SETTING THE POSTS

Gates get the most wear and tear of any part of the fence. Since they are opened, closed, slammed and swung on by children, they must be sturdily built, or they soon will sag and will be useless.

No matter what kind of hinged gate you build, start by installing strong posts on either side. One method of doing this is to create a concrete threshold. This approach will necessitate construction of the gate before the fence and the posts are in place (with other approaches, it is possible, and even desirable, to install the posts and the fence, then construct a gate to fit).

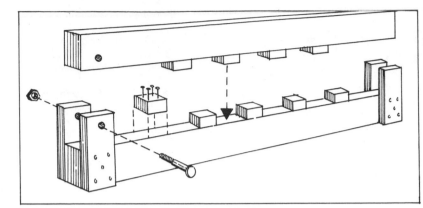

These jaws of fencing, which you can easily make, will enable you to build a horizontal basket-weave fence with a minimum of trial and tribulation.

Materials for Panel-Weaving

WOOD

1 pc. 2 × 4 × 14'	or	Jaws: 2 pcs. 2 × 4 × 6½'
1 pc. 1 × 2 × 4'	or	Jaw blocks: 15 pcs. 1 × 2 × 3''
1 pc. 1 × 4 × 4'	or	End pieces: 4 pcs. 1 × 4 × 8''

HARDWARE
6d nails
1 4'' × ¼'' bolt w/nut and washer

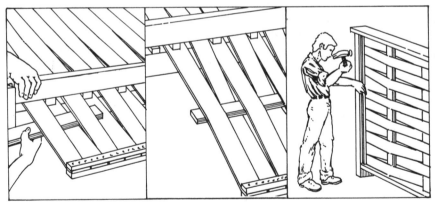

To make a horizontal basket-weave fence panel, you mount the slats, then use the fencing jaws to spread the slats just enough to slide a spacer in place.

Materials for One 8-Foot Panel of Basket-Weave Fence

WOOD

7 pcs. 1 × 2 × 12'	or	Spacers: 14 pcs. 1 × 2 × 6'
2 pcs. 1 × 1 × 12'	or	Panel frame vertical members: 4 pcs. 1 × 1 × 6'
2 pcs. 1 × 1 × 16'	or	Panel frame horizontal members: 4 pcs. 1 × 1 × 8'

2 shts. ¼'' ext. plywood (good two sides) or Slats: 15 pcs. 4'' × 8'

HARDWARE
Galvanized 8d nails
Galvanized 10d nails

Dig a 12-inch-wide trench the width of the gate and posts. The trench should be at least 18 inches deep at the outer extremities, but need only be a foot deep in the center.

Attach the hinge-post to the gate with hinges. Using scraps of wood, tack the latch-post and gate together as close as they must be for the gate to function properly, but do not install the latch. Remember that at least 18 inches of post should be in the ground.

Erect the gate and posts in position above the trench and secure it there with bracing constructed of scrap materials. Pour a few inches of gravel or crushed stone in the bottom of the trench, then fill with concrete. Trowel the threshold smooth. When the concrete has cured, remove the bracing and install the fence and the gate latch.

Another way to install strong gate posts is with a concrete strain plug.

Dig your post holes 24 to 36 inches deep and about 16 inches square. Use a 4-inch-square post, about 8 feet long. At the bottom, nail two cross-bars on opposite sides. Use 16-inch (or whatever width your hole is) pieces of 2 × 4s fastened with galvanized 10d nails.

Fill the hole with dirt and gravel and tamp it down tightly, to within about 12 inches of the

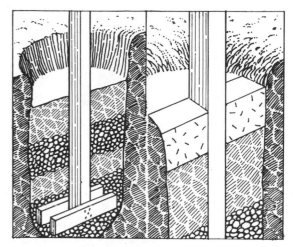

A gate post can be set with a concrete strain plug. The posthole must be quite large, since it must accommodate a post with crossbars attached to the bottom. Set the post and backfill with about 18 to 24 inches of earth and crushed stone in alternating layers. Complete the backfill with concrete poured on only two sides of the post, parallel with the fence line.

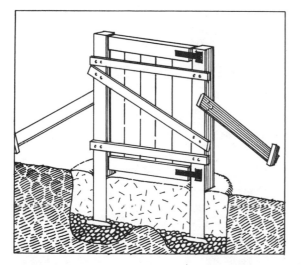

A very secure gate can be erected by setting it in a concrete threshold. The gate must be constructed, mounted on the posts and temporarily nailed together in a solid unit. It is then set up in a trench, rather than in postholes, and the trench is filled with concrete.

surface. Using about a cubic foot of concrete, form a horizontal block on opposite sides of the post, along the drag line of the gate (parallel with the fence line). Locating the concrete on either side of the post provides the needed strength, while allowing drainage away from the concrete and the post.

HINGES AND LATCHES

You will need to know a bit about hinges. Many hinges, such as strap or T hinges, can be mounted with either side up. Others, such as lag-bolt hinges, loose-pin hinges, and all those that are held together by gravity and the gate's own weight, must be specified to be either left- or right-hand hinges. To determine which you need, stand so the gate will swing away from you. If it swings to the right, it takes a right-hand hinge, and vice versa.

For most gates, strap or T hinges are used. Lag-bolt hinges are popular on wide farm fences. The halves of lag-bolt hinges separate into what are referred to as the male and female parts. The female part goes on the gate, the male on the fence post.

There is a wide variety of latches manufactured for gates: sliding bolts, hasps and hook-and-eye types.

SECTION IV
Creating and Maintaining Your Natural Landscape

18

Preparing the Soil

We've seen that, left to herself, Nature manages the soil with great efficiency. The vegetation and wildlife that are nourished and supported by the soil in life repay their debt when, after death, they decompose, replenishing the soil with the nutrients that were borrowed and making them available for new generations.

There are few areas of virgin soil left—that is, soil that has been managed solely by nature. The soils that come nearest to being like the soils the pioneers found lie along old, undisturbed fence rows, in road banks that have never been plowed or in woods that have not been severely grazed or burned.

If you are lucky enough to have virgin soil on your property, cherish it. It will be high in organic matter, porous, very crumbly and easily broken apart. It's more likely that the soil you find will have been cultivated, stripped or at least compacted. As a result of such treatment, the soil at your homesite may be heavy, poorly drained or inclined to drain too rapidly. Foreign objects, left on the site by the construction crew, may create small areas where the soil's texture is markedly different or its acid-alkaline balance disturbed. Because of the loss of up to half of its original organic matter, such distrubed soil will be lighter in color, harder and 10 to 30 percent heavier than nearby virgin soils.

Presumably you tested and analyzed your soil and planned your landscape with its characteristics in mind. You've chosen water-loving species for the poorly drained areas and planned your activities to take place in drier areas. Your task will be much easier than that of the unknowing homeowner who chose an azalea for his limestone soils. However, if your soils have been stripped or compacted, or if the existing soil conditions are not suitable to your proposed landscape plan, you will have to make some improvements if you want to have vigorous plant growth and a healthy landscape.

Fortunately, adding even one soil supplement may improve your soil's condition in several ways. Adding mulch, for example, not only improves the texture but also increases the nutrient levels present in your soil. Most organic soil supplements act in this way, both conditioning and fertilizing the soil. For purposes of discussion, however, we will talk about improving soil texture, fertilizing the soil and balancing soil pH as if they always required separate treatments.

Improving Soil Texture

The physical condition of the soil that has the most to do with air and water movement is called soil tilth. A soil in good tilth breaks up easily into crumbs or granules about the size of wheat grains or soybeans. These crumbs are porous and are made up of tiny bits of soil linked together, something like popcorn in a popcorn ball. These crumbs hold their structure even when soaked. Because of the pores in the crumbs themselves, and because the size of the crumbs keeps them from fitting together as tightly as smaller bits of soil, there is space for air and water. In other words, a soil with good tilth will have proper drainage and aeration.

The best method of improving soil texture is to increase its organic matter content. There are three general ways to do this: first, turn under cover crops; second, mulch regularly with organic materials, allowing them to decompose on the soil surface so that their nutrients are gradually released; third, add humus to the soil by composting, using any of several methods developed by organic gardeners.

GREEN MANURE COVER CROPS

The cover crop method is similar to what Nature does on her own. Good natural soils are continually being improved by the addition of organic matter from the decomposition of native vegetation. Disturbed soils, such as those on a building lot where a house has just been finished, can be reconditioned by the deliberate planting of cover crops that draw nutrients from the subsoil closer to the surface and improve soil texture by adding organic matter when they are turned under at peak growth. A year or two devoted to growing such soil-improving plants will reward the homeowner's patience with lush flowers, trees and shrubs on the entire property.

In warm weather, green manure crops that have been tilled into the soil decompose rapidly. In the South, especially in the humid areas, such organic matter breaks down so fast that other soil supplements must be added constantly to keep the percentage of humus high enough for good tilth. Green manuring is valuable there to prepare the soil for field crops, vegetables and flowers, but it is necessary to add a lot of compost and mulch to make these plantings flourish. In other parts of the country, by starting cover crops early enough in spring, two green manure crops may be grown in one season, preparing the soil for landscape planting the following year.

Legumes make good green manures because they fix atmospheric nitrogen in their root nodules.

Green Manure Cover Crops

Common Name	Description	Growing Locations	Soil Preferences
Alfalfa	Deep-rooted, perennial legume	Grown throughout the U.S.	Does well on all but very sandy, very clayey, acid or poorly drained soils
Alsike clover	Perennial legume	Grown mostly in the northern states	Prefers fairly heavy, fertile loams, but does better on wet, acid soil than most clovers
Alyce clover	Annual legume	Grown in the lower South	Prefers sandy or clay loams with good drainage
Barley	Annual nonlegume	Grown in the North	Does best on loams; not good on acid or sandy soils
Beggarweed	Annual legume	Flourishes in the South but grows fairly well north to the Great Lakes	Thrives on rich sandy soil but is not exacting. Will grow on moderately acid soils
Black medic	Legume	Grown throughout the U.S.	Grows well on reasonably fertile soils
Buckwheat	Nonlegume	Grown mostly in the Northeast	Tops for rebuilding poor or acid soils
Bur clover	A fine winter legume	Grown as far north as Washington, D.C., and on the Pacific coast	Prefers heavy loams but will grow on soils too poor for red or crimson clover if phosphate is supplied
Cowpea	Very fast-growing annual legume	Thrives practically anywhere in the U.S.	Does well on a wide range of soils
Crimson clover	Winter annual	Grown from New Jersey southward	Does well on almost any fairly good soil
Crotalaria	Annual legume	Grown in the South and as far north as Maryland	Does well on very poor soil
Domestic rye grass and Italian rye grass	Nonlegume	Grown in many areas	Does well on a wide range of soils
Fenugreek	Winter legume	Grown in the Southwest	Prefers loam soils
Field bromegrass	Nonlegume	Grown in the northern half of the U.S.	Widely adapted as to soils
Field pea	Annual legume	Wide climatic range	Prefers well-drained, sandy to heavy loam
Kudzu	Perennial legume	Grown in the South-Central states	Does well on all but the poorest soils
Lespedeza	Legume	Grown in the South and as far north as Michigan. Korean and Sericea varieties in the North	Does well on all types of soil, but Sericea is particularly good for poor acid soils. For these it is one of the best fertility builders available
Lupine	Legume	Grown in the Southeast to North	Prefers acid, sandy soils
Oats	Nonlegume	Widely grown	Does well on many soils

Planting Seasons	Sowing Instructions	Special Characteristics
Sow in spring in the North and East, late summer elsewhere	Sow 18 to 20 pounds of seed per acre on a well-prepared seedbed	Apply lime if pH is 6 or below and add phosphate rock
Sow in spring. May be sown in early fall in the South	Sow 6 to 10 pounds of seed per acre	
Sow in late spring	Sow 15 to 20 pounds of seed per acre	
In colder climates, sow winter varieties; elsewhere, spring varieties	Sow 2 to 2½ bushels of seed per acre	
Sow when all danger of frost is past	Sow 15 pounds of hulled seed per acre with 30 pounds of unhulled seed	Will spread in the South if seed is allowed to mature, so it may become a nuisance in borders and lawns
Sow in the spring in the North, fall in the South	Sow 7 to 15 pounds of seed per acre	Needs ample lime
Sow anytime after frost	Sow about 2 bushels of seed per acre	Has an enormous, vigorous root system and is a fine bee plant. Can grow 3 crops, 40 tons of green matter, per acre in a season. Use rock fertilizers very efficiently
Sow in September	Sow 15 pounds of hulled seed or 3 to 6 bushels of unhulled seed per acre	Spreads if allowed to set seed
Sow anytime after the soil is well warmed	Spread 80 to 100 pounds of seed over a large area or sow in 20 pounds in 3-foot rows	Fine soil builder. Its powerful roots crack hardpans
Sow about 60 days before the first killing frost	Sow 30 to 40 pounds of unhulled seed or 15 to 20 pounds of hulled seed per acre	Dixie hard-seeded strain spreads from year to year in the South
Sow seed in the spring	Sow 10 to 30 pounds of seed per acre, depending on the variety	Makes sandy, soillike loam
Sow in the spring in the North, fall in the South	Sow 2 to 25 pounds of seed per acre	
Sow in the fall	Sow 35 to 40 pounds of seed per acre	
Sow in early spring or late summer	Sow 10 to 15 pounds of seed per acre	Good winter cover, hardier than rye
Sow in early spring in the North, late fall in the South	Sow 1½ to 3 bushels of seed per acre, depending on variety	
Sow in early spring	Plant seedlings	Commonly allowed to grow for several years before plowing under
Sow in spring	Sow 30 to 40 pounds of seed per acre	Benefits from phosphate rock. Will spread if seed is allowed to set. Turn under early
Sow in spring in the North, late fall in the South	Sow 50 to 150 pounds of seed per acre, depending on the variety	Blue lupine is a fine winter legume in the South. White and yellow are most often grown in the North
Sow in the spring	Sow 2 bushels of seed per acre	Winter oats suitable for mild winters only

(continued next page)

Green Manure Cover Crops—*Continued*

Common Name	Description	Growing Locations	Soil Preferences
Pearl millet	Nonlegume	Grown as far north as Maryland	Prefers fair to rich soils
Persian clover	Winter annual legume	Grown in the South and Pacific areas	Prefers heavy moist soils
Red clover	Biennial legume	Grown in practically all areas, but does not like high temperatures so is most useful in the North	Does well on any well-drained, fair to rich soil
Rough pea (caley pea and single-tary pea	Winter annual legume	Grown in the southern half of the U.S. and the Northwest	Does well on many soils but best on fertile loams
Rye	Nonlegume	Grown mostly in the Northeast and South	Does well on many soil types
Sour clover	Winter legume	Grown in the South and West	Does well on most soils
Soybeans	Summer legume	Grown from the deep South to Canada	Does well on nearly all kinds of soil including acid soils where other legumes fail
Sudan grass	Nonlegume	Grown in all parts of the U.S.	Does well on any except wet soils
Sweet clover	Biennial legume	Grown in all parts of the U.S.	Does well on just about any soil. If reasonably well supplied with lime, will pierce tough subsoils
Velvet beans	Annual legume	Grown in the South	One of the best crops for sandy poor soils
Vetches	Annual and biennial legumes	Varieties for all areas	Does well in any reasonably fertile soil with ample moisture. Hairy vetch does well in sandy or acid soils and is the most winter-hardy variety. Hungarian is good for wet soils in areas having mild winters

Working in the green manure causes the root system to decay, releasing the stored-up nitrogen to the soil. By replanting the area within a short time after green manuring, the gardener can take advantage of this added soil nitrogen.

In sandy or poor soil, the benefits of green manuring are lost if the cover crop is tilled under, since surface water and groundwater will quickly wash away the nutrients added by the decomposing organic matter. To retard this leaching, take a scythe to the cover crop at the peak of its growth and allow the cuttings to decompose where they fall on the soil surface. In clay soils, however, it's best to incorporate the green manure into the soil, where it will break down faster, since leaching in such soils takes place slowly.

MULCH

Mulch is traditionally used on the soil surface around individual plantings to protect them from temperature extremes and drought. If there is sufficient existing vegetation on your property, you can use nature's technique of mulching. Simply allow dead plant material to remain on the ground, where it will protect plants from severe weather and eventually decompose, adding organic matter to the soil.

If you prefer to mulch specific areas, till the soil around the plant, add a nitrogen fertilizer and then mulch. These are some organic materials that are suitable: grass clippings, leaves, peat moss, compost, hay, straw, cornstalks, corncobs, plant

Planting Seasons	Sowing Instructions	Special Characteristics
	Commonly planted in 4-foot rows, 4 pounds of seed per acre	
Sow in fall	Sow 5 to 8 pounds of seed per acre	
Sow early in spring to allow time for 2 stands	Sow 15 pounds of seed per acre	Needs phosphorus
Sow in the fall	Sow 30 pounds of seed per acre	Needs phosphorus; will spread
Sow in the fall	Sow 80 pounds of seed per acre	Probably the best nonlegume for green manuring
Sow in early fall	Sow 15 to 20 pounds of seed per acre	
Sow from spring to midsummer	Sow 60 to 100 pounds of seed per acre	Will stand considerable drought. Use late-maturing varieties for best green manure results
Sow in late spring	Spread 20 to 25 pounds of seed per acre	Very rapid grower so good for quick organic matter production
Sow from fall to early spring	Sow 17.5 pounds of seed per acre	Especially adept at utilizing rock fertilizers. A fine bee plant
Sow when the soil is well warmed	Sow 100 pounds of seed per acre or 25 to 30 pounds in wide rows	Produces roots 30 feet long, vines up to 50 feet long
Sow in the North in spring, elsewhere in the fall	Sow 30 to 60 pounds of seed per acre, depending on the variety	

residues, wood chips, dried sludge, sawdust (broadcast only on the soil surface), pine needles and bark. When judging how good a material is for mulching, consider if it's heavy enough not to blow away; if it's free of any toxic chemicals that might cause plant injury; if it's fairly easy and inexpensive to obtain and apply; and if it will remain loose enough to allow air circulation down to the soil's surface.

COMPOST

Composting is one of the basics for successful organic gardening. Like natural landscaping, composting works with nature, encouraging bacteria to decay organic matter into humus. In its many forms and variations, compost is a beneficial substance that conditions the soil, fertilizes it and makes it more productive.

A great amount of research in composting methods has been done, resulting in the 14-day method, sheet composting, anaerobic methods and many variations of these. Behind them all, however, lies the original Indore method invented by the father of organic gardening, Sir Albert Howard. The Indore method is used all over the world and is still considered practical and productive.

THE INDORE METHOD

Howard worked in India from 1905 to 1934 as a British government agronomist, advising the Indians

Sowing a cover crop requires no special soil preparation. The goal usually is to get vegetation growing as quickly as possible to protect the soil from erosion. The soil improvement that results when the crop is turned under is an oft-overlooked bonus. A small area can easily be seeded by hand. A broadcast seeder will enable you to evenly seed a large area. Turn the crank, and it spins out seed, quietly and *efficiently. Let the crop grow until it blossoms, then cut it, as though you were haying. Use a scythe or a sickle-bar mower, here mounted on a walking tractor. You can collect the cuttings, but your soil will be the beneficiary if you leave it. In the early spring, use a big tiller or a tractor with a plow to turn the crop under. A small area can probably be chopped up with a mattock and turned under with a spade.*

about farming and learning from them as well. During these years, he tried to develop a consistently successful method of composting. Through experimentation, he discovered that a 3:1 proportion of plant matter to manure made the same kind of rich, loamy humus found in the woods and fields. To insure that these proportions were achieved, he decided to build his compost heap in layers. He began with a base of brush on the ground, then applied a 6-inch layer of plant residues such as clippings, leaves and husks. Next, he piled on a 2-inch layer of manure and topped this with a sprinkling of rich earth, ground limestone and phosphate rock. He repeated the layers of "green matter," manure and rock powders to build his compost heap. By experimentation, he found that a heap 5 to 10 feet wide and 5 feet high was ideal, although the length made no difference. After the

All sorts of materials, natural and man-made, can be—and are—used as mulches. Some are more appropriate than others for the natural landscape, particularly those, like leaves and pine needles, found mulching undisturbed areas. Straw is widely available and commonly used in vegetable gardening and on newly seeded lawns. Wood chips are long lasting and, when coarse and put down in thick layers, are often used for paths in natural settings. Newspapers are ubiquitous, smother weeds very effectively and look like the very devil; certainly you'll use such a mulch only temporarily.

compost heap had heated up during decomposition and begun to cool down, he turned it over to aerate it—once after 6 weeks and again after 12 weeks. At the end of 3 months, this simple method had produced a rich, crumbly compost, high in nutrient value and remarkable as a soil-structure builder.

In further research, Howard found that aeration could be improved in the compost heap by placing pipes or thick stakes through it as it was being built and then afterwards removing them. Taking this step allowed oxygen to reach all parts of the heap more quickly, permitting new bacteria to function and resulting in a more rapid breakdown of the composting materials. When the pile was finally cooled down, Howard added earthworms to it to keep it crumbly and well aerated.

There have been many modifications of the

Compost heaps are piles of rottables that are rotting. If you are a gardener, you'll want—or already have—a routine that supplies your garden with an annual dressing of compost. If you're not, a major heap to supply the one-time dressing your landscape will need to get established at planting is all you'll want. In any case, your heap should be erected on a spot with rich, fertile soil. Loosen this soil a bit, then start building layers: first of garden trash, leaves, grassy cuttings or hay, then of manure, then of garbage. Add more manure, more green matter and so forth. Put in a few thin layers of that soil you're building on. Sprinkle the heap with water as you build; you want it damp but definitely not wet or soggy. Don't compact it, just heap up your materials. Shredding is important if you want compost fast. If you haven't a shredder, give the heap time to work. Once the heap is done, just let it rot. It will slowly settle, diminishing in size. Eventually, you'll be ready to use it, and use it you should, whether it looks like what you expect—dark, crumbling, humusy matter, almost like peat—or like it's not quite done—with stems and lumps.

Indore method to meet the needs of today's modern farmers. Although some of these modifications are real refinements, all composting methods are based on the principles discovered by Sir Albert Howard in the early 1900s. The end product of whatever method is used will be a fine, dark brown or black humus, rich in all the needed soil nutrients, organic matter, fungi and earthworms. Enough of this material spread on the most shabby, run-down garden can bring about a miraculous rejuvenation.

THE 14-DAY METHOD

Using the 14-day method, you can make nine heaps of crumbly compost in six months in an 8 × 4-foot space. This is enough compost to spread in a 2-inch layer over 6,000 square feet of ground—the area of a 75 × 80-foot plot. If you have a smaller area of land to compost, you may not want to make as many piles.

You begin building your compost heap in early spring, making it 4 feet high in an 8 × 4-foot space. After two weeks, remove the finished compost, which will measure 110 cubic feet and weigh about 2 tons. You can put the compost directly on your soil, or you can store the finished compost and allow it to decompose into a fine humus. By mid-fall, six months later, your ninth heap should be finished, giving you a six-month total of 18 tons.

The 14-day method has passed many trials with flying colors. Initially devised by an agricultural team at the University of California, the method was first tried at Rodale's Organic Experimental Farm in 1954. Since that time, many Rodale readers have reported success with it. The basic procedure, described below, may be altered to suit your individual needs and supply of materials.

First day. To build your compost pile, you will need "green matter," manure and rock powders. Shred *everything*—including the manure—with a compost shredder or rotary mower, and mix the materials together in a mounded heap. Shredding is essential to the success of the 14-day method because it speeds up the decomposition process, breaking up the "green matter" (which tends to mat down) into particles that soil bacteria can readily digest.

If your compost-building materials are low in nitrogen, be sure to add a sprinkling of dried blood, cottonseed meal or some other nitrogen supplement to each shredded and mixed layer in the heap.

Second and third days. By now the heap should have begun to heat up, indicating that the bacteria present in the manure and plant residues are hard at work, breaking down the organic matter. To check the temperature, bury a thermometer in the heap. If you do not get a reading of at least 104°F. (40°C.), add more nitrogenous material. It is especially important, during the first few days, to keep the heap moist. If turning the heap shows it to be drying out at all, give it a good watering with the garden hose.

Fourth day. Turn the heap, check the temperature, and water the heap if needed. By now the temperature of the heap should have reached 160°F. (71°C.). It should stay this warm for almost a week.

Seventh day. Turn the heap again, check the temperature, and keep the heap moist.

Tenth day. Turn the heap once more. It should now begin to cool off, indicating that it is nearly finished.

Fourteenth day. The compost is ready for use. It will not look like fine humus, but the straw clippings and other materials will have broken down into a rich, dark, crumbly substance. You may want to allow the heap to decay further, but at this stage it is perfectly good for garden use.

SHEET COMPOSTING

By incorporating plant refuse or compost into the soil and allowing it to decay for a month or two before planting, you can greatly improve the condition of your soil and the quality of the vegetation it supports. Peat, manure or a variety of other organic materials can be composted. Some enthusiasts claim to have obtained very good results by sheet composting heavy organic mulches.

Trash for composting can be spread over the ground and simply turned in. It will rot in the ground and boost the fertility and organic matter content of the soil as it does. No need to build a compost heap and wait for it to ripen. Just lay straw, leaves, manure, even garbage on the ground, then turn it in with a shovel, tiller or, if you've a big area to work, a tractor and plow. The process is often called sheet composting.

Work whatever organic material you are using into the soil to a depth of 6 to 8 inches with a disk or plow. In a small garden, you can incorporate the material into the soil by hand, or work it in to a depth of 3 to 4 inches with a cultivator and then turn the soil with a spade, shovel or spading fork.

When a lawn is converted to a planting area, it may be sheet composted simply by turning over the sod. The subsoil can be spaded and enriched before the sod is inverted over it.

ANAEROBIC COMPOSTING

If you are renting a house and land and are reluctant to build a permanent compost bin, anaerobic composting may be for you. This airless composting method is also appropriate if you are living in suburbia, where neighbors might object to the odor and flies that may appear around a conventional compost heap.

Because anaerobic composting requires no turning or waterings after the heap is built, it is the method used most often for municipal composting. Through experimentation, home gardeners have found a way to make it practical on a smaller scale. First, an area of land is disked to bring earthworms to the surface. Manure is piled on this exposed soil in a long mound 5 feet wide and 3 feet high. This mound is then soaked with water from a garden hose and covered with a sheet of black polyethylene plastic. The plastic is "sealed" against the ground by a layer of dirt around its edges. (Because plastic can smother, it is wise to fence in the compost heap with chicken wire to protect children who might be tempted to play "king of the mountain.") After 2½ months, the plastic is removed to expose dark, rich, sweet-smelling compost. Using this method, little of the size of the original heap is lost, and few of the nutrients are washed away by rainwater.

Fertilizing the Soil

From the results of your soil test, you should know the level of the major nutrients—nitrogen, phosphorus and potash—available in your soil. If there are deficiencies, you can correct them by planting a legume cover crop that is tilled into the soil as a green manure at the peak of its development. This practice improves the very structure of the soil, making it porous to water and well aerated, as well as increasing the level of the nitrogen. Nutritional deficiencies can also be remedied by the use of processed natural fertilizers.

Commercial fertilizers, available at garden and farm supply stores, are described in terms of a three-part chemical formula that includes nitrogen, phosphorus and potash. The common fertilizer, 5-10-5, is 5 percent nitrogen, 10 percent phosphorus and 5 percent potash. Commercially manufactured fertilizers can be obtained in varying proportions of these nutrients to suit the needs of specific soils. Since applying either too little or too much nitrogen to your soil can damage plants placed in the area, it is tempting to buy fertilizer in "scientifically precise" proportions. However, the chemical elements in a synthetic fertilizer are immediately active, so there is danger of root burn, which can be fatal to a plant. Of the natural fertilizers, only

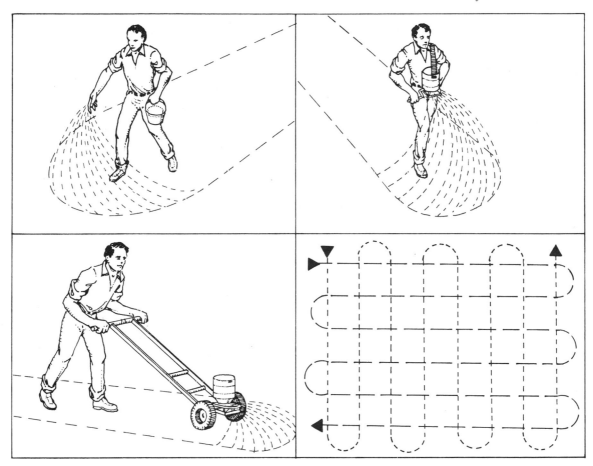

Spreading rock powders, dried manure and other commercial organic fertilizers can be done in several ways, but the goal is always to cover the ground as evenly as possible. For small areas, you can dust out a handful at a time from a bucket. A heavy-duty broadcast seeder, whether a hand-cranked or push model, can also be used to spread powdery fertilizers, easing the burden of covering a large area. Whichever method you use, walk back and forth over the area, lightly fertilizing parallel paths. Try to avoid getting too much overlap. Then spread in paths at right angles across the once-covered area.

fresh manure, with its relatively high nitrogen content, may cause root burn. Adding straw bedding to the manure will absorb the animal urine in which the nitrogen is concentrated. Then, as with other organic fertilizers, the nitrogen and other nutrients will be released to the soil gradually and gently over a period of years.

Many organic fertilizers benefit the soil in other ways than simply boosting the major nutrient levels. Manure, which supplies nitrogen, also adds humus; phosphate rock adds trace minerals as well as phosphorus. Greensand, which was once at the bottom of the sea, supplies potash and many other ingredients not to be found in a bag of man-made 5-10-5 fertilizer.

There are many other organic soil builders available in different areas. These can be worked into the soil in spring or fall, top-dressed around growing plants or added to the compost heap.

If you live in an area with extremely poor soil

or with very little rainfall, you should consider deep placement of fertilizers. By putting the fertilizer below the root systems of plants, you will encourage the roots to reach deep into the subsoil for nutrients. With a more extensive root system, the plants will be closer to the water table and better able to stand up under drought conditions.

Balancing Soil pH

When you analyzed your soil in Chapter 6, you determined its pH—the degree of acidity or alkalinity. If you found that your soil is more acid than neutral, you have probably included acid-loving plants like blueberry, cranberry, laurel and azalea in your landscape design. By choosing plants that grow in acid conditions, the need for changing soil pH should be minimal. If your soil is highly acidic, however, the nutrients may be locked in and unavailable to the plants. When the pH is below 5.5, phosphorus and other elements are tied up, and there may be no available calcium. In this case, it would be wise to cure your acid soil by adding lime. By acting on the aluminum and iron particles, lime releases the blocked-in plant foods and helps to decompose organic matter, free nitrogen and stimulate the work of microbes and root bacteria.

Hydrogen, which makes the soil acid, is displaced by the calcium supplied in lime. Calcium also improves the soil structure and helps to grow bigger crops by increasing the organic matter. Lime may be needed, therefore, not merely to control acidity but to bring vital calcium and its related services to soil and plant life.

Adding lime by guesswork is definitely a mistake. Too much can be as detrimental as too little. In addition, different sections of your property will probably have different requirements, so you will have to know how much to apply to each area.

In general, sandy and light-colored soils need less lime than silt or clay loams of the same pH, and soils containing a high percentage of organic matter need heavier liming than those deficient in it.

Areas receiving comparatively small amounts of rain require less lime than others. Where the annual rainfall is 20 inches or better, more is needed.

Different species have different lime requirements as well. Legumes (which depend on calcium to form their nitrogen-supplying nodules) and some grasses need liberal amounts. A few ornamental plants prefer an alkaline (pH above 7) soil. Some, like azaleas and rhododendrons, demand a quite acid soil to thrive.

The primary source of lime is ground limestone, which is usually 90 percent pure. Dolomite lime, also a natural ground rock, has some magnesium as well as calcium. Either of these is suitable for liming and will not leave harmful residues in the soil. Hydrated lime, burned lime and quick lime act more rapidly than dolomite lime but are caustic. These should not be used because they burn seeds and seedlings and destroy soil bacteria. In some localities, marl, marble and oyster shells (all of which contain some calcium) are used successfully, but limestone is the most widely available source of lime and generally costs the least.

The effectiveness of limestone varies with how fine it is ground or crushed. Finer grades go into solution and act more quickly to improve the soil, while coarser ones remain in the soil longer and are effective over a greater number of years. Fine limestone is pulverized so that all of it will pass through a 10-mesh screen, and 40 to 50 percent of it will pass through a 100-mesh screen. This grade of limestone has enough fine particles to provide immediate soil improvements and enough coarse particles to maintain its effectiveness for up to three years.

Lime may be applied during any season that the soil can be worked, but the more time it has to act before planting, the better the results will be.

There are several ways to apply limestone. For sizable areas, use a lime spreader for easy application. In many cases, the seller will spread the lime for you with his lime spreader and include this cost in the per-acre fee. For small-scale application, adapt a manure spreader, use a shovel or distribute the lime by hand in the garden. Best results are obtained if it is thoroughly mixed with the soil. This can be done by spading, plowing or trenching it in. Lime can also be added to the compost pile.

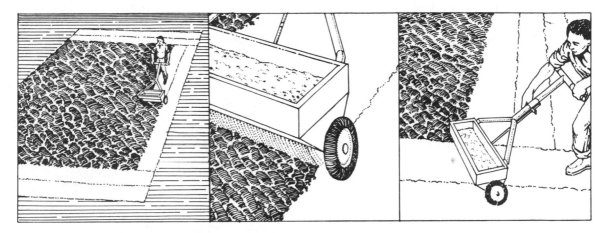

Hopper-type lime spreaders are useful for spreading lime and other powdered natural fertilizers on even ground. A sliding gate controls the flow from the hopper, making it easy to spread evenly if you work with care. First make a couple of parallel passes at each end of the area being covered. Roll the wheel just inside the area covered by the previous pass.

When you reach the end of a pass, shut off the flow and make your turn for the return. Then make similar passes at right angles, back and forth between the end strips, which provide room for turning. Remember to stop the flow while turning: there can be too much of a good thing.

Organic Soil Builders

Soil that is compacted, low in nutrients or poor in drainage will need to be improved if you want your natural landscape to flourish. Many organic materials are available for use as mulch, as ingredients in compost and as fertilizer. Some of these can be purchased at garden or farm supply stores; others are by-products or waste products of daily life and able to be recycled; still others, such as fish scraps, are available in sufficient quantities only to those who live in particular locales. The list of organic soil builders that follows is not all-inclusive. It should, however, make clear the diversity of soil amendments available to the organic gardener and help you to make wise use of the resources at hand to restore your soil to good condition.

Bark
Basic slag
Bone meal
Compost
Corncobs
  (ground)
Cottonseed meal
Feathers and
  feather meal
Fish
Granite dust
Grass clippings

Greensand
Hay
Hulls and shells
Leaf mold
Leaves
Lime
Manure
Newspaper
Peat moss
Phosphate rock
Pine needles
Plant residues
Sawdust
Seaweed and kelp
Sewage sludge
Straw
Sudan grass
Tankage
Weeds
Wood ashes
Wood chips

You'll undoubtedly know off the top of your head which of these materials are readily available to you. Further information on all of them can be found in Rodale's *Encyclopedia of Organic Gardening* (Emmaus, Pa.: Rodale Press, 1978).

Use the soil tests and analyses you conducted earlier to determine what kind of improvements your soil needs. Get advice from your county extension agent in order to decide which organic soil builders available to you will put your soil in top shape. The amount of work involved may be as slight as sprinkling powdered lime over a section of your plot—or it may be extensive and time-consuming. If the latter is the case, you may feel frustrated and impatient, especially if the idea of low maintenance was important to you in deciding to design and plant a natural landscape. Don't give up! A healthy meadow, prairie, woodland or desert will require very little attention on your part once it is established. The best way to ensure a flourishing natural landscape, however, is to provide your plants with soil that has good drainage and aeration and an adequate level of nutrients that are gradually released to your plants' roots. So accept whatever labor is necessary at the outset to prepare your soil for planting, and enjoy it! You'll get some good exercise, learn a skill that will stay with you for the rest of your life and give your native plants the best chance for survival in the habitat you've designed for them.

19 *Finding Native Plants*

When at last your site is prepared and all construction completed, you can begin to gather plants to fit the landscape you've planned. This is an odyssey, not a shopping spree. Some plants you will collect, some you will propagate. You may go to a nursery specializing in native plants and choose from hundreds, or you may scour your local garden center and find one or two. Friends may make contributions when they learn of your interest. Plant sales at wild-flower preserves can fill some gaps.

No matter how you approach the acquisition of plants, the more you know about the plants to begin with, the easier a time—and the more fun—you will have. Learn to identify the plants— common name and botanical name, flower, leaf, overall form, habitat, blooming season, winter habit. Only when you know a plant that well will

311

you be able to identify it in the wild—or in a garden center. Only when you know its whole growth cycle will you know whether you want it as part of your landscape—and what part. This is a pleasant part of gardening, the armchair part, if you will, but it goes hand in hand with the digging and the harvest. Any intelligent decision must be based on information.

It will be useful at this point to know some of the kinds of plants that you will be looking for in general. The ornamental gardener, thumbing through a seed catalog, planning the annual beds, encounters a great number of highly cultivated plants, most of them man-made hybrids created for very specific purposes, like compact form, color, self-branching habits or long flower life. These are not the plants that will interest a gardener working with native plants. That gardener is looking for species or selections of the native flora. There are some natural hybrids between two native species and a few man-made ones that will be of interest, and there are some ornamental plants that are creations from the native flora with the considerable help of horticultural science.

Some illustrations will help. *Phlox stolonifera* is one of our native phlox and would be of interest as a species to any gardener with wild plants. There is, however, a horticultural variety (cultivar) of this plant called *Phlox stolonifera* 'Blue Ridge', which is superior to the species as a garden specimen. It is not a hybrid but a selection of a superior plant from a native population, propagated vegetatively so that all the new plants carry the same qualities as the parent—in fact, they are simply parts of the parent. There are many selections of the flowering dogwood—the pink form, for example—that arose in the same way, a happy accident preserved for everyone's enjoyment.

Beyond selection, there is the plant engineered from a native species. The 'Gloriosa Daisy', for instance, was created by Burpee plant breeders from the common black-eyed Susan (*Rudbeckia serotina*) by doubling the chromosome number by treatment with colchicine, which causes the plant to "sport." The resulting form is more vigorous, bigger and showier than the wild flower. Still, it is a native plant. You can see that dabbling in native plants is not going to be simple. You really have to know what you're doing.

Native Plants from the Nursery
TREES AND SHRUBS

A large nursery-bought tree can cost hundreds of dollars. Although small trees will not give you the instant effect you want, take heart in the fact that most smaller plants will be easier to establish, will recover from transplant shocks sooner and will grow faster than the larger ones.

In inspecting a native tree or shrub on sale at a nursery, look for a good root mass, free of any jumping or crawling bugs that could indicate an insect problem. Wood with good turgor (crispness) will have firm heartwood, and its young branches will be supple rather than brittle. The bark should be smooth, with no evidence of fungi discolorations or bruises, or drought or water stress. A healthy plant will have plump buds rather than soft or empty ones, and firm leaves without brown edges or tips.

If you buy a tree from a nursery, it may come bare rooted, balled-and-burlapped or in a container. The way you buy it should be determined by the season of the year, the variety of tree and the climate in which you live.

Deciduous trees should be planted only when they are dormant (unless they are park grown, in which case they may be planted with the soil intact around their roots at any time). The best times for planting are in the fall after the first frost but before the ground freezes, and in spring after the ground thaws but before the leaves appear.

Broad-leaved evergreens should be transplanted between growth blushes. In northern areas, this means after the new spring growth has hardened in late summer or fall. In the South, it is any time when the evergreen is not putting out new growth.

BALLED-AND-BURLAPPED PLANTS
Balled-and-burlapped plants, often referred to as "B and B," are dug from the ground with a ball of soil around the roots. This ball is wrapped in burlap and tied with twine to keep it intact. Although usually more expensive, balled-and-burlapped plants suffer less from transplanting than bare-rooted plants. They take hold sooner and grow faster. Deciduous trees with trunks more than 1 inch thick should always be purchased balled-and-burlapped, as should any varieties of trees with delicate roots.

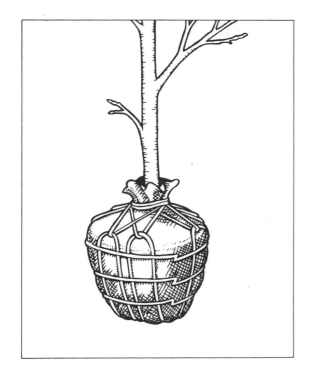

The condition of the ball of soil containing the plant roots is of prime importance. Don't spend a penny on a tree or shrub with a cracked, crumbly, loose or dried-out root ball. And after you've spent your money, make every effort to preserve the root ball. Carry the plant by the ball, supporting its bottom, not by the trunk or stems. If you can't hold it that way, set the root ball in a sturdy sling and enlist strong helpers to carry it. Failing that, have it delivered; nurseries use special hand trucks that allow them to move even large trees with modest effort.

Ball sizes should always be of great enough diameter and depth to encompass all of the fibrous and feeding root system necessary for the plant's full recovery. In certain soil and regional conditions, plants have root systems of proportionately less depth and greater diameter; these require a shallow but wider ball to encompass the roots. In other soils and regions, roots develop great depth and less spread and require an exceptionally deep ball. In most areas, balls with diameters less than 20 inches will have a depth not less than 75 percent of the diameter; balls with diameters of 20 to 30 inches will have a depth not less than two-thirds of the diameter; balls with diameters of 30 to 48

inches will have a depth not less than 60 percent of the diameter; balls with diameters over 48 inches will have the depth scaled down proportionately.

When buying a balled-and-burlapped plant, look for a firm, well-tied ball. Don't buy the tree if the root ball is soft or broken. Be careful with the plant—never use the trunk as a handle, and don't drop it. Cradle the root ball well with one hand supporting the bottom. If the plant is too heavy for you to carry from your vehicle to the planting site in the proper manner, get a friend to help you carry it in a sling of canvas or stout burlap.

Successful planting involves more than just digging a hole and putting your plants into it. The planting hole must be carefully prepared to ensure a good environment for the root system. You'll find many suggestions about how large the planting hole should be, but generally, if the hole is 6 inches wider and 6 inches deeper than the soil ball, it will be adequate. For very large specimens, such as trees with trunk diameters of 4 inches or more and large shrubs with a soil ball of 3 feet or more, the hole should be made up to 24 inches wider than the soil ball, but the depth of 6 inches deeper remains the same.

Although there are various methods of digging holes, from specially designed large-scale equipment to hand-held power augers, it is likely that you will be digging with a shovel. As you dig the hole, keep the topsoil separated from the subsoil. When you are ready to plant, mix the topsoil you saved with peat moss in a 2:1 proportion. Shovel a 6-inch layer of this mixture into the bottom of the hole, and then check the depth. Be sure that when the soil ball is planted, its top will be level with the surrounding ground and at the same time will be exactly the same depth as it was when growing in the nursery. Do not plant it too deeply, as this can easily kill the plant.

Backfilling the hole with topsoil and peat moss will cause a certain amount of settling, which is not harmful in most cases. However, if you live in a very wet climate, there may be enough settling to damage the roots. To prevent this, do not use 6 inches of backfill in the bottom of the planting hole, but instead dig a hole the same depth as the soil ball and place the soil ball directly in it. This is a transplanter's cardinal rule: Never replace a plant at a depth lower than it grew before.

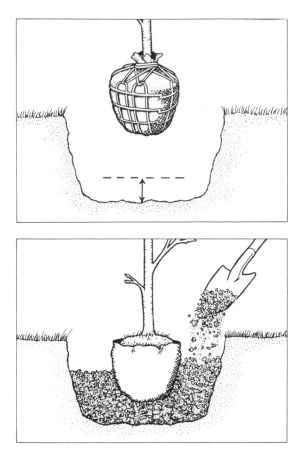

The most difficult part of planting a balled-and-burlapped plant is digging the hole and moving the plant. As you dig, set the topsoil aside, to be mixed with peat moss. Make the hole at least 6 inches deeper than the height of the root ball, and at least 6 inches larger all around than the ball's width. After

mixing the topsoil and peat, shovel a 6-inch layer (or more) into the hole. The goal is to have the top of the root ball even with the ground when the plant is in place, so add enough mix to the hole to ensure that. Carefully set the tree—burlapped ball and all—in the hole. Start packing more mix around the root ball. Saturating the newly backfilled area will help ensure that it settles properly. Cut away any twine or burlap that will stick above the ground; the rest will slowly decompose. As you complete backfilling, form a saucer around the base of the plant to collect rainwater. Adding mulch isn't a bad idea.

Balled-and-burlapped plants should be placed in the planting hole with the burlap intact. The fabric will decompose in time, since it is degradable, and it will help to condition the soil.

Only very huge trees—over 8 feet in height or 6 inches in trunk diameter—need to be supported. Smaller balled-and-burlapped or container-grown trees usually do not need wire, stakes or guys. When driving stakes, be careful not to damage the root ball. Remove all supports after one season. To prevent frost cracks and to keep water loss at a minimum in cold climates, wrap the trunk with tree-wrap paper or burlap.

BARE-ROOTED PLANTS

It is standard practice to move many varieties of plants bare rooted, especially when these plants are small or dormant. Bare-rooted plants are generally the cheapest form of nursery-bought material. As a rule, bare-rooted trees and shrubs require heavy pruning back of the tops to compensate for the loss of roots and rootlets. Set them into the ground in fall or early spring to provide the plants with a period in which the root system can recover before issuing spring growth. Never expose the roots to the sun while bare. Where circumstances permit, puddle the roots in

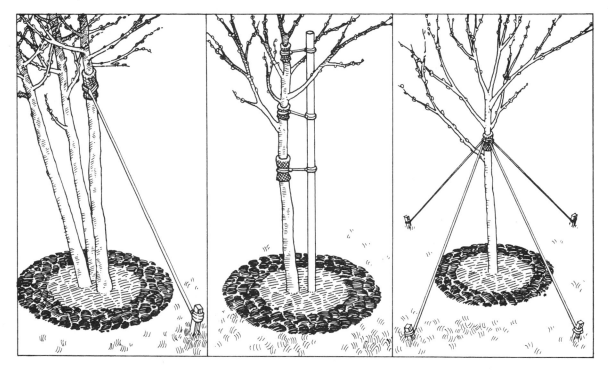

Trees and shrubs can be supported in a variety of ways during their first year in your landscape, but only quite large plants need it. One or more guy wires can be extended from stakes to the trunk. Or shorter wires can extend from a post or two driven next to the main stem (or trunk). Don't crack the root ball or damage the roots themselves with the stakes or posts. Slip a piece of hose or other padding around the wire so it doesn't cut into the bark.

If you live in a cold climate, wrap the trunk of a newly planted tree with burlap or special tree-wrap paper to prevent the sun and cold winds from drying out and cracking the bark. Such damage could allow the stem to dry out, thus killing the tree.

very wet clay to protect them from drying out, then cover them with a damp material like wet sphagnum moss or burlap to help them retain moisture. Bare-rooted plants must not be allowed to dry out before planting.

To prepare bare-rooted plants for planting, remove any covering and soak the roots for 1 to 24 hours. Dig a hole following the guidelines suggested above under "Balled-and-Burlapped Plants." After you have placed the plant in the hole, add the topsoil and peat moss mixture almost to the top. When the plant is straight and properly

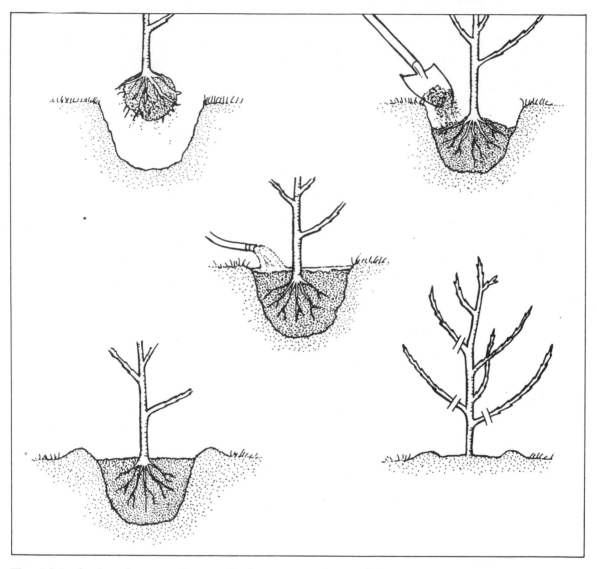

The trick in planting a bare-rooted tree or shrub is in getting the roots spread out without damage and getting them firmly embedded in the soil. After digging the hole, build up a mound of topsoil-peat moss mix in the center. Perch the plant on the mound and, while a helper holds it in position, carefully stretch the roots down its slopes. Be sure the plant won't be markedly above or below its original planted depth; a soil line should be visible on the trunk. Pack soil around the roots. Once you've backfilled enough and tramped enough for the plant to be self-supporting, puddle it in by saturating the soil. This should settle the soil and assure that it is in contact with all the roots. Finish backfilling and form a rainwater-collection basin around the plant. Finally, prune the plant, taking up to one-third the foliage area off.

positioned, gently work the soil around the roots. By filling the hole with water, you can firm the soil and get rid of any air pockets. After you are certain that the roots are in contact with the soil, finish filling the hole with the soil mixture. Firm the soil around the tree to form a saucerlike depression that will encourage rainwater to collect and seep down to the roots. Fill the saucer with a mulch of peat moss or wood chips. Give the newly planted tree a second drink; if a fertilizer is necessary, add it to the water in a mild solution.

Although broken or damaged branches should be removed from all trees, bare-rooted plants can be shorn of one-third of their leaf area at the time they are planted. Never remove the central leader of trees, and be careful not to destroy the natural symmetry of shrubs. Support the plant with wires, stakes or guys if its size requires it.

CONTAINER-GROWN PLANTS

Plants are grown successfully in earthenware pots, metal cans and wooden boxes. The advantage of buying a container-grown plant is that it can be transplanted with the smallest possible amount of shock. Such plants are usually small and expensive.

When selecting container-grown plants, look for root systems sufficiently developed to hold the soil solidly together during removal but not so far developed that the roots circle the trunk, hindering future growth. Plants that have been in containers too long become root bound and dwarfed and grow very poorly when planted.

Contrary to popular opinion, when container-grown plants are ready for transplanting, they should not be removed from their containers—the containers should be removed from them! Most container-grown plants can be removed by turning the plant upside down and giving the top edge a sharp tap. The soil ball should be carefully caught so that it doesn't break apart. Larger containers need to be cut away. Handled this way, a plant will grow immediately after transplanting with none of the interruption to its activity or recovery experienced by other plants after they are set out.

GROUND COVERS

Few of the most popular ground covers are native plants. Only the *Asarum* species (wild ginger), *Juniperus horizontalis, Pachysandra procumbens*

Ground covers should be planted in a gridwork layout, with individual plants or cuttings spotted about 4 to 6 inches apart in all directions. Within a year or two, the plants will have spread and filled in the intervening areas. This is the way to plant plugs of grass to create a lawn.

When planting ground covers—or other plants, for that matter—scoop out a pocket for the root ball, then mix a handful of compost into the soil. Set the plant and firm it into place. Be sure it is set at the same depth at which it grew in a pot or flat.

and *Dichondra* may be considered natives. Nurseries are likely to have these individually potted or in flats. For more unusual ground covers, you are likely to have to forage. (For names of native ground covers you can plant, see Section 2.)

Container- or flat-grown plants are generally more expensive than bare-rooted cuttings, but they can be spaced farther apart when transplanted. To achieve a fairly solid cover in two to three years, set your plants into the soil 4 to 6 inches apart and equidistant from one another, as if they were laid out on a grid.

If you plant ground covers that have been grown in plastic or clay pots, they should be watered the day before planting. This will make it easier to remove the pot without disturbing the root mass, while ensuring that adequate moisture is retained by the soil ball. Again, be careful to plant the ground cover at the same depth at which it was growing in the pot.

If you're using plants that are potted in peat containers, pull off the rim of the peat pot above the root ball before planting. Otherwise, the peat may dry out and inhibit root development. Peat pots must be thoroughly watered before planting, and the newly planted area must be watered on the same day it is planted.

A mulch spread around the newly planted cuttings will help the soil retain moisture and will encourage the rapid establishment of the ground cover. If you are planting on a steep slope, the mulch will reduce the chances of serious erosion.

LAWNS

If you have decided to include a patch of lawn in your landscape plans, you should be aware that some lawn grasses may be purchased as layers of sod or as sprigs or plugs. The initial investment for sod is quite high, but the effect is immediately gratifying. Most homeowners are content to prepare the lawnbed well, seed and wait. What appears to be a scraggly showing will become a dense stand of turf, given the proper care.

If you prefer "overnight" transformations, go to a reliable nursery and find out what sort of ready-made lawn they can supply. Usually only a few creeping grasses, like bent grass, are available as sod. Bent grass, centipede grass, St. Augustine grass, Bermuda grass and zoysia can be purchased in sprigs or plugs. When you want a very uniform lawn, using sprigs or plugs is to your advantage, since they are clones, identical to a parent plant, propagated by cuttings in the nursery. Bluegrasses, fescues and ryegrasses are most easily grown from seed.

Carefully inspect sod at the nursery before buying it. Check the edges to see if the soil has been allowed to dry out. Look for a uniform green color. The sod should be clipped close, to stimulate the spread of root systems after it is planted in your lawnbed. A thin layer of sod is better than a thick layer for the same reason.

Preparing your lawnbed for sodding is lots of work. You must clear the soil of all weeds, stones, sticks and other yard debris. Dig up and destroy any existing grasses. Till the soil deeply, then grade it smooth. Just before laying down the sod, broadcast a fertilizer (1 pound per 1000 square feet) so that major nutrients will be readily available to the roots. Lay the sod on the prepared soil and use a roller on it to ensure good contact between the roots and the soil. If you are laying sod on a slope, you should peg the squares in place temporarily so that rains will not wash them away. Fill in any cracks or channels between squares of sod with a light dressing of good topsoil. Water daily for the first two weeks to encourage the roots to penetrate the subsoil. After this, water your sod lawn heavily, but only when the soil is dry to a depth of 3 or 4 inches. Fertilize again after two months and at the end and the beginning of subsequent growing seasons.

If you choose to plant your lawn using sprigs or plugs, treat it much as you would any other ground cover. Two-inch plugs, planted 12 inches apart in a grid pattern, will spread to fill in the bare spots and give you good coverage in two or three years.

Perhaps you want a green spot out back to play ball with your kids. Maybe you want an area of low-clipped grass because you like to give garden parties. It's possible you've decided you just like the way it sets off your house. Whatever your reason for establishing a lawn, it is likely that you will grow it from seed purchased at a nursery or garden-supply center.

Look closely at the "ingredient list" under the label before buying. Most bags of grass seed contain several different varieties, sometimes including

Sod is expensive but quick and easy to lay: instant lawn. Prepare the soil as you would for sowing seed. Then simply unroll or unfold the strips of sod, butting one against another as tightly as possible. Stagger the ends of the strips from row to row. Use a large, sharp knife to cut the strips where necessary. On slopes, the sod can be secured with pegs or staples

made from wire coat hangers. Don't push them in too far; you'll want to remove them after the sod is established. Dress the seams with topsoil. Then, using a roller half full of water, roll the sod. Watch for the pegs or staples; pull them up and replace them as you go. Water the sod thoroughly. You now have lawn where only hours before you had bare earth.

crop grass and weed seeds. Such blends are fine for a farmer's cows to graze on in the pasture, but you are likely to be disgruntled if some of your carefully seeded lawn comes up in dandelions and clover. Although "pure" lawn grass blends are more expensive initially, they save you later aggravation and time spent hand weeding.

If you live in the North, sow your grass seed in the fall or early spring. The grasses that flourish in your region will begin to germinate at temperatures just above freezing, so have them in

place in the soil in time for spring thaw. Germination will proceed more quickly as temperatures rise, but the optimum conditions of 55° to 60°F. (12.8° to 15.5°C.) may occur as early as March.

Southerners can sow their seeds later in the spring or early summer. These grasses germinate quickly in a warm soil (60° to 65°F./15.5° to 18.3°C.), although they will begin the process when it is slightly cooler.

Prepare the soil for sowing by clearing it of weeds, stones and debris. Till it to provide good

Soil preparation is the hardest part of sowing a lawn. The area, hopefully a small one, should be cleared of weeds and detritus as much as possible first. Then till the soil well, perhaps turning in a fine-textured soil amendment. Clear all the rocks and roots you can from the soil. Level the surface carefully. You can cobble up a serviceable device for leveling by attaching ropes to a 2-foot by 4-foot piece of

plywood; put some stones or cement blocks on it for weight, and drag it across the ground. Then roll the area, using a roller about one-third full of water. The seed can be sown by hand or with a broadcast seeder. Finally, rake the area lightly and spread a thin layer of mulch—straw is traditional—over the seed. Water periodically, and eventually you'll have a lawn.

aeration and drainage for the new plants. Broadcast the seed as uniformly as possible over your lawnbed. (You may even want to use a mechanical seed spreader to make sure that your lawn is evenly seeded.) Rake the soil lightly just to cover the seeds, then mulch it with a shallow layer of weed-free straw, peat moss or hay. A thorough soaking will encourage the seeds to absorb water and the seed coat to break so that the plant can send out roots. Water often enough during the first few weeks to keep the soil moist under the mulch.

Once your patch of grass is thriving, help to keep it that way by watering only when the soil is dry to the touch down to a depth of 3 inches below the surface. More information on maintaining your lawn is provided in the next chapter.

Foraging for Native Plants

Plant collecting can be a satisfying and rewarding pastime and may be the only means available for getting the native plants you want. It requires hard work, patience and a willingness to accept some degree of failure. And you will need to take certain precautions.

Obtaining stock other than from a nursery requires permission from the owner of the property to guarantee that you are not removing plants that are wanted or protected. Although you may think of your efforts to obtain and preserve native plants as legitimate collecting, the owner may consider it stealing. Digging up trees or taking roots or other cuttings from public parks and nature reserves can also lead to prosecution.

Even with permission, never take more than half the specimens of any one kind of plant so it will reestablish itself. Push loose dirt back into the hole, and cover the soil around the plant with leaves or straw to give it the best chance of recovery.

Finally, as a plant collector, be able to recognize any plants in your area of the United States that are in danger of becoming extinct. Do *not* try to move even one of these plants unless you are certain that it otherwise will be destroyed. Even if you're an old hand at plant collecting and have confidence that you can successfully transplant an endangered species, you may be doing a public disservice by hiding such a plant in your own backyard.

In some areas of the United States, concerned people have organized public plant digs. One such group is the plant rescue team of the University of North Carolina in Chapel Hill. They remove plants from areas to be developed and reestablish them in native plant collections. In Tallahassee, where public plant digs have become community outings, some 40,000 people have joined in the effort to save native plants since the first dig was organized by a handful of nature lovers in 1970.

When the organizers of a dig are advised by developers and landowners that an area is being cleared, they make an announcement in the local paper. Townspeople grab shovels, bags and boxes, gather family and friends and troop to the wooded area that has been destined to feel the bite of the bulldozer. The organizers help with plant identification and arrange for traffic control.

Tallahasseeans have found the project so simple and satisfying that they have come to believe that each community should invent its own version and watch people and nature flourish. If you don't have access to a wild area or can't find a source of native plants, get in touch with your local garden club or ecology group to see if they hold plant digs. If not, why not try to drum up interest?

Anyone who has done any plant collecting develops his or her own method. Everyone admits, however, that plant collecting involves much trial and error. What works for one plant may not be successful for another, even if it is a member of the same species. Everyone agrees, too, that the larger the root ball, the better. Initial watering is very important, and the ecological conditions in your landscape must be the same as those of the plant growing in the wild.

Look at the site you want to plant in terms of sun, shade, wind, slope, drainage and water. Then find plants that grow in similar conditions. For example, ferns from the deep woods will be happy in a spot with dense shade from trees. Cattails, reeds, sedges, asters and shrub willows will all thrive in a sunny but wet place. Although shrubs and trees need room to grow, it's better to plant herbaceous plants close together.

Ideally, you should collect plants during their dormant period in early spring and late fall. Plants moved from June through September need a great deal of tender loving care to bring them through the shock of transplanting.

One legitimate reason for moving plants during their growing season is to save those growing in a habitat that is about to be destroyed by a bulldozer. In this instance, when you are certain that the plants would be lost anyhow, and you think you may be able to find or create a similar habitat, it is worth taking the risk to save them.

If your first attempts at "saving" native plants during the growing season meet with little success, pay more attention to the soil type, moisture conditions and light requirements of the plant as it grows wild, and carefully attempt to recreate similar conditions in the new surroundings.

Make frequent trips to undisturbed areas in all four seasons to observe the plants available and learn which will make the greatest contribution to your landscape plans. Make notes reminding yourself when a particular species leafs out, when it starts to flower and how long a flowering season it has—a single season or several months. You'll need to consider these things when selecting plants that will make your landscape attractive year-round.

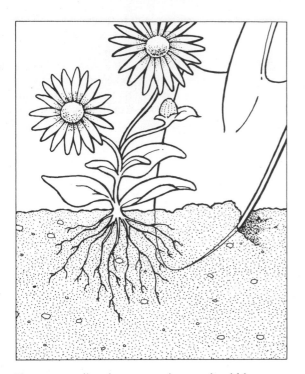

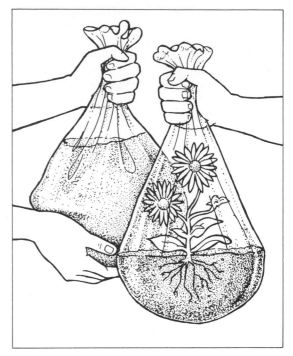

Plants you collect from natural areas should be replanted the same day in your landscape. The handiest plant containers for a short trip between homes are plastic bags. They come in all different sizes—from sandwich, through quart and gallon freezer bags, to huge garbage-can liners. Carefully dig

the selected forb from the ground, and, keeping as much soil around the roots as possible, settle it into a bag. It's not a bad idea to collect an extra bag of "native soil" for each plant, too. Use it to line the hole you dig for the plant.

GROUND COVERS

The natural-landscape gardener who forages for plants can choose a ground cover from a wide variety of wild flowers and other forbs and need not have his choice dictated by the limited selection made available through the nursery.

The "classic" ground covers—*Vinca*, ivy, *Ajuga*, *Pachysandra* and juniper—are all evergreens. The ground covers cultivated by nature may be evergreens or wild flowers or ferns. The blanket of white on a woodland floor in early spring is bloodroot; the blue haze growing on a stream bank the bluebell; the sunshine scattered across a meadow the creeping buttercup. Any of these wild flowers can make a good ground cover in the right habitat and will provide a showy seasonal spectacle of color besides.

To obtain your starter plants, dig up clumps from an established ground cover. Treat them just

as you would bare-rooted cuttings of a ground-cover plant from a nursery. Plant them a few inches apart from one another, as if they were laid out on a grid. Ferns, which spread very rapidly, should be given more room. In a year or two, the plants will multiply and spread to fill in the bare spots, and your low-maintenance natural ground cover will be in good working order.

TREES

Trees are very difficult to transplant. If you try to move trees, take very young ones. The larger the tree you dig, the more roots and earth you should take with it. The best size is 6 to 8 feet in height, with a trunk diameter of less than 3 inches. A tree larger than this should not be moved, since it will have more soil and roots than two people can lift without special equipment.

Inspect the native tree carefully before you

dig it. Look for damaged bark, especially near the ground, where it may have been eaten by small animals. If the damage is severe, don't remove the tree.

One of the advantages of collecting trees instead of buying them from a nursery is the ability to choose an interesting and natural shape. Nursery-bought specimens are often pruned to perfect symmetry, and this can be boring and sterile. Your collected tree may also benefit from a little pruning, even though your goal may be to preserve its unusual shape. For example, if the tree you have chosen grows near another tree, it may lean, and its roots may be hard to disentangle. Pruning its roots a year before you try to dig it from the woods will make it easier to transplant. Thrust the spade into the soil 6 to 12 inches from the trunk, depending on the size of the tree. This

If your circumstances permit, it is a good idea to help prepare a tree or shrub for transplanting several months to a year ahead of the event by pruning the roots. Drive a spade into the ground around the tree about 6 to 12 inches from the trunk, cutting through any roots that extend beyond what would be the root ball. A special balling or transplanting spade is a particularly good tool for this.

pruning will allow the plant to make new roots close to the trunk that will provide greater support when it is transplanted the next year. Prune the roots of any tree you plan to collect except for dogwood and pine. With these, remove only broken branches. If a tree requires further above-ground shaping, it should be delayed until after the second growing season and then should be as minimal as possible.

Contrary to popular opinion, most trees do not have a taproot. (Only tulip poplar and hawthorn do.) Usually the roots spread out quite close to the surface, where water and nutrients are most available. In most soils, small trees have very few roots below 8 inches. To protect such a shallow root system, rather than digging a traditional nursery ball, make a preliminary cut with the shovel a foot or two beyond the branches of the plant where there is no danger of cutting any roots. Then dig in a circle, pushing the shovel farther and farther under the plant, toward the center—much like lifting a piece of sod. Move the shovel back a few inches from the first circle of cuts and remove the wedge of earth in between, taking care not to cut any root over ¼ inch thick. Continue shoveling until you have made a shallow trench all around the tree. Follow large roots that are exposed by your shoveling until they branch and become smaller, and then cut them with the edge of your shovel. By taking these steps, you will find it a relatively easy task to lift the tree out of its hole.

Occasionally a tree will have a few roots going much farther from the trunk than others. In digging up the plant, leave as much earth on the roots as is convenient, but don't try to take too much. Soil that isn't secured by the roots will drop off when the tree is moved, and roots may be broken in the process. To transplant such a tree, just dig a hole the same shape as the roots but 6 inches larger. (Irregular root systems like this develop most often on trees that have grown up in dry, rocky soils. Such soils are difficult to collect from and should be avoided.)

When moving a tree you have dug up, try not to handle the root mass too roughly, as this can damage the roots. Any roots over ¼ inch thick that have been inadvertently broken should be trimmed with pruning shears, because jagged and damaged ends encourage disease.

Holding a ball of soil around the roots of a plant being dug up for transplanting is tricky, but it's vital for all evergreens and for deciduous trees that are in leaf. Several days before the move, soak the ground around the plant; this will help the soil cling to the roots. Tie up the branches. Then start digging, creating a deep, spacious trench all around the root ball. Once the plant is encircled, undercut the soil surrounding the roots to create a ball tapered from top to bottom. Cut a strip of burlap, stretch it around the root ball and sew the ends tightly together; this should hold the ball together while you jockey it around and get it wrapped and tied. Chicken wire could be substituted. Use a second piece of burlap—no substitutes—to surround the entire ball. Roll up about half the burlap and lay it in the trench with the roll under the ball as much as possible. Tip the ball from side to side, breaking it free of the ground and, simultaneously, working the burlap under the ball. Pull up the corners and tie them together. After binding the ball tightly with twine around and under-and-over the ball, hoist it carefully—by the ball, not the trunk—from the hole.

The roots of some plants, such as sumac, tend to grow in big spreading clumps in which all the stems are interconnected. The secondary or feeder roots are small and easily broken. When you dig sumac, you should try to get as much of the main root as possible by feeling for it with your shovel and following it along for a few feet. Even if the particular upright stem you get dies back, the underground stem will send up shoots, so give it plenty of room when you replant it.

Nurserymen use a special spade for digging up trees, which is longer and narrower than the usual garden spade and helps to keep the soil around the roots. If you plan to do a lot of collecting and transplanting, you should purchase a balling spade and learn to use it with care. Do not subject the tree or the ball to jolts that will loosen the earth from the roots. If you do, you may tear away many of the tiny feeder roots on which the uprooted tree must depend until it becomes established. Minimizing such transplanting shocks is especially important when you are relocating a native specimen.

EVERGREENS

If you're digging an evergreen, it may be easier to work if you tie the branches first. Attach the rope to the trunk at the base of the tree and wind it over the branches, pulling them in close to the trunk.

Evergreens are slow to establish a new root system and need a continuous supply of water due to the loss of moisture from the ever-present leaves. Consequently, you must be sure to retain an unbroken ball of soil with many undamaged roots capable of supplying the needs of the plant until new roots develop. In general, evergreen root balls should have the following dimensions:

Plant Height or Spread (whichever is greater) in Inches	Ball Diameter in Inches
18 to 24	12
24 to 30	14
30 to 36	16
36 to 42	18
42 to 48	20
48 to 60	22

To dig a ball without breaking it is not easy, and to move it intact to its new location requires that it be covered and carefully handled. Work slowly until you get the hang of it. Dig a trench at right angles to the plant to avoid breaking or loosening the soil. After you've cut below the depth of most roots (about three-quarters of the diameter in most cases), reduce the diameter of the column by

undercutting below most of the roots. Round off the upper surface close to the trunk where there are few roots, and remove any loose soil. Keep the back of the spade toward the ball and cut all roots flush with its surface. A pair of helpers can lift the ball onto a piece of burlap and tie or sew it tightly so that it holds the soil firmly.

Beginners should sew the burlap down the sides as far as the undercut permits before cutting the ball free. If you backstitch and pull each stitch taut, there is little danger of the ball breaking. Finish sewing over the base as soon as the ball is lifted out of the hole and laid on its side.

Never lift or tilt a balled or partially balled tree by the trunk. Even if you do not break the ball, you weaken it so it will be more likely to break in transit. Plant your forged balled-and-burlapped tree just as you would a nursery-grown specimen.

SMALL DECIDUOUS TREES

The easiest deciduous trees to move are ash, catalpa, crab apple, elm, hackberry, linden, locust, maple, pear and sycamore. Poplar and willow are also easy to move, but their spreading roots can cause property damage if you plant them near your foundation or water or sewer lines. Any of these trees may be moved bare rooted. More difficult to move are apple, birch, cherry, hawthorn, larch, mountain ash, plum and spruce. American hop hornbeam, American hornbeam, beech, butternut, hickory and many of the oaks and walnuts are the most difficult and require quick, carefully thought out transplanting.

To dig any small deciduous tree, start by tying branches in the same way as you would do with an evergreen. Dig a trench completely around the tree outside the spread of roots you think you can move. It's much better to start with a large circle and take off more roots than to start with a small circle and increase the shock to the tree to the point where its survival is in question. After you have dug your trench down several spade depths, start undercutting the roots and removing the soil. Then, with a slender stick, carefully comb out soil from between the roots, a little at a time. The soil that falls down must be dug out and more of the roots undercut before combing closer to the trunk. As soon as you can cut the main roots,

Digging up a deciduous tree while it is dormant means you needn't fret too much about maintaining a root ball. You still must be careful of the roots, however. Start by excavating a trench around the roots, then undercutting the root ball. Using a stick or hand trowel, cautiously brush soil away from the ball in an effort to expose the roots. Keep alternately undercutting and brushing soil until the lay of the roots is established. You need not completely remove the soil from the roots. Break the roots free, if they aren't already, and hoist the tree out of the hole, wrapping the roots and remaining soil in a piece of wet burlap. Keep the roots moist until the tree is replanted. Replant the same day if at all possible.

lift the tree and cover the whole root ball with a damp cloth.

Trees up to 1 inch in diameter should have a minimum root spread of 26 inches. Most homeowners will find larger trees too difficult to move (even 3-inch trees carry a root spread of 42 to 46 inches and may weigh well over a ton).

When you move a tree late in the season or work on a more difficult kind of plant, dig a larger

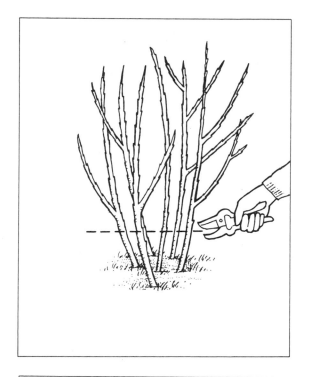

root ball. If roots are damaged or dried during moving, even taking this precaution may not be sufficient to guarantee the survival of the plant. If you move your tree during the leafy season, you will need to ball all plants in the same way as evergreens.

SHRUBS

Most deciduous shrubs are easy to dig if you work before growth starts or after it stops. All but the slowest growers should be pruned to within 6 inches of the ground before any digging begins. To unearth the plant, make a circle of vertical cuts to a full spade's depth as far from the trunk as necessary. Find a helper, if possible, to lift the shrub out of its hole. Staying on opposite sides,

A shrub should be severely pruned before transplanting, unless it is particularly slow growing. Cut all the stems to within 6 inches of the soil. Then cut into the soil a spade's depth all around the plant. Undercut and work the spade under the roots. Have your helper wield a second spade and together lift the plant from the ground. Here's where a transplanting spade is particularly useful.

insert a shovel into the soil at each cut and work it back and forth to loosen the ball, cutting deeper under the plant if possible. Most shrubs can be lifted this way without trenching and with sufficient roots intact. Protect the roots as soon as lifted.

Evergreen shrubs and a few deciduous shrubs like azaleas, blueberries and some viburnums must be provided with a ball of earth if they are to survive transplanting. If you must move shrubs in midsummer, dig them up with root balls intact or you will have to cut all the leaves off.

Perennials are best transplanted in the fall after the first hard freeze. The plant becomes dormant for the winter. The top-growth of nonwoody plants withers and dies, leaving few clues as to the plant's identity. If you mark the plant's location while the above-ground part is still growing, this problem will not defeat you.

Perennials have a root mass that may range from a few inches to several feet both in diameter and in depth. By experimenting, you will know exactly how wide and how deep you will need to dig in order to safely remove a plant with root system intact. You should always try to get most or all of the large main roots, but the small feeder roots are only a little less critical. The less you disturb the roots in the soil clump, the greater your chance of success.

20

Propagation

Propagation is what people do to make new plants from old, but, though it is based on nature's way, it is not nature's way. Nature is profligate: a thousand fertile seeds may yield one individual. But one is enough to keep the species going— temporarily—and nature is satisfied. The propagator, on the other hand, wants to make every seed count, wants every cutting to root, every layer to take. He is interested in speed, in uniformity, in control—none of which matters very much in nature.

As most gardeners encounter it, propagation is a simple thing: sowing seeds for the summer vegetable garden or rooting a coleus cutting in a glass of water. The seeds sprout, the coleus roots. No problems. Unfortunately, the lessons learned

329

there will not stand us in good stead when we come to propagating native plants. They, because they have adapted to a temperate climate, with its alternating seasons of warmth and cold, have evolved some barriers to premature germination that give the propagator fits. Vegetative propagation is not simple either: temperate zone shrubs and trees grow by flushes. What starts out green and supple in the spring is hard and woody in the fall and leafless in the winter. The propagator's success depends a lot on timing.

Still, even if propagation isn't easy, it isn't that hard either. Once you know the plants and something about their cycles of growth and reproduction, learning how to propagate them is a matter of getting a few basic ideas down pat. And what rewards! You will never have been so involved with your plants or the landscape into which they go as when you have been responsible for their growth from the beginning.

Sexual Propagation

The advantages of growing plants from seeds are several. It's an inexpensive way to produce the large numbers of plants that a natural landscape may require, and it's cheaper still if the seeds are collected rather than bought. If the seeds can be found nearby, one is certain of growing the genotype that is best adapted to local conditions, the purest form of gardening with native plants. The plant that provides the seeds continues its life undisturbed, which is a bonus, since many native plants are protected by conservation law, and removing the whole plant—or even part of it—is unwise and illegal. The seeds, however, were intended for dispersal.

BUYING SEEDS

With the rising interest in native plants, many new commercial sources of seeds have sprung up. Even the big seed companies, which normally sell vegetable and flower seeds, have introduced mixtures for meadows, prairies and natural landscapes in the last year. There are also many nurseries and "Mom and Pop" seed companies that specialize in wild flowers and native trees and shrubs, and that offer the seeds of these plants as well. The watchword is to try for as local a source as possible. Horticultural

societies (in large cities), plant hobby groups, county extension agents, university departments of horticulture, arboreta and conservation groups will help you find a reliable source of seeds in your area—and don't overlook the classified ads in gardening publications. Of course, you have to know what you're looking for (knowing the botanical as well as the common name would speed things right along). Hopefully, propagation instruction will be part of your seed package.

HARVESTING SEEDS

For hard-to-come-by seeds, commercial sources may be the only sources, but for the more common wayside plants, there is no reason why you should not collect the seeds yourself. Be sure to have the permission of any landowner before you invade his property, and remember to leave the site as undisturbed as possible.

Plants signal the ripeness of their seeds by activating their systems for natural dispersal. The pine cone dries, opens and releases its winged seeds. The berries of the viburnum redden to attract birds. The pods of the Kentucky coffee tree dry and split, releasing the hard seeds. The collector will have noted the passing of the flower and observed the state of the developing seed. Obviously, the optimum time for collection is just before dispersal occurs, when the seed is mature but still on the plant.

A small paper bag is ideal for collecting and storing seeds, since the drying process can continue inside (the moisture can escape), and you can write the name of the plant and collection date on the outside.

Seeds that have a fleshy seed coat (pulp or fruit) must be cleaned before they are stored. The pulp often contains inhibitors to germination and must come off before the seed will grow. In nature, this would happen in the digestive tract of a bird or animal, and the cleaned seed would be deposited with the droppings. You can macerate the pulp in a strainer and separate out the seeds by flotation. Mix the mashed-up pulp with water: the heavier seeds will sink to the bottom of the container while the pulp and "void" seeds will float to the top, where they can be poured off. Dry the cleaned seeds and store in paper like your other collections.

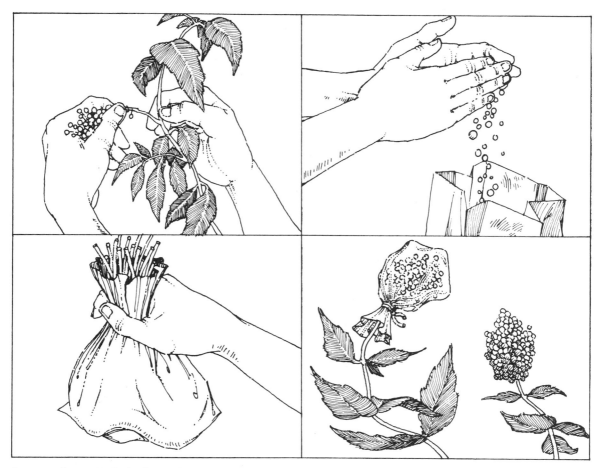

Some seeds, particularly those of many trees and shrubs, can be collected just as you would harvest produce in a garden: you just pick them one by one when ripe. But the seeds of other plants are tiny things encased in pods or tenuously attached to seed heads. Some plants you can allow to dry where they grow, then crush in your hands, catching the seeds in a

paper bag. Flowers can be cut as their seed heads mature and hung to dry with their heads in a paper bag; when dry, the seeds can easily be shaken from the heads in the bag, and the stems discarded. Still another approach is to tie a plastic sandwich bag over the blossom of a plant and leave it there until the plant dries; the bag will prevent the loss of the seeds.

MOVING TOWARD GERMINATION

Because most of us deal with seeds that come in packages just in time to be sown in the spring, it does not occur to us to wonder what seeds do in nature between the time they are shed (dispersed) and the time they come up (germinate). It should be obvious, however, that plants in a temperate climate must have some bar to premature germination, since they would be wiped out by the approaching winter before they had a chance to establish themselves.

Many seeds are capable of germination as soon as they are dispersed, needing only sufficient water, air (oxygen), warmth and light. It is the absence of one of those conditions—usually warmth, due to the season, or water, due to a hard seed coat, impenetrable by water until bacterial action has broken it down a bit—that keeps the seed from germinating immediately in nature. For the propagator, who can provide all the necessary external conditions, these newly shed seeds can be made to germinate on his schedule.

In collecting seeds, you often find that in the bargain you've collected stems and leaves and seed capsules and pulp you don't need. Separation of the seeds can be tedious but not difficult. Crush dried materials in your hands, then pick out the seeds by hand or with tweezers. If the seeds seem heavier than the chaff, try winnowing the material in front of a small fan. Seeds can often be separated from fruits by mashing them in a sieve, then placing the mass in a container of warm water for a few days. The seeds should settle to the bottom, and the pulp can be decanted off.

STRATIFICATION

But there are seeds that, while apparently mature, are not capable of germination even when all of the aforementioned conditions prevail. They must have a period of after-ripening under conditions of moist cold, during which the embryo changes and matures. In nature, this would be time spent under a layer of autumn leaves during the winter months. For seeds that are embryo dormant, the propagator must provide a similar period of moist refrigeration. This is called stratification.

Stratification is accomplished by mixing the seeds with a *moist* growing medium (sand and peat in equal parts at twice the volume of the seeds themselves) and storing the combination in an airtight plastic bag (sandwich size) for a period of one to four months. Though seeds have very specific requirements for stratification time (available in scientific literature), a period of three months is average and will take care of most dormancy problems. The temperatures of the family refrigerator are fine, but not those of the freezer.

SCARIFICATION

Another kind of dormancy is produced, not by an immature embryo, but by a seed coat that is impermeable to water until it has been eroded by bacterial action or cracked by the stress of freezing and thawing. Any member of the legume family is likely to have an impermeable seed coat. This physical barrier to germination is breached by scarification.

Scarification can be as simple as rubbing the seed on sandpaper until the coat is worn thin in one spot or nicking it with a file. For large batches of seeds, scarification can be accomplished by mixing the seeds with sand in a rock tumbler. In nature, scarification results from bacterial action—the seed coat decomposes over a long period of time, and water finally enters. This can be reproduced by the propagator, of course, but it is time-consuming. The process is called warm stratification and differs from cold stratification in two ways: the moist medium must contain garden soil for bacteria to be present, and the seeds are stored at fluctuating warm temperatures (60° to 100°F./15.5° to 37.8°C., in a shaded part of a greenhouse, for instance). The process takes about five months. A file is quicker.

For large batches of seeds with impermeable seed coats, soaking in hot water overnight will break the dormancy. Begin with an amount of hot water (190° to 200°F./87.8° to 93.3°C., just below the boiling point) five or six times the volume of the seeds. Pour the water over the seeds and let it stand—without further reheating—overnight. Sow the seeds before they dry out.

It is not uncommon for seeds to be doubly dormant. They may have a hard seed coat that requires scarification as well as an embryo that needs a period of after-ripening. To break this kind of double dormancy, one must scarify first (to allow water to penetrate the seed) and then stratify (to mature the embryo). It's simple, really, and requires only patience and a dated label.

So how do you know if the particular seed that you are trying to propagate has these complications? You read, primarily; but the niche that the plant inhabits in nature can give you a pretty good idea. If seeds are shed in the fall and germinate the following spring, you can figure that some kind of after-ripening took place over the winter.

GERMINATION, FINALLY

The time is late winter; the days are lengthening, and you are looking forward to spring. This is the time to sow your seeds indoors in preparation for planting. The hour of the propagator is come round at last. You will have already done one of the following things: (1) collected and stored your dry seeds over the winter in a paper bag; (2) stratified for three months the seeds you suspect (or know) need a period of after-ripening; (3) scarified, immediately before planting, those seeds that have a hard seed coat (usually the legumes); (4) scarified and stratified those seeds that are doubly dormant; (5) just received in the mail seeds ready for planting, which may have been pretreated for you by one of the previously mentioned methods. In any case, you are ready to put some seeds in some soil.

THE MEDIUM

You want your seeds to grow, of course—all of them. While the container is not important—a tin can will do as well as a flower pot or a seedling flat—the growing medium is of prime importance, especially the top layer, which contains the laboriously gathered and prepared seeds. One part sand, one part garden soil and one part peat moss makes a fine filler for the pot. But the top layer is key: over the main soil, add ¼-inch layer of milled sphagnum moss. This moss contains a natural antibiotic (produced by a bacteria in the moss) that prevents or greatly reduces the chances of the fungal infection known as "damping-off," the main killer of young seedlings. The seeds will be sown on this layer of milled sphagnum moss and covered with another layer of the same material (very fine seeds—powdery ones—can be sown uncovered on the moss layer and will germinate in the crevices).

WATERING

Initial watering is tricky. You want to dampen the entire medium without disturbing the carefully prepared "seed sandwich" on the top. A fine spray from the rose of a watering can or the mist from a nozzle, passed repeatedly over the surface, will wet the contents—ultimately—without disturbing the top. Better yet, you might soak the pot in shallow water until it is moist through and through. (Be careful not to plunge the pot into deep water:

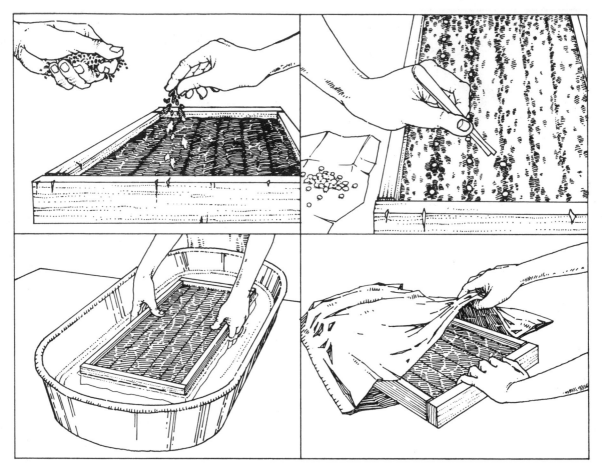

Seeding a flat begins with the preparation of the growing medium; a mixture of equal parts of sand, garden soil and peat moss is a good base. Fill the flat with this, then spread a thin layer of milled sphagnum moss atop it. Sow the seeds, either by gently sprinkling them over the surface or by placing them one by one on the moss with tweezers. Cover

them with another thin layer of the moss. The flat can best be watered by placing it in a tub with a few fingers of water in it; the medium will soak up water without disturbing the seedbed. When the flat is thoroughly damp, slide it into a plastic bag and seal the bag until the seeds sprout.

the whole dry contents will float up and destroy your construction.)

Once you are satisfied that the pot is thoroughly watered, enclose it in a plastic bag to maintain moisture in the top layer until germination actually begins. Remove the bag when seedlings begin to appear.

LIGHT

As anyone who has germinated vegetable seedlings on a windowsill knows, the late winter light that

comes through most windows is not strong enough to prevent seedlings from becoming "leggy." The problem—the scientific word for it is etiolation, from the French for "reaching for the start"—is characterized by long, weak stems instead of the short, squat seedlings that strong light would produce. Without a greenhouse, the home gardener's next best bet is fluorescent light from a two-tube fixture (4-foot 40-watt tubes, one cool white and one warm white) set 6 to 8 inches above the growing seedlings. Of course, one can avoid the

A time will come, not too long after germination, when your seedlings must be transplanted into more spacious accommodations. This can be a touchy project, since the seedlings are still particularly frail. After preparing their new home, either pots or flats, pick the seedlings out of the crowd, one by one, using the handle of a fork or spoon. Hold the seedling by its leaves in one hand and poke a hole in the new medium with a finger of the other. Lower the seedling into the hole and firm the medium in around it. If the seedlings have developed enough in their first home to have very long roots, they should be transplanted to individual pots. Lay the pot on its side, scoop in about half its capacity of medium, stretch the roots out on the medium, tip the pot upright while holding the seedling, then fill in with more medium.

whole etiolation problem by waiting until the whole process can be accomplished out of doors (but still in pots).

SEEDLING AFTERCARE

Seedlings should be removed from the germination pot or flat as soon as they can be handled (usually when they have a pair or two of real leaves). Further development will be hampered if they are allowed to remain too long in crowded conditions, and the chances of disease wiping out the whole crop is greater when they are in the mass. The first spring and summer can be spent in a seedling bed in the ground or in a larger flat that allows for wider spacing. (Planting in individual pots is not recommended because roots coil and may girdle the developing plant.) In areas with severe winters, the new plants will require some protection from hard freezing over the first winter; they must be allowed to go dormant in the cold, of course, but should not be exposed to conditions of frost heave or other temperature extremes. A cold frame would provide a winter vacation ideally suited to their needs.

DIRECT SEEDING

You can, of course, bypass these complex procedures in favor of direct seeding and let natural processes take care of themselves. Seeds sown or broadcast in the fall will stratify or scarify during the coming winter and will appear—albeit sporatically—the following spring, or perhaps the spring after that or the third spring. The disadvantage of direct seeding is waste—many seeds will simply never germinate at all.

Still, if a large natural landscape is contemplated, this may be the only way, and failure will have to be reckoned with in planning the number of seeds to be sown. Placement of individual plants will be random, of course, but that effect might be pleasant. Once some plants are established, they can always be moved to more favorable spots—whatever is demanded by the design. If direct seeding is contemplated, then preparation of the site is of utmost importance so that the seeds have the best chance of finding hospitable conditions for germination.

Vegetative Propagation

The alternative to growing plants from seeds is vegetative or asexual propagation. The idea is to take a piece from an existing plant and grow it into a new plant. Shoots or cuttings have the ability to regenerate roots, roots may produce shoots and the leaves of some plants recreate the whole. Of course, under laboratory conditions, a single cell will regenerate the entire plant, but this is not the concern of the home propagator.

For the gardener interested in native plants, vegetative propagation offers speed more than anything else: he can get a larger plant in a shorter time. This is especially true of layering or air-layering plant material, where large sections of a living plant can be induced to form new root systems while still attached to the parent plant.

For the commercial nurseryman, vegetative propagation is important as a way of producing many plants that have exactly the same genetic makeup as the parent. This is important when the horticultural value of the tree or shrub is based on a characteristic that is not carried by the seed, like a weeping habit, a particular hue or size of flower, or variegation pattern of leaf. These horticultural varieties are always propagated asexually so that the desirable characteristics will not be lost.

This will be a less important consideration for the propagator of native plant material, since, almost by definition, those plants will be the norm, not the exception. Of course, there are selections that horticulturists have made from native populations that do exhibit unusual characteristics, and these plants, which would be found in rare-plant nurseries rather than in the wild, would have to be propagated vegetatively.

Vegetative propagation does have one drawback. Viruses and other pathogens that inhabit the parent plant are propagated with the plant or may be introduced into an otherwise healthy strain by carelessness. One can't get carried away by this eventuality, however; not very much can be done about viruses. Reasonable cleanliness is advisable, and any knives or other cutting tools used in the preparation of cuttings should be sterilized when one moves from working on one species to another. With that caution, lets look at the options of vegetative propagation.

ROOTING HORMONES

The biggest advance in the history of propagation technology was the discovery in the late 1930s that certain substances would stimulate the rooting of cuttings. These have popularly been called rooting hormones and are available in several commercial preparations. Their effect is to intensify what happens in nature: to concentrate auxins at the base of the cutting. With hormones, it is possible to accelerate the speed of rooting, even in easily rooted plants (an important commercial consideration); to increase the number and mass of roots that a cutting produces (so that it gets off to a better, faster start); and finally, to induce difficult-to-root cuttings to produce roots. This last effect was commercially the most important, since many plants that had previously been grafted (a laborious process requiring great skill) could—with the hormones—be propagated inexpensively by rooting.

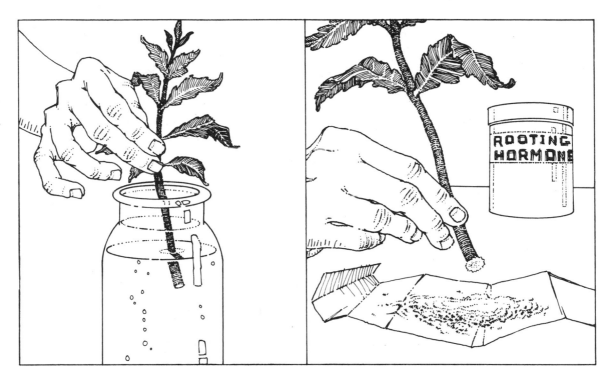

Using rooting hormone is as easy as dipping a chip. Sprinkle some hormone powder on a dish or paper towel. Dip the stem's cut end into the powder, which

should adhere only to the wounded area, not to the sides of the stem. If the wound isn't damp enough to hold the powder, dip it in water, then in the powder.

Rooting compounds are usually sold mixed in a talc base and are simple to use. Shake some of the compound onto a paper towel and dip the end of the cutting into it. Usually the cutting will be damp enough so that the talc adheres; if it isn't, wet the end of the cutting first. Avoid the temptation to dip the cutting directly into the can or envelope of rooting hormone: this contaminates the whole lot. All cuttings should have some hormone treatment, no matter how easy you think it is to root them.

Rooting compounds come in different strengths for use on different kinds of cuttings. Generally there is one strength for herbaceous cuttings like coleus and geraniums, a second for softwood cuttings and a third for hardwood cuttings. Read the directions on the label when you buy.

STEM CUTTINGS

One of the most common ways to propagate trees and shrubs is to "plant" a section of the stem cut from an existing plant. Very simply, you cut a piece anywhere from 4 inches to a couple of feet long, stick the end that was closest to the roots into the ground, leave the end with a bud on it up in the air and let nature do the rest. There is a bit more to it than that, of course. There are different kinds of cuttings, there are special ways of dealing with each, and there are pitfalls. But using stem cuttings will be a primary planting technique for most natural landscapers.

The two principal kinds of cuttings are hardwood and softwood. The designation has nothing to do with whether the parent plant is a hardwood—such as a hickory, walnut, oak or other deciduous tree—or a softwood—such as a hemlock, fir or other evergreen tree. It has everything to do with whether the cutting itself is a year or more old and thus hard and woody or whether it's young and pliant. The distinction should be obvious. In between is what is called a semi-hardwood cutting.

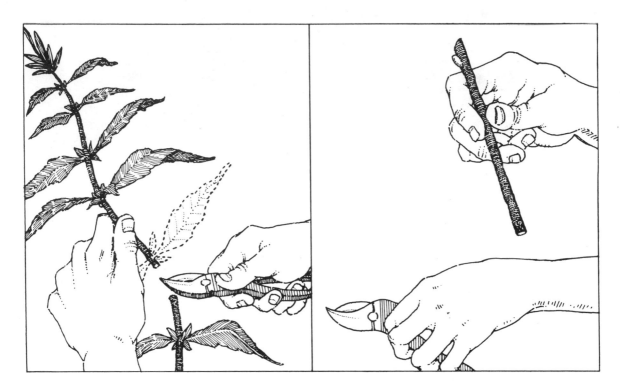

Collect cuttings for propagation while you prune. Softwood cuttings, which are young and pliant, are taken in the spring. They can be from 4 to 24 inches long. Nip the stem just a fraction of an inch below a leaf joint, then trim the lower leaves (there should be at least 1 or 2 inches of bare stem). Hardwood cuttings are taken in the early fall from woody,

mature growth. Usually the base of a stem is the section to use as a hardwood cutting. The base end of the cutting should be cut square. The top end must have a bud; if it is a lateral bud, make an angled cut, trimming off the excess stem just above the bud. The cutting should be 4 to 6 inches long.

With stem cuttings, the propagator is between a rock and a hard place. Keeping the cutting alive until it can form new roots is a function of keeping it turgid—that is, filled with water. Yet it is the roots alone that are responsible for replacing lost water, and the cutting doesn't have any roots. The ideal environment for a cutting is where the atmosphere inside the leaf and outside are equally moisture laden so that very little water is lost through transpiration. Such an environment reduces water loss in the plant to zero.

SOFTWOOD CUTTINGS

The softwood cutting—a piece of any tree or shrub's new growth that has not yet become woody (it should be supple but should break if bent sharply)—is the easiest kind of cutting to root—and

the one most difficult to keep turgid. Auxins, which are produced in the green leaves and move down the cutting to induce rooting at the base, are high in green-wood cuttings, and roots emerge easily from the nonwoody stem without the physical barrier of "bark." Sugars, the product of photosynthesis, are also high because of the food-making capabilities of the leafy cutting. But with photosynthesis and growth comes the necessity for transpiration, which is accelerated by the heat component of light. What you need is a simply constructed box for propagating green-wood cuttings.

A Rooting Box for Softwood Cuttings

The little bottle of water that works so well as a rooting medium for herbaceous (nonwoody) cuttings like coleus and ivy will not do for the

Softwood cuttings need the proper environment to root, and that environment can be provided by an easily made propagation box. Line a shallow wooden fruit crate with plastic, leaving about 2 inches of the liner overhanging the sides of the box. Fill it with a half-and-half mixture of sand and perlite. Insert the cuttings in the medium and water them. You must

cover the box with plastic, but it can't be supported by the cuttings. So fabricate a support from turkey wire and set it in place. The box should be located outdoors in a permanently shaded area. Once it has been placed, lay plastic over the support and seal the edges by heaping soil over them.

softwood cuttings of native trees and shrubs. Success with them is dependent on your making a propagation cabinet. The one described here was developed by Al Fordham, the propagator for many years at the Arnold Arboretum in Boston, Massachusetts. Its advantages are that it is simple to build, mostly from "found" materials, and it works for any softwood cutting that you stick in it.

There are two ways to go: the case can be mobile, or it can be built into the ground as a

permanent fixture. Either way, it is intended to be located outside in permanent shade (the north side of a house, for instance) to receive cuttings in the late spring, with the expectation that they will be rooted in a few weeks, certainly by the beginning of winter.

If a portable unit is desirable, its basis might be the shallow wooden crate that grapes or similar small fruit are packed in. For a permanent installation, the box can be a shallow excavation in the ground, framed with boards to prevent the earth from caving in and contaminating the propagation medium. The shallow box you have chosen is then lined with 2-mil polyethylene plastic sheets. Allow a 6-inch overhang around the sides. The lined box is then filled with the propagating medium. For most cuttings, a mixture of half builder's sand and half perlite is suggested. If you are going to root the cuttings of ericaceous plants primarily (rhododendrons, azaleas and their kin), the medium should be half sand or perlite and half peat moss to provide the acidity those plants require. (A second frame for rooting ericaceous plants would be a nice idea.)

Once the medium is in place, the box is ready to receive the cuttings. These should be inserted and watered in (which settles the medium around them). Now the whole unit is ready to be topped with a turkey-wire frame (2'' × 4'' welded-joint wire) that will support the humidity-conserving polyethylene tent. Cut the wire to fit inside the box and shape it like a staple—flat on top with sides folded down at right angles to meet the propagating medium. The tent top should be about 6 inches *above* tops of the cuttings, so plan accordingly. Put the frame in place and cover it with a sheet of polyethylene film, mounding up soil around the edges where the tent touches the ground. You want a tight seal.

The unit that you have constructed meets all the requirements for rooting softwood cuttings. There is light so photosynthesis can go on, but not sun, which would heat up the space under the plastic and turn it into a steam bath. There is plenty of water in the medium and in the atmosphere. In fact, you have created a closed system, waterwise. Evaporation from the surface or transpiration from the leaves will condense at night on the wire-supported plastic and, because the frame is flat on top, will drip back into the medium.

A cloudy day provides the opportunity to check on the progress of the cuttings and to pick up any leaves that may have fallen onto the medium. (If allowed to rot there, they will contaminate the soil and provide food for destructive fungi.) A tug on the cutting will give you all the information you need about its progress. Heavy resistance means good rooting, some resistance means that rooting is just beginning or is slight, no resistance (the cutting comes out in your hand) means that rooting hasn't started yet. (Don't worry that you've ruined something, just push the cutting back into the rooting medium.) When cuttings show signs of good rooting, they can be potted in a more complete growing medium.

A much simpler version of this softwood-cutting propagation box is a clear plastic bag closed at the top with a "twist-'em." This makes a "bubble" around the cutting and creates a closed water system. Cover the bottom of the bag with 2 inches of moist perlite, insert the hormone-treated cutting and close the bag. Success is ensured by remembering two things: never set the bag in sunlight, and expose the cuttings to the night air (for conditioning) as soon as roots have emerged (an inch of roots apparent in the perlite).

Aftercare of Softwood Cuttings

Since the softwood cutting has been rooted in an atmosphere of high humidity and weak light, its immediate return to a normal environment would be a severe shock. Gradual reconditioning is the key to success. If one is fortunate enough to have a number of cloudy days in a row, the process may take care of itself: the potted cutting will adjust (harden off) in a few days. If sunny weather prevails, the potted cutting should be grown under the protection of plastic during the daytime (out of the sunlight) and uncovered at night. Putting pot and all in a clear plastic bag (out of the sunlight) will do the trick. Once the cutting is established in its pot—and is no longer showing signs of wilting during the heat of the day (uncovered)—it is ready to begin life as an independent plant.

HARDWOOD CUTTINGS

Hardwood cuttings from dormant wood are important in the nursery industry because they can be propagated in great numbers without special equipment and without concern for wilting and desiccation (water loss), which is the plague of the softwood cutting.

Rooting plants from hardwood cuttings is low-energy technology that's practically as old as the science of propagation. It takes advantage of the soil temperature in winter, which hovers around 50°F. (10°C.) just a few inches below the surface. Many hardwood cuttings will either root or form

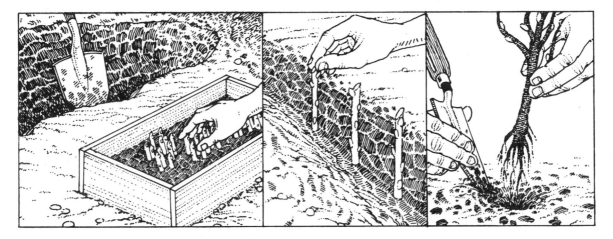

Hardwood cuttings are propagated directly in the ground. While they can be planted in the fall, immediately after a dip in rooting hormone, the usual practice is to dip the cuttings in rooting hormone, bundle them in groups of about ten and put them in a cool but not freezing place for the winter. A good approach is to bury the bundles in a box of damp sawdust or sand-perlite mixture, then to bury the box below the frost line. In the early spring, exhume the cuttings and plant them. Dig a hole for each cutting or a trench for all of them, and plant them base down with the topmost bud just sticking above the soil surface. Come the warm weather, the cutting should sprout nicely and be ready for transplanting—if that's in the plan—in the fall.

the preinitials of roots while they are held at that temperature. The cuttings can be recovered in early spring and allowed to root directly in the ground after the winter stratification. The cold period will also have broken bud dormancy, which, like embryo dormancy, requires that certain changes take place within the bud during the winter before growth can resume in the spring. Few plants are now rooted commercially from hardwood cuttings because of more efficient technologies for rooting softwood cuttings more quickly, but the technique is very appropriate for the home gardener, since it requires no special equipment and no special care of the dormant cutting while roots are forming. It is a totally "in-ground" operation.

Hardwood cuttings are taken in late summer or early fall after growth is woody and the plant is quiescent—even dormant. Generally, this method is used to propagate deciduous trees and shrubs. It is the absence of leaves and the generally reduced metabolism of the cutting that makes it so easy to handle: no worrying about lost moisture from transpiration and no need for photosynthesis, since there is a reserve of stored sugars in the mature stem.

The cutting is made from an average stem that grew the previous season. It should include a terminal bud, but one long stem may be cut into several pieces, as long as each ends in a lateral (side) bud. The end that is to form roots (the one nearest the trunk or crown) should be dusted with a root-inducing hormone. The cuttings are then bundled and stratified. The medium for this could be a dampened mixture of sand and peat moss, sand and perlite or it could simply be dampened sawdust. Stratification could occur in a pit outdoors or in a wooden box buried below the frost line. The cuttings should not freeze—that is the point—and the medium should stay moist over the winter, fed from water in the surrounding soil. Good results have been reported with cuttings stratified in the family refrigerator in the same manner recommended for seeds. Stratification can also take place with the cutting planted in the ground just as it is going to grow (only the top bud above the surface), if the area can be protected

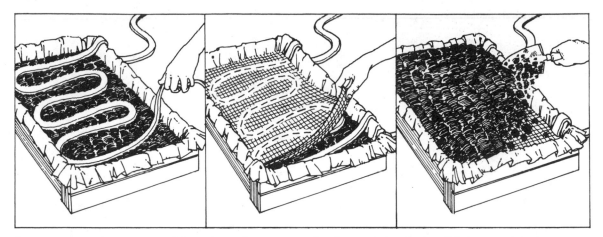

The propagation-box setup used for softwood cuttings can be converted for propagating conifer cuttings if you move it indoors and add a heating cable to it. Fill the box halfway with medium, then lay in a heating cable. Cover the cable with a piece of hardware cloth, which will help spread the heat evenly across the box. Add more medium to cover the cable and hardware cloth. The box is now ready for planting.

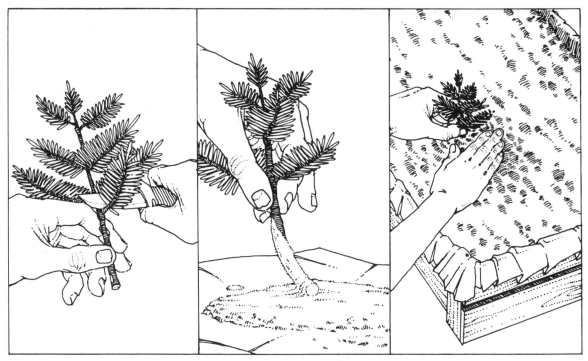

Propagating the conifers is different from propagating other cuttings, once the proper environment is provided, only in that it takes much longer for the cuttings to root. The proper environment is provided by the heated propagating box. Collect the cuttings in the fall, and strip the side branches, if any, and needles or leaves off the bottom third of the cutting.

Dust the stem with rooting hormone, covering in this case not only the stem end but all the little wounds where needles or leaves were taken off. Insert the cutting in the medium, water, cover with plastic and plug in the cable. And be ready to wait a year or more for the cutting to root.

from hard freezing by a polyethylene covering supported on a wire frame. But this is tricky and should be tried only in areas where the winter is mild.

By early spring, the cuttings should be ready to remove from stratification and plant in their permanent site or in containers. Rooting will continue with the coming warmth, and the terminal bud will finally break into growth, forming the basis of the new plant.

NARROW-LEAVED AND NEEDLED EVERGREENS

Because a hardwood cutting of an evergreen is not going to be leafless, it presents some special problems for the propagator. Since it will be composed of a single year's (or more) mature growth, it will be a hardwood cutting. But because they take so long to root—a year or more, even under optimum conditions—they stand a good chance of drying out. So they should be placed in moisture conditions similar to softwood cuttings.

Use a rooting box not unlike the one you would use for softwood cuttings. But this box should be kept indoors (or in a greenhouse), and it should have bottom heat from a heating cable. To prepare a propagating case for hardwood evergreen cuttings, lay down 2 inches of propagating medium (sand and perlite mixed half and half), and install a heating cable, coiled so that it covers the largest surface area possible at that level. Over the cable (and in contact with it), lay a piece of hardware cloth (½-inch mesh) to help in furthering heat distribution. More medium goes in over the mesh. Since the unit will be covered in polyethylene, the usual precautions about heat buildup from the sun apply.

To prepare a cutting for rooting, strip the leaves from the lower third of the cutting and dust the exposed stem, as well as the end, with rooting hormone. The small "wounds" where the leaves were taken off expose more of the stem to the action of the hormone.

SEMI-HARDWOOD CUTTINGS

This category is really splitting hairs and applies mostly to rhododendrons, holly and other so-called broad-leaved "evergreens." The cuttings are taken after the first flush, or growth, is mature but before it is woody. The cuttings are semi-hardwood.

To reduce transpiration through the big leaves—and to save space in the propagating case—the leaves of these cuttings are often cut in half to shorten them.

Root as for hardwood cuttings with hormone treatment and bottom heat. If rhododendron or azalea cuttings (or any of their ericaceous relatives) are contemplated, the propagating medium should be changed to half sand or perlite and half peat moss.

LAYERING

Layering in the ground is based on the same low-energy technology as rooting hardwood cuttings. The main difference is that the cutting is not completely severed from the parent plant before it is rooted. This is a particularly good way of propagating native shrubs *in situ*, bending a low branch to the ground and rooting it there over the winter, recovering and transplanting the layer the following spring.

The process is simple. A long supple stem is bent to the bottom of a trench that has been dug to receive it. Think of the trench as the stratification pit below the frost line. If the soil in the pit is hard and claylike, consider replacing it with a lighter, better-aerated stratification medium. With the pit prepared, bend the stem to the trench bed and wound the stem where it comes in contact with the medium. The "wound" is an angled cut halfway through the stem. Now, dust the wound with rooting hormone. Peg the stem to the bottom of the pit with a forked stick or wire staple so that the wound is in contact with the medium. Then bring the layer to an upright position and stake it there. Refill the trench. Roots will form at the wound during the period of winter stratification, and the layer can be unearthed in the spring, cut from the shrub and removed to another site. It can also be left there to grow for a few seasons if there is no rush to collect it—a larger, healthier plant would be the result.

ROOT AND LEAF CUTTINGS

Root cuttings can be particularly important for propagating some species of small trees and shrubs, particularly those that form clumps and colonies—like the sumac along the highways—by sending

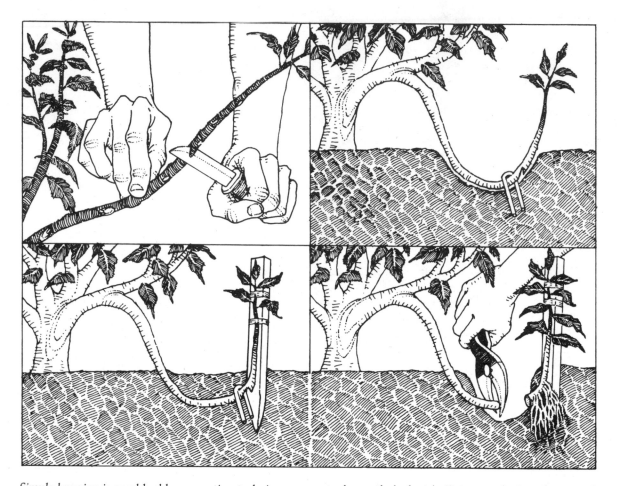

Simple layering is an old, old propagation technique. In early spring, trim the leaves from a section of a long, supple stem at a point where it will touch the ground, and wound the stem by cutting about half-way through it on an angle. Scoop out a pocket of soil where the wounded stem will touch, bend the stem into the pocket and pin it there with a wire staple or a forked stick. Drive a stake into the ground beside the stem and tie the trailing end upright to the stake; doing this should open the wound without totally severing the stem. Cover over the hole with soil and water. By the end of the growing season, the stem should have taken root; cut it from the parent plant and, if desired, transplant it.

up new plants from the old roots of the original colonizer. Some other native plants that are commonly propagated from root cuttings are the bottlebrush buckeye (*Aesculus parviflora*), dwarf juneberry (*Amelanchier stolonifera*), trumpet vine (*Campsis radicans*), American bittersweet (*Celastrus scandens*), sweet fern (*Comptonia peregrina*), bayberry (*Myrica pensylvanica*), phlox species, all the sumacs (*Rhus* species), black locust (*Robinia Pseudoacacia*), several roses such as *Rosa virginiana*, blackberry and raspberry (*Rubus* species) and sassafras (*Sassafras albidum*).

The age of the stock plant is important in taking root cuttings. Best results are with pencil-sized roots taken from two- to three-year-old plants. The roots of the plants will be well supplied with stored nutrients. The time to do it is in late spring, when the ground is workable but before active

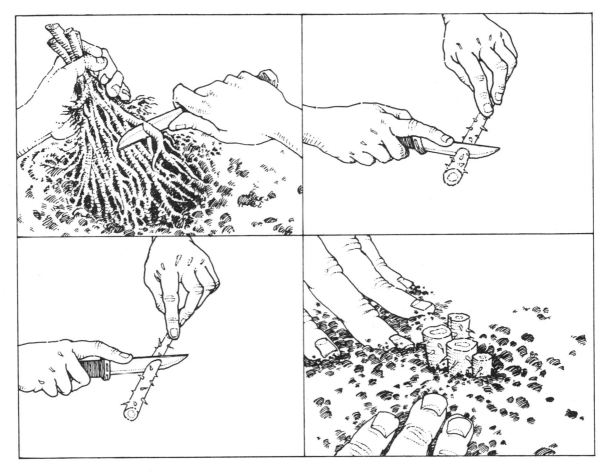

Root cuttings must be collected in the plant's dormant period, and it can be done without sacrificing the plant. Prune back the plant top, then carefully dig it up and rinse the soil from the roots. The cuttings should be taken from the young roots close to the crown. Since you must know which end is up, make the cuts that sever the cutting from the plant at right angles to the root stem; this will be the end that points up when you plant the cutting. Trim away the end of the cutting with an angled cut, clearly differentiating that end from the top. After you've taken a few cuttings, return the plant to its home in the soil.

growth has started. Since it isn't easy to take root cuttings, you might consider trying softwood cuttings or, later, seeds from the same plant, rather than digging around looking for an appropriate root to propagate.

Root cuttings like to know which way is up and which way down, something you won't remember unless you have a system for making the proximal end (nearest the crown, or "up") and the distal end (away from the crown, or "down"). Common practice is to cut the distal end at a slant and the proximal end straight across. The slanted end gets a treatment with rooting hormone.

Perhaps the easiest way to deal with root cuttings is to stratify them for a few weeks outdoors like hardwood cuttings, then root them directly in the ground. Since the soil has not warmed to any great depth in the late spring when you are preparing them, finding an underground spot where the temperature is about 40°F.(4.4°C.) shouldn't be a big problem. Stratify the hormone-treated cutting for three weeks, then plant it outside (right side up) with the proximal end just at or slightly under the soil surface. Wait for new shoots to appear.

Leaf cuttings, frankly, are more important in the propagation of houseplants than in the propagation of native species. Succulents, as every indoor gardener knows, can be grown from leaf cuttings, but if the aim is to produce succulents for a natural landscape, the gardener should consider rooting much larger pieces of the desired plant. Any succulent that will root from a leaf will root from a stem or, if the stem has been reduced to rosette, from the rosette complete with its central, compressed stem.

If you are bound and determined to try leaf cuttings, however, the process is so simple that it's really automatic. Remove the leaf from the plant and lay it on top of a flat or pot of sand. With time, the leaf will send out roots, which will grow into the sand. A little moisture helps at this point. As the roots establish themselves, the leaf will send up a shoot, which is the new plant. All you have to do is provide the sand-filled pot to receive the roots: the leaf does all the rest. This is a long-term method of propagation, but it works.

21 *Living with Your Natural Landscape*

Your soil is in good shape. You know how to forage for native species, what to look for when you buy them from a nursery and how to grow your own from seeds or cuttings. Now you must learn how to create and maintain your natural landscape—what plants must be established first, how to achieve the diversity of species necessary to eliminate "weeds" and attract wildlife, how often to mow or burn and how to defend your natural landscape from plant pests and diseases. All of this information is discussed in detail in this chapter.

Before you proceed to convert your yard into a wilderness habitat, however, there's another book you should consult besides *Nature's Design* —the "Book of Codified Ordinances" of your township or city. Most townships have a weed ordinance that specifies a maximum height for plantings that are not "ornamental or useful." While the original intent of this law—to protect property owners from lazy or careless neighbors—is valid, there are some obvious problems with its current interpretation. Who, for example, defines whether a plant is ornamental or useful? Why should ajuga or daylilies be acceptable, while the equally attractive black-eyed Susan or Queen-Anne's-lace is not? As more and more homeowners have revised their notions of landscaping, more and more weed cases are being won. Nevertheless, you should check your local ordinance and take some precautionary steps to avoid breaking the law.

Find a township supervisor to discuss how this law is defined in your area. To what plants does the height limit apply, and what is legally considered to be a weed? Tell the town officials of your plans and get them to identify any specific plants that are outlawed. Be careful not to ignore your neighbors. Let them know what you're doing and why you're doing it. If you cheerfully explain

yourself at the onset, people will be less likely to think you're trying to ruin the neighborhood!

If that doesn't work and push comes to shove, most natural-lawn cases have been won in court—but you must be prepared to prove that the vegetation growing on your property is not composed of noxious weeds but of natural and beautiful wild flowers. You might talk about noise pollution from your neighbor's mower and throw in some statistics about the energy consumed by mowers and fertilizers. Remember, you've got a lot of natural laws on your side. If you need solid information to back up your claims, contact a local nature center, conservancy or the botany department of a local college. It will help to bring in an expert to support your argument.

Prairies

The American prairie is a landscape of hundreds of diverse species of grasses and forbs that grow naturally from Indiana west to the shadow of the

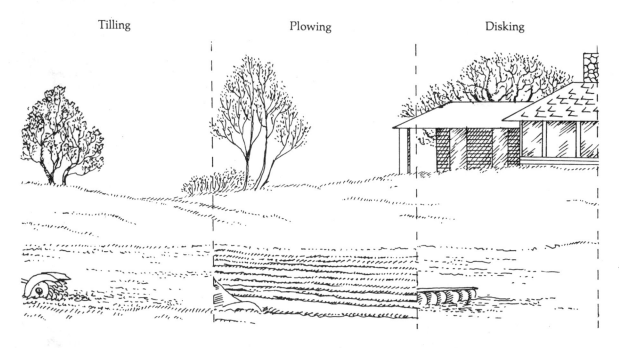

Tilling   Plowing   Disking

Establishing a prairie is a long-term process, which may take three years or more. The first year's work is the worst. The first several steps are intended to prepare a seedbed, but also to disrupt the germination

and growth of weeds, which will compete with the prairie plants you are cultivating. So till or plow in the fall, then again in spring. Disk the prairie-to-be, then seed, using a broadcast seeder. Lightly rake the

Rockies and from Canada south to mid-Texas. Its appearance and composition differ according to the amount of rainfall it receives. At the base of the Rockies, where rainfall is scant (but greater than the surrounding desert), the western wheatgrass, buffalo grass and blue grama seldom exceed 1 foot. Further east, where there is an extra 10 inches of rainfall, the midgrass prairie consists of 18- to 24-inch-tall side-oats grama, split-beard bluestem, needle-and-thread and prairie dropseed. Even further east, where there is a whopping 40 inches of rain per year, interspersed with periods of severe drought, the big bluestem, switch-grass and Indian grass can get to be as tall as 8 feet.

All of these species have adapted to their severe environments. Their thin leaves and stiff stems present the smallest possible surface area to the sun to minimize evaporation and prevent wilting. Some species have evolved upright divided leaves, which provide shade for each other, and all have underground perennial crowns that are protected from fire, the creator and conservator of the prairie.

The grass flowers appear at the tops of the plants to take advantage of their means of pollination—the wind. After 50 million years of evolution, prairie plants are neatly adapted to their environment and can take care of themselves, whether in the wild or in your home landscape.

An established prairie landscape requires minimal maintenance (once-a-year burning or mowing), but getting it started is hard work and takes a minimum of three years. Ideally, the prairie site should be tilled in the fall prior to planting to expose existing plant roots and weed seeds to the killing effects of winter frosts. Plow deeply in the spring, and follow with several diskings throughout the summer. This method is preferred because it will eliminate the weeds that would otherwise compete with the new prairie plants.

If you don't want to wait a whole season, till in the early spring and again two to three times before the middle of June, when you begin planting. These last tillings should be shallow so you don't bring dormant weed seeds up to the surface. If the

Seeding   Raking   Rolling

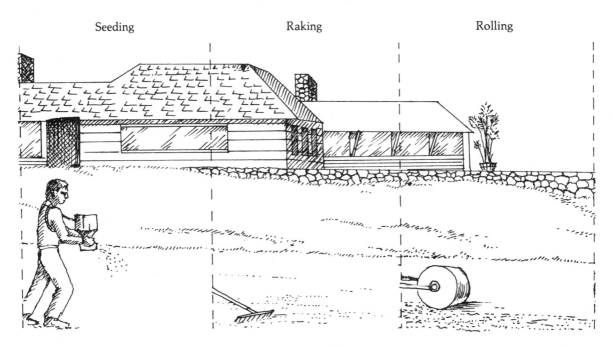

seeded area, then roll it. It's likely that the first plants to appear will be weeds. While you may want to and be able to pull the largest of these, if the area is large, you probably won't be able to hand weed the whole

plot and get every blasted exotic out. Rather, mow the plot periodically during the first growing season. At first, you can mow to a height of 3 to 5 inches. Subsequent mowings should be at greater heights,

(continued next page)

site is already weed-free, you can plant as early as April 1.

Seeding can be done by any of a number of methods—sow one at a time, broadcast or spread with a mechanical seeder. Sow at least four different grasses, and the more forbs the better—even a small area of virgin prairie contains as many as 40 species. Cover the seeds with ⅜ inch of soil, and roll or compact it to ensure contact between the soil and seeds.

Then sit back and wait for an abundant crop of exotic nonprairie weeds to appear. Don't despair—while your prairie plants don't look like much above the soil, below the ground they are growing at the amazing rate of about 2 inches per week. This is another adaptive mechanism of prairie plants, which need an extensive root system to get as much water as possible.

The exotic weeds, which could shade out your young prairie plants, must be mowed before they set seed. Set your mower at 4 to 8 inches to

protect the emerging prairie plants, and mow after the first month. At the end of another month, mow again, but set the blades slightly higher. Mow a third time with the blade set to 2 to 3 inches above ground at the beginning of the second year. Burning, which removes the previous year's debris and makes room for new growth, also helps to control unwanted weeds. Before burning, be sure to consult your local fire department and arrange to have fire protection. After this first burning, the prairie can be mowed or burned on an annual basis. In three years, you should have a stable prairie community, capable of taking care of itself with the minimal maintenance of an annual mowing or burning

Meadows

Meadows are quickly gaining popularity as an alternative to energy-consuming, high-maintenance lawns. Although people often refer to prairies and

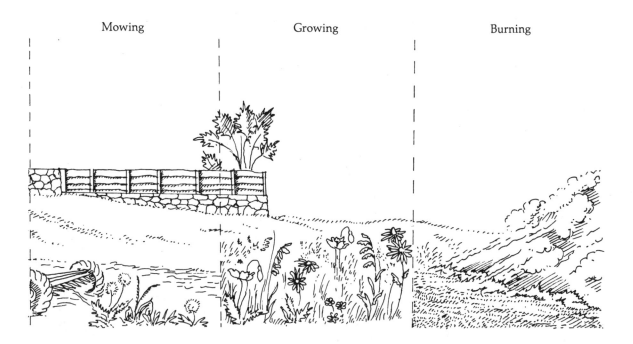

Mowing   Growing   Burning

since your prairie plants will eventually emerge, and you won't want to set them back by mowing them. Just keep the tops clipped off the weeds. Every fall, you should burn your prairie. Obviously, you'll have to exercise appropriate care and solicit the assistance

of local firefighters to do this. After the first year, the only maintenance you should have to perform is spot weeding to eliminate particularly pernicious weeds, and the annual, year-end burning.

Establishing a meadow takes a fair amount of work. Maintaining it does too, unlike maintaining a prairie. A meadow can be started either by frontal assault or by dividing and conquering. A frontal assault requires you to strip the sod from the lawn, plow and disk it, then sow a seed mixture of wild flowers and native grasses. Nurturing the meadow in this situation and staving off weedy infiltrators will be a lot of work during the first, and even the second, growing season.

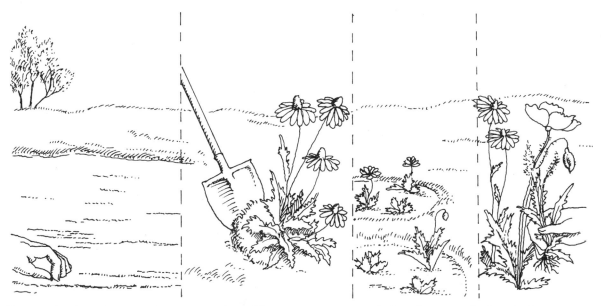

You can divide and conquer by stripping the sod from evenly scattered spots and seeding them with your seed mixture. Weeding only small plots will be somewhat less work. As the native plants mature, you can dig them up and divide them, replanting the existing spots with some of the plants and starting new spots with the others. It will take a bit longer to get the meadow started using this approach, but the chance of success is greater and the measure of work to be done is smaller. With either approach, the meadow must be scythed or mown every spring.

meadows interchangeably, there is a distinct difference between the two that will be important to your landscaping plans. While both are grasslands, prairies occur naturally in areas of low rainfall (like the Plains states) and, because they are ecologically fit for the late successional environment, require little maintenance. Meadows, which occur in areas of high rainfall (like the Northeast or Pacific Northwest), are usually the first stage of succession and require more work to maintain. Meadows demand a willingness on your part to keep after ever-encroaching tree and shrub seedlings, as well as the weeds that can successfully compete with early successional species.

Meadows can be created in any area with well-drained soils and full sunlight. There are several ways to establish a meadow—from doing nothing to planting meadow species as ground covers. If you try the do-nothing technique, it will take a minimum of four years for wild flowers to become established—if, in fact, they do—and by then you may have several nasty invaders, such as poison ivy, honeysuckle and bittersweet, not to mention some good-sized tree seedlings threatening to turn your meadow into a forest.

If you'd like to hurry this process, you can begin in the fall, before the first frost, by tilling and throwing seeds mixed with sand over the entire area. As an alternative, you can open up a number of soil pockets in your lawn and plant the wild-flower seeds in the pockets. Although these planted areas will have to be mulched for protection through the winter, you'll have a head start on establishing a meadow. In the spring, you can scratch away more lawn and plant native grasses.

If you are putting in young plants, you should follow the same techniques as for planting ground covers, but instead of spacing them evenly, place them in clumps of three or more of the same species. As these become established, they will reseed and spread rapidly until you can divide and transplant the clumps.

Meadows, like prairies, require an annual cutting. But because there will be woody species too tough for a lawn mower, you will need to scythe by hand or mow with a tractor. Cutting should be done in the fall, after the plants have gone to seed, although many meadow gardeners who like the winter appearance of the tall grasses mow in the early spring.

Meadows will also need to be weeded. Disturbed soil is an inviting environment for hundreds of unwanted species. You will need to keep an ever-wary eye out for invaders like poison ivy, blackberries and honeysuckle, which can quickly take over.

If the periphery of your meadow is wooded and if there are tree species like ash, maple or oak, you can expect a good number of seedlings to invade your open area. Keeping these from growing into a forest will be a constant maintenance problem, though the annual mowing is intended to keep these invaders down. A dense stand of evergreens at the edge of the meadow will discourage invading undergrowth, as will ground covers with tightly knit root systems. Hay-scented or New York fern can also prevent other plants from taking hold. Taking these measures will not prevent the spread of plants like black cherry, choke cherry, viburnum and ocean-spray. Since wildlife carry the seeds of these plants into your meadow area, you will have to be prepared to do some hand weeding.

Woodland Gardens

If you are developing a prairie or meadow, don't expect any compliments for at least three years. (But don't get discouraged either—the newly planted lawn with spindly specimens look pretty bleak for longer than that.) If you are creating a mid- to late-successional woodland, however, it is possible to develop a lush, finished-looking landscape almost immediately. Although a woodland requires even more work initially than either a prairie or a meadow, its long-term demands are far fewer.

Don't be intimidated by the term woodland—it doesn't have to be a forest. A woodland can be any size, height or density you wish, as long as you follow the example of natural woodland layers. With its herbaceous, shrub and canopy layers, woodland actually is the closest natural form to the standard residential landscape. The difference is the greater number of species, their fitness in your environment and their placement, which is based on the successional stage.

Woodland gardens can be planted in the early spring or late fall on an area of bare soil or existing grass. There are both advantages and disadvantages to removing the sod. Some experts

If you already have a mature tree or two, establishing
a woodland grove can be done easily and successfully
by using them as the focus of the landscape. A
woodland, remember, isn't necessarily a forest. The
initial step is to remove the plants that don't have a
place in your natural landscape. Till the area to
be replanted. Then plant the trees and shrubs,
and finally the forbs. If you've done your studies
well and created a good plan, your landscape can
look like a natural woodland from the moment you
finish planting.

Northern Coniferous Forest

Eastern Deciduous Forest

Southeastern Mixed Forest

North America is widely forested. Most of the heavily populated areas of the continent have native woodlands that you can visit, study and endeavor to duplicate in your natural landscape. Duplicating any woodland is not simply a matter of planting the same species, for the same species may appear in several forest types. You must study a variety of characteristics, match them to your property's characteristics, then work out planting schemes.

A series of trips, real or imagined, can help you draw distinctions among the forest types.

A trip from northern New York to southern Georgia or Alabama will take you through three forest regions. You'll begin in the Northern Coniferous Forest, one typified by a predominance of evergreens. This forest has little diversity and thus little to mark the change of seasons. Much of your time will be spent traversing the huge Eastern Deciduous Forest, a highly diverse forest dominated by deciduous trees and shrubs, which give this forest dramatic seasonal changes—showy springtime blooms, heavily green summers, splashy autumn colors and bare winters.

Prairie Grove

Rocky Mountain Evergreen Forest

Pacific Forest

The concluding hours of your journey will be spent in the Southeastern Mixed Forest. It is seemingly a blend of the first two types you saw, a mixture of evergreens and deciduous plants, with neither dominating. It's highly diverse with a rich understory, yet the relatively mild climate helps to moderate the seasonal changes.

A trip from the Mississippi to the West Coast will also take you through several types of woodlands. Depending upon where you start your western trip, you may find yourself in the fringes of any of the eastern forests, though you will quickly leave them and head into the plains. There you'll see prairie groves—small woodlands isolated in the sea of prairie grasses. Eventually you'll pass through the Rocky Mountain Evergreen Forest, dominated, of course, by towering evergreens, though some deciduous trees are mixed in. The woodlands will disappear almost completely, then reemerge in the Pacific Forest. Here the stupendous firs and redwoods dominate.

recommend tilling several times in the fall before the next spring's planting or tilling throughout the spring and summer for a fall planting. While this will get rid of the existing grasses and weeds, which will compete with your young plantings, at the same time it creates a hospitable environment for new weeds. If you till, you will need to cover the entire exposed area with new plants or be willing to keep after the unwanted invaders.

If you have a small site, you can remove existing vegetation by mulching it heavily (8 to 12 inches) with leaves.

Another school of thought advocates simply planting your woodland species in the lawn and allowing the shade these plants produce to get rid of the grass. Moreover, during the initial stages, the already established grass will be attractive still and will prevent an invasion of troublesome weeds.

Whichever method you opt for, the planting procedure must follow one of these courses. The whole idea is to duplicate the growing conditions of a woodland by planting a variety of species of different ages, sizes and heights. You can create the layers in miniature by using ground covers, low shrubs and small trees. You can keep a feeling of openness by using sun-loving species that grow at the edge of forests. If you want dense shade and privacy, you can create a solid canopy of large trees. Your best bet is to find a natural environment you like and use that as your guide.

Unless your property is bordered by another woodland or a wall, you will need to plant the edges to prevent harsh sunlight and wind from penetrating. Try to use rapid spreaders that will tighten the edge and control weedy invaders.

Within this edge, plant sun-loving species that will serve as the nurse crop for more shade-tolerant shrubs and ground covers. The less light reaching the ground, the less you will need to weed or water. In small gardens, where large shade trees may be out of scale, you can provide shade by adding walls or trellises.

Once you have established enough shade, you can plant any of the lovely herbaceous species that are native to your area—trilliums, mertensia, partridgeberry or any shade-loving understory trees and shrubs. There are thousands of beautiful woodland plants. Choose the species that fit the conditions of your environment as well as your individual taste.

Your newly installed plants should be mulched with leaf litter or peat moss, and they will need to be watered well during their first growing season. If you aren't able to fill the entire area with plants, cover any bare spots with a thick layer of leaf litter to discourage weeds.

Don't overlook the use of ferns and mosses for filling in areas of bare ground. There are hundreds of ferns that grow in a wide variety of habitats; many of these would enhance your landscape with their delicate forms.

Mosses can provide a serene, smooth-textured, green surface in which wild flowers and ferns will thrive. If you have a lot of shade and an acid (pH 5.5 or less), well-drained soil, you can establish moss by transplanting clumps in the early spring and keeping them moist for several weeks. The only maintenance requirement is an occasional brushing or raking-away of leaves, which might rot the moss.

A woodland garden takes about two to three years to become self-maintaining. Once established, your garden will involve only minimal maintenance—removing unwanted plants, transplanting wanted ones and restraining the overly exuberant with an occasional pruning. As the woodland matures, it will efficiently mulch itself each fall—none of this dead organic matter should be removed. By its second or third year, when the root system is well established, no watering will be needed.

Lawn

If you live in an area that will support a prairie, meadow or woodland, you also live in an area that will support a traditional lawn. And even if the natural landscape you've designed is a panoramic display of desert cacti and succulents, the less attractive but hardy buffalo grass, love grass or grama may grow for you. For whatever reason you decide to include a patch of lawn in your landscape design, understand at the outset that creating and maintaining it will be a lot of work.

Just as for any other area of your landscape, you must know the soil. Grasses grow best in a soil with a pH of 6.0 to 7.6. Good soil texture, drainage and aeration are important. Sandy soils leach away nutrients, as water seeps quickly down through them; clayey soils hold water and fertilizer for a longer period of time close to the surface, where plants' roots can utilize it, but are harder for roots to penetrate than more granular soils. A healthy balance of nitrogen, phosphorus and potassium will support lush green top growth and strong spreading root systems underground. Lawns fed the proper "diet" are also better able to resist disease and pests.

These conditions are important to the growth of many healthy plants besides grasses. So where does all the time-consuming maintenance come in? In order to appreciate the never-ending labor of maintaining a healthy lawn, it is necessary to understand a little about the way in which grasses reproduce. Most lawn grasses are perennials. If you were to be called away suddenly on business for the length of a summer, you would return to find your grasses tall and laden with flowers ripe with seed. Left to nature's care, these seeds would fall, germinate and grow next year. By mowing your lawn, however, you shortcut this process, and the plants use another method of spreading. Grasses spread by sending out runners (stolons) above ground and rhizomes (horizontal roots) below ground. Repeated mowings encourage the grasses to grow in the dense stand that we have come to consider the sign of a well-groomed lawn. Adequate water and fertilizer will aid in this vegetative propagation process. Keeping out weedy invaders is essential but becomes easier once the lawn is established.

Lawns can be started using grass seed, sod or sprigs, as detailed in Chapter 19. Whatever form you use, you must clear the soil of debris, till it deeply and fertilize it before planting. Seeds should be broadcast uniformly over your lawnbed and gently raked into the soil so that the soil just covers them. Sod should be laid down and rolled to ensure contact between the roots and the soil. Sprigs can be planted like other ground covers, 12 inches apart in a grid pattern. Thorough watering after sowing is essential for germination, and frequent watering during the next few weeks is important in getting the roots established.

Since you may have a meadow or prairie stand setting seed nearby, the thicker your lawn carpet grows, the less room there will be for weeds to take hold. The key to lush green growth is proper mowing. Set your mower to cut the grass to 2 to 3 inches. This may seem high, but research has shown it is optimal for weed prevention. In addition, it is a good height for play areas for children. You may want to cut grass shorter around patios, where you want a more formal effect.

Paradoxically, the wild flowers and meadow and prairie grasses will seem like weeds if they pop up in the middle of your lawn. The best way to prevent them from gaining a foothold is to get your soil in tiptop shape, till it deeply before sowing and follow good lawn-care practices regarding mowing, watering and fertilizing. Make sure that any topsoil you purchase is weed-free; the same precaution goes for the lawn seed you sow and the mulch with which you protect the seedbed. And, for love of a manicured lawn, be prepared to get down on your hands and knees and weed. The stubbornest invaders will surrender if you dig up their root systems. This is easiest after a rain or watering. You may get a little muddy, but your lawn will look good.

Deserts

Although there are many different environments within a desert, there are overriding conditions that are common to them all: intense light, temperature extremes and dryness. Because of these, plants have evolved that make the most of available moisture or do without it for large parts of the time, and that survive, if not thrive, in the intense light and heat of the days and the cold of the nights. The desert homeowner who takes advantage of the cacti and succulents and native trees and shrubs that have adapted to this harsh environment will be rewarded with an easy-maintenance landscape.

For the better part of a century, people who have moved to the Southwest have been trying to establish desert oases, with manicured and lush green lawns and flowers that thrived back East. Although many of their experiments failed miserably, their stubborn persistance has paid off. The desert homeowner can now grow forsythia, roses and magnolias, knowing they will flourish given a bit of extra attention and ample water. But such "foreign imports" are not necessary to create a beautiful desert landscape.

Instead of lawn grass under your feet, enjoy the bare earth of a courtyard or the paved texture of a patio floor. Get out of the hot sun in the shade of a blue palo verde tree snuggled against a high adobe wall. Watch the rock forms and desert plants, silhouetted by the sun into stark geometric cutouts, make patterns of light and shadow. The beauty of this garden is in contrasts: the smoothness of a cactus branch, the sharpness of its thorns, the softness of a bright desert flower, the roughness of the shimmering sand.

Making a desert garden bloom requires the same attention to climate and soil conditions as any other natural landscape. In the United States, the desert stretches from southern California into Nevada and Arizona, spans the Rocky Mountains in New Mexico and descends into the flatlands of Texas. Across such a large expanse, rainfall varies from 2 inches a year to 22; elevations range from 2.2 feet below sea level in Death Valley to 5,200 feet in Albuquerque, New Mexico; daytime winter temperatures may climb to 60°F. (15.5°C.) or higher, while the thermometer drops at night to −6°F. (−21°C.); spring brings winds of 40 miles per hour to some areas; and summer scorches the land, with temperatures in July averaging 106° to 108°F. (41° to 42.2°C.) in the low desert.

The soil in the desert has the moisture baked out of it, concentrating salts in the upper layers. Water used for irrigation may itself be high in salts, compounding the problem. The effect on plants is "salt burn" and stunted growth.

If the water used for irrigation is balanced, a gardener can simply wash the salts in the soil down into lower layers as rains would in another climate. Deliberately leaching the soil this way, several times a season, will give plants better growing conditions—if drainage is adequate. If not, root rot may become a problem.

When water used for irrigation is saline, as, for example, that supplied by the Colorado River, the problem must be addressed differently: soluble calcium must be supplied in the soil to bond with sodium and render the salts harmless to plants. This can be done by adding powdered gypsum, or hydrated calcium sulfate, with a lime spreader. However, desert soils often have the necessary element locked away in an insoluble form just below the surface. Caliche, which forms a crusty layer that roots cannot penetrate, is high in calcium as well as lime. Iron sulfate and sulfur can be spread on such soil and leached in to free up the calcium in caliche so that further accumulation of salts can be prevented.

Although proponents of organic farming methods consider iron sulfate a chemical dangerous to soil life, desert soil with a high concentration of salts doesn't support much anyway. As little as ½ to 1 percent of most desert soils is organic matter, and without much plant and animal waste on which to feed, the populations of soil microorganisms are kept small.

However, if your soil has lots of caliche as well as salts, even adding iron sulfate and sulfur will not solve all your soil problems. The crusty hardpan may extend from a few inches to several feet below the surface. Besides being impenetrable to roots, it utterly stops drainage. Because of this, the plants that manage to take hold above a layer of caliche are prone to Texas root rot; the high concentration of lime may induce chlorosis, or loss of leaf color, as well.

Unfortunately, there is no solution to this gardening problem but to remove the caliche and replace it with good soil. You will probably have to call in a backhoe unless the area of caliche is small and you are proficient with a pick and shovel. Dig deep! Good drainage is essential for all desert natives.

If this seems like too much trouble, consider making your planting in tubs or containers. Given the extremes of temperature, the salinity and alkalinity of the soil and the lack of organic matter, it may strike you as remarkable that any plants have adapted to life in the desert. In fact, the Southwest is a showcase garden for cacti and succulents, supporting a remarkable diversity of species. Cacti have adjusted to the near-perpetual drought by developing the ability to store water in branches and pads. In addition, the thorns or spines on some cacti shade the thick skin, reducing water loss through transpiration and protecting it from insects and animals who might be tempted to quench their thirst.

Some native trees and shrubs have evolved to fit the desert microenvironment of riverbanks and streambeds. Although they can endure the heat and drying wind of the desert, deciduous trees like the Arizona ash, the Arizona cypress, the cottonwoods, willows and hackberries need adequate water to thrive. The honey mesquite, an evergreen, also requires an underground water source or irrigation, even though its immediate

To plant in an area with lots of caliche, you've simply got to dig it out. Roots won't penetrate it, and the alkalinity is too high for most plants, even natives. Short of hiring a bulldozer and crew, you can use a pick and shovel to excavate pockets—albeit deep ones—here and there around the house. Replace the caliche in these pockets with more suitable soil and plant in them.

relative, the screwbean mesquite, can endure long periods of drought and still flourish.

Other natives are adapted to even drier conditions. By reducing leaf size, the blue palo verde saves water that would be lost through transpiration. Branches and stem take over the work of photosynthesis. The ocotillo drops its leaves and goes into dormancy when months without rain go on and on. The ironwood sends a taproot deep into the desert soil to find the water table; lateral roots on the surface stretch out to catch occasional brief rains. Some plants defeat the desert's demand for their water with a waxy or varnishlike coating on the leaves. The brittlebush and the creosote bush are two native shrubs that conserve water this way.

In designing your desert landscape, creating a visually pleasing arrangement of foundation, understory and canopy plants will not be your only goal. You must also consider the need to protect your plantings from cool winter and gusting spring winds. A high adobe wall, a fence or a double row of Arizona cypress or cottonwoods on the west side will do much to tame wild breezes. A more extensive planting arrangement of four or five different kinds of shrubs and trees, in rows of gradually ascending height, will direct the air currents up and over your house and garden. Choose hardy plants for this project, and anchor them in place, if necessary, with guy wires.

If you enjoy taking your meals out on the patio, by all means give yourself some shade. The honey mesquite grows as high as 30 feet, with evergreen branches expanding 40 feet across. The hackberry and the desert elderberry grow just as high if well watered, providing cool shelter from the rays of the desert sun. The Jerusalem thorn and the blue palo verde provide a more filtered

While most people think of the desert only as a hot, dry place, those who know the desert know there are degrees of hot and dry. The vegetation of individual desert locales reflects, as much as anything, the degree of dryness of the areas. There are rivers in the desert, and along their banks grow willows, cottonwoods and sycamores. At the opposite end of the moisture scale grow the cacti, including the saguaro, Joshua tree, rabbitbrush and the hardy creosote bush. Between the extremes, one finds mesquites, palms, desert willows and many other plants.

shade as well as a bounty of bright yellow flowers in spring.

For an understory layer, there are many attractive native shrubs you might use. The jojoba, an evergreen now being cultivated commercially for its oil, bears an edible fruit. Chuparosa puts on a showy display of red flowers in late spring; fairy-duster or false mesquite blossoms into powder-puff clusters in February or March; cassia dresses in gold flowers from June through September.

Cacti can also be a part of your understory layer. Plant several individuals of the same species together to create a strong geometric effect. Organ-pipe, fishhooks, barrel and Indian fig grow tall and striking. Cotton-top grows round and low to the ground. After flowering, it bears the white woolly fruit from which it got its name. Hen-and-chickens, or echeveria, is hardy enough to stand the deep cold of New Mexico's winter nights as well as the scorching summer sun. Sedum is also an excellent ground cover for a desert landscape. If you have foraged seeds, you may be able to enjoy the desert's spring spectacle—the delicate, bright colors of wild flowers—zinnia, *Calycoseris* and mariposa—forced into bloom by sudden rains.

Although the trees and shrubs, cacti and succulents mentioned are among the toughest plants in the world, they do not require severe conditions to flourish. In fact, these natives respond very well to a soil that is considerably higher in organic matter than the coarse sandy soils to which they've adapted. If your soil has good drainage, the only improvement you should make is to spread a 2- to 3-inch layer of ground bark or peat moss on the soil surface, sprinkle it with a high-nitrogen fertilizer like powdered bone meal or dried blood and then work these into the soil with a Rototiller 6 inches deep or more. Finished compost is also a good addition. The incorporation of such organic matter into desert soil has the same positive effects it does elsewhere: aeration and drainage are improved, and food is supplied to the plant's roots. If you must replace caliche-ridden soil with your own, aim for a blend that is equal parts good topsoil, coarse sand and organic matter. Even cacti will appreciate the extra nutrients suddenly made available to them.

Nurseries sell about half of their desert natives in containers and dig up the rest on the spot, wrapping soil balls in burlap or leaving the plants bare rooted. Deciduous trees and shrubs bought bare rooted are especially prone to drying out before they can be planted and during the two weeks after planting. You can lessen the danger of desiccation by planting only during the cool fall or early spring months. (Avoid winter planting because of temperature drops and high-velocity winds.) As with any bare-rooted plant, get it in the ground as soon as you get home from the nursery and water it.

Native trees and shrubs should be protected by a mulch 2 to 3 inches thick year-round. Mulches help prevent evaporation of soil moisture and keep the soil temperatures down to the livable maximum on the most blazing summer days in July. As mulches like ground bark decompose, they add to the organic matter content of the soil.

Desert cacti and succulents can get by very well with little help from you. However, they must be planted in rapidly draining soil (like the mixture suggested above) to thrive. Although the cacti and ground covers echeveria and sedum can stand the full intensity of the midday sun, some of the desert succulents enjoy early-afternoon shade, so design your landscape with this in mind.

As difficult as it is to survive in the desert, the native plants in your garden are so well adapted to their harsh environment that they'll manage to get by with very little attention from you; spend the time they save you in maintenance out on the patio lounge chair. Enjoy the rustle of the breeze in the blue palo verde, the cooling shade of the mesquite, the sweet fragrance of the blossom-laden smoke tree. Even the desert has gifts to give to those who know how to receive them.

City Gardens

Seventy percent of the American population lives in an urban environment. Although urbanites may feel themselves far removed from the cycles of nature, they are just as much a part of the natural system as any country dweller. There are obvious differences—dense concentrations of people, buildings, pavement, automobiles, less open space and fewer species of vegetation. Because of these factors, nature takes on an added significance in urban environments. In fact, a real psychological need for some visible and direct contact with nature has made city dwellers pioneers in natural landscaping.

According to Elizabeth Barlow, administrator of New York's Central Park, "When cities were small and wilderness everywhere, raw nature was frequently characterized as rude and horrid. Plants were ruled and made submissive by topiary and parterres. Then romanticism bred an elysian naturalism with gardens and parks of undulating walks and serpentine lakes. Now in a technocratic age, we have come full circle and want to create landscapes that are no longer a vision of paradise, but rather that rude and horrid nature itself. City dwellers have begun to domesticate wildness rather than lose it from their lives."

To landscape in the city, you must be just as knowledgeable about the ecology of your environment as if you lived deep in the country. You must understand the composition, distribution and microassociations of the species of the plant community you are using, as well as all of the ecological characteristics of your site. Whereas in the forest, these are solely nature's creation, in the city they are man-made as well.

Environmental factors make it difficult for many plants to survive in the city. Anyone who commutes from the country to the city knows that cities are warmer than the surrounding area— perhaps 10°F. warmer. Sidewalks, buildings and blacktop absorb heat from sunlight and release it slowly, increasing the temperature. This extra warmth makes it possible for some marginally hardy plants to survive in the city.

For most plants, surface rainfall is rarely adequate to enable them to cope with the heat of summer in the concrete jungle. Compounding the problem is the wind-tunnel effect created by the

Tree pits harbor city trees, but city circumstances ofttimes prevent them from being the sort of havens for trees that they should be. If you are going to plant a street-side tree as part of your urban natural landscape, make the pit large enough. Then install headers to bound the area that will absorb rainwater.

Wherever possible, keep the area within the headers unpaved, forming a saucerlike depression in the soil to channel water to the roots. If you must pave for some reason, pave the area with bricks set in sand. Water thus will be able to percolate between the bricks and to the roots.

tall buildings on both sides of the streets. Trees are desiccated by the wind year-round. Some survive, some languish, but none thrive.

The soil itself, compacted by years of building, demolition and rebuilding, is unable to absorb rain easily. Tree pits, which protect sidewalk trees, are rarely large enough to direct enough surface water to the roots.

In spite of having to cope with all the radiant heat absorbed from the sun by buildings, sidewalks and blacktop, plants often have a problem getting enough light for photosynthesis. Plants on the north side of tall buildings may get only two hours of sun at the summer solstice and less the rest of the year—not nearly enough to sustain healthy growth.

"When people observe a sick city tree, they often attribute it to air pollution," says Ruth Foster,

former assistant tree warden in Boston. "In fact, pollution is usually not the major cause of sickly trees in the city, except in areas that have high contaminant concentrations or very sensitive species. Given good growing conditions, most trees will do reasonably well. Pollutants, however, do take their toll in growth rate and longevity."

The cumulative effect of the stresses of the urban environment is to shorten the life span of plants, stunt growth and leave them in a weakened condition, easy prey for plant diseases and pests. While this stress response is familiar to foresters, its effect in urban settings is just beginning to be investigated.

Despite the harshness of these conditions, bright tulips and hyacinths flourish in window boxes, tomatoes ripen on rooftops and fire-escape landings, and city officials make sure that scarlet sage, white petunias and bachelor's-buttons dress up the formal parks for the Fourth of July. In the midst of so much noise and bustle, people have a need for simple, delicate beauty, defiantly bright color and a waft of sweet scent on the breeze. And the rewards of gardening—the sense of connectedness to the soil and the natural rhythm of the seasons, the self-forgetting that comes in witnessing living things grow—are as important to some city dwellers as they are to a farmer in the Ozarks. Determined city gardeners find space for planting indoors, on windowsills, in window boxes, in tubs and containers on balconies and terraces, in postage-stamp-sized backyards and even in vacant lots.

Those who succeed do so because they have carefully selected plants that will survive in an urban environment, both native and nonnative species. Sometimes plants like the ginkgo, sophora and katsura trees, which all originated in Japan, perform better than natives. It is impractical for most city gardeners to eliminate nonnative species that flourish in the city from their plans, unless they have a backyard or access to a vacant lot where there will be space enough to grow the diversity of plants found in most natural landscapes.

Those who garden on a terrace or balcony may still choose native trees and plants as a preference. Instead of the usual tub crab apple, why not choose a shadblow or serviceberry for a small flowering tree, or use the elegant sourwood, with its rich autumn color, instead of the Japanese maple. If evergreens are desired, there's the Canadian hemlock and the hollies, as well as mountain laurel, white pines and white cedar—all natives. And who could overlook dogwood and redbud, certainly two of the most popular native trees.

Tub-planted trees need root management, of course, to keep them from becoming pot-bound over a long time. They can probably go for three to five years without any attention to the roots, but eventually all of the feeding roots (the growing tips) will be on the periphery of the root ball with little soil around them. This condition will cause the tree to wilt quickly, since the water-holding soil will be in the center of the ball and the roots—growing in roots, essentially—on the bottom and outsides. You can borrow a technique from bonsai at this point and prune the roots, reducing the size of the root ball by one-third overall. The smaller ball is then replanted in the same container with new soil under and around the reduced root system. The pruned roots will branch and grow out into the new soil masses—just the way things should be underground.

Rather than worry about pruning tubbed plants, it is a good idea to choose small trees to begin with (all of the above are small except the white pine, of which there are dwarf forms).

Don't overlook ferns, cacti and other herbaceous plants for window boxes and small plots. The same toughness that stands them in good stead in their natural environments makes them tough and adaptable in the city.

The city dweller with a backyard can attempt to create a natural landscape typical of the wild habitats nearest to the city where he lives. Procedures for creating a prairie, meadow, desert or woodland are the same, with one exception: prairie-makers will have to mow each year—rather than burn—to maintain the landscape they've created.

And what of the vacant lot? The soil is generally sandy and humus deficient, as well as coarse, unstable, highly erodible and low in nutrients. It has little oxygen because it is highly compacted or covered with a nonporous material; it is usually high in sulfur compounds and other toxic materials. Some wind-pollinated and familiar grasses, annuals, biennials, perennials and tree species can grow and reproduce in such soil—if they can get enough water. Trees that can live in these conditions often have long taproots and get both water and oxygen by penetrating the clay drains of city sewage and water systems. The dominant woody species of the vacant lot climax generally are: *Ailanthus* or tree-of-heaven; *Prunus pensylvanica* or bird cherry; *Acer Negundo* or box elder; *Acer platanoides* or Norway maple; *Acer rubren* or red maple; and *Catalpa speciosa* or Indian bean.

Vacant lots are tough environments to survive in and are generally poor in all species—especially wood ones. Reclaiming a vacant lot is a matter of tilling and planting it. The simple penetration of roots into the soil will help to aerate it; legumes like clover or alfalfa will restore nitrogen to it; and the decay of plant matter over time will improve the soil tilth. New York City's Green Guerillas, who help community groups acquire and use vacant lots for gardens, recommend broadcasting some of these seeds: clover, alfalfa, ground cherry,

Landscaping in the city can get pretty desperate. Tall neighboring buildings block out the sun, the space for landscaping itself may be minuscule, and the soils may seem unable to support even weeds. Planters can help solve these problems. First, they help you solve the soil problem: you just fill them with top-quality soil. They allow you to surround yourself with plants and allow you to place plants on a variety of levels, thus making a small space seem larger. And depending upon your situation, they can tie man-made surroundings into your natural landscape.

dandelion, sunflower, cosmos, marigold, sheep sorrel, milkweed, lamb's-quarters, mustard, goldenrod, burdock, flax and plantain. Even if you don't have ownership rights to convert a vacant lot into a full-fledged natural landscape, you do the soil a service by creating such a weed patch.

The lack of free space and a strong urge for some contact with nature has encouraged many urbanites to band together to develop community gardens. These gardens, often occupying what was once a vacant lot, have gained popularity as more and more people experience the rewards of sharing work and enjoyment. Most popular are cooperative vegetable and flower gardens, but gaining in popularity are parks for toddlers with sandboxes, tricycle freeways, playgrounds equipped with recycled Volkswagens or motorboats, and park areas with barbecues and picnic tables.

Planners agree that some general procedures must be followed in developing mid-city gardens. First, the initiators of the plan must be well organized. Once a site is found (preferably an eyesore that would benefit by its new use), a site-feasibility study must be done. This is similar to the site analysis described in Section 1, but in addition to

the ecological characteristics of the site, the social environment must be analyzed as well. There must be enough interested people living nearby who are willing to work to ensure success. The needs and desires of the community—for a vegetable garden, for park benches, for a play area for children—must be taken into account, and any conflicting needs must be resolved in the plan for the proposed site. (If you are interested in establishing a community garden, you might consider initiating the formation of a neighborhood land trust, a nonprofit organization with tax-exempt status that can acquire property and assets.)

In less urban areas, communal gardening can take place on a larger scale. Citizens concerned with the rapidly deteriorating environment have joined organizations dedicated to preserving and reclaiming areas of natural beauty. Preservation of open space, control of development, beautification of roadsides (controlling billboards and signs) and improved community planning are some of these organizations' goals. For information on what's being done in your area, contact your township office, your watershed association, your local branch of the Environmental Protection Agency or your county extension service.

Organic Disease Protection

A meadow, blooming with Queen-Anne's-lace and asters, may seem an unlikely site for plant diseases; a woodland, soft with the delicate blossoms of mountain laurel, looks impervious to blights or cankers. In fact, native species are subject to many of the same viral, bacterial and fungal infections as are their domesticated relations.

It is a cliché to say that the best protection is prevention, but this is indeed the case. Make all cuttings from healthy plants; use disinfected tools to make cuttings and to plant and transplant; sterilize any soil that is part of the rooting medium. Before choosing native species to transplant, inspect the specimens available to you for signs of disease. Whenever possible, eyeball both top growth and root system.

You will be unable to inspect the root ball if you buy balled-and-burlapped or container-grown plants from a nursery. Since there is no practical way to sterilize the soil supporting an acre of cedars or rhododendrons, nurseries cannot guarantee that such plants will be disease-free. Reputable nurseries, however, will often make a verbal or written agreement to replace a tree or shrub struck down by disease with another like it. Buying such plants, which are often expensive, is an indication to a wise nursery owner that you are serious about landscaping your property. If he wants you as a repeat customer, he will be anxious to provide you with landscaping materials that flourish in your garden—so don't hesitate to ask about the nursery's policy on returns and replacements when you make your purchase.

Finally, in planting seedlings or transplants, be gentle with them. Any wound or bruise to the bark, stem, twig, leaf or petal is a potential entryway for germs, viruses and fungi. Strip off damaged leaves, petals or twigs. Prune wounded trees or shrubs with a sterilized pruner.

Some horticulturists recommend painting the cut with a fungicidal sealing compound, although there is some dispute about the value of wound sealants. There is some evidence that sealants retard the healing process of the tree. Nevertheless, a sealant will prevent water loss through the wound, encourage new branching at the point of the wound and provide a barrier to infection.

Not all viruses, bacteria and fungi are harmful to plants, of course. Associations of fungi and roots (mycorrhizal associations) help many of our evergreens—pines especially—to take up water and nutrients. Nitrogen-fixing bacteria, which can remove nitrogen from the air and share it with the plants whose roots they inhabit, are important to all the legume crops—clovers, soybeans, peas and their ilk.

Both aerobic and anaerobic bacteria are welcome in the compost heap. They are responsible for decaying plant refuse into rich humus.

Just as there are beneficial garden insects, natural enemies of plant pests, so are there beneficial viruses, bacteria and fungi that help to keep plants healthy. *Bacillus thuringiensis* has been approved by the USDA for use as a microbial insecticide. It does not harm man, animals or plants but has a devastating effect on the grub stage of many harmful insects, like Japanese beetles. Research into other microbial pest and disease controls shows promising results as well.

The viruses, bacteria and fungi that produce disease are pathogens. Bacteria and fungi that require a living host are parasitic; those that can survive by consuming dead organic matter—plant husks, shells, cobs and so on—are saprophytic. The microbes that heat up a compost heap, decaying plant refuse and producing rich, well-aerated humus, fall into this latter category.

Viruses require a living host in order to multiply. However, they can be transmitted when they are in an inactive state in a number of ways. Aphids, leafhoppers, mealybugs and whiteflies may carry pathogenic virus infections from plant to plant. Using infected tools can do the trick, as can making plantings in infested soil.

Pathogenic viruses, which are so small they cannot be seen without the aid of an electron microscope, can strike any part of a plant. Symptoms may include mottled, yellowed or spotted leaves, leaf curling, dwarfing or excessive branching.

Once a virus has infected a plant, the plant is doomed. Remove it and destroy it. Direct your attention toward the control of the plant pests that act as carriers, if you want to prevent the virus from striking in your garden again.

Bacteria are one-celled plants that live off other animals or plants, either living or dead. Some bacteria that thrive in the tissue of a living plant (as parasites) can overwinter in husks, stalks, shells or other plant refuse (as saprophytes).

Bacteria move by means of tiny hairs or flagella. They cannot move themselves very far, but rainwater, stream water or soil particles can carry them to new sites. They can enter plants most easily through wounded or bruised plant tissue, but healthy stem and leaf tissue is not impenetrable to them. Once inside the plant, they move by swimming in the tides of sap.

Bacterial diseases are often readily identifiable. Rots dissolve leaf, stem and branch tissue, turning them into a soft, smelly slime. Wilts occur when pathogenic bacteria block the transport of nutrients, water and oxygen to all parts of the plant. Galls occur when some parts of the plant are overstimulated to produce new tissue as a result of interference with the plant's vascular system.

Bacterial diseases can most easily gain a foothold in warm, wet soil and a humid atmosphere. An imbalance in a plant's diet can make it more susceptible to these pathogenic microbes. Too much nitrogen, for example, encourages bacterial wilts. Avoid this problem by using fertilizers that release their nutrients to the soil slowly and gently over a season or more.

When a bacterial disease strikes, there is little you can do but remove and destroy the affected plants to prevent the contagion from spreading. If you were growing vegetables, you could try crop rotation; growing native species, however, you may simply have to stop growing an affected plant family for three or four years until the bacteria that may be present in the soil die from lack of food. Removing plant refuse at the end of the season may also help defeat bacteria that overwinter.

Fungi also cause a large number of plant diseases. Powdery mildew, rust, leaf spot, gray mold and damping-off are all attributable to the work of parasitic fungi. Some of these diseases are not really damaging to plants; others can be fatal. If you can live with the looks of powdery mildew on your phloxes, or leaf spot on your mountain laurel, there's no necessity for you to remove the diseased plants from the garden. Other fungal diseases require corrective measures.

Another set of diseases may strike in a garden where soil and atmospheric conditions are less than ideal. Dieback, leaf scorch, hollow heart and sunscald may lead you to the conclusion that your plants are under microbial attack, when in fact the environment is the culprit. A soil on which chemically treated plants have been grown can be purged of pesticides and herbicides by mixing 300 pounds of activated charcoal into each acre of soil. Chemical-supply houses can provide activated charcoal in this quantity. If the quality of the air is in question, as it sometimes is in the city, there is little you can do except to grow varieties that have shown themselves to be hardy under urban conditions.

Healthy plants, just like healthy people, are resistant to disease and stress. Keeping a plant healthy is a matter of supplying it with sufficient nutrients, soil in good tilth and the amount of water, humidity and sunshine it needs to thrive. As has been said before, knowing your plant's identity, characteristics and preferred habitat will improve your chances of growing it successfully in your natural landscape.

Organic Pest Protection

Lack of diversity in a man-made landscape is responsible for lack of diversity in the insect population. Just as intensive single-crop agriculture creates an unstable condition by giving up its natural controls, the simplification of natural landscapes makes them dangerously prone to insects, disease and the loss of valuable wildlife. Thus, a few species of insects attracted to a concentration of particular plants can increase their numbers to epidemic proportion, creating havoc in the garden. A naturally diverse group of plants, on the other hand, supports many insect species, including the predators that provide natural checks on unwanted pests.

Plant-feeding insects are labeled pests if their diets include plants of economic or aesthetic importance. In nature, a balance exists between plant pests and their natural enemies. To provide this balance in your natural landscape, you must consciously plant associations, rather than individual species, of native plants in their correct habitat. By using a generous blend of native plants to create canopy, understory and ground cover, you will provide the food and shelter needed to attract beneficial birds, insects and wildlife. Thus, your landscape will be not only aesthetically pleasing but practical as well.

To protect your natural landscape, you might take these preventive measures:

- Select resistant varieties of forbs and grasses, trees and shrubs
- Schedule your plantings against insect emergence times
- Keep back weeds
- Clean up plant residues
- Use companion planting
- Cultivate in spring and fall to eliminate overwintering insects

Establishing vigorous plants by fertilizing and watering is important, since most pests are more easily controlled on healthy plants but are very destructive to those that are weak, dry or malnourished. Also, vigorous plants can tolerate minor insect damage while weak plants are more apt to be overwhelmed by pests.

Unfortunately, no matter how thorough you are about landscape maintenance, you may still encounter pests in the garden. There are a number of ways you can address the problem. You *can* rush out and buy the latest chemical spray. This will have a detrimental effect on your soil and may poison some wildlife. At the very least, it will kill off not only your insect pests but their natural enemies as well.

A safer and more effective solution is to let the natural system work for you. Organic pest control is a three-pronged system of biological controls, physical controls and the use of repellents and poisons. A successful pest-control program for your landscape will involve an integration of all three.

Biological control involves the use of parasites, predators and pathogens; it is based on the idea of using living organisms to reduce the number of destructive insects and other pests. Many organisms contribute to this effort: bacteria and fungi, predatory and parasitic insects, birds, frogs, salamanders, toads, moles, shrews, skunks and others. Insect predators and parasites such as lady beetles, trichogramma wasps, praying mantises and lacewings are highly valued for their beneficial effects and can be purchased for introduction into your landscape. It is usually preferable, however, to encourage the residents that you already have

rather than importing insects. The table on the next page mentions some organisms that are particularly useful against specific pests.

Physical controls can involve such techniques as handpicking pests or placing collars around plants. These types of methods are particularly well suited to the scale of the homeowner, who may have to deal with minor infestations in a single tree or small garden plot.

Repellents and poisons are usually employed for more serious infestations. Natural derivatives such as pyrethrum or rotenone are only suggested for extreme cases. Milder solutions like soapy-water sprays or dusts of diatomaceous earth can also be quite effective.

One of the best control methods—because it involves no poison spray, requires little work for the gardener and brings additional bonuses in enjoyment—is to invite birds to stay in your garden. Birds eat 100 or more insects a day and will help you weed your garden by finding and consuming weed seeds before they sprout. The key to attracting such good guests is knowing how to plan your landscape with wildlife in mind.

Inviting Wildlife into Your Natural Landscape

If you want to bring wildlife to your landscape, you must provide food, water, cover and reproductive areas. To do this, you must first evaluate what vegetation you have on your property. If you have a new lot, you can incorporate some basic principles of wildlife management into your landscape plan. If your lot is already established, there are a number of ways it can be modified to make it more attractive to wildlife.

The key to a successful wildlife planting plan is variety. Offer a wide selection of vegetative species that will give your yard a good blend of closed and open spaces and will create a practical combination of plant sizes. Choose your species carefully and look for multipurpose types that can provide both food and cover. By doing this, you will be creating a vast number of animal niches, the special combination of physical requirements that are unique to every creature. The more niches you can make, the more wild residents and visitors you can expect.

Landscape Pest Primer

Areas	Pest	Species Affected	Symptoms
Trees & Shrubs	Cankerworms	Many species, common in apple and cherry trees	Defoliation; holes in leaves; presence of silken threads
	Codling moth	Fruit trees, especially apple and pear	Tunnels through fruit; cocoons in bark crevices
	Gypsy moth	Many species	Defoliation; large masses of feeding caterpillars present
	Tent caterpillar	Many deciduous trees and shrubs; favor cherry and apple trees	Defoliation; large silken nests in forks of branches
	Carpenter worm	Locust, ash, oak, maple	Large wounds on trunks and branches
	Flat-headed borer	Many deciduous trees and shrubs, orchard trees	Stunted growth; sawdust material exuding from holes in bark; look for brown, black metallic beetles in summer, stains on bark
	Twig-girdlers (group)	Many species	Irregularly broken branches hanging from trees in late summer, fall or winter
	Aphids	Virtually all species	Sticky, honeydew substance on leaves; mold spots; sometimes cottony masses on trunk and twigs
	Lacebug	Broad-leaved evergreens, sycamore, basswood, hawthorn, cherry, white oak	White or yellow spots on leaves; molasseslike drops on underside of leaves
	Scale	Many species	Some leave honeydew secretions on foliage, twigs, branches; black fungus; small shell-like lumps on branches and trunk
	Gall insect	Many species	Small bulblike swellings on leaves, twigs and branches
	Mites	Many species	Leaves turn yellow and die; webbing at base of leaves
	White pine weevil	Pine	Terminal shoots wither and die; forked, crooked trunk; drops of resin on bark
	Spruce budworm	Fir trees	Webs holding needles together
	Bagworm	Evergreens	Baglike nests hanging from branches
	Dogwood borer	Dogwood	Swollen, gall-like areas on lower trunk
	Hickory bark beetle	Hickory	Girdled branches; dead foliage; small round holes in bark

Biological Control	Other Controls
Fall species—spray *Bacillus thuringiensis* in April or May; spring species—trichogramma wasps	Place sticky material such as tanglefoot around trunk
Woodpeckers, braconid wasps, trichogramma wasps	In spring wrap trunk with corrugated paper, then in September remove and burn; scrape larvae off bark in spring; spray with dormant oil solution when pest is in egg stage
Trichogramma wasps, white-footed mice, tachinid flies, predaceous ground beetles, *Bacillus thuringiensis*	Wrap burlap around trunk, folding over the top to form shelter; crush caterpillars or shake into container of water topped with kerosene; scrape off and destroy egg clusters
Baltimore orioles, digger wasps, *Bacillus thuringiensis*	Tear out nests with pole and destroy; in winter cut off infested twigs; scrape off egg bands and destroy; attract adult moths with light traps
	Remove and destroy infested branches; dress and paint over all wounds; attract adult moths with light trap
Woodpeckers, crows, wasps, predatory beetles, vireos	Wrap strips of burlap, sticky paper or corrugated cardboard around trunk; prune to remove injured or weak branches; burn infested branches; probe holes with wire
Bug-eating birds, especially fall tree dwellers	Rake up and burn infested branches late in fall
Lacewings, lady beetles, syrphid flies	Spray with the following solution: heat 1 gallon of water mixed with ½ pound hard soap; add to 2 gallons of boiling kerosene; churn with force pump and spray nozzle for 5–10 minutes; to use, dilute 1 part of this emulsion with 9 parts of cold water
	Spray or dust with nicotine or pyrethrum
	Some types of trees can be treated with a petroleum oil spray. CAUTION: not all trees are tolerant to this spray and can be damaged; scrape pests from branches and trunk
	Little can be done, but they usually do not cause any significant damage
Ladybugs, lacewings	Wash tree with spray from garden hose
	Remove infested tips well below dead portions and destroy; plant in shade; select varieties with thicker bark and wider trunk diameter
Birds, red squirrels, spiders, trichogramma wasps, *Bacillus thuringiensis*	Cut off and destroy infested tips
	Pick bags during winter and destroy; handpick caterpillars
	Wrap young trees with kraft paper until well established (2 years); prune deadwood; paint tree wounds with shellac; fertilize and water
	Cut off and burn affected areas; attacks mainly weak trees, so fertilize and water to maintain vigor

(continued next page)

Landscape Pest Primer—*Continued*

Areas	Pest	Species Affected	Symptoms
Lawn	Chinch bug	Lawn	Small spots of yellowing grass; large irregular dead patches; odor
	White grubs (larvae of June beetles, chafer, Japanese beetle, Asiatic garden beetle	Lawn	Brown patches of dead grass that can be rolled back like a carpet
	Cutworm	Lawn	Grass blades cut off at base leaving small, elongated or irregular closely cropped brown spots
	Nematode	Lawn	Lawn appears off-color, yellow, bunchy and stunted; grass blades dying back from tips; wilted and dead in irregular areas
	Sod webworm	Lawn	Irregular brown patches; grass dies back from shoot; worm can be seen when sod is lifted
Garden	Aphid	Most garden plants	Honeydew deposits; black mold
	Blister beetle	Many vegetables and flowers	Insect can be seen on plant; defoliation; damaged fruit
	Cabbage worm	Cabbage, cauliflower and related plants, flowers	Chews large holes in outer leaves, leaving behind green excrement
	Colorado potato beetle	Flowers	Insect can be seen on plants; defoliation
	Cucumber beetle	Fruit trees and flowers	Holes in leaves, flowers and fruits; wilting
	Cutworm	Most garden plants	Defoliation; stems cut off at ground level or several inches below
	Grasshopper	Most vegetable crops, grains	Plants defoliated during dry periods
	Flea beetle	A number of vegetables and flowers	Leaves riddled with tiny shot holes gnawed from underside
	Japanese beetle	Most garden plants	Leaves look like a leafy skeleton
	Nematode	Virtually all garden plants	Malformed flowers, leaves, stems, roots; dwarfed plants; dieback; galls
	Slug and snail	Variety of garden plants	Silvery mucous trails; holes scraped in foliage
	Squash bug	Vine crops	Wilted, crisp leaves; egg masses beneath leaves
	Stink bug	Some flowers, vegetables and fruits	Malformed tomatoes, wartlike growths on bean pods; pitted fruits
	Thrips	Many flowers and fruits	Blossoms appear stained with dark streaks; leaves twisted and discolored; pitted fruit
	Whitefly	Many garden plants	Fruits stunted; foliage yellows and dies; sticky honeydew; black fungus; large numbers of insects on underside of leaves

Biological Control	Other Controls
Big-eyed bugs	Shade lawn with trees and shrubs; seed lawn in soil made up of $1/3$ sharp builder's sand, $1/3$ crushed rock and $1/3$ compost; fertilize and water
Wild birds, domestic geese and ducks, milky spore disease, moles	Rake off loose turf and turn over the soil under it; continue to turn it up every few days until fall; fertilize and water; remove any fallen fruit
	Flood lawn with water until puddled; collect worms and destroy
Fungi	Keep grass growing vigorously through proper watering and fertilizing
Milky spore disease	
Ladybugs, lacewings, syrphids, flies, spiders, assassin bugs, braconid wasps	Dust with diatomaceous earth; place aluminum foil on ground under young plants; grow nasturtiums between vegetable rows; use soapy spray and rinse
	Wearing gloves, you can handpick and destroy; dust with rotenone
Bacillus thuringiensis, trichogramma wasps	Handpick caterpillars and crush egg masses; cover seedlings with netting; dispose of garden trash
Ground beetles	Mulch well with a 1-foot layer of clean hay or straw; apply rotenone if necessary; grow potatoes on top of ground; handpick adult, crush eggs
Tachinid fly	Rotenone or pyrethrum for serious infestations; heavy mulching, late planting
Bacillus thuringiensis, meadow larks, toads, moles, shrews, parasitic wasps	Border garden with sunflowers; scatter crushed eggshells at plant bases; put down chicken manure and a mulch of oak leaves; place a cardboard collar around young plants; tie stems of wild onions around vegetables pushed 1 inch below soil
Ground squirrels, field mice, birds, snakes, toads	Fall tillage, right after harvest; spray with hot pepper, soap and water; trap in mason jars partly filled with molasses and water buried in garden
	Dust with diatomaceous earth; spray foliage with a garlic or onion infusion; good garden sanitation
Milky spore disease, parasitic wasps, starlings	Handpick and drop in can with some kerosene; spade soil deeply in spring; rotenone spray
Fungi (supplement soil with organic matter to develop)	Rotate with immune or resistant crops; interplant marigolds; for small areas, sterilize soil
Garter snakes, lightning bugs, box turtles, salamanders	Set out saucers or jar lids of stale beer; handpick and destroy; dust with diatomaceous earth
	Good garden sanitation, rotate crops; handpick insects and crush egg masses
	Weed control; handpick and destroy; dust with sabadilla
	Tobacco dust; diatomaceous earth; promptly remove infested flowers and buds
	Spray leaf surfaces with tobacco tea or ryania solution; repeat several times

A natural landscape is a landscape that is attractive to birds and wildlife. It has a diversity of plantings that provide food and shelter year-round, that mix tall trees with low shrubs and that provide a blend of open and closed spaces. As you plan and plant your landscape, try to achieve the necessary diversity, but once the plants are established, back off and let them develop naturally. As they develop, they'll bring birds and insects and wild creatures to your landscape.

If you are planting a new lot, follow these practical tips:

• Frame your yard by providing a backdrop of species that will grow into large trees (30 feet and over). This will become your forest canopy and will create nesting sites, protective cover and food for small mammals and birds.

• Create an understory by planting small flowering trees near the tall trees. These should be massed in small groups and also planted at various other points on the perimeter of your lot. Not only will you be adding an important source of food for songbirds, but the flowers will draw butterflies and other useful insects.

• Flank small trees with a mixture of tall and low shrubs, thick herbaceous growth or brambles. This ground cover will provide homes for small mammals and some birds and is a ready escape area for ground-feeding creatures.

• Select plants that will provide a year-round food supply, as well as being adapted to your yard's soil, moisture and light conditions.

• Create foundation plantings of low herbaceous growth and shrubs around your home. Be sure to select shrubs that will not obstruct your view when they mature.

• Provide a constant supply of water. To draw the most wildlife, a small pond large enough to support vegetation is recommended. This can bring such creatures as raccoons, turtles, frogs and ducks to your yard and will become a focal point of activity.

If you are converting an established lot into a natural landscape, make these simple adjustments to attract wildlife:

Sawing up fallen trees and cleaning up other natural forest debris may make it easier for you to move through your landscape, but these actions won't help you attract wildlife. A fallen tree provides natural shelter for many woodland critters, shelter you can supplement with prunings that must be taken for one reason or another. You can save yourself a lot of work, and help attract wildlife to your landscape in the bargain, by letting nature maintain your landscape.

• Surround or interrupt your lawn with small groupings of trees and shrubs.

• Plant small shrubs and low herbaceous growth around solitary trees.

• Let leaf litter stay under your deciduous trees. Insects that come to feed on them will make mealtime fare for insect-eating ground-feeders.

• Don't prune shrubs at ground level. This is where cover is most critical. Create a rock pile or rambling stone wall. This is especially inviting to small mammals and reptiles.

• If ground cover is scarce, build some brush piles. To build, heap brush over rocks, stumps or logs. Be sure to keep the pile loose to prevent matting and to allow native vegetation to grow.

• As long as they pose no safety hazard, save dead trees. Though they may seem ugly, they provide food, homes and viewing perches for a wide variety of mammals and birds.

• Put out a birdbath as well as a supply of water at ground level. You can use such common materials as clay saucers or inverted trash-can lids.

• Supply materials to encourage nest building on your property. Don't try to keep your yard immaculate. By leaving such things as feathers, bark, grass clippings, moss and fur bits, you are supplying birds with a valuable source of nesting materials.

• Allow fence rows to develop naturally.

The National Wildlife Federation suggests the combinations of foundation, understory and canopy plants listed in the table, "Plant Associations That Attract Wildlife." In studying the table, keep in mind that these recommendations are very general.

Your soil tests and site analysis will allow you to choose the plants from among those listed that are best suited to your landscape design.

Don't expect hoards of wildlife overnight. Your newly created habitat will take from 30 to 40 years to fully mature, but if you follow the simple steps mentioned, you can expect to see birds such as robins and ground-feeding sparrows once your planting is complete. And you have a lot to look forward to. Within 5 to 10 years, shrubs and small trees will have become large enough to bear flowers and fruit that will attract additional birds and insects. This new growth will provide nesting sites for birds and cover for small mammals such as chipmunks and rabbits.

A good way to provide more shelter for wildlife, especially if your plantings are young, is to construct birdhouses. But building a birdhouse involves careful consideration. Many birds have individual and very strict specifications for their adopted homes. Size and placement of the home and the dimension of the entrance hole are all crucial. Attention to detail is the key to success here.

When your natural landscape is established and thriving, you will enjoy the variety of birds that will come to nest and feed there. Many of

Plant Associations That Attract Wildlife

Region	Herbaceous Growth	Low Shrubs	Tall Shrubs	Small Trees	Tall Trees
Northeast	Panic grass Timothy Sunflower	Blackberry Blueberry Huckleberry Snowberry	Sumac Dogwood Elderberry Winterberry Autumn olive Wisteria	Flowering dogwood Crab apple Hawthorn Cherry Serviceberry Red cedar	(Coniferous) White pine Hemlock Colorado spruce (Deciduous) Sugar maple White oak Red oak Beech Birch
Southeast	*Lespedeya* spp. Panic grass Sunflower	Blackberry Blueberry Bayberry Spicebush Huckleberry	Sumac Dogwood Elderberry	Holly Dogwood Serviceberry Cherry Persimmon Red cedar Palmetto Hawthorn Crab apple	(Coniferous) Longleaf pine Loblolly pine Shortleaf pine (Deciduous) Ash Beech Walnut Live oak Southern red oak Black gum Pecan Hackberry
Northwest	Turkey mullein Timothy Sunflower Filaree Lupine Fiddlenecks Tarweed	Blackberry Blueberry Snowberry Oregon grape	Sumac Bitterbrush Russian olive Elderberry Buckthorn Madrone	Serviceberry Dogwood Hawthorn	(Coniferous) Douglas fir Ponderosa pine Western white pine Lodgepole pine Colorado spruce (Deciduous) Oregon white oak California black oak Big-leaf maple
Southwest	Turkey mullein Sunflower Filaree Lupine Fiddlenecks	Utah juniper Blackberry Spicebush Prickly pear Algerita	Mulberry Lote bush Sumac Manzanita Madrone	Serviceberry Dogwood Mesquite Crab apple	(Coniferous) Arizona cypress Pinyon pine (Deciduous) Live oak Pine oak Bitter cherry

these birds will return the favor you have done them in providing food and cover by operating as very efficient pest controllers. The table, "A Gardener's Avian Friends," lists some of these beneficial birds and the insects on which they prey.

TIPS ON CONTROLLING UNWANTED GUESTS

Supplying attractive food and cover plants may bring you some unwanted avian guests, as well.

Blue jays, crows, starlings and house sparrows— "weed" birds—can often take over birding areas, intimidating and even driving away more desirable species. These birds become "squatters" in other nests and may peck through eggs or at fledgelings. By gang feeding, starlings and house sparrows scare more timid visitors away. In addition, the loud clucks and calls of these unwanted intruders may seem unwelcome noise to those of us who delight in the gentle chirping of songbirds. There are, fortunately, some safe and simple ways of encouraging these birds to leave:

Build a Better Birdhouse

Species	Floor of Cavity in Inches	Depth of Cavity in Inches	Entrance above Floor in Inches	Diameter of Entrance in Inches	Height above Ground in Feet	Color	Location	Success Quotient		
								City	Suburbs	Country
Bluebird	5 × 5	8	6	1½	5–10	Light brown, tan	Post, open sun	Poor	Fair	Excellent
Chickadee	4 × 4	8–10	6	1⅛	6–15	Light brown, tan	Post, 40–60% sun	Good	Good	Excellent
Titmouse	4 × 4	8–10	6–8	1¼	6–15	Light brown, tan	Post, sun or shade	Fair	Fair to good	Excellent
Nuthatch	4 × 4	8–10	6–8	1¼	12–20	Light brown, tan	Tree limb	Poor	Poor	Fair
House wren	4 × 4	6–8	1–6	1	6–10	White or light brown, tan	Post or limb, 60% sun	Good	Excellent	Excellent
Bewick's wren	4 × 4	6–8	1–6	1¼	6–10	Light brown, tan	Post, 50% sun	Fair	Good	Excellent
Carolina wren	4 × 4	6–8	1–6	1½	6–10	Light brown, tan	Post, sun or shade	Poor	Fair	Good
Violet-green swallow	5 × 5	6	1–5	1½	10–15	Light brown, tan, gray	Post, 50–100% sun	Poor to fair	Fair to good	Good to excellent
Tree swallow	5 × 5	6	1 5	1½	10–15	Light brown, tan, gray	Post, 50–100% sun	Poor to fair	Fair to good	Good to excellent
Purple martin	6 × 6	6	1	2½	15–20	White	Post in open area	Poor to fair	Poor to good	Fair to excellent
Phoebe	6 × 6	6	1	Leave 1 or more sides open	8–12	Natural wood	Side of building	Poor	Fair	Fair
Flicker	7 × 7	16–18	14–16	2½	6–20	Light brown, tan	Post	Fair	Good	Good

A Gardener's Avian Friends

Region	Bird	Time of Year Present	Pests Eaten	Some Native Plants for Food and/or Shelter
Northeast	Rufous-sided towhee	All year	Beetles, moths, caterpillars, grasshoppers	Dogwood, oak, huckleberry, wild blackberry
	Downy woodpecker	All year	Wood-boring larvae of beetles, moths, adult beetles and ants	Various oak varieties, hop hornbeam, dogwood
	Slate-colored junco	Summer in northern states, winter in southern states	Caterpillars, beetles, ants, other insects	Sumac, pine, native grasses, weeds
	Black-capped chickadee	All year	Eggs of moths and plant lice, caterpillars, flies, leaf-hoppers, treehoppers	Pine, hemlock, birch
	Evening grosbeak	Winter	Some beetles, caterpillars	Maple, dogwood, wild cherry
	White-breasted nuthatch	All year	Beetles, weevils, ants	Oak, pine
	American goldfinch	All year	Some aphids and caterpillars	Balsam fir, spruce, pine, garden flowers
Midwest	Yellow-shafted flicker	All year	Ants, beetles, caterpillars, other insects	Oak, dogwood, native fruit bearers
	Mockingbird	All year	Beetles, ants, bees, wasps, grasshoppers	Dogwood, cedar, hackberry, hawthorn
	Brown thrasher	All year	Beetles	Dogwood, oak, hawthorn
	Robin	All year	Caterpillars, beetles, sowbugs, termites	Dogwood, huckleberry, hawthorn
	American goldfinch	All year	Some aphids, caterpillars	Native garden flowers, weeds, grasses, conifers
	Slate-colored junco	Winter	Caterpillars, beetles, ants, other insects	Native grasses, weeds
	Eastern bluebird	All year	Ground beetles, weevils, caterpillars, sowbugs, other insects	Dogwood, hackberry
Northwest	Red-shafted flicker	All year	Ants, beetles, grasshoppers, crickets	Oak, grape, elderberry
	Steller's jay	All year	Wasps, beetles, grasshoppers	Oak, elderberry, raspberry
	Robin	All year— more common in summer	Caterpillars, beetles, sowbugs, termites	Raspberry, grape, dogwood
	Evening grosbeak	All year	Some beetles, caterpillars	Dogwood, cedar, hemlock
	Pine siskin	All year	Caterpillars, aphids, true bugs and fly larvae	Pine, weeds
	White-breasted nuthatch	All year	Beetles, weevils, ants, moths, caterpillars	Oak, pine
	American goldfinch	All year	Some aphids and caterpillars	Filaree, oak, native grasses, weeds
Southeast	Red-bellied woodpecker	All year	Beetles, ants, caterpillars, true bugs	Pine, oak
	Eastern bluebird	All year	Ground beetles, weevils, caterpillars, sowbugs, other insects	Native fruit bearers

A Gardener's Avian Friends—*Continued*

Region	Bird	Time of Year Present	Pests Eaten	Some Native Plants for Food and/or Shelter
	Cardinal	All year	Caterpillars, grasshoppers, true bugs, beetles	Native fruit bearers, grasses
	Slate-colored junco	Winter	Caterpillars, beetles, ants, other insects	Grasses, pine, weeds
	Robin	All year	Caterpillars, beetles, sowbugs, termites	Black gum, native fruit bearers
	White-breasted nuthatch	All year	Beetles, weevils, ants, moths caterpillars	Oak, pine
	Tufted titmouse	All year	Caterpillars, wasps	Oak
Southwest	Downy woodpecker	All year	Adult beetles, wood-boring larvae of beetles and moths, snails, aphids, scales	Large shade trees, pine, other evergreens
	Bewick's wren	All year	Great variety of insects including weevils	Native underbrush, thickets, pinyon, juniper
	Mockingbird	All year	Beetles, ants, bees, wasps, grasshoppers	Native underbrush, hackberry, elderberry, honeysuckle
	Lesser goldfinch	All year in southern states, summer in northern states	Some caterpillars, aphids	Native grasses and weeds, filaree, sunflower
	Bullock's oriole	Summer	Caterpillars, beetles, ants, wasps	Shade trees such as oak, dogwood, elderberry
	Rufous-sided towhee	All year	Beetles, moths, caterpillars, grasshoppers, bees, wasps	Native underbrush and weeds, oak, native fruit bearers
	Chipping sparrow	All year in southern states, summer in northern states	Grasshoppers, caterpillars, beetles, leafhoppers, true bugs, ants, wasps	Filaree, native grasses and weeds, evergreens

• Remove perches from your birdhouses. The natives don't really need them, and this will prevent the pest birds from intimidating your tenants in their homes.

• Scatter bread crumbs on the ground to lure pest birds from your plantings. These birds prefer to feed off the ground, and this will ensure a supply of more valuable food for other birds.

• Try constructing an artificial owl. This is quite effective in driving starlings and sparrows away. Even though the likeness is immobile, birds respond to the size and shape as if the threat were real.

• To drive away starlings that have already taken up residence in your trees, tie ropes to the branches below the nests and shake them. After a few such sessions, the birds should seek more stable territory.

Of course, birds are not the only creatures that will be drawn to your natural landscape. You may expect visits from other wildlife as well. Because of the services they perform in keeping your soil and plants healthy, you will want to encourage some of these guests; others, who may be a little too hungry or too friendly, you will want to dissuade from stopping in. The table, "Critters in Your Landscape," presents reasons and methods for encouraging or discouraging the social calls of wild creatures.

Sometimes it may be your own family cat that is wreaking havoc in your wildlife area. You can't fault him for his natural instincts, but you

Critters in Your Landscape

Mammal	Region Inhabited	Likelihood			How to Encourage a Visit
		City	Suburbs	Country	
Mole	Throughout most of U.S. except mountain-desert regions and arid western plains	Unlikely	Likely	Common	Grow grasses and develop meadow areas
Shrew	Widespread throughout U.S.	Unlikely	Likely	Common—more likely near fields and wooded areas	Provide rock piles for cover; plant pines, hemlock
White-footed mouse (deer mouse)	Throughout U.S.	Unlikely	Likely	Common	Build stone piles and walls; develop hedgerows and low brush cover
Meadow mouse (vole)	Throughout U.S.	Unlikely	Likely	Common	Considered a pest
Chipmunk	Present in most of U.S. except for dry regions, prairies and extreme southern portions	Likely	Likely	Common	Build stone piles and/or walls; develop hedgerows and low brush cover; plant nut- and fruit-bearing trees such as maple, oak or cherry
Red squirrel	Present in forested areas of Northwest, Northeast and West	Likely, especially in park areas	Common—more likely near forested areas	Common	Plant cover and food producers such as conifers, hickory, oak, beech, maple, other nut trees, apple trees
Eastern gray squirrel	Eastern half of U.S.	Common	Common	Common	Plant nut-producing trees such as oak, walnut, hickory and beech; develop hedgerows and windbreaks; leave dead trees
Cottontail rabbit	Various species occur throughout U.S.	Unlikely	Likely	Common	Provide plenty of brushy cover such as shrub thickets; develop fence rows; build brush piles; plant clover and grasses, legume stands; plant conifer clumps
Common skunk (striped skunk)	Throughout most of U.S. except some parts of the Coastal Plain	Unlikely	Likely	Common—more likely near agricultural or wooded areas	Develop hedgerow and shelterbelt areas; provide adequate, dense cover for this usually nocturnal guest
Raccoon	Throughout U.S. except the northern Rockies and drier portions of the Great Basin	Unlikely	Unlikely unless near large wooded or agricultural area	Likely near wooded areas	Develop hedgerows and low dense cover; put out sweet corn or grow corn for wildlife
Opossum	Eastern half of U.S. excluding northern New England; also on west coast	Unlikely	Possibly near wooded area	Common near wooded area	Plant fruit- and nut-bearing trees; provide ground cover; develop hedgerows

Advantages	Disadvantages	Controls
Eats grubs and many harmful insects in adult and larvae stages; aerates and tills soil	Creates mounds and ridgelike humps on lawn areas; may cause damage to root crops and flower bulbs	Intersperse garden plants with caster beans; apply a heavy mulch around garden crops
Eats large amounts of insects for its body-weight, including larvae and adults of beetles and caterpillars; also will eat mice and supplement diet with seeds from cones	May eat some garden crops, fruits	Place vine fruits in half of a plastic jug cut lengthwise, put a hole in each tray for water to run out (shrews don't like to climb in jugs)
Eats large amounts of grasshoppers, beetles, moths and other insects; important food for predators	Can enter dwellings and cause damage	Trap; seal all entrances to home
Important food for predators	Girdles trees; eats garden crops; can enter dwellings and cause damage	Trap; seal all entrances to home; inter-plant garden plants with caster beans and edge with comfrey
Entertaining to watch; eats small amounts of insects	May cause damage to garden flowers and crops	Screen garden areas and/or protect with wire cloches
Has very entertaining antics; useful tree planter	Can kill young birds, eat eggs; if gains entry to dwelling, can chew on bedding and clothing; may cause structural damage	Seal all entrances to home, especially those under roof overhangs; trap and relocate
Useful planter of nut trees; entertaining and friendly visitor around home	May enter attics	Seal all entrances
Entertaining to watch	Often invades garden crops	Sprinkle crops with blood meal; screen off garden areas, cover vegetables with wire cloches
Useful destroyer of mice, small rodents and insects in both larvae and adult stages	May invade garden crops; may spray if frightened	Screen off garden area; do not attempt to approach
Useful destroyer of mice and insect pests	May enter garden (especially fond of sweet corn)	Fence off garden areas; trap and relocate
Destroys mice and many insects	Can invade garden crops	Fence off garden areas, trap and relocate

(continued next page)

Critters in Your Landscape—*Continued*

Mammal	Region Inhabited	Likelihood			How to Encourage a Visit
		City	Suburbs	Country	
Woodchuck	Northeastern quarter of U.S.	Unlikely	Unlikely	Likely in open agricultural lands	Considered a pest
Muskrat	Throughout most of U.S. except some extreme southern and southwestern portions	Unlikely	Unlikely	Possible near wooded areas with running water, lakes and ponds	Build a pond large enough to encourage a good stand of aquatic vegetation
White-tailed deer	Throughout U.S. except for California and northern portions of the Southwest	Unlikely	Possible	Possible near large wooded areas	Provide bushy cover and low brush such as dogwood, young hemlock and red maple; also viburnum, clover, alfalfa, mountain ash, apple trees; plant windbreaks and hedgerows

can confine him during early morning and evening hours when most birds feed. (If you have supplied all your wildlife visitors with adequate cover, they should be fairly safe from him during the rest of the day.) Many natural-landscape gardeners enjoy taking the first cup of coffee sitting in an easy chair by a picture window and watching the world come alive with the sun. Having your cat curled up beside you is a double comfort: a friendly creature, who has adopted you, close at hand, and curious wild creatures, who've adopted your natural landscape as a second home, just outside.

Choices

A sandstorm shreds a leaf of a desert succulent, and no one picks it off the plant because it is ugly or an entryway for germs. It weakens and falls to the sand. The stem calluses over in the dry air, and tiny new roots form, seeking a home in the desert soil. In time, new leaf growth develops and takes

hold. The shredded leaf withers away altogether, its purpose served by beginning a new plant life even as its own life leaves it.

A tree branch comes down with a crash in the forest, struck by lightning. Its parent plant dies slowly, the wood rotting away over many years. Canopied mushrooms cling to its weakened roots. Bugs infest it. Woodpeckers drill it full of holes, in search of tree ants and other insects. No one thinks to remove it because it could harbor overwintering leaf spot fungi.

Wheat rust ruins acres of prairie grass, spreading to the very edges of the habitat. The grasses die, and the prairie withers until seeds of hardier grasses are blown across it by the wind.

In the wild, the tree seedlings that invade a meadow grow up in time and draw birds and squirrels instead of field mice. The leaves that fall to the woods floor are left where they fall, and whether or not they harbor hosts of leaf-eating

Advantages	Disadvantages	Controls
Burrows protect rabbits in winter; holes allow water to enter soil	Invades garden crops	Construct electric fences around gardens
Entertaining to watch; helps control aquatic plants	Can cause structural damage to man-made ponds requiring the practice of regular checks and maintenance	Trap
Entertaining to watch	Can cause orchard and garden crop damage (deer especially relish apples)	Attach pieces of human hair to garden and orchard areas; construct fencing

insects, they decompose into a rich, fine humus just right for wild flowers.

There is no human caretaker in nature's garden and none needed. Events happen on a time scale we are too short-lived to appreciate. Nature works, with a seeming intelligence, to foster all life. In planting a landscape, we must make a choice: do we leave the "maintenance tasks" to nature, or do we actively participate in the process? We *can* step out of the picture entirely. Or we can try to do what so many others have done before us and force our will on the land, with plenty of money and time and effort to back us—growing a green lawn in the low desert.

Perhaps there is a natural role for us to play, too—one in which we neither absolve ourselves from any responsibility for our natural landscape nor attempt to control it according to some rigid plan. We can use our intelligence to decide whether to clear a woodland of debris to prevent disease or leave branches where they fall as a cover for wildlife. We can learn to recognize which leaf-spot diseases are dangerous to the life of our plants and live with the looks of others.

Nature is superb at making accommodation for change—or you would not be able to establish a natural landscape in your backyard, no matter how careful you were in attempting to create the proper habitat. If we take Nature as a teacher, we will accept some of the "ills" that befall our natural landscape without attempting to correct them, and we will use our intelligence to recognize situations that require action in order to support the continued life and health of our plants—and ourselves. If the rotting tree harbors a hive of wasps and your child is allergic to the poison, destroy the hive and take down the tree. Your natural landscape is strong enough to make some accommodations for you, too.

Bibliography

Adams, LeRoy. *Illustrated Flora of the Pacific States.* Vol. 1, Ferns to Birthworts, 1923; Vol. 2, Buckwheats to Kramerias, 1944; Vol. 3, Geraniums to Figworts, 1951; Vol. 4, Bignonias to Sunflowers, 1960. Stanford, Calif.: Stanford University Press.

Aiken, George D. *Pioneering with Wildflowers.* Taftsville, Vt.: Countryman Press, 1978.

Andersen, Robert N. *Germination and Establishment of Weeds for Experimental Purposes.* Weed Science Society of America, 113 N. Neil St., Champaign, Illinois 61820, 1969.

Appalachian Mountain Club. *Mountain Flowers of New England.* Boston: Appalachian Mountain Club, 1977.

Barlow, Elizabeth. *The Forests and Wetlands of New York City.* Boston: Little, Brown & Co., 1971.

Barrington, Rupert. *A Garden for Your Birds.* New York: Grosset & Dunlap, 1972.

Birdseye, Clarence, and Birdseye, Eleanor G. *Growing Woodland Plants.* New York: Dover Publications, 1972.

Brady, Nyle C. *The Nature and Properties of Soils.* 8th ed. New York: Macmillan Publishing Co., 1974.

Brainerd, John W. *Working with Nature: A Practical Guide.* New York: Oxford University Press, 1973.

Braun, E. L. *Deciduous Forests of Eastern North America.* 1950. Reprint. New York: Hafner Press, 1967.

Briggs, Shirley A. *Landscaping for Birds.* Washington, D.C.: Audubon Naturalist Society of the Central Atlantic States, Inc., 1973.

Brown, Clair A. *Wildflowers of Louisiana and Adjoining States.* Baton Rouge, La.: Louisiana State University Press, 1972.

Brown, Lance J., and Whiteman, Dorothy E. *Planning and Design: A Workbook for Community Participation.* School of Architecture and Urban Planning, Princeton University, Princeton, New Jersey, 1973.

Brown, Lauren. *Weeds in Winter.* New York: W. W. Norton & Co., 1976.

Bruce, Hal. *How to Grow Wildflowers and Wild Shrubs and Trees in Your Own Garden.* New York: Alfred A. Knopf, 1976.

Carpenter, Philip L., et al. *Plants in the Landscape.* San Francisco: W. H. Freeman & Co., 1975.

Chiara, Joseph. *Site Planning Standards.* New York: McGraw-Hill Book Co., 1978.

Clements, Edith S. *Flowers of Mountain and Plain.* 1926. Reprint. New York: Hafner Press, 1955.

Clements, F. E., and Clements, E. S. *Rocky Mountain Flowers: An Illustrated Guide for Plant-Lovers and Plant-Users.* 3d ed. New York: Hafner Press, 1963.

Cobb, Boughton. *Field Guide to the Ferns and Their Related Families.* Peterson Field Guide Series. Boston: Houghton Mifflin Co., 1977.

Costello, David F. *The Prairie World.* New York: Thomas Y. Crowell Co., 1969.

Craighead, John J., et al. *Field Guide to Rocky Mountain Wildflowers.* Peterson Field Guide Series. Boston: Houghton Mifflin Co., 1974.

Crockett, James, and Allen, O. *Wildflower Gardening.* Time-Life Encyclopedia of Gardening Series. Alexandria, Va.: Time-Life Books, 1977.

Curtis, John. *Vegetation of Wisconsin: An Ordination of Plant Communities.* Madison, Wis.: University of Wisconsin Press, 1959.

Dean, Blanche, et al. *Wildflowers of Alabama and Adjoining States.* University, Ala.: University of Alabama Press, 1973.

Dorman, Caroline. *Flowers Native to the Deep South.* Baton Rouge, La.: Claitors Publishing Division, 1958.

Dowden, Anne O. *Wild Green Things in the City: A Book of Weeds.* New York: Thomas Y. Crowell Co., 1972.

Duncan, Patricia D. *Tallgrass Prairie: The Inland Sea.* Kansas City, Mo.: Lowell Press, 1978.

Duncan, Wilbur H., and Foote, Leonard E. *Wild Flowers of the Southeastern United States.*

Athens, Ga.: University of Georgia Press, 1975.

DuPont, Elizabeth N. *Landscaping with Native Plants in the Mid-Atlantic Region*. Brandywine Conservancy, P.O. Box 141, Chadds Ford, Pennsylvania 19317, 1978.

Edminster, Frank C., and May, Richard M. *Shrub Plantings for Soil Conservation and Wildlife Cover in the Northeast*. Washington, D.C.: U.S. Department of Agriculture, 1951.

Fairbrother, Nan. *The Nature of Landscape Design*. New York: Alfred A. Knopf, 1974.

_____. *New Lives, New Landscapes*. London: The Architectural Press, 1970.

Federal Water Pollution Control Administration. *Water Pollution Aspects of Urban Runoff*. Chicago, Ill.: American Public Works Association, 1969.

Ferguson, Mary, and Saunders, Richard M. *Wildflowers*. New York: Van Nostrand Reinhold Co., 1976.

Fernald, Merrit L., et al. *Edible Wild Plants: Of Eastern North America*. Rev. ed. New York: Harper & Row Pubs., 1958.

Flawn, Peter T. *Environmental Geology: Conservation, Land Use Planning and Resource Management*. New York: Harper & Row Pubs., 1970.

Foster, Ruth S. "Roots: Caring for City Trees." *Technology Review* 79 (no. 8):29-35.

Geiger, Rudolf. *Climate Near the Ground*. 4th ed. Cambridge, Mass.: Harvard University Press, 1965.

Gilkey, Helen. *Handbook of Northwestern Plants*. Corvallis, Ore.: Oregon State University Bookstores, 1973.

Gill, Don, and Bonnett, Penelope. *Nature in the Urban Landscape: A Study of City Ecosystems*. Baltimore, Md.: York Press, 1973.

Gleason, H. A. *New Britton and Brown Illustrated Flora of the Northeastern United States and Adjacent Canada*. 3 vols. Rev. ed. New York: Hafner Press, 1968.

Gleason, Henry A., and Cronquist, Arthur. *The Natural Geography of Plants*. New York: Columbia University Press, 1964.

Graves, Arthur H. *Illustrated Guide to Trees and Shrubs*. New York: Harper & Row Pubs., 1956.

Gray, Asa. *Manual of Botany*. 8th ed. New York:

Van Nostrand Reinhold Co., 1950; corrected printing, 1970.

Greene, Wilhelmina F., and Blomquist, Hugo L. *Flowers of the South: Native and Exotic*. Chapel Hill, N.C.: University of North Carolina Press, 1953.

Gress, Ernest M. *The Grasses of Pennsylvania*. Harrisburg, Pa.: Pennsylvania Department of Agriculture, 1924.

Hanson, A. A. *Grass Varieties in the United States*. U.S. Department of Agriculture Handbook No. 170. Washington, D.C.: U.S. Government Printing Office, 1972.

Haskins, Leslie L. *Wild Flowers of the Pacific Coast*. New York: Dover Publications, 1977.

Heckscher, A. "Nature and the City," *Natural History* 77 (1968):6-10.

Hitchcock, A. S. *Manual of the Grasses of the United States*. 2 vols. 2d ed. New York: Dover Publications, 1971.

Holt, Joseph Bixby. *Man and the Earth*. Englewood Cliffs, N.J.: Prentice-Hall, 1962.

House, Homer D. *Wild Flowers*. New York: Macmillan Publishing Co., 1974.

Hull, Helen S. *Ferns*. 1969. Reprint. New York: Brooklyn Botanic Garden, 1979.

Hull, Helen S., ed. *Gardening with Wildflowers*. 1962. Reprint. New York: Brooklyn Botanic Garden, 1979.

Hunt, Charles B. *Physiography of the U.S.* San Francisco: W. F. Freeman & Co., 1967.

Jaeger, Edmund C. *Desert Wild Flowers*. Rev. ed. Stanford, Calif.: Stanford University Press, 1941.

Justice, William S., and Bell, C. Ritchie. *Wild Flowers of North Carolina*. Chapel Hill, N.C.: University of North Carolina Press, 1968.

Kenfield, Warren G. *Wild Gardener in the Wild Landscape*. New York: Hafner Press, 1972.

Kindilien, Carlin. *Natural Landscaping: An Energy-Saving Alternative*. Lyme, Conn.: Weathervane Books, 1977.

Knobel, Edward. *Field Guide to the Grasses, Sedges, and Bushes of the United States*. New York: Dover Publications, 1977.

Kuchler, A. W. *Potential Natural Vegetation of the U.S.* New York: American Geographical Society, 1964.

Leggett, R. F. *Cities and Geology*. International Series in Earth and Planetary Sciences. New York: McGraw-Hill Book Co., 1973.

Leopold, L. B. *Hydrology for Urban Land Planning: A Guidebook on the Hydrologic Effects of Urban Land Use*. U.S. Geological Survey Circular 554. Washington, D.C.: U.S. Government Printing Office, 1968.

Leopold, Luna B., and Langbein, Walter B. *A Primer on Water*. Washington, D.C.: U.S. Government Printing Office, 1960.

Leveson, David. *Geology and the Urban Environment*. New York: Oxford University Press, 1980.

Lipp, Lewis F., ed. *Propagation*. 1957. Reprint. New York: Brooklyn Botanic Garden, 1980.

Logsdon, Gene. *The Gardener's Guide to Better Soil*. Emmaus, Pa.: Rodale Press, 1975.

Lyman, Benson. *Cacti of Arizona*. 3d ed. Tucson, Ariz.: University of Arizona Press, 1969.

McGourty, Frederick, ed. *The Environment and the Home Gardener*. 1977. Reprint. New York: Brooklyn Botanic Garden, 1980.

——. *Nursery Source Guide*. 1977. Reprint. New York: Brooklyn Botanic Garden, 1979.

McHarg, Ian L. *Design with Nature*. Garden City, N.Y.: Natural History Press, 1971.

Margolin, Malcolm. *The Earth Manual*. Boston: Houghton Mifflin Co., 1975.

Miles, Bebe, and Loeur, Peter. *Wildflowers: Perennials for Your Garden*. New York: Hawthorn Books, 1976.

Munz, Philip A. *California Desert Wildflowers*. Berkeley: University of California Press, 1962.

——. *California Mountain Wildflowers*. Berkeley: University of California Press, 1963.

——. *California Spring Wildflowers: From the Base of the Sierra Nevada and Southern Mountains to the Sea*. Berkeley: University of California Press, 1961.

——. *Flora of Southern California*. Berkeley: University of California Press, 1974.

Natural Vegetation Subcommittee, Plant Resources Division, Soil Conservation Society of America. *Wildflower Seed and Native Plants*.

Natural Woodland Nursery, Ltd. *A Guide to Natural Woodland and Prairie Gardening*. Waterloo, Ontario

Nehrling, Arno, and Nehrling, Irene. *Easy Gar-dening with Drought-Resistant Plants*. New York: Dover Publications, 1975.

Newcomb, Lawrence. *Newcomb's Wildflower Guide: An Ingenious New Key System for Quick Positive Field Identification of the Wildflowers, Flowering Shrubs and Vines of Northeastern and North-Central North America*. Boston: Little, Brown & Co., 1977.

Niehaus, Theodore F. *Field Guide to Pacific States Wild Flowers*. Peterson Field Guide Series. Boston: Houghton Mifflin Co., 1976.

Niering, W. A. *The Life of the Marsh*. New York: McGraw-Hill Book Co., 1966.

Niering, William A., and Goodwin, Richard H. *Energy Conservation on the Home Grounds: The Role of Naturalistic Landscaping*. The Connecticut Arboretum Bulletin Series, no. 21. New London, Conn.: The Connecticut Arboretum, 1975.

Odum, Eugene P. *Fundamentals of Ecology*. 3d ed. Philadelphia: W. B. Saunders Co., 1971.

Olyay, Victor V. *Design with Climate*. Princeton, N.J.: Princeton University Press, 1963.

Oosting, Henry J. *The Study of Plant Communities: An Introduction to Plant Ecology*. 2d ed. San Francisco: W. H. Freeman & Co., 1956.

Patterson, J. C. *Planting in Urban Soils*. Soils Planning Guide (Guide 6). Southeastern Wisconsin Regional Planning Commission.

Peterson, Roger T., and McKenny, Margaret. *A Field Guide to Wildflowers of Northeastern and North-Central North America*. Boston: Houghton Mifflin Co., 1974.

Peterson, Roger T., et al. *Gardening with Wildlife*. Vienna, D.C.: National Wildlife Federation, 1974.

Pohl, Richard W. *How to Know the Grasses*. 3d ed. Dubuque, Iowa: W. C. Brown, 1978.

Rickett, Harold W. *New Field Book of American Wild Flowers*. Putnam's Nature Field Guide Books. New York: G. P. Putnam's Sons, 1978.

Rickett, Harold W. *Wildflowers of the United States*. Vol. 1, The Northeastern States, 1966; Vol. 2, The Southeastern States, 1967; Vol. 3, Texas, 1969; Vol. 4, The Southwestern States, 1970; Vol. 5, The Northeastern States, 1971; Vol. 6, The Central Mountains and Plains, 1973. New York: McGraw-Hill Book Co.

Robinette, Gary O. *Landscape Planning for Energy Conservation*. Reston, Va.: Environmental Design Press, 1977.

_____. *Plants, People and Environmental Quality*. Portland, Ore.: National Book Co., 1977.

Rock, Harold W. *Prairie Propagation Handbook*. Alfred L. Boerner Botanical Gardens, 5879 South 92nd Street, Hales Corners, Wisconsin 53130, 1974.

Rydberg, Per A. *Flora of the Rocky Mountains and Adjacent Plains*. 1922. Reprint. New York: Hafner Press, 1954.

Schramm, Peter, ed. *Proceedings of a Symposium on Prairie and Prairie Restoration*. Biological Field Station Special Publication No. 3. Biology Department, Knox College, Galesburg, Illinois, 1970.

Sharp, W. Curtis. *Conservation Plants for the Northeast*. U.S. Department of Agriculture, Soil Conservation Service Program Aid No. 1154. Washington, D.C.: U.S. Government Printing Office, 1977.

Sharples, Ada W. *Alaska Wild Flowers*. Stanford, Calif.: Stanford University Press, 1938.

Slosson, James E. *Engineering Geology—Its Importance in Land Development*. Urban Land Institute Technical Bulletin Series, no. 63. Washington, D.C.: Urban Land Institute, 1968.

Small, John K. *Ferns of the Southeastern United States*. 1938. Reprint. New York: Hafner Press, 1964.

Small, John Kunkel. *Manual of Southeastern Flora*. 1933. Reprint (2 vols.). New York: Hafner Press, 1972.

Smith, W. H. "Trees in the City." *American Institute of Planners Journal* 35 (1970):429.

Sperka, Marie. *Growing Wildflowers: A Gardener's Guide*. New York: Harper & Row Pubs., 1973.

Spurr, Stephen H., and Barnes, Burton V. *Forest Ecology*. 3d ed. New York: John Wiley & Sons, 1980.

State University Geological Survey, University of Kansas. *A Pilot Study of Land Use Planning and Environmental Geology*. Topeka, Kans.: Kansas Department of Economic Development, 1968.

Storer, John. *The Web of Life*. New York: New American Library, 1968.

Taylor, Kathryn S., and Hamblin, Stephen F. *Handbook of Wild Flower Cultivation*. New York: Macmillan Publishing Co., 1962.

Teal, John, and Teal, Mildred. *Life and Death of a Salt Marsh*. New York: Ballantine Books, 1974.

Tenebaum, Frances. *Gardening with Wildflowers*. New York: Charles Scribner's Sons, 1973.

U.S. Department of Agriculture. *Yearbook of Agriculture, 1941: Climate and Man*. Washington, D.C.: U.S. Department of Agriculture, 1941.

U.S. Department of Agriculture. *Yearbook of Agriculture, 1948: Grass*. Washington, D.C.: Government Printing Office, 1948.

U.S. Department of Agriculture, Research Service. *Selected Weeds of the United States*. USDA Handbook No. 366, 1970. Reprint. Washington, D.C.: U.S. Government Printing Office, 1978.

U.S. Department of Agriculture, Soil Conservation Service. *Hydrology, National Engineering Handbook*, Section 4. Springfield, Va.: National Technical Information Service.

Vines, Robert A. *Trees, Shrubs, and Woody Vines of the Southwest*. University Station, Tex.: University of Texas Press, 1960.

Wali, Mohan K., ed. *Prairie: A Multiple View*. *Proceedings of the 4th Midwest Prairie Conference*. Grand Forks, N.D.: University of North Dakota Press, 1974. (Order from The University Bookstore, Memorial Station, Grand Forks, North Dakota 58201.)

Watts, May T. *Reading the Landscape*. Rev. ed. New York: Macmillan Publishing Co., 1975.

Whyte, William H. *The Last Landscape*. Garden City, N.Y.: Doubleday & Co., 1968.

Wiley, Farida. *Ferns of the Northeastern United States*. New York: Dover Publications, 1973.

Zimmerman, James H., ed. *Proceedings of the Second Midwest Prairie Conference*. University of Wisconsin Arboretum, 1207 Seminole Highway, Madison, Wisconsin 53711, 1970.

Index

A

acetate, transparent, for drawing base map, 7
acid soil, 50
adobe soil, 51
aerial photograph
    distortion with, 6
    drawing base map from, 5–6
    Soil Conservation Service for, 5
alkaline soil, 50
anaerobic composting, 304
analysis checklist
    climatic, 59
    functional, 93
    geological, 12
    hydrologic, 37
    physiographic, 25
    soil, 48
    vegetation and wildlife, 76
    visual, 100
angle of incline, 30
angle of repose, grading land and, 17
angles, measuring of, 7
aquifers, 41
asexual propagation, 336–46
augers, for digging holes, 313
auxins, 338

B

Backyard Habitat Program, wildlife and, 91
balled-and-burlapped trees, 312–14
    buying of, 313
bare-rooted plants, 314–17
    preparation for planting, 315–17
barrier plants, controlling circulation with, 228–29
base map, 3
    aerial photograph for, 5–6
    drawing of, 6–8
    establishing scale for, 7–8
    survey for, 3–5
bedrock geology map, 20
berm, grading land for, 17
biological pest control, 366–67
birdhouse, building of, 375
brick(s), 271
    medium-weathering (MW), 254
    no-weathering (NW), 254

paving with
    crowned bed, 271–72
    headers for, 271–72
    laying of, 273–75
retaining walls, 253–55
severe-weathering (SW), 254
building site
    sinkholes and, 14
    suitability for construction, 14–15

C

California Region, 202–5
    climate, 202
    forbs, 204–5
    shrubs, 203–4
    trees, 202–3
        edible ornamentals, 220
        flowering, 230
        shade, 209
canopy spread, estimating of, 5
capillary soil water, 51
circulation, barrier plants to control, 228–29
city gardens, 361–64
    tub-planted trees, 363
    vacant lot, 363
climate
    analysis checklist, 59
    of California Region, 202
    of Desert Region, 195
    of Great Basin Region, 192
    micro-, 59, 66
    modifying with plants, 63–64, 207–10
    of Pacific Forest Region, 198
    of Prairie Region, 184
    regional, 59–61
    of Rocky Mountain Evergreen Forest Region, 189
    of South-Central Swamp Region, 181
    of Southeastern Mixed Forest Region, 176
    zones, 59–61
climatic regions, 59–61
    elements affecting comfort, 61
Coastal Plain Region, 173–76
    forbs, 175
    shrubs, 174–75
    soil, 173

trees, 173–74
    edible ornamentals, 220
    flowering, 230
    shade, 209
communal gardening, 364
composting
    anaerobic, 304
    14-day method, 307
    improving soil with, 301–4
    Indore method, 301–4, 307
    sheet, 307–8
    Sir Albert Howard on, 301–3, 307
concrete, paving with, 275–81
    ingredients, 276
    mixing of, 276
    pouring foundation, 277–80
    procedures for, 277
    tools for, 277
construction phase, 134
container-grown plants, 317
contour lines
    determining elevation from, 28
    drawing of, 34
contours. See contour lines
core samples, obtaining soil for, 53
creosote, treating wood with, 283
Critters in Your Landscape (table), 378–81

D

damping off, milled sphagnum moss and, 333
Desert Region, 195–97
    climate, 195
    forbs, 197
    shrubs, 196
    trees, 195
        edible ornamentals, 220
        flowering, 230
deserts, 357–61
    soil, 358
diagrammatic analysis, of property, 100–106
direct seeding, 336
disease protection, organic, 365–66
    bacteria, 366
    fungi, 366
    insecticide for, 365
    viruses, 365
    wound sealant, fungicidal, 365

drainage
    grading your yard for, 42
    paving and, 267–68
    recording water movement for, 45
    subsurface, 244–46
        dry well, 246
        French drain, 244–45
    surface, 242–44
        creating swale for, 243–44
driveway, paving of, 266
dry well, for subsurface drainage, 246

E
earth moving. *See* grading
earthquakes, damage from, 13–14
Eastern Deciduous Forest Region,
    167–72
    Appalachian Oak Forest Area,
        167–69
    climate, 167, 169
    forbs, 169, 171–72
    Oak-Hickory Forest Area, 169–72
    shrubs, 168–71
    trees, 167–71
        edible ornamentals, 220
        flowering, 230
        shade, 209
elevation
    determining by map contours, 28
    establishing on map, 34
energy efficiency, landscape and,
    94–96
engineering geology map, 21
environment, improved with plants,
    206–7
Environmental Protection Agency
    floodplain maps and, 42
    on land preservation, 364
erosion, 16, 28, 43
    water, 210–11
        control of, 210–11
            plants for, 212–14
        grading to prevent, 17
        preventing with vegetation, 40
        runoff, 210–11
            gull, 210–11
            rill, 210–11
            sheet, 210–11
    wind, 210
        control of, 210
eskers, glacial deposits and, 15
etiolation, of seedlings, 334
evaporation, hydrologic cycle and, 38
evapotranspiration, by plants, 62

F
faults, 21–22
    locating on maps, 13
fertilizers, natural, 214
finish grading, 240–42
flagstone, 275
floodplains, 40–42
flowering trees, 229–30

footings
    for masonry retaining walls,
        256–57
    for mortared stone walls, 252
forbs. *See* individual region listings
form plants, 230–33
foundation
    igneous rocks, 14
    suitable site for, 14–15
14-day composting method, 307
French drain, for subsurface drainage,
    244–45
frost, effect on vegetation, 65
frost heave, 65
    clay soil and, 15–16
frost line, concrete footings and, 256
functional analysis, 92–98
    checklist, 93
    lists for, 96–98
    measuring energy efficiency,
        94–96

G
galls, 366
Gardener's Avian Friends, A (table),
    376–77
geologic contacts, 21–22
geology, 11–23
    analysis, 20–24
        checklist, 12
        collecting information for,
            20–21
        recording of, 21
    assets from, 19
    earthquakes and, 13
    and use of native plants, 19–20
glacial deposits, 15
glacial drift, 15
glacial till, 15–16
grading, of land, 12, 19, 48, 237–42
    angle of repose, 17
    around homes, 43
    do-it-yourself, 238–42
        finish, 240–42
        rough, 238–40
    operations for, 238
    ordinances, 237–38
        utility companies and,
            237–38
    protecting existing plants
        cutting around trees, 260–61
        filling over tree roots, 261–62
grass seed, 318–20, 357
    preparing soil for, 219–20
gravitational soil water, 51
Great Basin Region, 192–94
    climate, 192
    forbs, 194
    shrubs, 193–94
    trees, 192–93
        edible ornamentals, 220
        flowering, 230
        shade, 209

ground covers, 145–46, 317–18, 322
    plant species for, 150–51
groundwater, 41
    pollution, 16, 44–45
    recharge area, 41
    water table, 41
groundwater pollution, 44–45
    limestone areas and, 16
growing medium, for seeds, 333

H
hardiness, of plants, 64
high water tables, 15
    seasonal, 17
Howard, Sir Albert, on composting,
    301–3, 307
humus, soil formation and, 48
hydrologic cycle, 37–38
hydrology, 36–46
    analysis checklist, 37
hydroscopic soil water, 51

I
igneous rocks, building foundation
    on, 14
Indore method of composting, 301–4
infiltration
    determining rate of, 45
    hydrologic cycle and, 38–40, 41
    nonporous paving and, 43
insecticide, USDA approval of, 365
instruments, surveying, 31, 33
insulating vines, 210

K
kames, glacial deposits and, 15
kettle lakes, glacial deposits and, 15

L
landscape
    base map for, 3
    color, 106
    design of, 100, 118–36
    energy-efficiency of, 94–96
    form, 104
    plan of, 2–3, 119–28
        sketching, 119–23
Landscape Pest Primer (table), 368–71
landscaping
    analyzing property for, 100–106
    effect of soil on, 47–48
    spaces, views and screens, 101–3
    texture, 104–6
    vegetation and, 78–79
    wildlife and, 80–81
lateral bud, 341
lawn, 318–20
    grasses for, 151
    grass seed, 318–20, 357
        broadcast method for, 320
        preparing soil for, 319–20
    pH level of, 356
    plugs for, 318

lawn (continued)
    sod for, 318, 357
    sprigs for, 318, 357
layering, of plant stems, 343
leaf cuttings, 346
light, for seed germination, 334–35
    fluorescent, 334
limestone areas, ground water
    pollution and, 16
loam soil, 50

M
maps
    base, 3–8
    bedrock geology, 20
    engineering geology, 21
    surficial geology, 20–21
    topographic, 28–30
masonry
    retaining walls, 253–60
        bricks and blocks, 253–55
        footings, 256
        laying up, 256–60
        mortar for, 255
        tools for, 255–56
meadows, 144–45, 350–52
    creation of, 352
    plant species for, 144–45
microclimate, 59, 66
milled sphagnum moss, antibiotic for
    fungal infection, 333
mineral fraction, of soil, 19
moisture
    requirements for plants, 65
    testing soil for, 46
mulch, improving soil with, 300–301
mylar, for drawing base map, 7

N
National Weather Service, 70
National Wildlife Federation
    on attracting wildlife, 273–75
    Backyard Habitat Program and,
        91
noise control, 217–18
    plants for, 218
Northern Coniferous Forest Region,
    154–58
    Appalachian Area, 154–55
    climate, 154, 156
    forbs, 154–56, 158
    Great Lakes Area, 155
    New England Area, 156–58
    shrubs, 157–58
    soil, 155
    trees, 154–57
        edible ornamentals, 220
        flowering, 230
        shade, 209

O
ordinances
    grading, 237–38
    weed height and, 247–48

organic matter fraction, soil
    composition and, 50

P
Pacific Forest Region, 198–201
    climate, 198
    forbs, 200–201
    shrubs, 199–200
    trees, 198–99
        flowering, 230
        shade, 209
paving, 263
    blocks for, 280–81
    brick
        crowned bed, 271–72
        headers for, 272–73
        laying of, 273–75
    concrete, 275–81
        ingredients for, 276
        mixing of, 276
        procedures, 277–80
            curing, 280
            finishing, 280
            foundation, 277–80
            pouring of, 280
        tools for, 277
    drainage and, 267–68
    driveways, 266
    layout for, 268–70
        tools for, 268
    loose aggregates
        crushed stone, 270
        specialty rocks, 270
        wood chips, 270–71
    materials for, 267
    planning for, 263–64
    soil cement, 281
    steps, 264–65, 283–84
    stone, 275
        flagstone, 275
    terraces, 266–67
    utility line installation and, 268
    walks, 364
    wood, 282–83
        creosote for, 282
        drawbacks of, 282
pest protection, organic, 366–67
    biological control, 367
    physical control, 367
    preventive measures, 367
pests, tips on controlling, 375, 377, 380
pH
    balancing of, 308
    of grasses, 356
    of soil, 50
phasing plan, 134–36
    construction, 134
    planting, 134
    synthesizing of, 135–36
photograph, aerial
    distortion with, 6
    drawing base map from, 5–6
    Soil Conservation Service for, 5

photosynthesis, 338, 340
physical pest control, 367
physiographic characteristics,
    determining of, 31
physiographic provinces, 24–25, 31
physiography, 24–25, 28, 30–35
    analysis checklist, 25
    availability of surface water and
        groundwater, 28
    determining of, 30
plane survey, 3
plant(s)
    aesthetic uses of, 222–33
        as barriers, 228–29
        flowering trees, 229–30
        form plants, 230–33
        plant walls, 225
        screening and privacy,
            225–28
    attracting wildlife with, 374
    bare-rooted, 314–17
    barrier, 228–29
    classifications, 141
    container-grown, 317
    control of temperature with, 62
    distribution of, 76–78
    ecological regions for, 139–40
    existing, 85, 88–89
    functional uses of, 206–21
        climate control, 207–9
        edible ornamentals, 220–21
        erosion control, 210–14
        insulating vines, 210
        natural fertilizer, 214
        noise filters, 217–18
        pollution control, 214–17
        shade, 209
        windbreaks, 209–10
    habitats, 81–82
    hardiness zone classification of, 64
    modifying climate with, 63–64,
        207–10
    moisture requirements of, 65
    native, 138–39
        benefits of, 139
        foraging for, 320–31
            ground covers, 322
            shrubs, 327–28
            trees, 322–27
        from nursery, 312
            balled-and-burlapped,
                312–14
            bare-rooted, 314–17
            container-grown, 317
    selection, 137–43
    source of water for, 43–44
    succession process, 78
plant charts, regional, 152–205
    California Region, 202–5
    Coastal Plain Region, 173–75
    Desert Region, 195–97
    Eastern Deciduous Forest Region,
        167–72

Great Basin Region, 192–94
Northern Coniferous Forest
    Region, 154–58
Pacific Forest Region, 198–201
Prairie Region, 184–88
Rocky Mountain Evergreen Forest
    Region, 189–91
South-Central Swamp Region,
    181–83
Southeastern Mixed Forest
    Region, 176–77
Subtropic Region, 178–80
planting phase, 134
planting plan, 128–34
    cautions for, 132–34
    domestic gardens and, 132
pollution, groundwater, 16, 44–45
pollution control, 214–16
    plants for, 216–17
polyethylene covering, to prevent
    hard freezing, 343
Prairie Region, 184–88
    climate, 184
    forbs, 186–88
    Great Plains Area, 185
    Prairie Brush Area, 184
    Prairie Parkland Area, 184–85
    shrubs, 185–86
    soil, 184
    trees, 184–85
        edible ornamentals, 220
        flowering, 230
        shade, 209
prairies, 145–50, 348–50
    plant species for, 146–50
    seeding of, 350
precipitation, 72–73
    effect on comfort, 62
    hydrologic cycle and, 37
professional surveying, 31
propagation, 329–46
    sexual, 330–35
        seeds for, 330–35
            buying of, 330
            germination of, 331–35
            harvesting, 330
            scarification of, 333
            storage of, 330
            stratification of, 332
    vegetative or asexual, 336–46
        drawbacks of, 336
        root and leaf cuttings, 343–46
        rooting hormones, 336–37
            compounds for, 337
        stem cuttings, 337
            hardwood, 337, 340–43
            narrow-leaved and
                needled evergreens,
                343
            preparation for rooting,
                343
            semi-hardwood, 343
            softwood, 337–40

R

railroad-tie retaining walls, 246–49
reagents, soil testing and, 55
regions, climatic, 60–61
reflection, 217
refraction, 217
retaining walls
    masonry, 253–60
        bricks and blocks, 253–55
        footings, 256
        laying up, 256–60
        mortar for, 255
        tools for, 255–56
    railroad-tie, 246–49
        building of, 248–49
    stone, 249–52
        cutting of, 249
        drywall construction, 249–52
        mortared construction, 252
rhizomes, 357
rock, identifying, 22
Rocky Mountain Evergreen Forest
    Region, 189–91
    climate, 189
    forbs, 191
    shrubs, 190–91
    soil, 189
    trees, 189
        edible ornamentals, 220
        shade, 209
root cuttings, 343–46
rooting box, 343
    preparation of cutting for, 343
rooting compounds, 337
rooting hormones, 336–37
rots, 366
rough grading, 238–40
runners, 357
runoff, 40
    homes and, 42

S

sandy soil, 50–51
scale, establishing, 7–8
scarification, of seeds, 333
seasonal high water table, 42–43
seed(s)
    buying of, 330
    germination of, 331–35
    growing medium for, 333
    harvesting, 330
    lighting for, 334–35
    scarification of, 333
    storage of, 330
    stratification of, 332
    watering of, 333–34
seedling(s)
    aftercare of, 335
    leggy, prevention of, 334
septic tanks, soil conditions and, 16
sexual propagation, 330–35
sheet composting, 307–8

shrubs. See also individual region listings
    for fruit production, 221
    transplanting of, 327–28
sinkholes, building site and, 14
site plan, 119–28
    simulating, 127–28
    sketching, 119–23
slopes, 30
sod, used for lawns, 318, 357
soil, 47
    acid, 50
    alkaline, 50
    analysis checklist, 48
    analyzing of, 48, 52–53
    composition, 50
    fertilizer for, 304–7
        organic, 305
        soil builders, 305–7, 309–10
    formation of, 48–50
    improving of, 297–304
        compost for, 301–4
            anaerobic, 304
            Indore method, 301–4
        green manure cover crops,
            297–301
        mulch for, 300–301
    lime for, 308
    mineral fraction of, 19
    nutrients, 51, 54–56
    obtaining core samples, 53
    organic matter fraction and, 50
    pH, 50
        balancing of, 308
    porosity of, 51
    preparation for grass seed, 319–20
    structure, 51, 53–54
    survey, 23, 51–53
    testing
        kits for, 54–56
        for moisture, 46
    texture, 50–51, 53
    types of, 50–51
    water, 51
soil cement, 281
Soil Conservation Service
    aerial photographs and, 5
    soil survey and, 51–52
soil structure, 51, 53–54
soil survey, 23, 51–53
soil water, 51
solar radiation
    effect on comfort, 61–62
    natural comfort devices against, 66
South-Central Swamp Region, 181–83
    climate, 181
    forbs, 182–83
    grasses, 182–83
    shrubs, 182
    soil, 181
    trees, 181–82
        edible ornamentals, 220
        flowering, 230
        shade, 209

Southeastern Mixed Forest Region, 176–77
  climate, 176
  forbs, 177
  shrubs, 176–77
  trees, 176
    edible ornamentals, 220
    flowering, 230
    shade, 209
sprigs, 357
stem cuttings, 337
  hardwood, 337, 340–43
  narrow-leaved and needled
    evergreens, 343
  semi-hardwood, 343
  softwood, 337–40
    aftercare of, 340
    rooting box for, 338–40
steps, paving of, 264–65, 283–84
stone
  cutting of, 249
  paving with, 275
  retaining walls, 249–52
    drywall construction, 249–52
    mortared construction, 252
stratification
  of cuttings, 341–43
  of seeds, 332
subsurface drainage, 244–46
Subtropic Region, 178–80
  forbs, 180
  shrubs, 179–80
  soil, 178
  trees
    edible ornamentals, 220
    flowering, 230
    shade, 209
succession process, 78
sun, measuring direction and altitude of, 70
sunlight, effect on vegetation, 65
surface drainage, 242–44
surface materials, reflective qualities of, 70–71
surficial deposits, 23
surficial geology map, 20–21
survey
  making your own, 4–5
  soil, 23
  triangulation method and, 4
  types of, 3–4
surveying
  do-it-yourself, 31–33
  instruments for, 31, 33
  professional, 31
  using a map, 31
synthesis
  map, 110–11

rural property, 114
suburban property, 113–14
urban property, 111–13
synthesis map, 110–11
swale, for drainage, 243–44

T

taproot, transplanting and, 323
temperature, 73–74
  effect on comfort, 62–63
  use of plants for control of, 62
terminal moraines, glacial deposits and, 15
terraces, paving of, 266–67
testing kits, for soil analysis, 54–56
topographical maps, 28–30
  contours on, 28
  slopes on, 30
topographical survey, 4
transit survey, 4
transpiration, by plants, 211
  reduction of, 343
transplanting trees, 322–27
  deciduous, 325–27
  evergreens, 325
tree(s). *See also* individual region listings
  balled-and-burlapped, 312–14
  canopy, 62
  flowering, 229–30
  for fruit production, 221
  for nut and seed production, 220
  shade, 209
  for sugars, drinks or seasonings, 221
  transplanting of, 322–27
tree canopy, 62
triangulation method, developing boundary lines with, 4
trowel, cement pouring and, 280
T-square, measuring angles with, 7

U

United States Department of Agriculture (USDA)
  on floodproofing, 42
  on hardiness zones, 64
  on insecticide approval, 365
United States Geological Survey (USGS), topographic maps and, 28, 31
utility companies
  grading ordinances and, 237–38
  paving and, 268

V

vegetation
  analysis, 81–89

analysis checklist, 76
classifications of, 141
effect of frost on, 65
effect of sun on, 65
effect of wind on, 65
geology and, 19–20
landscaping and, 78–79
pattern of, 76–77
preventing erosion with, 40
vegetative propagation, 336–46
vertical zonation, 28
vines, for insulation, 210
visual analysis, 99–109
  checklist, 100
  designing a landscape, 100
  diagrammatic, 100–106
  drawing of, 107–9
  of property, 100–106

W

walks, paving of, 264
walls, retaining. *See* retaining walls
water erosion, 210–11
  runoff, 210–11
watering, of seeds, 33–34
water movement, recorded for drainage, 45
water pollution, possible sources of, 44–45
water table, 41
weeds
  characteristics of, 78
  ordinance on, 347–48
wells, underground water for, 16, 43
wildlife, 367
  analysis, 89–91
  analysis checklist, 76
  attracting with plants, 374
  Backyard Habitat Program and, 91
  landscaping and, 80–81
wilts, 366
wind, 68–69, 71–72
  chill factor and, 62
  damage from, 65
  effect on comfort, 62
  erosion, 210
  prevailing, 71–72
windbreak plants, 209–10
wind erosion, control of, 210
woodland gardens, 352, 356
wood paving, 282–83
  creosote for, 283
  drawbacks of, 282

Z

zones, climatic, 59–61